Flamenco and
Bullfighting

Flamenco and Bullfighting

*Movement, Passion and
Risk in Two Spanish Traditions*

ADAIR LANDBORN

McFarland & Company, Inc., Publishers
Jefferson, North Carolina

LIBRARY OF CONGRESS CATALOGUING-IN-PUBLICATION DATA

Landborn, Adair.
    Flamenco and bullfighting : movement, passion and risk in two Spanish traditions / Adair Landborn.
        p. cm.
    Includes bibliographical references and index.

    ISBN 978-0-7864-9616-7 (softcover : acid free paper) ∞
    ISBN 978-1-4766-1957-6 (ebook)

    1. Flamenco—Spain. 2. Bullfights—Spain. 3. Arts—Spain. 4. Performing arts—Spain. 5. Ethnology—Spain. 6. National characteristics, Spanish. 7. Spain—Social life and customs. I. Title.
    GV1796.F55L36 2015
    793.3'19468—dc23   2015028448

BRITISH LIBRARY CATALOGUING DATA ARE AVAILABLE

© 2015 Adair Landborn. All rights reserved

No part of this book may be reproduced or transmitted in any form or by any means, electronic or mechanical, including photocopying or recording, or by any information storage and retrieval system, without permission in writing from the publisher.

On the cover: flamenco dancer © 2014 iStock/Thinkstock; matador © 2014 Hemera/Thinkstock

Printed in the United States of America

McFarland & Company, Inc., Publishers
   Box 611, Jefferson, North Carolina 28640
   www.mcfarlandpub.com

To Dr. Joann W. Kealiinohomoku,
teacher, colleague, and very dear friend,
for her impeccable and visionary scholarship,
kind mentoring presence, generosity of spirit,
and deeply inspiring example.
I will be ever grateful for her invitation to
the transformative adventures of dance scholarship.

Acknowledgments

With heartfelt gratitude I wish to thank the following people who helped me to better understand my subject and helped to make this book possible: Dr. Joseph Meeker, Dr. Joann W. Kealiinohomoku, Dr. John M. Wilson, and Dr. Cynthia Knox for their guidance of my initial research; Ms. Tere Aguirre for help with Spanish language translations (any remaining errors are mine alone) and for sharing her wealth of knowledge and experience of all things flamenco; Marla Howard for introducing me to Jaime, my first tauromachy teacher, and Jaime, for his enthusiasm and careful teaching; Coleman Cooney, director of the California Academy of Tauromachy, for his patient instruction and willingness to answer "just one more question"; my many flamenco dance teachers, especially Tere Aguirre, Carmela Greco, Manolete, Maria Magdalena, and Teo Morca, with a special shout out to Eva Enciñias-Sandoval and her family for their inspiring example. I also wish to thank the late Matteo Vittucci for his generosity, enthusiasm, and encouragement. Many thanks also to the National Institute of Flamenco, the University of New Mexico Department of Theater and Dance, and the New Mexico Hispanic Cultural Center for making it possible to study with world-class flamenco artists and see them perform here in New Mexico.

I especially want to thank the photographers: Melissa Lind for her can-do attitude and for making our photo shoot fun; Elke Stolzenberg for her candid photos of behind-the-scenes activities at the old Amor de Dios dance studios in Madrid where we first met; Juan Pelegrin for his photos that capture the action but also the inherent drama of the bullfight; Ray Fisher, Raúl Gordon Blasini, Marcus Obal, Manuel González Olaechea y Franco, and the many other talented photographers who have contributed to this book. For their assistance with photographs and publication permissions, I wish to thank Mike Markiewicz at ArenaPAL; Julio Cordal Elviro of the Biblioteca Virtual del Patrimonio Bibliográfico; Thomas Lisanti and Alice Standin at the New York Public Library, Dance Division; and Dale Stinchcomb at the Houghton Library of the Harvard College Library. ¡*Muchas Gracias!* to Josefa

Ramos Parra of the Fundación de Caballero Bonald in Jerez de la Frontera, Spain, for helping me track down one especially obscure image. My thanks to the many librarians at the Fundación de Flamenco, Centro Andaluz de Flamenco, Biblioteca Municipal de Jerez de la Frontera, and the Biblioteca Nacional de España in Madrid for their generous advice and assistance.

I thank Lois Ann Abraham for reviewing chapter drafts and providing clear feedback, positive encouragement, and moral support, and for collaborating with Coda Hale to provide the generous photo grant that made it possible for me to illustrate my ideas. I am deeply grateful to Melinda Lightfoot of Wordsmith Writing & Editing for her patience, expertise, and support with this project, first as a dissertation and now as a book. Her insightful comments and suggestions have always been greatly appreciated. I extend my thanks to Cheryl Cutler and Pedro Alejandro for their supportive colleagueship, to the Wesleyan University Dance Department for their support of my research sabbatical, to Cross-Cultural Dance Resources for supporting my research through the HKK Memorial Research Choreographer-in-Residence Award, and to Dorothy Richmond for her support, friendship, and good company on my tauromachy adventure in Tecate, Mexico. My thanks also to Cee Bearden and Ellie Quick for their generous friendship, to the Fear Not Dance Foundation for providing accommodations as I completed this book, and to the Peña Flamenca de Taos, my local cohort of flamenco aficionados, for good times and opportunities to deepen my flamenco practice. ¡Olé!

Table of Contents

Acknowledgments — vii
Preface — 1
Introduction: Kinesthetic Culture — 9

One: Flamenco and Bullfighting: An Ongoing Discussion — 35
Two: Somatic Ethnography — 55
Three: Overlapping Worlds — 72
Four: Ritual and Performance Events — 99
Five: An Aesthetic Topography: *Gitanismo,* Romanticism and *Duende* — 123
Six: Movement Repatterning and Culture — 146
Seven: Gaining the Emic Edge — 163
Eight: Movement Analysis — 191
Nine: Movement Parallels: From Structures to Motifs — 223
Ten: Kinesthetic Culture — 244

Appendix 1: Laban Movement Analysis Overview — 261
Appendix 2: Notes on Language Use — 263
Glossary of Spanish Terms — 267
Chapter Notes — 273
Bibliography — 281
Index — 291

Preface

By some measures this book was over thirty years in the making, from my first naive forays into the flamenco dance genre in 1982 to this writing in 2015. In 1982, I took my first flamenco dance classes, driven by the confluence of three things: a feeling, an experience, and a memory. First, I felt my own cultural hybridity. As a displaced New Mexican, I felt my latent inner Latina spirit rising up in reaction to the Nordic-flavored culture of Seattle, Washington, where I was living at the time. One rainy Seattle afternoon this feeling led me to a darkened theater where I experienced the visually brilliant flamenco dance film of Federico Garcia Lorca's play *Blood Wedding* directed by Spanish director Carlos Saura. Watching, I felt called to action by the emotional intensity of the choreography of Antonio Gades. And this led to the third thing, a distinct memory of having said "I want to do that some day" after attending a 1975 performance by Eva Encinias-Sandoval and her flamenco family in Albuquerque, New Mexico.

And so, I added to my already busy modern dance career a sporadic element of flamenco dance training. From 1982 to 1989, as I studied with flamenco teachers Teo Morca, Eva Encinias-Sandoval, Manolo Rivera, and Tere Aguirre, I noticed that references to bullfighting as an important cultural influence were often made. Teachers sometimes employed bullfight imagery to help us better shape our bodies and embody the dynamic intensity and physicality demanded by the flamenco dance style.

On my first visit to Spain in 1989, I studied flamenco dance at the Paco Peña Festival Internacional de la Guitarra in Córdoba, Spain, and three weeks later in Barcelona, the day before my flight home, having exhausted all of the other tourist tours on offer, I overcame my trepidation and went to my first Spanish bullfight at the Plaza de Toros Monumental in Barcelona, Spain. I rationalized that the experience would increase my knowledge of Spanish culture and so might (somehow) improve my style as a flamenco dancer. I told myself that if I didn't like it (and as a pacifist Quaker I fully expected that I would not), I would simply stand up and walk out. I guess it was fate,

The Spanish bullfight tradition began as a contest between a Spanish nobleman on horseback and a bull. This method is known as *rejoneo*, in reference to the *rejon* (lance or spear) used by the horseman. Today, the extraordinary horsemanship skills of control and balance required for *rejoneo* are rarely demonstrated in the bullfight arena (efecreata mediagroup/Shutterstock.com).

but for some reason a special feature of the bullfight on that afternoon was a demonstration of *rejoneo*, the historic form of Spanish bullfighting from horseback. And I did not stand up and walk out. Instead, what I saw had a powerful, deep, soul-rocking effect on me; it was so aesthetically beautiful that I was moved beyond words and beyond understanding.

The *fiesta de toros* has long been a national addiction and obsession in Spain. Many Spaniards are bound economically to bullfighting; for them it is an occupation, a business, and a way of life, and for some bullfight aficionados the real-life and real-death drama of the *corrida* transcends entertainment and comes closer to being religion.

The bullfight reveals fundamental human choices: to risk oneself, or not; to bravely face the fact of one's own mortality, or not; to empathize with suffering, or not. These choices reveal more than our personal sensitivity or lack thereof; they reveal the beliefs that we have collected via our cultural circumstances and life experiences. If a bull is seen as a food source or if our cosmological worldview does not include notions of animal sentience, then we may exempt ourselves from empathic feelings. In the highly stratified cosmology of most bullfighting cultures, the bull is seen as a lower life form that God has provided for the sustenance of his human children. Whether or not, as some say, the Spanish bullfight evolved from ancient roots (hunting practices of Paleolithic tribes, fertility rites of early matriarchal cultures, or bloody contests between humans and animals in the Roman coliseum), the fact is that today bullfighting remains deeply entrenched in Spanish life.

In this book, I take bullfighting as a cultural given and focus primarily on movement analysis, dance, and performance. But bullfighting is a controversial practice, and, since some readers will want to know where I stand on these issues, I will discuss it briefly here. I am not "in favor of" bullfighting. I still prefer and am committed to the ethics of nonviolence. I appreciate the reasons behind the public protests in Spain and elsewhere against bullfighting practices. I am convinced by most of their arguments, and am relieved whenever I hear of the practice of bullfighting being banned. From a broad perspective, I see such decisions as a step forward for humankind, a step away from a long tradition of gratuitous cruelty to animals and needless loss of human lives.

While I agree with the goal of anti-bullfighting organizations, and appreciate the powerful effect of slogans proclaiming that "torture is neither art

The long history of philosophical and religious arguments against bullfighting practices extends from ancient Rome to modern *antitaurino* (anti-bullfight) street protests and public demonstrations. Organized in Spain as well as internationally, anti-bullfight activists have gained significant momentum as a result of the popularity of the Internet, social media, performance art, animal rights, and vegetarianism. The banner in the background reads "*La tortura no es cultura*" (Torture is not culture). More information is available at www.latorturanoescultura.org (©Lawrence JC Baron/Demotix).

nor culture," it seems to me that it is precisely because the bullfight *is* cultural, and is a long-practiced and deeply ingrained way of life, and it is precisely because the artistry practiced by many generations of toreros has been admired and emulated by so many generations of Spaniards, that great effort on the part of many people will be required before the bullfight can ever be abolished.

Beneath it all, I am baffled by my own contradictory responses. My first bullfight made me aware of an inexplicable fissure between my beliefs and my experience. The mystery of this chasm was unnerving and has exerted a strangely alluring pull on my curiosity about the world and my own nature. The honest truth is that I still treasure the aesthetic experience of that one afternoon in the Barcelona bullring when the swirling, spiraling movements of an elegant man, a supremely agile horse, and a phenomenally powerful bull thrust forward into my heart an overwhelming emotion made of love for all three and pride in their stunning natural beauty. Watching as these three live beings engaged in the deadly contest of the *corrida*, the bullfight

The natural, elemental power of the bull was revered by many ancient cultures as a fertility symbol, and today the bull still serves as an important symbolic figure in many human rituals, myths, and cultural practices. Spain's fighting bulls, *toros bravos*, are deliberately bred to exhibit aggressiveness, energy, and stamina. These wild herd animals have minimal contact with humans before their emergence alone into the bullfight arena (Juan Pelegrin/Flickr.com).

was dramatic and riveting, but I believe that it was *in the movement*, the dynamic tensions and interplay between these remarkable beings, that I found beauty. I also find that rare combination of beauty, skill, fierceness, risk, and passion in flamenco dance.

Prior to flamenco, most of my dance training and experience was in abstract contemporary modern dance and academic dance studies. By contrast, the uninhibited emotionality of flamenco dance appeared glamorous and exotic. The flamenco arts unearth, express, and celebrate the full range of human emotion. Emotional outpouring is flamenco's primary purpose. In flamenco, light emotions rise to the surface, but so, too, do the deeper emotions of grief, anger, bitterness, fear, loneliness, sorrow, and anguish. I have come to believe that in the flamenco arts, as in the bullfight, we see the workings of a fundamental spiritual task of humanity—the reconciliation of beauty and tragedy.

In 1992, I returned to Spain to live and study flamenco dance for an extended period. During this time, I had the opportunity to study bullfighting movement directly with a Colombian matador, with the side benefit of attending bullfights with him and his family. Because this formal training, as well as informal opportunities to spend time with people who knew a great deal about bullfighting, occurred concurrently with my intensive flamenco dance training, it greatly expanded my understanding of the links between these two cultural forms. In 1996, I presented a paper outlining my initial discoveries at the First Biannual Flamenco History Conference (sponsored by the Congress on Research in Dance) at the University of New Mexico in Albuquerque. In subsequent years, I lectured on this topic and continued to incorporate what I had learned into my flamenco performances. I also taught my flamenco dance students using these firsthand insights into the cultural roots and kinetic imperatives of the flamenco dance form. Then, while on sabbatical from Wesleyan University in 1999, I again visited Spain, this time spending long hours at the Biblioteca Nacional de España in Madrid and the Fundación de Flamenco in Jerez de la Frontera, researching the existing Spanish scholarship on the cultural links between bullfighting and flamenco.

Finally, in 2003, my inquiry went deeper as I undertook doctoral research using the interdisciplinary perspectives of the anthropology of dance and somatic studies. My initial somatic awareness of the connection between these two cultural practices quickly expanded into direct experiential research as I undertook practical field research with Coleman Cooney at the California Academy of Tauromaquia in San Diego, and had the opportunity to put my fledgling bullfighting skills to the test in an informal arena in Mexico. As a certified movement analyst, my exploratory work inevitably transitioned into an analysis of the respective movement phenomena of bullfighting and flamenco dance.

By way of caveat, this book offers little history and does not aim to prove anything regarding these two cultural practices, but rather offers a report based on my research into the existent scholarship and my direct personal experiences. I hope it may guide and inform readers curious about these two art forms and interested in understanding why they so often appear in reference to one another in popular culture, in academic literature, and in the artistic imagination. I expect readers will bring to the reading of this book multiple perspectives, divergent interpretations, and a range of interests and areas of expertise. Specialists in one area addressed in this book may be unacquainted or less familiar with other areas. My goal is to provide both sufficient background information for readers who are unfamiliar with these topics and sufficient new information to keep the interest of more expert readers. I give priority to those aspects of flamenco dance and bullfighting that are most pertinent to my own interests and emerging perspectives. There are many fascinating directions (i.e., history, religion, music, gender, etc.) that, despite their great interest and importance, I do not pursue, but only discuss as they emerge naturally in the process of analyzing the movement phenomena of bullfighting and flamenco dance. I especially hope this information will serve other dancers immersed in the flamenco arts.

As a general organizing principle, this book progresses from theory to direct experiential research and movement analysis, and concludes with an overview of the similarities in bullfight and flamenco movement vocabularies and performances. The Introduction presents my theory of kinesthetic culture and provides an overview of the book's topics and the various theoretical frameworks that informed my original investigation. In my experience, it was by combining theories from different disciplines that I gained the mental leverage needed to pry open my subject and gain deeper insights, and my hope is that by providing these intellectual resources, my readers may have the pleasure of constructing their own cultural and artistic perspectives.

Chapter One surveys various written works, both Spanish and English texts, that address bullfighting and the flamenco arts, and examines why the role of somatic experience seems to have been largely avoided within this ongoing cultural discussion. Chapter Two introduces perspectives and methods from somatic studies, movement analysis, and ethnographic writing that provide access to and insight into the lived experience of the culture and movement practices of flamenco dance and bullfighting. Chapter Three examines how the worlds of flamenco and bullfighting are known to overlap, focusing on the social behaviors and sense of sociality that these two cultural practices share. Chapter Four compares the performance contexts of bullfighting and flamenco dance, noting similarities and differences in their institutions, spatial attributes, and temporal parameters. Chapter Five reviews the aesthetic rules that inform and give structure to flamenco dance and bullfighting, as well as the influence of class and ethnicity on performance aesthetics. Also discussed are the influence of the *gitano* (Gypsy) culture and the concept of *duende* (spirit) as a measure of a performance. Chapter Six takes a broad view of the processes of cultural continuity and change as they relate to the traditions of flamenco dance and bullfighting, and discusses the interplay between life experience and cultural research.

Chapter Seven describes my experiential field research, the physical risks, artistic experiences, and cross-cultural adventures that increased my somatic/kinesthetic understanding of both movement traditions. Chapter Eight summarizes my analysis of the movement vocabularies of flamenco dance and bullfighting, describing their unique and shared attributes in relation to space, shape, timing, and movement expressivity. Chapter Nine identifies movement principles that inform both cultural practices, showing how movement imperatives in the high-risk context of bullfighting correlate with similar patterns in the passion-filled movements of flamenco dance.

Chapter Ten applies my theory of kinesthetic culture to further illuminate areas of correlation between flamenco dance and bullfighting, from the internal experience of individuals to the social settings of their performances to the broader surround of Spanish culture. Also included are a Laban Movement Analysis Overview, Notes on Language Use (an explanation of how issues of gender and translation are handled within the text), and a Glossary of Spanish Terms.

My study of two movement forms that function within the same culture constitutes an intracultural investigation into what I call kinesthetic culture. Both sensory and kinetic attributes of movement are important in this discussion because no movement, however active and outward-directed it may be, is without its sensate root in the body. Ultimately, I am interested in how culture resides in bodies and, transformed by the human genius for art making, emerges as dance. My hope is that readers will enjoy the cultural and artistic adventures recounted in this book, remember it as a user-friendly reference volume, and recommend it as a "fascinating read" to their friends and aficionados of Spanish arts and culture.

Introduction:
Kinesthetic Culture

Culture, all those shared and complexly interconnected behaviors, experiences, thought patterns, and ways of living that signal the common ground of a cultural group, functions as a whole system, multifaceted and many-layered. While knowledge of the discrete parts that make up the whole system is useful, understanding the relatedness, symbiosis, and synthesis among elements is critical to comprehension of the whole.

When we consider our own knowledge of the world, including knowledge of our own culture, we can see that it is largely constructed through the actualities of embodiment. The body has ways of constructing meaning within itself, noting references and connections between the inner realms of sensation, volition, and affect, and the outer realms of personal, social, and cultural significance. It is largely through interaction that we come to know our immediate environment and gain impressions of the wider world around us. And so movement is key. Cultural meaning, which is, after all, human meaning, is expressed through movement in all of its diverse forms, dynamics, and expressions.

Bullfighting and flamenco dance give expression to a Spanish worldview. They function as cultural rituals, as performance and social events, and as expressions of unique individuals and groups of human beings. As a comparative analysis of their movement vocabularies, performance conventions, and social traditions soon demonstrates, flamenco and bullfighting are overlapping domains with many shared cultural values. These shared values are embodied and sustained through somatic processes and kinetic enactments, making study of movement phenomena and the first-person lived experience of flamenco and bullfight practitioners a useful tool for understanding the Spanish worldview.

Anthropologist Michael Kearney defines *worldview* as "culturally organized macro thought: those dynamically interrelated basic cognitive assumptions of a people that determine much of their behavior and decision making, as well as organizing much of their body of symbolic creations—myth, religion, cosmology—and ethnophilosophy in general" (Kearney 1984, 1). Human movement, in its daily form and as it is elaborated through dance and ritual, is the means of our participation, our fundamental agency within the culturally constructed and inflected worlds we inhabit. Movement expression is particularized through both its sensory function and the human agency it actualizes within a cultural context. In Spanish culture, bullfighting and flamenco dance provide people with opportunities to enact personal identities, social belonging, and cultural values through mindful, soulful, embodied acts of performance.

Bullfighting is practiced in many countries outside of Spain, particularly in those areas of the world influenced by Hispanic culture. However, Spain is recognized as the historical and cultural epicenter of the bullfighting practice. The flamenco arts are also widely distributed, and Spain, particularly the southern region of Andalusia, is recognized as the center of the flamenco tradition and practice. Outside of Spain, from an international perspective, both bullfighting and flamenco dance are commonly linked and recognized as practices that are iconic of Spanish culture. In Spain, the social and aesthetic connections between the two practices are common knowledge.

Together, the movement practices of flamenco dance and bullfighting constitute a widely recognized cultural complex. Within a cultural group, elements that function as a cultural complex are thought of as "forming an integrated whole whose every part is not only accepted but held as symbolically essential" (Herskovits 1964, 93). Comparative analysis of the movements of these two performance practices clarifies the location, function, and role of each as a key element within the cultural complex. Flamenco dance and bullfighting are linked somatically, aesthetically, and socially, yet they also contrast in significant ways. Each cultural practice has numerous aspects open to analysis, such as personnel (gender, phenotype, age, class, and ethnicity), costumes (history, construction, as social indicator, and effect on movement performance), the architectural constructs that support public performance (public arenas, theaters, and nightclubs), and performance paraphernalia (swords, capes, shawls, and fans).

While bullfighting is not dance, neither is it considered a sport. Rather, bullfights are considered cultural events, and the bullfighter is appreciated for his (or her) artistry in the arena to such a degree that one commonly finds articles that report on bullfights and flamenco performances printed side by side on the cultural events pages of Spanish newspapers. "Which came first, the chicken or the egg?" This rhetorical question is just as puzzling

Spain is recognized internationally as the home of the flamenco arts and bullfighting. This postcard features a painting by Juan Giralt Lerin, a Spanish impressionist painter born in 1907. This postcard, titled *Zapateado*, is one of a series of Lerin postcards with flamenco dance titles; some others are *Bulerías, Peteneras, Zambra*, and *Alegrías*. Embroidered vintage postcards such as this one were especially popular in the 1950s. Like many other postcards created for the Spanish tourist trade, it combines images of flamenco and bullfighting to represent Spain's most commonly recognized cultural complex.

when applied to the cultural complex of flamenco and bullfighting. I think of flamenco and bullfighting as twins, developing together embryonically, born nearly simultaneously, and continuing to develop naturally side by side in their home culture over a period of centuries, first in informal and later in more formal, formulated, and even formulaic ways. Whatever the exact history of their emergence may be, most certainly over many centuries of development, it was in human flesh, action, and feeling that they maintained their twinship before finally emerging around the eighteenth century as public ritual and performance. And one result of their shared developmental history is that any pedagogical or aesthetic discourse focused on either flamenco or bullfighting is likely to express awareness of the significant links between the two cultural practices.

My own investigative adventures took place in the context of artistic and cultural endeavors. In such investigations, one's relationship to the culture, as an insider or outsider, is influential, as is whether one only observes or actually participates directly in a movement practice. Those of us who attempt to embody another culture's values through direct participation in movement/performance traditions gain special insights and perspectives. This learning process is fun, often challenging, sometimes frustrating, and can ultimately be deeply transformative.

I entered the cultural terrain of both flamenco and bullfighting as a cultural outsider, with my status as a student, teacher, dancer, scholar, and curious foreigner gaining me entrée and sympathetic treatment. The pedagogical methods I encountered as a student were influential in forming my initial impressions, as were my earliest experiences watching performances. Flamenco and Spanish bullfighting movement techniques are written about in books but are most commonly transmitted from person to person as kinesthetic and oral traditions. The pedagogical methods of flamenco dance and bullfighting, whether written down, communicated orally, or conveyed through a teacher's physical demonstration, provide a valuable source of information from the insider's point of view. Such communications also articulate the aesthetic and cultural values that guide the complex structures, patterns, and movement forms so essential to flamenco and bullfighting. Through a teacher's words and movement example, one often learns the proper intention and thought behind each movement, and thus becomes more aware of the deeply inscribed cultural values. The more I learned about the specific functional and aesthetic concerns that bullfighting movements address, the more I realized the extent of their influence on the movement vocabulary of flamenco dance.

The art of bullfighting, tauromachy (in Spanish, *tauromaquia*), has its own pedagogy and aesthetic standards, yet it shares many of the postures and expressive attitudes of the flamenco dance style and has similar aesthetic standards. Flamenco dance teachers evoke the imagery of the bullfight just as teachers of bullfighting try to elicit from their students the postures and expressive control of the dance. Flamenco dance teachers may accentuate style elements suggestive of bullfighting and its culture to help students to engage in flamenco dance with more authentic movement qualities and deeper emotional content. In Carlos Saura's 1984 film *Carmen*, renowned flamenco dance teacher María Magdalena is shown telling her students, "Your arms should rise smoothly and meaningfully. The hips must be detached from the waist. The breasts are like a bull's horns, warm yet soft. Head up. A princely posture."

Dynamic and complex, dance and movement phenomena are superbly effective as carriers of cultural meaning. While it is useful to consider the

María Magdalena is seen teaching in 1986 at the Amor de Dios dance studio, one of Spain's most historically influential dance studios, at Calle Amor de Dios 4 in Madrid. Her pedagogical methods are comprehensive, brilliantly organized, and highly consistent. Teaching numerous weekly technique classes (footwork, arms, castanets, choreography) at the studio for over 30 years, María Magdalena has greatly influenced current standards of style and technique in the flamenco dance genre in Spain as well as internationally (photograph by Elke Stolzenberg).

individual elements that contribute to a cultural system, knowledge of the relation and synthesis between cultural elements is essential to building a more comprehensive view of a particular culture. And it is to be hoped that a better understanding of any single culture will contribute to anthropological knowledge regarding the basis of human culture itself. In the same way, cultural events such as a public bullfight or flamenco dance performance contribute both to the unique life experience of each participant and/or witness, and to the wider cultural context in which they function. Human movement and dance, as aspects of affective culture, participate in and contribute to the larger cultural context. However, many of the patterns regulating and influencing human movement function below the level of conscious awareness. How can we learn more and bring these patterns up for conscious consideration?

One productive area of research in the anthropological study of dance and movement is the relationship between normal everyday human movement patterns and the highly formulated movement patterns of cultural events and performances. Anthropologist Dr. Joann Kealiinohomoku notes that "cultural phenomena are subsumed by these two large categories of ordinary and super-ordinary" (1976, 55). "Super-ordinary experiences are the highlights and the punctuations in ongoing existence; they make up affective culture" (56). Using Kealiinohomoku's definition, both flamenco dance and bullfighting constitute super-ordinary performative events within a shared cultural context.

Movement phenomena constitute a deep source of information about the social values and human behaviors that identify cultures. Anthropologists sometimes investigate the relationship between dance and non-dance movement patterns within the same culture to gain deeper understanding of a specific culture. For example, the Choreometrics Project authored by Alan Lomax (1968) sought to establish intracultural movement correlations within a broad-based cross-cultural study of dance forms.[1] This extensive research project was flawed by its assumption of a causal relationship between the movement patterns that pertain to the work and economy of a culture and those pertaining to the culture's dance forms (Kealiinohomoku 1979, 170). In this regard, Kealiinohomoku points out that "it is imperative to look for correlations, but it is equally imperative that correlations not be confused with causes" (1974, 22). While looking for identifiable correlations between the movement practices of flamenco and bullfighting, I felt it was important to honor this principle.

As I see it, all people have what I call *kinesthetic culture, kinesthetic* meaning the sensation and experience of motion, and *culture* meaning the patterns of living passed from one generation to another within a human group. Through the processes of enculturation (learning how to be human in our original cultural context) and acculturation (learning contrasting ideas about how to be human as we adapt to other cultural groups) our movement patterns are formed, and through movement we demonstrate agency by effecting change within our environment. A single individual's movement patterns constitute a collection that may be studied. As specific elements and patterns of an individual's kinesthetic life are identified, they may be interpreted as providing evidence of the individual's personality. However, such an analysis also provides evidence of the patterns of living unique to the human group responsible for the individual's enculturation as well as any other cultural groups that have had an acculturating influence on the individual.

This theoretical collection and sum total of an individual's movement patterns—his or her kinesthetic life—includes movements of the individual's work, play, and artistic expression. It includes movements affected by societal expectations and religious inhibitions. It includes movement limitations that individuals experience, however subtly, due to the terrain they move through on a daily basis, the clothing they wear, or the climate in which they live. It is made up of the many normative ways of both moving and understanding movement that are integral to the culture and unconsciously enacted. The kinesthetic life of an individual includes movements patterned during peak experiences of love, joy, risk, faith, or ecstasy, as well as movements patterned in response to emotions of desperation, anger, loss, fear, or grief. Intense life experiences are embodied in individual bodies, but are also given collective form when ritualized and celebrated formally through movement traditions and public rituals such as flamenco and bullfighting.

Individuals' movements are affected by their personal surroundings, the degree of emotional volatility they bring to living, the state of their health, and all the many other realities of their lives. Whether an individual lives the life of a U.S. American city dweller driving a car and watching television or computer screens, or an Andalusian ranch hand working closely with animals, the realities of that everyday life will affect and distinguish the individual's kinesthetic life. Spaniards making a living in rural Andalusia perform very physical work—kinetic and somatic—that entails significant interspecies interaction and considerable physical risk. The constant proximity of horses and bulls leads rural Spaniards to both identify with and differentiate themselves from their animals. They value their empathic knowing of the animals in their care. Through the ritualized movement and embodied practice of the bullfight they celebrate the power and elegance of bulls and horses as well as their own human will and ability to dominate these animals.

Collectively, the lived realities of individuals create the shared kinesthetic life of a cultural group. Kinesthetic culture, then, is the collection of actual movement sensations, movement memories, and vicarious movement experiences that connects members of a cultural group at the somatic level. Spain's kinesthetic culture embodies the totality of Spanish culture, including the somatic, emotional, and cognitive experiences and philosophical concepts that nourish Spanish cultural life. Bullfighting and flamenco dance both influence and express the kinesthetic culture of Spain.

Kinesthetic culture also includes assumptions about the significance of certain movements, gestures, or postural attitudes. In Spain I witnessed a large theater audience break into spontaneous applause at the last, subtle gesture of a flamenco dancer's tug on his vest at the exact culminating moment of the musical phrase, a gesture that might be lost on an audience outside this culture. Kinesthetic culture includes intrinsic attitudes or tendencies affecting responsiveness, impulsiveness, passivity, and activity. It includes affinities for rhythmic interactions and entrainment.[2] It also embodies many nonphysical aspects of culture by giving expression to its members' assumptions about life, death, space, time, reality, human nature, animal nature, and the organization of the cosmos, i.e., the unique worldview of the cultural group. Dance emerges from, takes its form, and is made manifest in this rich matrix.

The concept of kinesthetic culture has integrative value; it addresses cultural phenomena as both sensation and action, and examines their manifestations in both the personal and the collective realms. This broader view is important because, while engaging multiple theoretical perspectives results in the discovery of diverse attributes, ultimately it is a sense of the integrative whole that one hopes to construct.

Theory is important. Without theory, one cannot help but view flamenco and bullfighting as a tourist would, seeing the drama, color, action, and emotion, and making sense of the experience based on the norms of one's home culture. With a working knowledge of some of anthropology's key concepts, one is better equipped to reduce the distorting effect of one's own cultural prejudices, expectations, and judgments. The concept of ethnocentricity, understanding how *etic* perspectives (which rely on objective methods and facilitate cross-cultural comparisons) and *emic* perspectives (which examine the implicit cultural knowledge of a cultural group) combine to provide a more complete picture of a human culture, and the concepts of cultural relativity and performativity are especially useful in developing one's understanding of flamenco and bullfighting beyond the tourist's view.

Horses are vital to the cultural life of Spain. Breeding horses, grooming and caring for horses, training and riding horses, showing horses in competitions, selling or trading horses: these are major activities in Andalusia. This photograph illustrates the tradition of Spanish men riding their elegantly groomed horses through the streets of Jerez, de la Frontera, during the annual horse fair, Feria del Caballo. Ready to celebrate, the women of Jerez ride behind them dressed in festive *sevillanas*-style dresses with an abundance of ruffles (Kiko Jimenez/Shutterstock.com).

Ethnocentrism

Ethnocentrism has long been acknowledged in the field of cultural anthropology as the primary mechanism that affects our evaluation and understanding of human cultures.

> Ethnocentrism is the point of view that one's own way of life is to be preferred above all others. Flowing logically from the process of early enculturation, this characterizes the way most individuals feel about their own culture, whether or not they verbalize the feeling. Outside the stream of Euro-American culture, particularly among nonliterate peoples, this is taken for granted and is to be viewed [positively] as a factor that facilitates individual adjustment and social integration [Herskovits 1964, 54].

Ethnocentrism presents distinct challenges to the field of cultural anthropology. Writing about ethnocentrism, German American anthropologist Franz Boas characterized as "untenable" the modernist assumptions of continuity and progress that people from Western cultures attempt to project onto the map of human culture (1951, 1–6).

Postmodern scholarship, in general, expresses distrust of the phenomenon of ethnocentrism, often using the term to convey a negative value. In its negative aspects, ethnocentricity "can be politically harmful" (Kealiinohomoku 1990, 2), effectively reinforcing patterns of distrust between cultural groups. If used as justification for exclusion or prejudicial mistreatment, the ethnocentrism of dominant groups may damage the well-being of any disrespected or excluded cultural groups. The term often produces an immediate negative response in the popular mind and in much of the academic world, because it is linked to the historical and ongoing horrors of the European and Euro-American hegemony that, through colonialism, imperialism, and neoimperialism, denigrates, destroys, and exploits people of non–Western cultures. Presenting a mask of ethnocentric superiority, Western culture has played a devastating role in this global political context. A cloud of negativity surrounds ethnocentrism as a result of its association with Western culture's abuses of power, but, without that negative baggage, what is ethnocentrism?

Paradoxically, ethnocentrism functions *both* as a problematic blindness that impedes human tolerance of cultural diversity *and* as a sign of cultural health. Ethnocentrism has positive contributions to make to cultural homeostasis. If a society is functional, responsive to human needs, and conducive to living with enjoyment, any human may grow happily within that cultural context and remain convinced that their way of life is the best. This healthy attitude will be evident in a group's belief that their natural environment is more beautiful, that their bean soup is tastier, their gods more powerful, their songs more pleasing. In short, their way of life, their culture, represents to them the *right way* to be human. I am reminded of humorist Garrison Keillor's ethnocentric appreciation of his fictional Midwestern hometown, Lake Wobegon, which he describes as a place "where all the women are strong, all the men are good-looking, and all the children are above average."[3]

So, ethnocentrism is not an odd, unusual, politically incorrect, or pathological quirk restricted to Western culture; rather, it constitutes a healthy sign of successful enculturation in any culture. Ethnocentrism is actually a human universal, signaling the sense of belonging and rightness that people feel within their own cultural surround. Unless a culture is endangered from without or seriously dysfunctional within, the sense that one's own family, village, and country, one's own cultural ways of being, doing, and believing, are best will typify the experience of being human. Ethnocentrism signals the health, or striving toward health and survival, of a culture, cultural complex, or social group.

A corollary of ethnocentrism is that, typically, a person's own culture will remain obscure, less visible to him or her as a result of its very familiarity. A general consensus of anthropologists and philosophers supports anthropologist Edward T. Hall's statement that "culture hides much more than it reveals, and strangely enough what it hides, it hides most effectively from its own participants" (1969, 39). Because we remain blind to the familiar and ubiquitous elements of our own culture, some of the most deeply ingrained assumptions that rule our lives may never rise to the level of conscious acknowledgment. Such tacit assumptions affect many of the movement behaviors that constitute human cultural practices. In some instances it is precisely the outsider, in the process of learning and acculturation, who lifts up such tacit assumptions for conscious examination.

Anthropologist Melville J. Herskovits wrote that "culture fills and largely determines the course of our lives, yet rarely intrudes into conscious thought" (1964, 4). This would seem to be especially true where movement phenomena are concerned. Movement is a natural ongoing attribute of the cultural surround; the role of movement in culture is so obvious that it is often underreported. The presence of movement at cultural events and its remarkable transformative qualities within social contexts are so normative that they may generate few comments. Yet movement is a key aspect of culture; it is through moving, acting, speaking, and interacting that humans are enculturated.

Human culture surrounds us from birth onward; in fact, some prenatal psychologists assert that enculturation begins to affect us before birth. It is widely understood in the human sciences that human nature exists and is formed through an intensive nurturing process. We learn how to be human, and the formative learning of each person is richly endowed by culture. Ethnocentrism is implicit in the enculturation process; it is basic to human experience and its roots are nourished by the somatic processes of embodied living. True, there are biological potentialities, but which behaviors and characteristics emerge from that broad spectrum of human potential will depend greatly on the specific environment, socialization, and enculturation affecting a person's development.

"Even the facts of the physical world are discerned through the enculturative screen, so that the perception of time, distance, weight, size, and other 'realities' is mediated by the conventions of any given group" (Herskovits 1964, 49). In relationship to enculturation processes, the body functions as a mediating mechanism; each person actively screens cultural information through sensory experience. Individuals also test cultural precepts experientially through kinetic experience and the practical movements

Meticulously dressed up in her fancy miniature *sevillanas* dress, this little girl holds hands with her mother as she participates in the Spanish tradition of the promenade during Seville's annual spring fair. Spain's promenade tradition entails seeing, admiring, and socializing with other people as well as being recognized and admired by others in your community. The Spanish have a great affinity for this kind of round-the-clock socializing and their children are introduced to such traditions early in life (Francisco Javier Alcerreca Gomez/Shutterstock.com).

of the body. Through the function of human memory, a person's ability to maintain and transmit culture depends upon the body serving as a resource and repository of cultural knowledge. The body is culturally generative, through dance, through improvisation, and through play; the body participates in the creative moments that give impetus to cultural transformation.

Although ethnocentrism is deeply embedded in human experience and has positive aspects, it remains problematic for the study of dance, movement, and culture. Anthropologist Kealiinohomoku states that "ethnocentricity interferes with cross-cultural understanding" (1976, 78). Providing an example, she explains that, in the United States, Americans commonly presume that males professionally active in the dance field are effeminate. This belief is culture-specific, emerging from the social history of Western culture. Committed to this skewed interpretation of reality, many Americans might be surprised to learn that "on a worldwide basis ... there are more male dancers than female dancers, and in most societies the male dancer is considered to be especially virile" (1976, 78).

In Spain, such attitudes vary, reflecting the African continent's acceptance of and the European continent's ambivalence toward male participation in dance. These contrasting attitudes may also reflect differences between Africa's "participatory dance" and Europe's "presentational dance" practices (Nahachewsky 1995). In flamenco dance, there is a strong tradition of male participation as performers, teachers, and choreographers, and a gendered movement style that emphasizes *macho* (masculine) characteristics. However, flamenco dance also functions within the Western cultural context that Kealiinohomoku describes, and therefore the masculinity of male flamenco dancers is sometimes questioned.

It is ethnocentrism that largely explains the importance in Spanish culture of the expression of personal, familial, and regional pride (*orgullo*) and the general sanctioning of indulgence in the social pleasures of "being Spanish." In Spain a strong ethnocentric attitude is expressed on many levels and easily observed in daily life. It may be expressed through an individual's sense of self-esteem (*amor propio*, which translates as "self-love") and touch deeply upon a person's gendered expectations. It may be expressed through a family's sense of honor, tradition, and legacy. It may be seen in a village's parochialism and pride in local products, crafts, and customs or in a Spaniard's nationalistic devotion to indigenous folk art forms and ritualized customs (such as flamenco and bullfighting). Pride of place, self, and cultural traditions expresses the indigenous Spaniard's affiliation with, and embodiment of, the normative values and beliefs that rule Spanish life.

One cannot comprehend the cultural significance of the movements and behaviors performed in Spain's public ritual life without first acknowledging Spanish ethnocentrism as a sign of a robust and vital culture. Without such awareness, normative behaviors may be wrongly interpreted by observers from outside of the culture as examples of stereotypical Spanish arrogance. Similarly, the pride exhibited through a matador's or flamenco dancer's behavior may erroneously be judged excessive.

For the Spanish Gypsies, the *gitanos*, ethnocentric attitudes may be tinged with a passionate defiance colored by the history of their social oppression. Within Spain, the *gitano* subculture is identified by language, occupation, and by specific art practices. The *gitano* language, known as *caló*, is a blend of Romany and Spanish idioms (Pohren [1962] 1984). Their most traditional occupations have been horse dealing, blacksmithing, peddling, and fortune telling (Gay y Blasco 1999). The *gitanos* are also known for their musicianship and dancing, especially for their contributions to the development of the flamenco arts. As a marginalized people, their lives have historically been difficult, yet their nomadic lifestyle afforded them some unique freedoms as well. For a *gitano* or *gitana*, a fervent dedication to the *gitano* way of life, family, tribe, and cultural constructions of honor and purity represents a point of individual pride as well as a much-tested survival strategy of their cultural group.

Anglo-European and Anglo-American ethnocentrism may affect one's view of flamenco and bullfighting. Though both are European nations, the contrast between English and Spanish cultures is significant. Spain's unique cultural location between Moorish (North African) and European cultures is summed up in Alexandre Dumas' often-quoted phrase "Africa begins at the Pyrenees," which indicates the historical nature of Spain's inherent geographical and cultural isolation from the rest of Europe. Furthermore, the many earlier acts of competition and conflict between the nations of Britain and Spain were then reiterated in various confrontational interactions of these two cultures throughout the history of the Americas. Some Anglo-Americans may not be conscious of having absorbed implicit negative judgments of Spanish customs as part of their cultural legacy. However, evidence of such bias emerges when the passion ascribed to flamenco arts is noted as unusual, excessive, or titillating, the flamenco arts are admired as exotic, or the bullfighting arts are dismissed as bloody and barbaric. Through such obvious language constructions both cultural practices are brought into the category of "the primitive," a maneuver that serves to uphold Anglo-American ethnocentric bias in relation to Hispanic cultures.

It is important to understand the effects of ethnocentrism. If unacquainted with the positive function of ethnocentrism in strengthening a culture, a non-Spaniard might be irritated by the exclusivity of a Spaniard's enthusiasm for Spanish cultural life above all others. If unaware of the potentially distorting effects of his or her own ethnocentrism, the powerful emotions and dramatic public ritual life of Spanish culture may be misinterpreted

Emotional intensity is culturally sanctioned in the flamenco dance genre and the Spanish bullfight. This 2012 photograph of matador Rafael Rubio "Rafaelillo" captures an intense moment as the spiraling forms of matador and bull are tightly entwined in the heat of the contest. Generally, there is a direct correlation between the intensity of a matador's kinesthetic experience and the intensity of the emotional response of those watching the bullfight (Juan Pelegrin/Flickr.com).

as signs of exotic behavior or inherent pathological excess. It is important to know that we inevitably perceive the cultures of other people through the filtering shadow of our own enculturated inhibitions and expectations.

Etic and Emic Perspectives

Two contrasting perspectives, known as *etic* and *emic*, contribute to the development of cultural knowledge. These terms (derived from linguistic theory) were coined by Kenneth L. Pike (1967) and are used to describe perspectives, methodologies, data, or types of knowledge being sought in relationship to culture.

Etic perspectives employ general criteria that are external to the cultural system being studied and enable objective measurement of parts within the system. Pike notes the usefulness of etic approaches in conducting cross-cultural research that makes comparisons among many cultures: "Through the etic 'lens' the analyst views the data in tacit reference to a perspective oriented to all comparable events (whether sounds, ceremonies, activities), of all peoples, of all parts of the earth" (Pike, 1967, 41). Using etic methodologies a researcher attempts to document phenomena objectively. Such research data may then be interpreted for cross-cultural or intracultural research. Etic perspectives enable cross-cultural comparisons, so that bullfighting might be studied in relation to the rituals of other cultures that also involve humans and animals.

In contrast, *emic* knowledge is culture-specific and integrative; it results when data is interpreted based on the implicit understandings of the culture itself. Through an emic lens a researcher may view "the same events, at the same time, in the same context, in reference to a perspective oriented to the particular function of those particular events in that particular culture, as it and it alone is structured" (Pike 1967, 41). Employing emic perspectives, the answers to questions about the practice of bullfighting would be sought within the bullfighting context itself and would be interpreted based on syntactical, philosophical, and ethical concepts drawn from that context. Employing emic perspectives to better understand flamenco dance requires extensive knowledge of the other art practices (such as music or poetry) that contribute to flamenco's performance and culture.

Anthropologist Drid Williams suggests that the etic perspective examines "all those concerns with universals and invariants that preoccupy investigators in the sciences, the social sciences, and linguistics." She points out that the value of the etic approach is its "search ... for universal, culture-free elements of the world that transcend or in some way overarch the diversity of local usages and references" (2004, 191).[4] Thus, etic perspectives often aspire to subsume a multiplicity of cultures within an overarching theoretical system. Interestingly, the desire to contain cultural multiplicity within a single theoretical system (and thus make human diversity more manageable) may itself be a function of Western cultural hegemony.

Any theoretical system (or methodology) should be examined carefully for its inherent cultural bias. Take, for instance, Laban Movement Analysis, the system of movement analysis used in my study of the movements of flamenco dance and bullfighting. The theories of Laban Movement Analysis, named after their creator Rudolph von Laban, emerged in the process of developing an effective movement notation system.[5] While Laban Movement Analysis provides valuable conceptual tools for an etic analysis of movement, it is not entirely free of cultural bias. Laban's theories reflect the Eurocentric values prevalent during the early twentieth century, the historic period during which Laban and his associates developed the system. Laban Movement Analysis relies upon dualistic frameworks, idealizing mechanization, modernity, and progressive social change, and valuing drama and high-intensity, expressive dynamics. It emphasizes spatial mobility rather than stability of form, presumes an investigation of the individual mover's psyche, and endorses collective political action. These were valued by its creators and so are implicit within the system.

The existing European system for music notation provided a rough model for Laban's research, which focused on the analysis of dance and movement phenomena. This specialization is advantageous for research focused on movement only, though it potentially obscures the holistic nature of the music-dance dyad. The scientific values and etic approach of Laban Movement Analysis make it reliable as a data-gathering methodology.[6] Although its values contrast greatly with the romantic values inherent in flamenco dance and bullfighting, Laban's system is a useful research tool for objectively identifying and categorizing the movement elements of flamenco dance and bullfighting.

Etic perspectives provide the valuable quality of detachment and objective observation, yet emic perspectives are of critical importance as well, and comprehensive understanding of a cultural phenomenon requires a synthesis of information gained through both etic and emic perspectives. According to Pike, "etic and emic data do not constitute a rigid dichotomy of bits of data, but often present the same data from two points of view" (1967, 39). Sound ethnographic research takes the form of a progression, from an initial and tentative etic analysis to a final, comprehensive synthesis with emic knowledge: "In the total analysis, the initial etic description is gradually refined, and is ultimately—in principle, but probably never in practice— replaced by one which is totally emic" (1967, 39).

Ideally, study of a cultural practice provides for a synthesis of objective information that enables cross-cultural comparisons (etic) and is capable of explaining the practice using its own vocabulary, concepts, beliefs, and values (emic). Ethnicity, class, gender, and culture (as well as many other factors such as disability, age, sexual orientation, etc.) add complexity to the integration of the etic and emic perspectives through which cultural knowledge is gained. Such factors may affect whether one has access to the type of education that provides knowledge of etic methodologies, or, by determining whether one is an insider or outsider in relation to a cultural practice, such factors may determine one's access to emic knowledge.

Ethnicity

The subculture of the *gitanos* (Spanish Gypsies) is an interesting example. The tribal nature of *gitano* culture results in a marked boundary between belonging and ostracism, and an intense awareness of an individual's location in relationship to the innermost circle of the cultural group. The widespread European prejudice against Gypsies reinforces the *gitanos'* pleasure of social belonging and fear of ostracism from their tribe. Their outsider status in relationship to Spanish society intensifies their need to belong as an insider in the *gitano* social group and, in general, intensifies the importance of the insider/outsider dichotomy. Paradoxically, although *gitano* ethnicity is cause for social marginalization within mainstream Spanish culture, *gitano* culture and flamenco constitute a cultural complex that serves Spain as a distinctive cultural icon. Based on their unique ethnicity and cultural history, *gitanos* often claim special authority in relationship to the flamenco arts. Through their claim to special authenticity, *gitanos* are empowered as aesthetic arbiters and cultural authorities. In many cases, this claim on emic knowledge translates into status, both economic and social.

Social Class

Economic status may also affect a person's access to emic and etic perspectives in relationship to flamenco dance and bullfighting. Speaking broadly, the flamenco arts traditionally belong to the Spanish lower classes (including the *gitano* subculture) and are supported by the patronage of upper-class aficionados (scholars, enthusiasts, fans) and *patrones* (financial patrons of the arts). Although emic knowledge of the flamenco arts is available across Spain's social spectrum, a person's social position affects his or her access and perspective. Etic perspectives are often acquired through travel opportunities or higher education, which are more readily available to Spain's middle and upper classes.

In contrast, control of the cultural practice of bullfighting traditionally belongs to the landowning upper classes of Spain. The entertainment industry surrounding professional bullfighting and the agricultural production of Spanish beef for the public marketplace are economically profitable and necessarily interdependent. In Spain, emic knowledge of bullfighting is widely shared. Bullfighting is the rich man's sport that interests all, a public display of nobility and drama to which the poor aspire (Collins and Lapierre 1968). Professional bullfighting performances are open to the general public and so can be witnessed by any person who can afford the ticket price. And while ticket prices may exclude Spain's poorest classes from direct attendance, their absence at professional events should not be taken as evidence of their lack of interest or lack of emic knowledge. Professional bullfights are televised and widely disseminated through various media with the result that the *corrida de toros* (public bullfight event) is a mainstay of Spanish popular culture.

Gender

Similarly, gender can affect a person's insider or outsider status in relation to flamenco dance and bullfighting. When cultural sanctions for or against a person's participation are based on the person's sex, these gendered constraints are generally compelling. Bullfighting is identified primarily as a masculine domain; its practitioners are predominantly male, although a few women, too, now kill bulls in the arena as professional matadors.[7]

The cultural practice of flamenco also exhibits sexual politics. As a cultural activity, flamenco dance is associated with the feminine, while flamenco music is associated with the masculine. In having more female than male performers, flamenco dance tends to follow Western cultural norms. This is not to say that there are no male flamenco dancers or female flamenco singers and guitarists, but those who deviate from gender conventions will be outnumbered and gender bias may negatively affect their participation. People may feel less welcome or comfortable in various roles and realms depending on their sex, sexual preferences, and the culturally gendered behaviors they choose to enact.

A male flamenco dancer may endure direct ridicule or have his masculinity questioned or challenged.[8] A female matador also faces challenges in proportion to the stringency of the cultural enforcement of sex differences.[9] The famous contemporary *matadora* Cristina Sánchez accomplished much during her years as a professional bullfighter. As a result of her status as a cultural insider and a professional practitioner of the bullfighting arts, her emic knowledge of bullfighting is undeniably authoritative. However, Sánchez retired early from her professional career, citing sex discrimination as the reason for her exclusion from the more important professional *corridas* (bullfights) and bullrings. Being female made her an outsider within bullfighting's male domain (Sánchez 1998).

The contexts of bullfighting and flamenco involve very complex and deeply entrenched gender issues, bullfighting serving as the prototypical test of masculinity and flamenco dance serving as the prototypical display of female charms. These gendered behavioral norms are based on Spanish cultural assumptions (worldview) regarding the male/female dichotomy.

Joaquín Cortés is seen performing at Foro Italico in Rome, Italy. A multi-genre dancer, Cortés toured with the Spanish National Ballet from 1984 until forming his own company in 1992. In 1995, Cortés' noted choreography *Pasión Gitana* (Gypsy Passion) helped expand the choreographic possibilities within the flamenco genre by incorporating theatrical ballet and contemporary modern dance aesthetics. In a revolutionary move that freed subsequent male flamenco dancers to dance with more overt sensuality and a greater range of emotions, Cortés broke tradition with flamenco's reserved *macho* prototype by dancing shirtless (Domenico di Bona/Shutterstock.com).

CULTURE

There is a significant contrast between Anglo-American and Spanish perspectives in relationship to the cultural practices of flamenco and bullfighting.[10] Recognizing the effects of Anglo-American enculturation on my own cross-cultural experience, I also see its influence on many of the Anglo-American authors who write about Spanish culture. Anglo-Americans generally express ambivalent attitudes toward both flamenco performance (wanting to participate, yet feeling inhibited) and Spanish bullfighting (enthralled by the spectacle, yet appalled by the cruelty). Anglo-Americans generally consider the cultural practice of bullfighting moralistically, judging it to be cruel and inhumane. Despite this, some Anglo-Americans have become bullfight aficionados and even matadors. Anglo-Americans may also express fascination with bullfighting for its ritual, pomp, and drama, and fascination with flamenco dance for its earthiness, sensuality, and passion.

The puritan roots of Anglo-American culture generally lead to attitudes that reject dance itself as an inappropriate activity. In some cases, these attitudes express an unconscious distrust of dance as sinful and dangerous to one's moral and physical health (Wagner 1997). As a result, many Anglo-Americans view flamenco dance voyeuristically. To them, flamenco dance represents a tantalizing, forbidden area of human experience (and excess) against which Anglo-American cultural sanctions are aligned. Witnessing the freedom and abandon of others, but with conflicted feelings about their own level of participation, Anglo-Americans may be simultaneously judgmental and envious of flamenco's open emotional expressivity and sensual energy.

Nevertheless, gaining knowledge of flamenco culture may become a goal for some. Most Anglo-American or non–Spanish aficionados, whether they are fans of the flamenco arts or the bullfight, begin by employing etic perspectives and eventually seek out emic perspectives in their efforts to understand these cultural practices. In doing so they may follow Kenneth L. Pike's model (1967), progressing from an initial and tentative analysis that relies on etic perspectives, gradually gaining emic perspectives over time by learning from cultural insiders, and finally achieving an understanding that involves a synthesis of etic and emic knowledge.

Pike points out that knowledge gained through processes of acculturation may never result in knowledge that is "totally emic" (1967, 39). This is because our sensibilities, our capacities to respond emotionally and aesthetically, are created through the processes of our original enculturation. Each culture has its own style of enculturation; all enculturation involves somatic patterning of the body itself and reinforces cultural attitudes toward the body. Living in Spain and being directly engaged in the embodied cultural practices of Spain on a daily basis greatly strengthened my awareness of the significant contrast between Spanish and Anglo-American attitudes toward the body. I saw the people of Spain accept physical embodiment matter-of-factly in situations that would generally cause Anglo-Americans to experience embarrassment, shame, or discomfort. For example, I have seen Spanish people stop a friend on the street to take a close look at a blemish on their skin, an injured arm, an infected ear, or a sore throat. And in my flamenco dance class one day, the students were comparing belly fat by pinching their middles, each holding their roll of fat up, belly fat next to belly fat. The Spanish openly give each other nicknames based on physical attributes, such as the nickname "El Cojo" (the lame one) given to the flamenco dancer Enrique Jiménez (1912–85), who danced well despite disabilities.

The research of Seymour Fisher and Sidney Cleveland helps explain the psychosomatic basis of an Anglo-American's difficulty in acquiring emic knowledge of flamenco and bullfighting. Fisher and Cleveland use a measure called the "Barrier score," which they described as "an indicator of the degree to which the individual has been able to establish a separate stabilized identity" (1958, 151).[11] Describing the process through which these patterns of body perception, identity, and behavior are established, they explain that "the way in which an individual experiences his [or her] body from the very beginning is a function of his [or her] family experiences and social milieu" (110). They assert that the combination of "impulse restraint and contradiction in values," such as typifies Anglo-American culture, leads an individual to experience himself or herself as having indefinite boundaries (285).

This experience of having indefinite boundaries is enculturated, particularly during an Anglo-American child's formative years, through low tolerance of expressive behaviors and the secrecy, shame, or denial associated with natural bodily functions. This, when combined with the sometimes confusing diversity, uncertainty, and variability of Anglo-American social values, may result in a person having undefined personal boundaries. "The indefinite-boundary cultures are marked by multiple contradictory standards from which the individual makes his [or her] choice in a relativistic fashion" (Fisher and Cleveland 1958, 283). The behavioral attributes of people who experienced themselves as having indefinite boundaries are described as being "more impersonal. They remained relatively inactive in group participation and sought guidance for their conduct in objective rules and regulations" (216).[12] Thus, Anglo-Americans may tend to cautiously hold themselves back from participation and hesitate to assert themselves socially due to uncertainty about the behavioral rules.

In contrast, people who tend to experience themselves as having definite boundaries, and this would apply to most of the people of Spain, are enculturated with behavioral patterns that "provide considerably more freedom for the developing child to indulge his [or her] impulses" (Fisher and Cleveland 1958, 283). The social roles and expectations of Spanish culture are more restricting and inflexible compared to those of Anglo-American culture, and it is precisely this quality of containment that provides secure cultural and social boundaries within which Spaniards may express their individuality with relative freedom and abandon. Thus, Spain's tolerance of personal expression combines with stable Spanish social structures, or what Fisher and Cleveland describe as "well codified and noncontradictory belief systems," allowing individuals to experience themselves as having well-defined personal boundaries (283).

Fisher and Cleveland assert that people from such cultural groups "demonstrate an interest in people and feelings. They press forward and stimulate one another in their search for human contact" (1958, 216). I recognize in this description a behavior that I often saw enacted in Spain, and that never failed to surprise me. Seeing two people engaged in a vigorous dispute, as an Anglo-American I expected trouble or possibly even violence, and I would then be amazed to see them part with big smiles (and often a farewell embrace), apparently quite satisfied by the heightened level of self-expression and human contact they had achieved together through arguing.

Fisher and Cleveland's research confirms and highlights my experience of the positive role of conflict within the cultural practices of flamenco dance and bullfighting. Spanish enculturation supports the creation of separate, stabilized identities, and any conflict that erupts between them is often enjoyed. Bullfighting and flamenco are enduring traditions within Spanish culture because they provide culturally sanctioned opportunities for individual expression, contained and stabilized within the public arena or a social circle.

Cultural Relativity

Cultural relativism is a fundamental principle of anthropology and follows logically upon the recognition of the effect of ethnocentrism. The theory of cultural relativity establishes that "evaluations are *relative* to the cultural background out of which they arise" (48; Herskovits's italics). Both our ability to perceive and how we interpret our perceptions are formed by, and dependent on, our initial experiences within our own native culture, and this is an unavoidable bias that ethnographers contend with as they study the behavioral patterns and beliefs of other cultural groups.

Discussing relativism (both cultural and historical), anthropologist Clifford Geertz notes that "we can never apprehend another people's or another period's imagination neatly, as if it were our own" (2000, 44). Anthropologists generally agree that complete comprehension of the emic perspectives of another culture is not possible. "We can apprehend it well enough, at least as well as we apprehend anything else not properly ours; but we do so not by looking *behind* the interfering glosses that connect us to it but *through* them" (44; Geertz's italics). Thus, discovering the assumptions intrinsic to and tacit within our own culture is an essential part of the process of coming to know another culture.

Discussing cultural relativism, Herskovits wrote that "with a means of probing deeply into all manner of differing cultural orientations, of reaching into the significance of the ways of living of different peoples, we can turn again to our own culture with fresh perspective, and an objectivity that can be achieved in no other manner" (1964, 64). This statement reframes the scientific purpose behind anthropology's goal of objectivity, revealing the ethnographer's desire to be free of the blinding constraints of (his or her) ethnocentrism. Etic methodologies, cross-cultural research, and cultural relativism provide opportunities for a reexamination of one's own cultural roots. As a result of my experiences with Spanish culture through the embodied movement practices of flamenco dance and bullfighting, I better understand American culture. I recognize that my earliest enculturation emphasized individualism as a value, reality, and realizable goal. This basic tenet of individualism is securely interwoven with many other attitudes, behaviors, and beliefs that together constitute a U.S. American worldview. The American ideology of individualism values independence and reducing social conflict by maintaining the distance between people, and this contrasts sharply with a Spanish ideology of individuality that values unbounded sociality as a playground for the uniqueness of strong personalities.

Performative Practices

Both flamenco and bullfighting function as public spectacles; their audiences gather to witness impressive performances by those who dare to express their emotions with intensity through dance or dare fate itself in the bullring. These two performance practices are notable for their risk taking, both physical and emotional. Just as bullfighters seem to be playing with death, in performance, flamenco artists call upon an uncanny transcendent quality called *duende* (spirit) that enables the elusive spirits of the dead and the rough edge of pain and loss to guide their artistry.

The spectacular nature of these two dramatic performance activities makes examination of their details challenging. Given such intensity, it is often difficult for observers to look beyond the immediate, overt display that first commands their attention. In fact, objectivity runs counter to the fundamental purposes of flamenco dance and bullfighting. Those who know flamenco or bullfighting from personal experience, from the somatic perspective of a practitioner, have a categorically different type of knowledge. Many aspects that seem fundamental, essential, and obvious to those directly involved in these two cultural practices may be invisible or less apparent to outside observers. Western theatrical traditions enjoin fantasy and pretense in the creation and performance of imaginary worlds, and presume that enactments onstage are separate and distinct from offstage realities. In contrast, the performance practices of many non–Western cultures are based on the assumption of an integral interconnection between performance and daily life.

As performance practices, flamenco and bullfighting function within a romantic aesthetic that values nature, freedom of expression, and the heroism of the common man, and are both firmly based in (embodied, physical) actuality and risk. They are valued for their ambiguity, the tension between idealism and realism that they provide. The word *performative*, originally a linguistics term,[13] is used to describe statements that by being uttered signify an action (as saying "I promise" is understood to constitute an actual promise). Persons participating in flamenco and bullfighting as primary performers engage in the performative aspects of these activities on at least two levels, the personal and the social. For example, performing in the bullring is a performative act that directly and in itself affects a person's courage, affirming it, increasing it, or undermining it. Before one can publicly make a show of one's bravery, one must first, in actuality, face one's fear and summon courage. Thus a courageous performance constitutes a real-life event that has the power to affect an individual's sense of self-worth as well as his or her social standing. Similarly, the character, behavior, and sense of self of a flamenco artist (dancer, singer, or guitarist) are not enacted through pretense, but are generated in actuality through the quality of his or her performances. Thus, public (as well as private) performances of flamenco and bullfighting constitute performative acts affecting real-life relationships and economic opportunities, with the more successful flamenco artists and matadors enjoying much greater economic rewards for each performance event than those who are less accomplished.

CHAPTER ONE

Flamenco and Bullfighting
An Ongoing Discussion

Flamencology and Tauromachy

Because flamenco and bullfighting constitute important practices within the popular culture of Spain, many types of people engage in discussions about them, and the wide range of the resulting discourse reflects this diversity. The discourse, which is also supported through the public media, radio, films, and television, as well as the Internet and social media, ranges from the views of intellectuals and scholars to the views of members of the public at large, some of whom, due to illiteracy or preference, may only participate through informal conversation.

Flamenco and bullfighting don't often come up in regular conversation in the United States, but in Spain these are normal topics of conversation that come up often and about which most Spaniards have strong opinions. Whether for or against bullfighting, whether enthusiastic or uninterested in the flamenco arts, whether rural or urban, whether young or old, most Spaniards fully understand these two cultural practices to be deeply linked. The average Spaniard, supposing there to be such a person, is very likely to be able and eager to add emic perspectives, anecdotal evidence, historical details or philosophical viewpoints to any such discussion. This is an ongoing discussion on the streets, in the bars and clubs, in family homes, through phone and online conversations, through television, theater, and film, in training situations for both flamenco and bullfighting, and in the formal scholarship that addresses these two cultural practices.

The challenge is how to sort through the many sources of information that contribute to this discussion. There are many resources, none of them perfect, and many pitfalls; you can't believe everything you hear or read. Poetic embellishment and exaggerated tales of personalities and events are the mainstays of these conversations. In fact, the Spanish people love a good argument; they take pleasure in expressing their own opinions with passion and both enjoy and respect the partisanship of those with opposing views. Since partisanship itself is often the point, how is a non-Spaniard to make sense of the arguments? Patience is key, and fortitude helps.

Living and traveling in Spain, I had numerous opportunities to speak with people enthusiastic about the flamenco arts, bullfighting, or both; accessing the informal ongoing conversation is not particularly difficult. Once, at three o' clock in the morning, the time that in Spain is known as *la madrugada*, the hours between midnight and dawn, I was sitting with my Jerezana friends in the dark at an outdoor table in Jerez. I was cold and exhausted after a very long day and on the verge of excusing myself to head back to my room at the *pension* and a warm comfortable bed when a renowned aficionado of tauromachy showed up. Knowing of my interest, my friends introduced us and the conversation took on new life. I don't remember when I finally got to bed.

In 1999, accessing archives in Spain, the Fundación de Flamenco, the Biblioteca Municipal de Jerez de la Frontera, and the Biblioteca Nacional de España, I began to investigate how the relatedness of flamenco dance and bullfighting were addressed in two areas of specialized knowledge within Spanish scholarship: flamencology and tauromachy.[1] Flamencology is scholarship focused on the culture, social history, and aesthetics of flamenco performance, while the literature of tauromachy discusses the philosophy, aesthetic values, and history of the art of bullfighting. Within these literatures recognition of the relationship between flamenco and bullfighting is virtually obligatory, though references are often metaphoric or vague. Most commonly conducted in the Spanish language, both areas of scholarship tend to rely on anecdotal material and emphasize historical narrative or personal memoir.

Scholarly discussion of flamenco dance and bullfighting most often has produced social critiques or cultural analyses. There are many cross-references within the scholarship of flamencology and tauromachy; both direct and tangential references to bullfighting exist in flamencology texts, and flamenco receives comparable attention in tauromachy texts. Still, the two cultural practices are most often studied separately, and little scholarship seems to address the links between them on the embodied or phenomenological level.

The correlations between the movement phenomena and protocols of flamenco and bullfight performance events are not usually addressed in Spanish scholarship. I believe there are several reasons that this may be so, and foremost among them is the fact that movement is notably difficult to describe accurately using words. Perhaps it is partly for this reason that movement as a cultural phenomenon has generally been underrepresented, given a cursory explanation, or, in some cases, been ignored within the scholarly discourse surrounding flamenco and bullfighting. Instead, the existing scholarship generally focuses on performance personalities, historic events, aesthetic issues, or sociological and cultural aspects of these two cultural practices, topics that do not require descriptions of specific movement phenomena.

Substantive discussion is lacking regarding the role of cultural embodiment, namely, how the deep cultural connection that exists between flamenco dance and bullfighting is evidenced, formed, and maintained through movement praxis (practice). I use the term *praxis* to emphasize that human bodies practice for hours daily over a lifetime to perfect flamenco dance performances or to gain the necessary skill in manipulating a cape so as to survive the repeated charges of a bull with artistry and style. The absence of this discussion may also be due to a mistaken assumption on the part of many scholars that analysis of movement phenomena and the complexity of discourse in this area pose insurmountable challenges. Many non-dance scholars are simply unaware that scholars in the dance field have developed methodologies for the analysis of movement phenomena for a wide range of research purposes.

In addition, cultural beliefs that ascribe an instinctive quality to movement itself also have a negative influence on the production of meaningful scholarship on this topic. Because movement phenomena are complex and belong to the realm of nonverbal expression and behavior, many assume that such phenomena are beyond analysis and verbal representation. That the practices of flamenco dance and bullfighting are strongly influenced by the romantic aesthetic further hinders objective scholarship; a scholar's choice to gloss over the details of movement phenomena or to resort to poetic exaggeration is implicitly validated by the romantically oriented value system in which flamenco dance and bullfighting function.

Spanish-language texts that address flamenco or bullfighting often provide valuable emic perspectives. However, when Spanish-language texts lack etic perspectives entirely, the accuracy of their information becomes suspect. Texts written in English are also available, some of which strive to achieve a balance between emic and etic perspectives. Exclusive reliance on English-language texts is problematic, as the authenticity of the author's information is subject to question. Whether a text is written in English or Spanish, the author's location, perspectives, and methodology will significantly affect the contributions it makes to the broader discussion.

An issue affecting both English- and Spanish-language texts is language style. Because both flamenco and bullfighting function within the romantic aesthetic, many authors writing under this influence produce poetic descriptions that, for the purpose of scholarship, are marred by exaggeration and poetic license. Furthermore, within the cultural contexts of flamenco and bullfighting, enthusiasm and partisanship are highly valued. Rationality and objectivity? Not so much. Whether an entertaining travelogue written by a foreign aficionado or a philosophical treatise written by a Spaniard, many texts reflect the fact that their authors write from enthusiasm and often with overt partiality. Whether an author satisfies the romantic expectations of his or her readership also determines whether a written work will be publishable and successful.

Flamenco practices emphasize sociality; therefore, affective relationships and sociocultural expectations play a large part in how flamenco arts are critiqued, assessed, and valued. Social, cultural, or financial pressures related to membership in *peñas* or social clubs may also indirectly affect how authors choose to participate in the ongoing discussion. Flamencologists are social beings, and the emphasis on historical anecdotes and the personality of great performers in the scholarship of flamencology reflects their investment in the social dynamics of the flamenco subculture. The bullfighting context functions similarly.

Anecdotes are commonly used as a means of transmitting knowledge in both these literatures and readable books are often the result. The anecdote itself is accepted as genuine and legitimate information because both cultural practices function largely as oral traditions. Once an anecdote has passed through a certain number of tellings, for all intents and purposes, it becomes true. Many of the best Spanish-language texts on flamenco and bullfighting do not cite sources for the information they provide. Instead, they reflect the emic values of subjective opinion, intense partisanship, poetic ramblings, and passionate excess; their substantial value lies in the fact that they "tell a good story." The wealth of anecdotal evidence within the flamencology and tauromachy scholarship has yet to be examined objectively or organized to reveal unifying patterns within the two cultural practices.

Yet another language issue affecting these two areas of scholarship is the importance of nonverbal transmission of knowledge in these traditions. Scholarly texts pertaining to the flamenco arts are influenced by the nonliterate nature of the cultural practice, by the art form's significant reliance on oral and kinesthetic traditions. The poetic verses (*letras*) of flamenco song (*cante*) are part of Spain's extensive oral tradition. Collections of traditional flamenco *letras* have been published as text, and, since the development of modern recording technologies, flamenco *letras* have also been widely disseminated through public media. Although published musical notation for the guitar contributes somewhat to the transmission of flamenco music, the nonliterate process of person-to-person transmission and artistic mentoring continues to be primary. Learning how to play the flamenco guitar through direct observation, listening, or some form of one-on-one mentorship reflects both traditional and current practice, and, in a newer development, modern media such as online video sites or Skype now are further extending the tradition of flamenco's nonliterate transmission.

Even more than flamenco music, flamenco dance is a nonliterate tradition; its transmission involves oral and kinesthetic processes. Systems for its notation are rare, and rarely published, though that is changing.[2] As an unwritten tradition, flamenco dance relies on the remarkable human capacity to encode and remember complex patterns of sound and movement. Improvisational practices in the flamenco arts also reflect the nonliterate values of the cultural context. The qualitative and emotional aspects of dance and music expression are highly valued in the flamenco arts. Especially in the case of superlative flamenco performances, the phenomena of performance are generally considered to be beyond the scope of language. This represents an emic point of view: the written word is highly respected, but reverent expressions of awe and cries of "¡Olé!" are reserved for the ineffable qualities of lived experience.

Flamencology

In flamencology, the evidence of connection between flamenco and bullfighting is typically indicated in three ways. First, it is pointed out that direct references to bullfighting are made within the language of flamenco *letras* (song verses); second, that there are overlapping social and familial relationships between the participants of each cultural practice; and third, that shared aesthetic and cultural values nourish the roots of both flamenco and bullfighting.

Many flamencology texts attempt to provide a comprehensive overview of the range of flamenco arts, namely, the song (*cante*), guitar music (*toque*), and dance (*baile*). This scholarship typically emphasizes music, particularly the *cante,* while dance is mentioned less frequently. Perhaps this is because scholars not trained in dance or movement analysis have difficulty differentiating movement details and so hesitate to articulate their thoughts regarding such phenomena. It may also reflect a bias within the practice of flamenco itself that values the *cante* over the *baile, cante* being a male-dominated and more language-oriented domain and the *baile* being a domain that is more closely associated with females, bodies, and nonverbal expression. That *cante* generally receives greater attention in flamencological texts reflects this hierarchical relation between flamenco music and dance.

More rare in the flamencology literature are those texts that focus on dance. In *El arte del baile flamenco* (The Art of the Flamenco Dance), author Alfonso Puig Claramunt (1977) provides a useful historical survey of flamenco dance with an abundance of visual images dating from approximately 1832 to 1971. Puig Claramunt focuses on the development of flamenco dance, describing the first emergence of flamenco artists into venues of public performance in the *cafés cantantes* (the singing cafes), and their eventual arrival as established artists in the more formal theatrical setting of the concert stage.

Puig Claramunt includes useful information about early theatrical productions and ballets in which flamenco dance was influential, but does not clarify the distinction between flamenco dance and the genre of Spanish classical dance, which may confuse some readers.[3] Puig Claramunt probably assumes that he is writing for Spanish readers who will readily comprehend the nuances of class and the contrasting artistic contexts of flamenco and classical Spanish dance. There may also be an unconscious understanding between Puig Claramunt and his readers that they are literate, educated, and are of the same (upper) class. And so it may pose no problem to his Spanish readers that Puig Claramunt does not address the contributions of indigenous flamenco artists, except as they may have eventually appeared on the professional stage.

The photos and artwork in Puig Claramunt's text include images that indicate the influence of bullfighting. Despite significant visual evidence (seen in costume, posture, and theatrical scenario), overt reference to bullfighting in the text is minimal. Although Puig Claramunt's book contains no footnotes and provides no bibliographical information or index, it is a very rich and valuable resource, and its value is further increased through the inclusion of an extensive description of the flamenco dance technique of Flora Albaicín.

El baile flamenco (The Flamenco Dance) (1998) by Ángel Álvarez Caballero focuses on notable performers and performances in the history of flamenco dance and is a rich source of information, providing emic knowledge of flamenco personalities and flamenco's social climate. Álvarez Caballero provides chapter notes, a listing of prize-winning performers, a glossary of flamenco terminology, an index, and an extensive bibliography, making this text a useful reference. Interestingly, Álvarez Caballero dedicates about nine pages of his book to the discussion of the relation between flamenco dance and bullfighting. He does not believe the connection to be direct, but admits "a certain affinity between both arts, especially in the atmosphere they produce, the temperament of their important participants and some singular possibilities of comparison, especially as concern the dance" (Álvarez Caballero 1998, 87).[4] This last point made by Álvarez Caballero identifies precisely the area of research examined in this book.

Another text, richer in photographic evidence and more cognizant of the indigenous roots of flamenco as a cultural practice, is *Luces y sombras del flamenco* (Lights and Shadows of Flamenco) by J. M. Caballero Bonald (1997). It describes the development of the *baile, toque,* and *cante* as they function synergistically in the performance of culture. Caballero Bonald emphasizes the development of flamenco music in his writing, while flamenco dance is represented primarily through the inclusion of many fine photos. Thus, flamenco dance is used to heighten the book's visual interest for readers, while conveying an implicit message that dance phenomena are too ephemeral to be brought directly into scholarly discourse. This acceptance of dance primarily for its visual contribution is a common strategy in publications dealing with the flamenco arts. *Las Máscaras de lo Jondo* (Faces of Deep Flamenco) (1992) showcases flamenco photography by Elke Stolzenberg and includes text by Álvarez Caballero. Stolzenberg's unique strategy is to show not just photographs of dancers, but photographs of all types of flamenco artists in performance, singers, dancers, and guitarists. The result is a deeper look into the personalities and aesthetics of flamenco performance.

Spanish texts that provide information on the flamenco arts, and address specific attributes of the flamenco dance, include: *El enigma de España en la danza española* (The Enigma of Spain in the Spanish Dance) by Vicente Marrero Suárez (1959); *El baile* (The Dance) by Concepción Carretero (1981); *La danza española* (The Spanish Dance) by Trini Borrull (1982); *Tratado de bailes* (Treatise of Dances) by José Otero (1987); and *El baile flamenco* (The Flamenco Dance) by Ángeles Arranz del Barrio (1996). There are, of course, many others.

Scholarly writings also include reports of flamenco dance and bullfighting being linked in the public's creative imagination particularly through theatrical portrayals onstage or in films. A story line that appears quite often in dance drama scenarios is that of a romance between a handsome bullfighter (male) and a beautiful Gypsy dancer (female). An example of this is the *Romance del torero eterno ballet* (Ballad of the Eternal Torero Ballet) by Enrique Alarcón Sánchez-Manjavaras (n.d.).

Also of interest is the book *Carmen: El sueño del amor absoluto* (Carmen: The Dream of Absolute Love) (Saura 1984), which reports on the making of the movie *Carmen* by film director Carlos Saura and dance choreographer Antonio Gades. The film itself includes a scene of rivalry between a matador

The ballet *Carmen,* whether presented onstage or in film, typically includes the iconic figure of the matador. The 1983 film version of *Carmen,* directed by Carlos Saura and choreographed by Antonio Gades, includes a scene in which flamenco dancers playfully enact the formal traditions of the Spanish bullfight. This 2008 photograph of the Ballet Teatro Español de Rafael Aguilar performing *Carmen* at the Jichen Theater in Chengdu, China, includes the figure of the matador with the impressive specter of a bull looming in the background (Jack.Q/Shutterstock.com).

and the primary male protagonist of the story, danced by Antonio Gades. The film also includes a notably lighthearted dance scene that enacts formal bullfight protocols; through their performance of this familiar cultural ritual the dance protagonists demonstrate their emic knowledge of bullfighting and thus their belonging within the cultural group.

English-language texts that address the flamenco arts vary in their level of usefulness. Some of the more informative texts offer an overview of the art, such as *Flamenco,* edited by Claus Schreiner (1990; first published in German in 1985). In attempting to provide a comprehensive overview of the flamenco arts, these often provide many details concerning song styles, dance forms, the functioning of the music-dance dyad, historical developments, and regional variations; the connection between flamenco dance and bullfighting may only receive a brief mention.

Many of the English-language texts that address flamenco culture are firsthand reports of cross-cultural experience provided through a mixture of ethnographic narrative and autobiographic memoir. It is often due to contrast with our own cultural habits that we come to identify the unique attributes, manners, and values of another culture, and some English-language texts, particularly flamenco travelogue-type memoirs, have that as their strength. These reflections can be very informative: *In Search of the Firedance* (1992) by James Woodall; *Song of the Outcasts* (2003) by Robin Totton; and *The Flamencos of Cadiz Bay* (1994) by Gerald Howson. Another notable contribution is *Flamenco Deep Song* (1994) by Timothy Mitchell, which provides a more sociological analysis than is found in the other works listed.

The writings of D. E. Pohren were particularly influential in first drawing the attention of a U.S. American readership and providing potential new aficionados with hard-to-obtain information on the flamenco arts. Books by D. E. Pohren include *The Art of Flamenco* ([1962] 1984); *Lives and Legends of Flamenco: A Biographical History* (1964); and *A Way of Life* (1980). Pohren, a flamenco guitarist, provides exhaustive detail regarding flamenco music; as a result, his books are useful references, especially when one has a specific question. However, if one is seeking useful and balanced information on flamenco dance, they can be disappointing. Unaware, perhaps, that dance as a universal human activity contributes significantly to affective culture worldwide, Pohren is summarily dismissive of the role of dance and its function within the flamenco genre, expressing misogynistic and homophobic attitudes and specifically targeting flamenco dance and dancers in his remarks.

In *The Art of Flamenco*, Pohren describes the connection between bullfighting and flamenco as "undeniable, and vital for an understanding of either" ([1962] 1984, 30). However, his discussion of the topic is remarkably brief. In fact, most of Pohren's three short pages on the subject are taken up with the poetry of Federico García Lorca. Pohren explains his use of Lorca's poetry to point out the connection between these two cultural practices, saying that Lorca "wrote inseparably of flamenco and the bulls" (30). Pohren mentions that flamencologist Anselmo González Climent has "dedicated an entire book" to the subject of flamenco and bullfighting, but does not provide the book's title (30).

While researching flamenco and bullfighting in Spain, I followed Pohren's hint and searched for the works of Anselmo González Climent, who, though a noted flamencologist, was originally from Argentina, South America. I found two texts especially interesting, *Andalucia en los toros, el cante y la danza* (Andalusia in the Bulls, the Song, and the Dance) (1953) and *Flamencología: (toros, cante y baile)* (Flamencology: Bulls, Song, and Dance) (1964), in which González Climent expanded and developed ideas from his earlier book.

González Climent's writing describes and discusses the aesthetic values and the philosophical connections between bullfighting and the flamenco arts. Like many other flamencologists, González Climent was primarily interested in the aesthetics of flamenco *cante* (song) and writes less about the role of movement or flamenco *baile* (dance). González Climent also wrote specifically on flamenco arts in *Bulerías: Un ensayo jerezano* (*Bulerías*: An Essay from Jerez) (1961). In this latter work, González Climent points out that the informal qualities of the *bulerías* song and dance style allow it to draw from everyday life in its themes, providing a natural opportunity for religion, bullfighting, and flamenco to mix and share their influences within the artistic context of flamenco performance. This last point is quite significant; it begins to answer the question of how and under what circumstances the movement practices and practitioners of dance and bullfighting were brought together and intermingled.

Other flamencologists have also addressed the connections between flamenco and bullfighting. In *Cancionero popular taurino: Antología* (Popular Bullfight Songbook: Anthology) Manuel Martinez Remis (1963) provides an anthology of popular song lyrics that reference or celebrate bullfighting. In *Flamenco y toros* (Flamenco and Bulls) David González (1991) takes up this theme through the visual arts, namely painting. Focusing more specifically on flamenco *cante*, Alfredo Arrebola, in his book *Cante y toros: Un ensayo de aproximación* (Song and Bulls: A Reflective Essay) (1991), provides a listing of toreros involved with flamenco arts and flamenco artists involved with the arts of tauromachy. In *Toros y flamenco* (Bulls and Flamenco) (1997) author Antonio Parra discusses the historical relationship between the two cultural practices, especially the social connections and the significant lineages of the flamenco and bullfight worlds. His list of individual and familial ties between the two overlapping social domains of bullfighting and flamenco provides extensive evidence in this regard.

Recent flamencological scholarship, in both English and Spanish languages, provides more complex perspectives. This more reflexive contemporary scholarship includes works such as *Libertad o tradición: Una especulación en torno a la estética del flamenco* (Freedom or Tradition: A Speculation on the Aesthetics of Flamenco) by Juan Vergillos Gómez (1999); "El arte flamenco como campo producción cultural: Aproximación a sus aspectos sociales" (The Flamenco Art as Rural Cultural Production: Reflection on its Social Aspects) by Francisco Aix Gracia (2002); and "El flamenco como patrimonio cultural o una construcción artificial más de la identidad andaluza" (Flamenco as Cultural Patrimony or an Artificial Construction of the Andalusian Identity) by Gerhard Steingress (2002).

Steingress also published a chapter titled "Social Theory and the Comparative History of Flamenco, Tango, and Rebetica" in *The Passion of Music and Dance: Body, Gender and Sexuality,* edited by William Washabaugh (1998). This edited book also provides examples of new approaches in flamencological scholarship, including two chapters by Washabaugh, "Flamenco Song: Clean and Dirty" and "Fashioning Masculinity in Flamenco Dance" (1998), and a chapter titled "Gendering the Authentic in Spanish Flamenco" by Timothy deWaal Malefyt (1998). Washabaugh contributes additional useful contemporary perspectives in his book, *Flamenco: Passion, Politics and Popular Culture* (1996). His chapter outlining the alternative histories assigned to the flamenco arts provides important perspectives on flamenco's shifting political significance within Spanish culture.[5] Author Michelle Heffner Hayes elucidates flamenco's alternative histories further in her book, *Flamenco: Conflicting Histories of the Dance* (2009), with emphasis on changes in the aesthetics and social politics of flamenco dance.

As embodied practices, flamenco dance and bullfighting function within Spanish life as public forums serving various social, political, and cultural ends. Washabaugh, writing on the subject of flamenco, its history, and its social function, addresses instances in which performances enact cultural fictions. The performance of any particular social identity, belief, individual characteristic, or cultural value need not be entirely genuine in order to have meaning or be effective in a performative sense. Outlining the "relevant agendas, ideologies, and political forces that operate, however covertly, in moments of flamenco performance," Washabaugh generously provides the contextual background for "detailing flamenco's metonymic politics" (1996, 9). For example, he discusses how General Francisco Franco's propaganda adopted the flamenco arts, fashioning from them a fiction that served his nationalistic agenda.

Tauromachy

In the scholarly literature of tauromachy are numerous Spanish-language texts that discuss the behaviors and customs surrounding bullfighting: Carlos Abella's *Derecho al toro! El lenguaje de los toros y su influencia en lo cotidiano* (Right to the Bull! The Language of the Bulls and Its Influence in Daily Life) (1996) and Vicente Zabala's *La entraña del toreo* (The Core of the Bullfight) (1968). There are also many books in English on the topic of bullfighting: Roderic Bright's *Toros without tears: A simple explanation of what you will see at a bull-fight* (1961) and Vincent J. R. Kehoe's *Aficionado! The Pictorial Encyclopedia of the Fiesta de Toros of Spain* (1959); both provide non–Spaniards with basic information on bullfight protocols. Vincent J. R. Kehoe's

Wine, Women & Toros! The Fiesta de Toros in the Culture of Spain (1961) and *The Sevilla of Carmen* (1985) by Robert Vavra (which features Vavra's excellent photos of Andalusian culture) provide more expansive treatment of the overall cultural context in which both flamenco dance and bullfighting function. Excellent bullfight images by photographer Ricardo B. Sánchez are published with essays by José Luis Ramón and Rosa Olivares in *Passes: The Art of the Bullfight: Seduction, Deception, Illusion and Truth* (2001).

Blood Sport: A Social History of Spanish Bullfighting (1991) by Timothy Mitchell comprehensively examines the complex sociohistorical issues surrounding bullfighting as a cultural practice. This very useful volume also includes an essay and extensive bibliography on bullfighting contributed by Rosario Cambria. Mitchell's work provides a convincing portrait of the modern *corrida* as a formal version of the many complex and diverse ritual bull-baiting practices that have taken place in Spain throughout its history and that continue today.

Another example of contemporary scholarship is Sarah Pink's *Women and Bullfighting: Gender, Sex, and the Consumption of Tradition* (1997). Gender is an important topic in relation to both cultural practices, and especially so when it comes to the discussion of movement practices because the stylistic choices and personal expression of individual performers are generally quite strongly affected by sexual identity and cultural expectations regarding gender and sexuality. Pink's book includes extensive information on the career of *matadora* Cristina Sánchez, who has also written her own autobiographical account, *Matadora* (1998).

Gitanos

To better understand the flamenco arts and cultural practices, knowledge of the *gitanos*, Spanish Gypsies, is helpful. There are many useful English-language texts pertaining to European Gypsies and *gitano* culture in particular: *Gypsies in Madrid: Sex, Gender, and the Performance of Identity* by Paloma Gay y Blasco (1999); *The Spanish Gypsy: The History of a European Obsession* by Lou Charnon-Deutsch (2004); *Gypsies and Flamenco: The Emergence of the Art of Flamenco in Andalusia* by Bernard Leblon (1995); *Gypsies: Wanderers of the World* by Bart McDowell (1970); *The Gypsies* by Jean-Paul Clébert (1963); and *The Gypsies of Granada*, with paintings and drawings by Jo Jones (1969). In English-language texts, the subject of the Spanish Gypsies is sometimes given a romantic gloss that appears less frequently in the following Spanish-language texts: *Los gitanos españoles* (The Spanish Gypsies) by María Helena Sánchez Ortega (1977); and, by Teresa San Román, *Gitanos de Madrid y Barcelona: Ensayos sobre aculturación y etnicidad* (Gypsies of Madrid and Barcelona: Essays on Acculturation and Ethnicity) (1984) and *Entre la marginación y el racismo: Reflexiones sobre la vida de los gitanos* (Between Marginalization and Racism: Reflections on the Life of the Gypsies) (1986). Spanish-language texts are often concerned with the very real racism, social inequalities, and economic struggles that Gypsies face in Spain and throughout Europe.

The *gitanos*, as a cultural group, and the *gitano* way of life, worldview, and aesthetics, have had and continue to exert a significant influence on the flamenco arts. While credited with influencing flamenco, the degree to which *gitano* culture may have influenced the development of bullfighting or affected the stylization of bullfight movement techniques is less documented. This difference is likely a result of the economic factors and social class distinctions which in some eras made being a matador an unreachable aspiration for Spain's poorer classes, whereas participation in the flamenco arts was easily accessible to all. As a result, although both the influence of the *gitano* culture on the flamenco tradition and the link between flamenco and bullfighting traditions are recognized, questions remain about the degree to which the *gitano* culture may have influenced bullfight practices.

Pedagogy

Cultural values and social intentions are expressed implicitly within the movement phenomena of flamenco dance and bullfighting. The tacit nature of this communication makes precise identification and interpretation of its meanings difficult for cultural outsiders. Cultural insiders need little clarification on these points; as a result, explicit explanations of this cultural information are rare. However, both flamencology and tauromachy contain within them two areas of discourse, aesthetic criticism and pedagogy, where these implicit values and intentions are clearly articulated. Aesthetic criticism often explains the technical standards and performance expectations that pertain to a high level of artistry in the context of professional flamenco and bullfighting. Emic perspectives in the area of aesthetic criticism are generally found in Spanish-language texts (Abella, Caballero Bonald, Álvarez Caballero, González Climent, and Zabala).

Pedagogical texts related to flamenco dance and tauromachy routinely address technical standards and artistic expectations, though usually in the context of movement training rather than performance. Their central purpose is to instruct readers in the complex patterns of structure and form underlying the movement techniques of flamenco dance and bullfighting. Those written in Spanish provide emic perspectives regarding the specifics of movement stylization, technique, and form, and in the process they often articulate the aesthetic and cultural values of both movement practices. Pedagogical texts not only provide Spanish cultural perspectives, but sometimes provide intimate perspectives, expressing the points of view of experts and seasoned performers.

A useful example written in Spanish is *Todas las suertes por sus maestros* (All of the Cape Passes from the Masters) by José Luís Ramon (1998), which describes unique tauromachy movements created by famous matadors. For those interested in studying movement details, this book provides ample evidence of the creativity and artistry of individual bullfighters, discussing the unique moves they created and employed in their performances in the *corrida*. Examples of texts addressing the movement techniques of flamenco dance include the descriptive summary of Flora Albaicín's flamenco dance technique in the back of Puig Claramunt's *El arte del baile flamenco* (1977) discussed earlier; *Spanish Dancing: A Practical Handbook* by Lalagia (1985); and *Becoming the Dance: Flamenco Spirit* by Teodoro Morca (1990). A useful article, "The 'Trained' and 'Natural' Gypsy Flamenco Dancer" by Miriam Phillips (1990), provides a culturally nuanced examination of the movement aesthetics of flamenco. *The Language of Spanish Dance* by Matteo Vittucci with Carola Goya (1990) gives a broad overview and provides dance notations for common flamenco steps and movements. Matteo's book also describes both flamenco and Spanish classical dance movements that constitute direct movement references to the bullfight.

All of these details and specifics are fascinating, but they are even better appreciated in context—which means not just the context of Spanish culture, but in relation to the underlying capacity that all humans share to experience and enact culture. It is in that broad realm of anthropology that the mysteries of flamenco and bullfighting become even more nuanced and compelling. One of the purposes of this book is to cull information and emic perspectives gained through the study of flamencology and tauromachy and integrate them into a broader interdisciplinary framework: cultural anthropology, anthropology of dance, movement analysis, somatic studies, ethnochoreology, and ethnography.

Cultural Anthropology

At present the discourse of cultural anthropology, particularly as it appears in descriptive ethnographic writing, reflects a high degree of concern about a researcher's position in relationship to his or her research subject. As contemporary ethnographers examine the ambiguity of their own position within the cultural context they are researching, their writing demonstrates a sophisticated appreciation of cultural diversity and political consequences. Questioning and examining theoretical issues is often considered integral to the research process by authors: Ruth Behar (2003), Edward M. Bruner (1986), James Clifford (1988), Clifford Geertz (2000), Michael Jackson (1989), Arnold Krupat (1992), George Marcus (1998), Richard Shweder (1996), Loïc Wacquant (2003), and Margery Wolf (1992).

In general, however, the writings of these contemporary ethnographers do not provide a balanced overview of the general theoretical frameworks of anthropology or systematically outline the key underlying principles of ethnographic inquiry. To better understand the anthropological principles at work in contemporary ethnographic research, one needs to refer to their roots in the earlier writings that first identified cultural relativity and outlined the principles and methods of participant observation, such as *Cultural Dynamics* by Melville J. Herskovits (1964) and *Participant Observation* by James P. Spradley (1980). Herskovits outlines the theory of cultural relativity and the function of ethnocentricity, and reviews the many challenges these principles present to ethnographic researchers. Spradley discusses the possible permutations of participant observation research methodologies, describing their relative advantages and disadvantages. Because definitions of anthropological concepts as they are first provided by their originators are often clearest, I use the terms *etic* and *emic* as they were first defined by Kenneth Pike (1967), the term *worldview* as it was first presented by Michael Kearney (1984), and refer to the early research of Seymour Fisher and Sidney E. Cleveland (1958) in addressing issues of Spanish body image, personality, and cultural expressivity.

Why Humans Have Cultures: Explaining Anthropology and Social Diversity by Michael Carrithers (1992) provides anthropological perspectives on the human attribute of sociality and its important function within a cultural context. In identifying sociality as an anthropological concept, Carrithers opens a productive line of thought in relation to the cultural practices of flamenco dance and bullfighting. Accepting sociality as a fundamental human capacity opens the way for an examination of how sociality contributes to dynamic processes (such as performance) within a particular cultural context. *How Societies Remember* by Paul Connerton (1989) discusses the commemorative ceremonies and bodily practices through which social memory is maintained. Connerton's concepts also apply to the intergenerational transmission of and innovation in flamenco dance and bullfighting movement traditions.

An area addressed by both cultural anthropology and the anthropology of dance is the role of embodiment and movement behavior in relationship to culture: *Body Thoughts* by Andrew J. Strathern (1996); *The Anthropology of the Body* edited by John Blacking (1977); and "Embodiment as a Paradigm for Anthropology" by Thomas J. Csordas (2002). Csordas' work is particularly clear regarding the importance of the body and embodiment as phenomena for anthropological study. Embodiment, nonverbal communication, and performance studies are also part of the discourse: *Kinesics and Context: Essays on Body Motion Communication* by Ray L. Birdwhistell (1970) and the works of Edward T. Hall (1959, 1969, 1975, 1976, 1983, 1992) offer etic perspectives on movement phenomena in relation to culture.

The Anthropology of Dance

A significant trend in the anthropology of dance is to examine dance as a form of communication, as a nonverbal text with implicit cultural meanings to be decoded and interpreted; these ideas are examined in the writings of Brenda Farnell (1995), Judith L. Hanna (1979b, 1983), Adrienne Kaeppler (1972, 1985, 2000), and Drid Williams (1996, 1999, 2000). Writings that address anthropology of dance theories generally, such as *To Dance Is Human* by Judith L. Hanna (1979a), *The Anthropology of Dance* by Anya P. Royce (2002), and *Anthropology and the Dance: Ten Lectures* by Drid Williams (2004), are also informative and useful. *Researching Dance: Evolving Modes of Inquiry* edited by Sondra H. Fraleigh and Penelope Hanstein (1999) also provides useful perspectives on dance research methodologies.

Ethnochoreology, a specialized area within the anthropology of dance field, provides methods for the structural analysis of dance forms. These methods, such as those described in several texts by Anca Giurchescu (1983, 1991, 2000), facilitate a microanalysis of dance movement phenomena. Microanalysis is useful in identifying the unique movement components and analyzing the formal structures of particular dances; Laban macroanalysis is useful when making broader comparisons such as those between a dance genre (flamenco) and non-dance movements (bullfighting).

The field of performance studies also provides insights applicable to flamenco and bullfighting. *The Body, Dance and Cultural Theory* by Helen Thomas (2003) addresses current perspectives in dance theory, and *Performance Studies* by Richard Schechner (2002) and *The Anthropology of Experience*, edited by Victor W. Turner and Edward M. Bruner (1986), address the specific role of dance as a performative behavior that both gives expression to culture and affects the social standing of the performer.

Anthropologist of dance Joann W. Kealiinohomoku, in her dissertation, "Theory and Methods for an Anthropological Study of Dance" (1976), provides support for the examination of dance and human movement as cultural practices functioning within a complex social context. Kealiinohomoku focuses on dance as an element of affective culture and recognizes the importance of somatic experience. The dissertation of Cynthia Knox, "Embodied Knowledge: The Cultural Patterning of Movement and Meaning" (1992), also affirms that the connections between flamenco and bullfighting may be examined through somatic perspectives.

Ethnographic Narratives

Anthropologist Melville J. Herskovits asserts that "'culture' is a construct that describes the similar modes of conduct of those who make up a given society; that, in the final analysis, behavior is always the behavior of individuals however it may lend itself to summary in generalized terms" (1964, 41). He recommends that researchers read the biographies and autobiographies of persons native to the culture being studied, pointing out that such sources "reveal many things about a culture," and that they serve anthropological knowledge in part because they

> afford a corrective to exclusive preoccupation with institutions. Cultural behavior is institutionalized, but the range of accepted variation in individual conduct must be analyzed if the institution and the culture are to be seen in perspective. Intangibles such as values, goals, and other motivating drives come out in such documents, as does the play of differing personalities within a society [80].

Herskovits' phrase, "the play of differing personalities," is consonant with Carrither's use of "sociality." Both expressions denote factors (play, sociality, personalities) that constitute a central motivation and interest of people living and acting within the flamenco and bullfight contexts. Surrounded by a social circle, a flamenco dancer dances to assert both uniqueness and belonging; alone in the center of a bullfight arena, a matador fights to assert his or her courage and artistic prowess before the assembled crowd.

Personal autobiographical narratives such as *Death in the Afternoon* ([1939] 1994), an information-rich memoir of the bullfight aficionado and U.S. American author Ernest Hemingway, and *Matadora* (1998), the memoir of the Spanish professional female matador Cristina Sánchez, provide emic cultural perspectives along with the rich nuance of lived experience. Very much worth reading is the biographical narrative *Or I'll Dress You in Mourning* by Larry Collins and Dominique Lapierre (1968). In describing the life story of matador Manuel Benítez, known as "El Cordobés," Collins and Lapierre provide useful emic perspectives on human experience and behavior in the bullfight context.

The most useful ethnographic narratives emphasize emic perspectives or strive to achieve a balance between emic and etic perspectives. Texts in English often romanticize the cross-cultural experience of the author; this approach may result in good storytelling and increase the commercial value of a work, but it generally lessens its research value. Nevertheless, autobiographical ethnographies, such as *The Flamencos of Cadiz Bay* by Gerald Howson (1994), *The Gachí: My Gypsy Flamenco Quest*, a personal memoir by Susan Salguero (2009), or the fictionalized memoir *Returning to A* by Dorien Ross (1995), offer emic details and unique cross-cultural perspectives.

Through such ethnographic narratives, one gains emic knowledge directly related to flamenco and bullfighting as well as insights into Spanish and Andalusian attitudes and beliefs about the human condition. They offer cultural immersion into distinctly foreign worlds. Ethnographic narratives can help us to comprehend how deeply human cultures touch and form our lives, and how powerfully culture influences our interpretation of the many events and relationships contained within a human life. By personalizing the effects of culture, ethnographic narratives demonstrate that culture is not just an interesting component of human life; culture constitutes a necessary framework for human living.[6]

Laban Movement Analysis

The theoretical framework and methods of Laban Movement Analysis allow one to analyze performance contexts and movement phenomena experienced firsthand as well as those observed on video. Standard reference texts that address this area of specialized knowledge include two theory texts written by Rudolph Laban: *The Language of Movement: A Guidebook to Choreutics* ([1966] 1974), which addresses the analysis of spatial forms in relation to movement phenomena; and *The Mastery of Movement* ([1950] 1971), which focuses on the analysis, description, and interpretation of expressive movement qualities. Similar information is outlined in: *A Primer for Movement Description Using Effort-Shape and Supplementary Concepts* by Cecily Dell (1977) and *Space Harmony: Basic Terms* by Dell, Crow, and Bartenieff (1977).

Four Adaptations of Effort Theory in Research and Teaching, written by Irmgard Bartenieff, Martha Davis, and Forrestine Paulay (1970), provides insight into the systematic application of Laban's movement theories in cross-cultural research. The first essay, "The Root of Laban Theory: Aesthetics and Beyond," provides a careful interpretation of Laban's early writings by Irmgard Bartenieff, one of his former students. Although Laban's theories often rely on dualistic constructs, his understandings of movement phenomena and culture are highly sophisticated, and other researchers have benefited from them: *Research in Dance: Problems and Possibilities* (1967), a publication of the Committee on Research in Dance (CORD); *Beyond Words: Movement Observation and Analysis* by Carol-Lynne Moore and Kaoru Yamamoto (1988); "An Experiment in Looking: Reexamining the Process of Observation" by Allison Jablonko and Elizabeth Kagan (1988); and "Dialogue in Dance Studies Research" by Ann Dils and Jill Flanders Crosby (2001).

Videography

The ongoing discussion of flamenco and bullfighting often revolves around visual and kinetic evidence found in film and video sources; the nature of the discourse is significantly influenced by which movement material is available to be viewed as well as which material is selected for analysis. The flamenco dance genre is quite broad; its range includes Andalusian folk dance forms, traditional solo and couple dance forms, informal, private performances between friends, theatrical large group choreographies for the public, and both highly codified and highly improvisational dance forms. Flamenco dance has an interpretive function in relationship to flamenco music; furthermore, the flamenco arts are based on emotionality. The palette of human emotions expressed through flamenco includes sorrow, joy, anger, aggression, playfulness, happiness, and more. As a result, the dynamic range and stylistic differences between the different types of dances within the flamenco genre are considerable.

Clear references to the bullfighting movement vocabulary exist within flamenco's more playful dances, such as the *bulerías*, an improvisational form, and the *sevillanas*, a folk dance form and social dance for couples. Given the intensity of the bullfight, it is not surprising that movement references to bullfighting also appear in the more emotionally intense dances within the flamenco dance genre. Solo dance forms traditionally performed by males, such as the *farruca*, often provide evidence of the phenomenon of bullfighting movement crossing over into the stylistic vocabulary of flamenco dance; however, movement references to bullfighting also occur in dances performed by female dancers, particularly in the cape-like manipulation of the fabric of flamenco shawls and skirts.

A useful set of twelve videos of flamenco dance performances is available through the Spanish television series Rito y geografía del baile (Rite and Geography of the Dance). This is the dance counterpart to the 100-program series Rito y geografía del cante (Rite and Geography of the Song) that focuses on flamenco song traditions. Both series were aired by Radio Television Española "toward the end of the Franco years" (Washabaugh 1996, xv). Anthropologist William Washabaugh provides detailed sociopolitical analyses of programs within the Rito y geografía del cante series in his text *Flamenco: Passion, Politics and Popular Culture* (1996), noting the likelihood that these programs constituted a revising of the parameters of the authenticity of the flamenco tradition for purposes related to internal Spanish politics.

This political revisionism placed emphasis on the rural character of flamenco's cultural context. Rural, in this instance, implies connection to an agricultural lifestyle and thus connection to the Andalusian agribusiness that provides horses and bulls for Spain's many public bullfight arenas. As a result, relying exclusively on the Rito y geografía del baile series could increase the likelihood of finding evidence of correlation between flamenco and bullfighting; reviewing a wide selection of video materials will help to counter any inherent bias.

It is also advisable to view at least some portions of audiovisual material without their accompanying soundtracks. This common movement research practice reduces auditory distraction and increases the viewer's visual acuity and the accuracy of observation. On the other hand, when listening to the accompanying sound tracks, one may notice that verbal cues used in the context of the Spanish bullfight sometimes occur also in flamenco performances. Audiovisual materials of Spanish bullfighting come from both documentary and public entertainment sources. Observation of audiovisual materials is useful, primarily as a method for double-checking the validity of emergent perceptions; ultimately, the richest resource for knowledge of flamenco dance and bullfighting movement is the lived experience.

CHAPTER TWO

Somatic Ethnography

Experiential Inquiry

I am not writing from neutral ground; my bias leans decidedly toward the human body as a glorious wellspring of movement and sensation at play in the realm of culture. As a dancer, I revel in embodiment, so grateful that it allows me to be an active agent in the creation and enactment of human culture. I marvel at the neurological basis of human movement capacity, the neurological loop that links sensory experience with physical action. As a dancer, I know this loop intimately; I value its functionality and revere its poetry. I agree with dance anthropologist Judith Hanna who wrote, "Dance, it should be noted, is more like poetry than prose" (1979b, 80). To enter into research without this poetic element, without appreciation for the miraculous fact that it is through human bodies that art and culture emerge, that, in my estimation, would be a dull slog. Here I am, embodied American-style, with whatever inhibitions, cultural values, body image, and worldview that may entail, venturing into the foreign realm of Spanish-style embodiment, the culture, art, movement, sensation, and expressivity of flamenco and bullfighting. What can my body learn? How can I translate my embodied learning into words? That is the dance of this book.

Dance scholar Maxine Sheets-Johnstone affirms that an important task of dance research is to describe the totality of lived experience, including the somatic and kinetic "inner experience" of dancing itself. In her view such research "begins with the direct intuition of the phenomenon" (1966, 12). She points out that "if dance is the phenomenon, the phenomenologist describes the immediate encounter with dance, the lived experience of dance, and proceeds from there to describe the analyzable structures, such as temporality and spatiality, inherent in the total experience" (12). Thus, a dance researcher incorporates many modalities within an investigative process that seeks to discover and "elucidate *structures* apparent in the phenomenon" (1966, 12; Sheets-Johnstone's italics). Embodied experiential investigation is central to

An iconic flamenco dance motif, near-to-but-not-touching, is exemplified in this 2007 photograph as a torero reaches out to touch a bull's horn at Madrid's Plaza de Toros de Las Ventas. Rooted in the quixotic human desire to play with danger, the dynamic tension inherent in the near-to-but-not-touching motif evokes the magical power accorded to the bull in ancient fertility rites. This powerfully felt tension still functions today in the modern bullfight as matadors deliberately entice the bull to pass close by their bodies. In movement analysis terms, the phrase "near-to-but-not-touching" simply describes a spatial relationship of relative closeness. However, in the context of the bullfight, nearness entails danger. To elicit the drama of the bullfight, a flamenco dancer adds spatial tension to the movement motif near-to-but-not-touching (Reuters/Susana Vera).

dance and movement research because "without returning again and again to this lived experience, one cannot hope to arrive at a valid and meaningful description of dance, the nature of, and structures inherent in, its appearance, creation, and presentation" (29). To translate into words that which is fluid, changeable, and ephemeral—the body's lived experience of movement—is a challenging task, but one that offers exciting opportunities for completing the important meaning-making cycle between bodily experience and culture.

Culture is the most human facet of the grand macrocosmic reality that we inhabit and through which we move. "Culture is the manmade [human-made] part of the environment" (Herskovits 1964, 3). To the body, movement is a necessity. Through the body and its deep movement imperative, we act to fulfill desires and needs, accomplish our intentions, and demonstrate our beliefs. Close analysis of human movement phenomena in their natural context reveals the important influence of culture on human life. The details of a specific culture are consciously and unconsciously enacted through each individual's postures, gestures, rhythms, spatial choices, shifts of weight, and full-bodied actions. Relationships emerge clearly outlined when an individual faces different directions, makes or breaks eye contact or physical contact with others, manipulates objects or live beings within the environment, or changes location in relationship to others or the environment. Knowledge of the macrocosm (culture) provides essential contextual understanding for the study of the microcosm (dance).[1] The relationship is reciprocal; evidence revealed through study of the microcosmic phenomena of dance and human movement also informs us about the macrocosmic phenomenon, culture.

This book presents perspectives gained by viewing Spanish culture from afar, the macrocosmic view, as well as perspectives gained through close examination at the microcosmic level of human movement. The two cultural practices under examination, flamenco and bullfighting, promote and enrich human sociality, provide ritual space for the expression of all human emotions, and constitute a form of collective human knowledge. Their movement vocabularies constitute kinesthetic and somatic encoding of a unique set of cultural values identified with European Spanish culture, elements of which are also evident in Hispanic cultures worldwide.

In *Researching Dance: Evolving Modes of Inquiry*, Joann McNamara points to "the value of understanding the very essence of the subject itself, within its various settings" (1999, 163). Called phenomenological hermeneutics, this research method synthesizes lived experience with word-based knowledge. To understand "the very essence" and "elucidate *structures* apparent in the phenomenon"—these are my goals. As I shift between analysis and synthesis, between etic and emic perspectives, examining the microcosmic clues of movement phenomena and the macrocosmic context of the cultural surround, and between broad perspectives and movements scrutinized close-up and personal, what emerges is a somatic ethnography.

Engaging Somatic Perspectives

Dance scholars sometimes borrow from literary theory, semiotics, and linguistics, examining dance representations as cultural texts. However, this approach may not help in understanding the actualities of how dance embodies culture. In his book *Body Thoughts*, Andrew J. Strathern discusses the deeply embedded nature of culture and the need to "reject the (implicitly Cartesian) mentalism that informs the semiotic or linguistic theory of society."

> Our bodies and minds are clearly complex layerings of different times and kinds of learning and habit formation, and certain types of habit may be harder to discard than others, so that at any time we literally encode our own histories. But, if this is so, it also underlies the fact that we do indeed inhabit "mindful bodies" [2004, 36].

Understanding how dance embodies culture requires somatic perspectives.

The field of somatic studies relies upon the precept that the first-person perspective informed by bodily experience is a fundamental component in the construction of knowledge. Somatic research methods provide for the examination of embodied experience unique to the individual and are appropriate for both dance research and anthropological research. As anthropologist Victor W. Turner states in *The Anthropology of Experience*, "Of all the human sciences and studies, anthropology is most deeply rooted in the social and subjective experience of the inquirer. Everything is brought to the test of self; everything observed is learned ultimately 'on his [or her] pulses'" (Turner and Bruner, 1986, 33). I love Turner's poetic choice of the word "pulse" in conjunction with the human task of "learning." Unique knowledge is gained as the rhythmic hit of dancing feet, inner heartbeats, and pulsing drumbeats synchronize and merge; dance has much to teach us.

Thomas Hanna (1928–1990), a key philosopher and practitioner in the field of somatic studies, asserts somatic perspectives as an epistemological principle.

> It is fundamental to recognize that the same individual is categorically different when viewed from a first-person perception than is the case when he [she] is viewed from a third-person perception. The sensory access is categorically different as are the resultant observations. The categorical distinction between these two viewpoints establishes the ground rules for all studies of the human species. Failure to recognize the categorical difference between first-person observation and third-person observation leads to fundamental misunderstandings in physiology, psychology, and medicine [1986, 341].

Resisting the pervasive Western cultural and academic bias against subjectivity, Hanna asserts that

> the life sciences in general and the sciences of physiology, psychology, and medicine in particular lack grounds for what they assert to be established fact and sound theorizing exactly to the degree that they ignore, willfully or innocently, first-person data. To avoid evidence that is "phenomenological" or "subjective" is unscientific. To dismiss such data as irrelevant and/or unimportant is irresponsible [T. Hanna 1986, 343].

Inquiries into dance/movement phenomena and culture are necessarily qualitative in character, and the body has its own story to tell. As a dancer,

I hold embodied knowledge in high regard; I seek direct experience and trust the intelligence of the body as a resource of integrity and wisdom. Clearly, since "even the constant physiological rhythms of breathing and the beating of the heart are culturally influenced" (Kealiinohomoku 1976, 169), somatic perspectives are essential to the study of the embodiment and physical expressions of culture. And so, to better understand the movement phenomena of flamenco dance and bullfighting, my own bodily experience serves as an investigative tool.

Culture as Sensation and Emotion

Study of the sensory world is critical to the understanding of culture and cultural difference. Discussing this point, Kealiinohomoku notes, "the senses, far from being limited to the commonly cited five senses, are enumerated in scientific literature as being from ten to fourteen" (1976, 172). Our senses provide impressions of the world around us, but also the world within us. Thus, perceptions of equilibrium, temperature, or pain are affected by culture, as are experiences of internal organic functioning, pleasure, or movement.

The role of the sensory realm in the construction of knowledge is complicated by the dual use of the word "feeling" to signify both emotional affect and sensory impressions (Williams 2004, 57). Further complicating matters, emotions and sensations do, in fact, function together within a complex dynamic. The classical James-Lange theory of the emotions proposes that the experience of emotion results from physiological changes, while the later Cannon-Bard theory argues that physiological changes occur in response to the experience of emotion (Cannon 1927). In relation to dance, it may not matter whether emotion or sensation occurs first; within dance there is ongoing play between the two. Ultimately, what is important to remember is that the relation between human emotion and physiology is fundamental and reflexive; each informs each the other, or as psychologist James Hillman puts it, "biological systems are psychological fields asking to be read for their intelligence" (Hillman 1999).

It has been proposed that humans are motivated to dance by the need to discharge excess emotion and energy. Although this perspective is no longer accepted as adequate in anthropological scholarship, it continues to hold a place in the popular imagination. However, even more interesting and significant is that through the act of dancing, a person can change his or her emotional state and potentially his or her surroundings. This is the power of dance in culture, and flamenco is an interesting case in point. Flamenco provides a range of behaviors that opens up expressive opportunities for individuals both personally and socially. The transformative magic of flamenco may emerge at any moment depending on the volatility of a person's emotional state and whether the immediate external environment is conducive.

Particularly for the Spanish Gypsies, the *gitanos*, dancing and singing are considered integral to human living; these are capacities they carry within themselves always. These capacities give them the ability to transform any everyday situation into a celebration of life in general and their own existence in particular. Dance, as a human power that can change everything in an instant, provides a pathway to the experience of the super-ordinary, and *gitanos* live their lives knowing themselves to be rightful owners of this human power.

In contrast, some Anglo-Americans or Anglo-Europeans may view flamenco with distrust. They may associate flamenco's intensity of emotion and sensuality with morally, socially, or sexually transgressive behaviors. They may associate the open emotionality and expressive intensity of flamenco dance with impropriety, lack of (proper) self-containment, lack of emotional control, primitive immaturity, and inappropriate personal boundaries. Suppose that a person of Anglo heritage witnesses a flamenco dance performance in which a performer is actually behaving rather conservatively in relationship to the conventions of the flamenco tradition. Despite the flamenco performer's circumscribed behavior from an emic perspective, due to cultural bias the witness may see uninhibited emotionality and interpret it as evidence of the individual performer's flawed character. They may also take the phenomenon of group catharsis as evidence of primitive social development. The importance of the theory of cultural relativity, which reminds researchers to be wary of the distorting influence of their own enculturation, is made clear in this example.

Greater etic knowledge of human affective behaviors can reduce the influence of cultural bias, while greater emic knowledge of the specific cultural and social values being served through performance can make the interpretation of such activities more accurate and less judgmental. Still, objectivity may not be possible. Flamenco dance and bullfighting are cultural events that purposefully engage the spectator emotionally and viscerally. The primary purpose of these events is to incite emotion and somatic response. So if spectators are able to view one of these events with no increase of emotion, if they experience no inner turmoil or emotional catharsis, then from an emic perspective the event has failed.

Anglo-Americans unaccustomed to the emotional intensity of flamenco and bullfighting may react defensively, clinging to the rules, standards, and expectations of their own culture. The few who choose to become active participants or aficionados of flamenco or bullfighting were probably, first as observers, enthralled and perhaps transported (by sensation and/or emotion) beyond the constraints of their own cultural norms.

Culture as a Verb

To maintain our culture of origin, we must take actions (repeatedly), and much more action is required if we wish to learn a new culture, but the results are worth the effort. My adventure started innocently enough. I simply wanted to be a better dancer. But dance is not simple, and flamenco dance, in particular, is rhythmically complex, exceptionally nuanced, and physically demanding. Additionally, one is called upon to perform with authenticity, meaning that within the dance you should be fully yourself and express exactly who you are honestly and without shame. But, at the same time, being authentic in the context of flamenco performance means dancing in a way that truly represents flamenco's indigenous culture. As a result, authenticity is the holy grail of many cross-cultural learners of the flamenco arts, always sought after and rarely attained. Meanwhile, there are layers upon layers of rich, culturally inscribed movement patterns to discover, practice, master, and pass on to others.

Some might say this process is like learning a new language, but it is not that simple. While both language and dance are human universals, the non-verbal nature of dance does not mean it is universally accessible. Clarifying the issue, Kealiinohomoku explains, "To call dance a 'universal language' is useless and misleading. Although dance (or phenomena generally recognizable as dance) is universal in human societies, that is not to say dance is a 'universal language,' just as verbal language is a human universal but clearly there is no universal spoken language" (2002, 1). Dance anthropologist Judith L. Hanna concurs: "Dance is not a universal 'language' but many languages and dialects. There are close to 6,000 verbal languages, and probably that many dance languages" (J. Hanna 2002, 6).

In dance, as in language, there are also issues of dialects, accent, and poetic nuance. Kealiinohomoku explains that "to move in a culturally appropriate way requires the appropriate phenotype [body type]; special training with prolonged habituation, often from early childhood; and motivational social context" (1976, 318). She specifically credits "prolonged habituation" as a key factor in the development of "movement dialects" (320). In their joint article, "Thinking with Movement: Improvising Versus Composing?" Rajika Puri and Diana Hart-Johnson consider the usefulness of the linguistic analogy in understanding the variations that occur within single dance traditions and between the dance traditions of different cultures. They point out that "knowing a language or idiom of dance means that one is familiar with the conventions, assumptions, and structures that inform it" (1995, 163–64).

My original goal was to gain knowledge and skill in relation to the flamenco dance idiom, and achieving it involved just such an effort on my part as these authors describe. I first went to study flamenco dance in Spain, hoping that through direct contact and "prolonged habituation" with Spanish culture I might improve my style as a flamenco dancer. While seeking to identify movement attributes that would denote an authentic "accent" within the flamenco dance idiom,[2] I noticed that references to bullfighting were made in my flamenco dance classes. At the time, bullfighting seemed like a missing clue to the fascinating puzzle of flamenco dance. And so, after gaining a degree of mastery of the flamenco dance idiom, when the opportunity arrived, I was ready to act.

> *SPAIN:*
> *The year is 1992; the location is the Casa de Campo park, located on the right bank of the Manzanares River just west of Madrid, where I am taking private lessons from a Colombian matador, Jaime, in the art of bullfighting. Jaime praises my movement style and urges me to try these movements in a tienta, an informal arena setting where students of bullfighting test their skill and courage as well as the bravery of yearling calves. I resist, saying, "No, thanks. I just want to study the movements of the bullfight."*
> *The sun is hot and Jaime is patient as he explains the animal psychology and behavior that is intrinsic to his movement technique and passion for the art. Suddenly, my body senses a direct link. As I practice a movement with the* capote, *the heavy, brightly colored canvas cape of the matador, knowledge arises out of a distinctive rotating movement of my wrists and hands, and I speak up, "I practiced this same movement this morning in my flamenco class!"*

Theory, tested and confirmed by direct experience, transforms into embodied knowledge. Leverage, strength, countertension, visual acuity, core support, alertness, readiness to react, focus, adversarial energy, self-protection, strategy, animal behavior, and so much more were part of my first lessons in the movements of the bullfight. The connection between flamenco dance and bullfighting is not a secret; it is openly addressed in various texts. Matteo in *The Language of the Spanish Dance* notes that "the torero's [bullfighter's] basic body line and stance with a lifted chest and pelvis thrust forward are at times synonymous with those of a male dancer (*bailaor*)" (Matteo with Goya 1990, 243). Perhaps it was my dance training, vertical posture, and performance ability that had caused Jaime to suggest I was ready to take my bullfighting to the next level. Perhaps, the movement patterns of flamenco dance that I had already absorbed into my body caused him to see the potential torero in me.

Ultimately, curious about the disruptive effects that a bull's unpredictability might impose on the bullfighter's careful technical training and aesthetic intentions, I undertook additional formal training in the arena with a live animal. I wanted to experience the unpredictability that an animal presents so that I could later explore the implications of that unpredictability in relationship to improvisational practices within traditional flamenco dance forms.

Approaching the bull with *muleta* and sword in hand, this matador presents the ideal posture of the Spanish *torero*. His hips are pressed forward. His chest is lifted high. His chin and focus are inclined downward. His hands are anchored near the body, while his elbows expand wide. Similar postures are developed through dance training, occur often in flamenco performance, and inform the aesthetic standards of flamenco dance (efecreata mediagroup/Shutterstock.com).

MEXICO:

The year is 2005; the location is an informal arena on a ranch in the remote and beautiful desert mountains south of the border town of Tecate, Mexico. I am receiving instruction from Mr. Coleman Cooney, director of the California Academy of Tauromaquia, San Diego, California, as I prepare to put my fledgling bullfighting skills to the test for the first time in the tienta arena with a yearling. What new perspectives will emerge from the experience of learning to use the smaller red felt cape, the muleta? How will testing my courage by using my skills with an animal transform my understanding of flamenco dance? I am here to find out. I am here to learn the constraining rules of the game of bullfighting and use that knowledge to develop my potential in the flamenco dance genre. I am here to conduct somatic lived-experience research—and to test my courage.

My focus is on the yearling, even as I try to manipulate the muleta using the techniques I have just learned. I am not as afraid as I thought I would be when

Jaime on that long-ago afternoon in Madrid first suggested that I give this a try. Now encouragements in Spanish and English are called out to me from the sidelines around the small arena—advice and reminders and suggestions. The yearling and I are intent upon each other. She charges me repeatedly, each pass unique. We are alone in the center of the circle, as the eyes of those surrounding us remain focused on the improvisational moment as it plays out again and again. Leaving the circle of the arena, I am relieved and energized. I have experienced self-confidence, courage, power, and agency that I hope to apply as a flamenco performer.

The energy of the arena, being surrounded by supporters, the adrenaline in my body, the dust and reality, the interactive edge, the proximity to danger, playing with risk, the complex moment when practiced technique attempts to juggle with the unexpected, and much more were part of this new lesson. Having now moved deeper into the territory of the bullfight and its cultural surround, I had a deeper appreciation for the performative values of flamenco—sociality, personality, risk, and passion. And these attributes of flamenco culture are meant to be passed on.

NEW MEXICO:
The year is 2009; the location is the high mountain plateau of Taos in northern New Mexico where I am teaching a group of eight dancers how to participate improvisationally in the art of flamenco dance—how to enter the flamenco social circle, how to relate to the other participants, how to feel the music and maintain the rhythm in their bodies while their minds recognize signals coming from the musicians and absorb energy coming other participants, how to keep a cool head despite the intensity building around and within them so that they can make artistic decisions in the moment. Strategy is imperative. I draw from the remembered emotions and kinesthetic sensations of facing the yearling in the tienta arena. Urging students to express their individuality and passion while maintaining the formal elements of the performance recognized by the collective group, I am teaching the skills through which humans come together to create the super-ordinary.

"Enter the social circle. Don't be shy. Maintain direct eye contact. Really look at people as you walk around the flamenco social circle. Be present. Let yourself be seen. This is your social circle. Focus. Let the group support you, clap a rhythm for you, call out encouragement to you. Enjoy the music. Let yourself respond to this situation. Express yourself. Enjoy the opportunity for deep play opening up between you and the music. Don't worry. There is a formula for leaving the circle when you are ready. Remember the formula and follow it. There! You are out! You took risks. You return now to the outer circle of community, creative spirit brimming with success, energy heightened, and courage recharged."

Culture calls for action, whether one is learning something new, observing the performance of others, performing in public, or teaching new dance steps and cultural traditions to students. In the contexts of the bullfighting and flamenco traditions, there are many possibilities, and how we choose to participate will determine what we learn.

Ethnographic Inquiry

Current usage defines ethnography as "social research based on the close-up, on-the-ground observation of people and institutions in real time and space, in which the investigator embeds herself near (or within) the phenomenon so as to detect how and why agents on the scene act, think, and feel the way they do" (Wacquant 2003, 5). The model of participant observation has long served as the primary method of ethnographic research. Discussing traditional parameters for participant observation field research, anthropologist Drid Williams notes that "'participation' means living with (or as close as possible to) one's chosen people for at least twelve months. 'Participant field research' means conducting one's investigation in the language spoken by the community—not the anthropologist's language" (1999, 28).

Anthropologist James P. Spradley outlines five types of participation that distinguish participant observation methods; these are identified by the degree of researcher involvement and are known as nonparticipation, passive participation, moderate participation, active participation, and complete participation (1980, 58–62). Nonparticipation relies entirely on the techniques of observation, as, for instance, when I gather impressions by observing videos of flamenco dance and bullfighting. Passive participation signifies a low level of researcher involvement; it relies heavily on observation but the researcher is present in the social context. Spradley describes the role of the passive participant-researcher within the research context as that of "'bystander,' 'spectator,' or 'loiterer'" (59).

However, this conventional model is problematic because both flamenco dance and bullfighting are performances and require observers. And given the high levels of sociality, emotion, and adrenaline involved in both practices, I would not categorize a flamenco or bullfighting spectator's experience as passive participation. Nor is being a spectator at a flamenco dance performance or a public bullfight equivalent to being a "loiterer" or "bystander." Due to the performative and public ritual nature of flamenco dance and bullfighting, both participant and observer roles are intrinsic, necessary, and vital. Flamenco dance and bullfighting are, in general, public spectacles. Observing and witnessing are therefore key actions within these traditions. By observing a bullfight, one is participating in the bullfight tradition.

It may be more accurate to say that spectators of flamenco dance and bullfighting events are engaging at the level of moderate participation. Moderate participation implies that one strives to "maintain a balance between being an insider and an outsider, between participation and observation"

As a matador engages with the bull, an attentive *torero* watches the action from behind the *burladero*, the protective wooden wall around the inside of the arena. Lives are at risk (Juan Pelegrin/Flickr.com).

(Spradley 1980, 60). Spradley identifies the penultimate level of researcher involvement as "active participation."

"The active participant seeks to *do* what other people are doing, not merely to gain acceptance, but to more fully learn the cultural rules of behavior" (1980, 60; Spradley's italics). Recommending this approach, Spradley notes that "the *less* familiar you are with a social situation, the *more* you are able to see the cultural rules at work" (62; Spradley's italics). This applies, too, when one is seeking to understand the rules that govern a performing art. For example, when I first began taking flamenco dance technique classes regularly in Madrid, I found it very beneficial to take classes with American flamenco dance artists who had lived and performed in Spain for many years. They were able to explain the tacit rules of flamenco performance explicitly, in a way that many Spanish dance teachers could not. These rules represent an implicit knowledge base that the Spanish flamenco dance teachers may never have had reason to question or define. Teachers native to Spain often could not explain the rules and appeared not to understand why they were being asked about what were, to them, such obvious matters. Interesting exceptions to this were those flamenco dance teachers of Spanish origin who had extensive experience teaching abroad (in Japan, the United States, or other parts of Europe). In that case, their own cross-cultural experience seemed to have made them more conscious of tacit knowledge within the flamenco dance practice.

According to Spradley, the highest level of researcher involvement, complete participation, occurs when ethnographers "study a situation in which they are already ordinary participants" (Spradley 1980, 61–62). Pointing out that this highest level of participation can be problematic, Spradley cautions that "the more you know about a situation as an ordinary participant, the more difficult it is to study it as an ethnographer" (61). Being a flamenco dance performer myself, my involvement might be categorized as complete participation research; however, in actuality, my participation in flamenco dance performance remains, even after many years, an exploration into territory that for me is not ordinary. The experience remains cross-cultural, and it retains significant technical, linguistic, and social challenges.

Implicit in my decision to take a soma-based and active participation approach is the recognition that intelligence resides not only in the gray matter of the brain, but throughout the body. I rely on what body psychotherapist Susan Aposhyan calls "natural intelligence," a quality she defines as

> synergistic intelligence that arises out of ... all the resources of every tissue and fluid in the body down to the cellular level. Every system of the body has its own unique abilities to perceive and respond. For both cultural and evolutionary reasons, we ignore and override both sensory input and behavioral responses which arise outside of the nervous system. Including and integrating the intelligence and creativity of the entire body is natural intelligence [1999, 186].

Aposhyan's phrase "natural intelligence" has attributes in common with what Howard Gardner calls "bodily-kinesthetic intelligence" (1999, 42). Discussing the deep connections between soma and culture, Cynthia Knox points to the sensory aspect of somatic intelligence, noting that "our embodied knowing is an essential component of the way we experience the world" (1992, 2). Like Aposhyan and Gardner, Knox acknowledges the kinetic aspect of somatic intelligence, stating that "our ways of making meaning, including the ways we practice our art, are intertwined with and informed by culture-specific ways of moving" (2).

My body and person serve as a somatic laboratory, providing immediate sensory, affective, and cognitive feedback in response to the kinetic phenomena of flamenco dance and bullfighting, enabling me to identify, describe, and interpret the somatic cues that arise as I move within these contrasting movement vocabularies. Previous acculturation to the flamenco dance style serves as a somatic field, an information matrix through which I trace my impressions of bullfighting movements.

Laban Movement Analysis

In this somatic ethnography, I identify the movement characteristics of flamenco dance and bullfighting based upon observation of audiovisual materials as well as my own lived experience with each cultural practice. The information gathered reveals recurrent patterns of posture, gesture, spatial use, movement dynamics, and body use, and possible correlations between these two movement practices. Through a process of analysis, reflection, and synthesis, new understandings and new knowledge coalesce.

A mainstay in my process is the use of Laban Movement Analysis (also known as Labananalysis or LMA). Describing the attributes of the LMA system, dance scholars Ann Dils and Jill Flanders Crosby note its reliance on the "habit of comparison" as a means of distinguishing between different types of movement phenomena. The Laban Movement Analysis system relies on knowledge accumulated through embodied learning; for the trained Laban movement analyst, "the body acts as a notebook, storing information and providing a means of comparison" (2001, 71). The Laban system is holistic in character; it facilitates seeing not just isolated movement elements, but "the nexus of elements in relationship" (70). Dils and Crosby concur with other researchers that the theoretical and practical training that Laban movement analysts receive results in "an automatic and cumulative resource upon which subsequent observations are based" (Jablonko and Kagan 1988, 161). "This kinesthetic sympathy with the observed movement provides rapid and efficient access to the perception of complex patterns" (161–162).

The importance of somatic experience and body intelligence is implicit within Laban's methods. Experiential knowledge of the full range of spatial and qualitative dynamics of movement phenomena is essential to the development of reliable observation skills and is therefore deliberately developed through stringent training. Similarly, somatic knowledge of flamenco dance gave me emic perspectives for assessing the attributes of bullfighting movements. Both flamenco dance and bullfighting involve high levels of tension and urgency; in contrast, the tranquil environment of a dance studio reduces feelings of tension, intensity, urgency, and anxiety, and so facilitates detailed examination of movement phenomena. Through a process of comparison and experimentation, correlations between the two distinctive movement vocabularies of flamenco dance and bullfighting emerged.

Each new somatic experience in the bullfighting realm sets off a ripple of awareness regarding its possible correlations to the movement vocabulary and performance protocols of flamenco dance. My experiences are filtered through the intrinsic intelligences of a substantive living body, through mind

The commercial aspect of flamenco ranges from informal street performers who dance for gratuities to large international touring companies that charge significant fees. Street performances share a spontaneous quality with the *espontaneo* of the *corrida*, in which a member of the public unexpectedly (and illegally) leaves the stands and enters the arena to challenge the bull. This photograph, taken in 2011 in central Madrid, Spain, shows how easily an informal public spectacle can attract a crowd and draw the attention of a diverse group of witnesses: tourists, passersby, and photographers (Anastasia Petrova/Shutterstock.com).

and emotion, and through that entity anthropological theory addresses as the person.

Person and Culture

I often ask myself, "Who am I to try to address the intrinsic connections between these cultural practices?" I am a particular collection of human intelligences, and my findings reflect the particularity and uniqueness of that collection. Howard Gardner, known for developing the hypothesis that human beings function using multiple intelligences, defines intelligence in relation to culture. Each intelligence, he writes, is "a bio psychological potential to process information that can be activated in a cultural setting to solve problems or create products that are of value in a culture" (1999, 33–34). Human intelligences are potentials that "will or will not be activated, depending upon the values of a particular culture, the opportunities available in that culture, and the personal decisions made by individuals and/or their families, schoolteachers, and others" (34).

Outlining this multiplicity of intelligences, Gardner produces a list that includes linguistic, logical-mathematical, musical, bodily-kinesthetic, spatial, interpersonal, and intrapersonal intelligences (41–43). Of these, musical, bodily-kinesthetic, spatial, interpersonal, and intrapersonal intelligences are especially relevant in considering the role of dance and movement in the embodiment of cultural values.

Writing Ethnographic Narrative

In *The Anthropology of Experience* Edward M. Bruner suggests that ethnographic writing functions "as a genre of storytelling" and that "ethnographies are guided by an implicit narrative structure, by a story we tell about the peoples we study" (1986, 139). Supporting this view, anthropologist Michael Carrithers asserts that anthropology as a field depends on the human capacity to "imagine the stories of others, others with whom one has at first no imaginable connection" (1992, 75). Thus, the human capacity to imagine the cultural lives of others is as essential to ethnography as is the human capacity for recognizing patterns of behavior. But first there must be the original spark of interest created through the felt experience of contrast and cultural difference.

Tribe to tribe, explored and explorer, region to region, and across national or natural boundaries, humans of different cultures meet one another, notice differences, and self-reflect. Eventually, stories (with the characteristics of ethnographic narratives) are told. My ethnographic narrative focuses on the somatic aspects of my lived experience, drawing comparisons and noting distinctions between the movement vocabularies of flamenco dance and bullfighting; however, locale, personnel, sound, language, temperature, and interactions also matter and contribute significantly as the story unfolds.

The subjectivity of ethnographic writing is part of its value. Ethnographer Ruth Behar, describing a significant shift toward intersubjectivity in her own perspectives, wrote, "Identification and connection rather than distance, difference, and otherness are what I would seek as an ethnographer. I would use not only the observational and participatory methods of classical anthropology but the subtle forms of knowledge found in ineffable moments of intuition and epiphany" (Behar 2003, 23). Therefore, my somatic ethnography also reports the many "Aha!" moments that made this cultural investigation so compelling and valuable to me.

I accept the storytelling nature of the endeavor, taking pleasure in articulating each intimate impression of the lively play between movement and culture. Part method of thinking, part vehicle for the conveyance of thought, writing helps me gather and synthesize new information and bring ideas to the larger discussion. Calling upon qualities of intuition, creativity, and curiosity, I take this task to heart, believing that "ethnography is most of all a method for converting lived experience into memorable, even beautiful, writing" (Behar 2003, 18). This book communicates a synthesis of ideas— facilitated by moving from close examination of the microcosmic phenomena of human movement to consideration of their implications in relationship to the macrocosm of Spanish culture. I hope that articulating my process of discovery will serve to bring transparency to the process of interpretation whereby cultural significance is attributed to movement phenomena.

CHAPTER THREE

Overlapping Worlds

Looking at the overlap between the cultural practices of bullfighting and flamenco dance, one notices that an extensive sociality enlivens each cultural practice and they are connected by a free-flowing exchange of people, a high level of participation, and an intense celebratory energy. Both flamenco and bullfighting provide tremendous opportunities for individual achievement; public expression of emotion and displays of unique personal idiosyncrasies are encouraged and celebrated. This volatility is counterbalanced by the fact that the cultural forms containing these practices are relatively stable. The play between fluidity and innovation on one side and stability and tradition on the other is a compelling feature of both practices. The play between change and stability keeps flamenco audiences coming back to see what will develop next. They may enjoy arguing about the modernisms of Israel Galvan and Joaquín Cortés as much as they enjoy the nostalgia or take regional or national pride in seeing traditional forms performed well—yet again. The play between the certainty of formal traditions and the uncertainty of fate keeps spectators of the *corrida* returning to the arena to see how individual matadors will fare this time within the age-old tradition of the bullfight.

Looking at the intense human sociality that surrounds the cultural practices of bullfighting and flamenco, I see people, full of creative energy and passionate expressivity; I see many individuals, each presenting a unique voice and contributing a unique presence. I see unending generations of people, passing through cultural practices held firm by tradition. Cynthia Knox (1992, 8) states with poetic simplicity, "I perceive movement as multidimensional and unremitting." And within that complex ongoing flow of human movement, there is also a continuity, as generations of aesthetic, social, and performative human beings flow through the more fixed formal constructions that enable their public ritual life.

Sociality and Lifestyle

Human beings are social animals, living in interactive community, participating in social networks through affective behaviors that are patterned at the cultural level (Bowlby 1969; Carrithers 1992; de Waal 2005). Knox, addressing the embodiment of knowledge, adds that "successful enculturation dictates that the values, thoughts and acts deemed acceptable by a group become the template for and measure of reality" (1992, 72). Knox's statement speaks to my experience of the Andalusian cultural life as a complete, closed system within which flamenco and bullfighting are practiced.

American cultural life tends to offer many options on a given day, and in general it is socially acceptable when individuals choose not to participate, celebrate holidays, go to sporting events, or attend performance events. I experienced a highly contrasting situation in Jerez de la Frontera, where the entire city is organized around an ongoing annual schedule of cultural events. Businesses change their hours or close, streets may be closed and traffic diverted, and the entire population appears to have changed their schedule to focus on an event. Community events are highly anticipated, actively prepared for, and draw participation from a very high percentage of the population. Participation appears to be unanimous. For as long as a week, a community celebration trumps other activities and any other options are extremely scarce. This corresponds with Edward T. Hall's definition of a *high-context* culture, a complex culture with extensive, specialized knowledge that is quite difficult for outsiders to comprehend.[1] Although there is heterogeneity within the Andalusian population, ethnic, economic, gender, and age differences, Andalusians often appear to be seamlessly bound within a homogeneous, high-context system of meaning; they are united in worldview.

While within the sociality of flamenco and bullfighting there exist social pressures toward conformity, there is an equally pervasive imperative for individuals to achieve distinction within the behavioral boundaries deemed acceptable by Andalusian social conventions. This combination of contrasting drives—social conformity and individuality—results in people accustomed to watching each other carefully even as they monitor their own behavior with self-conscious awareness. A sense of social homogeneity and homeostasis are maintained through the restraints of high-context culture and closely monitored lives (Hall 1976, 113). Visual perception is emphasized as individuals attend to the appearance and behaviors of others and carefully consider their own in relation to social connections and status. This does not necessarily have an inhibiting effect on an individual's everyday behavior or expressivity in performance situations. The Andalusian tendency is to appreciate the emotional content and intensity of a performance, interpreting them as evidence of an individual's sincerity. Those gathered to bear witness to a performance tacitly affirm and validate for each other each individual's human right to hedonistic expression. An individual's personality and unique performing style (*estampa*) serve as fundamental evidence through which human existence, character, and value are acknowledged and appreciated.

This tendency to perceive and interpret direct experience through the filter of enculturation is referred to by Segall, Campbell, and Herskovits as "perceptual inference habits" (1966, 214). Asserting that perception itself is affected by enculturation, they conclude that:

> To a substantial extent we learn [how] to perceive; that in spite of the phenomenally absolute character of our perceptions, they are determined by perceptual inference habits, and that various inference habits are differentially likely in different societies. For all mankind [humankind], the basic process of perception is the same; only the contents differ and they differ only because they reflect different perceptual inference habits [214].

Thus, too, everyday Andalusian discourse is subtly governed by an enculturated ability to discern which performative phenomena are important and worthy of comment.

Socializing is a central activity within Spanish and Andalusian culture, and flamenco performances and *corridas* (bullfights) provide occasions and opportunities for much social relating and communicating. Anthropologist Michael Carrithers points out that "on balance ... individuals in relationships, and the interactive character of social life, are slightly more important, more real, than those things we designate as culture" (1992, 34). And so, while ostensibly conversations may focus on the attributes of a particular performer or performance, the subtext of these words and behaviors is likely to express a collective concern with social relationships. In Andalusia, the people attend performance events to see and be seen, to meet and be met, to assert themselves as effective members of the social group by making their presence, opinions, and personality known within their community. Flamenco and bullfighting generate lively cultural and artistic discourse and general socializing; many individuals will take advantage of this heightened sociality to advance personal and social objectives.

That sociality is central to human affective culture is particularly evident in the case of flamenco and bullfighting. Carrithers states, "Human character and human experience exist only in and through people's relations with each other" (1992, 55); this coincides with the view that humans learn humanness from other human beings. Carrithers regards sociality as an evolutionary result of the development of the human capacity for intersubjectivity, which he defines as "an innate human propensity for mutual engagement and mutual responsiveness," two qualities that are key attributes in the social behaviors surrounding flamenco and bullfighting (34–55).

American anthropologist Franz Boas defines dance very generally as the "rhythmic movements of any part of the body" and considered "the two forms of expression" (music and dance) to be "mutually determined" (1951, 344). Kealiinohomoku makes this point also, noting the occurrence of synesthesia as an important aspect of dance phenomena. "The music is heard but transferred neuro-muscularly so that the listener's body responds to the sound and the feedback to the auditory stimulus is kinaesthetic" (1976, 195). The resulting construct is referred to as the music-dance dyad. Franz Boas, in order to counter the bias of his own era, which saw dance as primarily a discharge of excessive energy, stressed the importance of formal elements in the practice and appreciation of dance. He noted that the value of dance, as with other arts, is based primarily on form and technical proficiency (1951, 344–346).

Standards and expectations of form and technique are important to the flamenco dance practice even though its aesthetic goals center on the display of emotion. The formal rules contain the energy of the event; this allows an emotional charge to build up so that a cathartic discharge may be experienced. In discussing the attributes of flamenco dance, British anthropologist of dance Janet Goodridge notes, "Performance is heightened by characteristic acceleration at times, and the sense of a dancer's conflict—with the rhythm of inner demons, perhaps" (1999, 50). In support of this perspective, Goodridge quotes from Joanna Cole's published interview with flamenco dancer Joaquín Cortés (*The Guardian*, 22 March 1996). Cole reports that "Cortés talks much as he dances—faster and faster. His fingers leap, his arms spin as he describes flamenco as a 'fight. A fight against oneself. It's erotic, angry, yet spiritual and mystical'" (Goodridge 1999, 50). Flamenco's formal traditions and artistic structures serve as a framework that facilitates shared experience of emotional highs and lows.

Sociality takes different forms in response to the performance circumstance. When flamenco is performed in large public theater venues, the audience and performers are often placed on different levels within the space, and the effect of height, distance, and separation between them may create a more impersonal experience. Spanish audiences attend large theater productions with the expectation of witnessing a spectacle, and with high expectations for the enjoyment of sociality and exchange between audience members before, during, and after the performance event, as well as in the intermission (which in Spain is often quite extended). In the case of large-scale dance productions, the sociality surrounding flamenco practices resembles that which is present in the context of the public bullfight arena.

Flamenco is also performed in more private venues such as family homes, *peñas* (private flamenco social clubs), or at the sites of *juergas* (impromptu flamenco gatherings or parties). In such informal circumstances few, if any, barriers separate performers from observers; also, the distinction between observer and performer is less fixed. This is especially so since those performing often emerge from the circle of witnesses and will return again to the social circle after their performance. Part of the suspense inherent in a *juerga* is generated by the improvisational nature of the performances as well as not knowing who will dance or sing next. Such performances, contained within the social or familial circle, facilitate intensely intimate sharing.

Bullfighting practices also take place in a variety of contexts, ranging from informal to formal. Bullfighting is best known in its manifestation in the public arenas of large municipalities, but bullfighting practices also occur in smaller venues as part of informal events, i.e., fiestas (parties, festivals, or

In Spain, spring is the season for joyful social dances such as the *sevillanas*. Supported by the *cante, jaleo, palmas*, attention, energy, and encouragement of the traditional flamenco social circle, a couple dances in celebration during the Romería de El Rocío, the annual pilgrimage in honor of the Virgen del Rocío, in El Rocío, Spain, in May of 2012 (Cornfield/Shutterstock.com).

celebrations), *capeas* (rural fiestas), small town plazas (town squares), and on haciendas (cattle ranches) as part of the *tienta*, the testing of the bravery of young female calves for breeding purposes.[2] In the biography of the matador, El Cordobés, *Or I'll Dress You in Mourning*, a very private manifestation is described in which El Cordobés as a young man engages in the illegal practice of fighting bulls secretly at night in the fields (Collins and Lapierre 1968, 129–149).

The synergy between performers and audience members can invoke profound social ties; through the act of bearing witness audience members validate the performative testimonials of their compatriots and affirm the cultural values shared within their community. Within the public ritual life of Spain, the role of the witness is an active role. For example, in both bullfight and flamenco contexts the overt vocalizations, known as *jaleo*, of audience members affirm their direct empathic connection with performers and signal

As seen in this proscenium theater production of *Carmen* by the Antonio Gades Company for the 2010 Theater, Music and Dance Festival in the Canary Islands, Spain, the flamenco social circle is often staged in flamenco shows as a representation of Spanish culture and folk traditions. This break with the conventions of the formal theater setting provides an opportunity for audience members to feel included in the flamenco social circle. It also provides opportunities for solo dancers to perform more colloquial flamenco dance forms, such as the *bulerías* (criben/Shutterstock. com).

their active support of the event.³ Within Andalusian communities, the act of bearing witness has social import. Community members generally take turns appearing within the busy public ritual life of their community. As they alternate between the roles of performer and witness, they affirm Andalusian cultural values and secure their own place within the social group.⁴ For insiders within this high-context culture, the empathic ties between performers and witnesses are especially strong, heightening their appreciation of public rituals and performance events. Psychologically, there is a flexible, permeable boundary between performing and observing. In informal situations, an observer may decide to join in by performing, or a performer may decide to shift to the role of witness and support the performance through *jaleo*.

The flamenco term *jaleo* (commotion, noise, uproar, ruckus, or hubbub) refers to the supportive sounds, handclapping (*palmas*), finger snapping (*pitos*), and vocal responses or comments (*jaleo*) used to encourage performers.⁵ Sociality is fundamental to flamenco arts; the flamenco performance arts model is one of interactivity. This applies also in the bullring, where vocal participation is not only accepted, but forms part of the aesthetic expectation. Anthropologist Anselmo González Climent compares the *jaleo* of spontaneous verbal responses in flamenco performance to the shouts of "¡*Olé!*" heard in the bullfight arena (1964, 256). *Olé* is a hispanicized version of the Arabic word meaning Allah, or God, and thus it often expresses a quality of transcendent spirituality or reverence inspired by a unique moment of lived experience within an aesthetic context.

Social bonds are formed through the affective culture of flamenco and bullfighting. The social bonds of dependence and interdependence are implicit in the mutual support enacted in the arena between the matador and his support team, *cuadrilla* or *equipo*. Similar bonds are enacted onstage between the *cuadro flamenco* (half circle of performers providing support) and individual performing artists. The social bonds of performance also manifest behind the scenes. It is commonplace for social ties forged in performance to continue beyond the temporal or spatial boundaries of the performance event. Marriages between performing artists are common, and marriages between male flamenco guitarists and female flamenco dancers are perhaps the most common. The overlap of the social worlds of flamenco and bullfighting is commonly recognized in the scholarship of flamencologists who catalog intermarriages, social ties, and family legacies that link the two contexts (Arrebola 1991; Parra 1997). In Arrebola's extensive listing of the social connections linking bullfighting and flamenco, he also points out a number of professional toreros who have retired from the arena to become flamenco singers or dancers (1991, 51–67).

In his discussion of the social connections between the bullfighting and flamenco worlds, flamencologist Alfredo Arrebola quotes from Fernando de Palencia's book, *Los toros y el flamenco* (*The bulls and flamenco*), to explain why names of the great bullfighters and flamenco singers are so often linked. Palencia describes the overlapping of personal and emotional energies that unites the two cultural practices. "After attending a bullfight, it is traditional that enthusiastic fans will get together to comment on it, finishing off the night by going to a flamenco nightclub" (Palencia, quoted in Arrebola, 1991, 13).[6] Thus, flamenco artists who came to witness the bullfight in the afternoon would still be emotionally affected by their experience as they sang and danced at the *tablao* (flamenco nightclub); and after the bullfight, the toreros would celebrate their success by going to enjoy the flamenco arts and *ambiente* (ambiance) at the *tablao*. Flamenco artists go to the bullfight to get wound up with excitement in preparation for their performance; toreros go to the *tablao* so that the expressive intensity of flamenco performance can help them

The *tablao* or flamenco nightclub provides employment opportunities for professional performers, and its competitive stage is often associated with both the technical advancement and the commercialization of the flamenco arts. At the Café de Chinitas, a popular tourist destination in Madrid, Spain, dancers perform in the *cuadro flamenco* formation with the audience seated informally at tables around a raised stage (Pavel L Photograph and Video/Shutterstock.com).

to wind down after the anxiety, adrenaline, and excitement of the *corrida*. And so affective experience is shared by some of the same personnel in the same two contexts, flamenco and bullfighting. Both contexts promote intense sociality and cathartic emotional release. The two cultural practices overlap and affect one another through this dynamic interplay between sociality, artistry, and catharsis.

Two separate films produced by Films for the Humanities, *Matador* (1988) and *The Heritage of Flamenco* (Pachon 1992), provide an understated nonverbal acknowledgment of the overlapping worlds of flamenco and bullfighting. In *Matador*, the moving image of a female flamenco dancer repeatedly interrupts a scene focused on a matador as he practices movement techniques with his *muleta* (small red cape). Likewise, *The Heritage of Flamenco*, with its primary focus on flamenco singing, includes long scenes in the countryside showing bulls being chased down from horseback.[7] These scenes, accompanied by a sound track of flamenco singing, convey the Andalusian lifestyle that seamlessly combines flamenco and bullfight practices.

In neither documentary film is any verbal commentary provided to explain the juxtapositions of flamenco and bullfighting; rather, these two cultural activities are presented as complementary and congruent aspects of a single lifestyle. The overlap between flamenco and bullfighting practices is not articulated directly through narration, but is conveyed instead nonverbally through visual and aural images. The intimate relation between flamenco and bullfighting within the Andalusian lifestyle was expressed by the famous matador Manolete, who was killed in the bullfight arena in 1947 (Hooper 1986, 164). Flamencologist González Climent quotes Manolete as having said, "The countryside, riding horseback, and above all flamenco song and dance: that excites me; not in the theater or in public, but in small gatherings with friends" (1964, 233).[8]

Personal experience in an atmosphere of intimacy shared with others is an important and sought-after pleasure within the Andalusian lifestyle.

Sensory Modalities

Key to understanding the human sociality surrounding flamenco and bullfighting practices is an examination of "the interplay of sensory modalities, social interactions, and meaning attribution" that function within them (Csordas 2002, 71). Concurring with Thomas J. Csordas [2002] regarding the importance of understanding sensory experience as a component of culture, Edward T. Hall, in his many writings on the subject of human behavior and culture, suggests that touch behaviors, heat sensing, olfaction, visual signaling, hearing, and other sensory influences on proxemics (the scientific study of the effects of spatial proximity on the behavior of human beings) be used to elucidate human behavior (1959, 1969, 1975, 1976). Sensory modalities are an important substrate of the affective culture and lifestyle surrounding flamenco and bullfighting. Furthermore, somatic and kinesthetic experience constitute key modalities through which sensory information contributes to cultural knowledge. Probably because of their contrast with my own Anglo-American sensory habits of perception and behavior, there are three components of Andalusian sensory experience that I find particularly interesting: proximity, eye contact, and the experience of personal boundaries.

Proximity

Because of geographical proximity and historical connections, North African, Moorish, and Arabic influences run deep within Andalusian culture (Fletcher, 1992). Edward T. Hall's writing often draws attention to the differences of sensory perception and behavioral patterns between Arabic and Anglo-American cultures. These ideas pertain also to Andalusian culture, and Hall acknowledges this cultural link, saying, "The European Spanish, having been occupied by the Arabs for over five hundred years, incorporated many Arab culture patterns" (1976, 159).[9] Andalusia is also influenced by its proximity to Mediterranean cultures and so, especially in comparison to Anglo-American culture, Andalusian culture exhibits many attributes of a people with a polychronic sense of time and intense sensory involvement with one another (1969, 173–174).

The people of Andalusia are habituated to the heightened sensory awareness of smells, temperature, and skin contact that accompanies human closeness. Tactile senses are heightened through close proximity. Visual senses are stimulated and aural sensibilities are heightened in the contexts of performance. Within the contexts of flamenco and bullfighting, individual and group behaviors indulge enculturated tastes and satisfy enculturated expectations. The sociality surrounding flamenco and bullfighting characteristically includes close proximity and comfort in relationship to touch. Human emotions and bodily sensations are celebrated in Spain and Andalusia as evidence of life's actuality.

These attributes contrast significantly with Anglo-American patterns. Commenting on the sensory involvement typical of Anglo-Americans, Knox states, "Anything that permeates our boundaries is experienced as intrusive or even threatening—odor, touch, prolonged gaze" (1992, 120). Noting that olfactory suppression and acuity are culturally patterned, Hall links habituated spatial proximity between humans to acuity of olfaction and suggests that for the American middle class, "when olfaction is present it usually signals intimacy" (1975, 1015). Less proximity and a more restricted sensory awareness typify Anglo-American culture; by comparison, Andalusians enjoy being near one another and are enthusiastically sensual.

Laban Movement Analysis theories describe the human experience of touch as occurring within a range of movement phenomena from the withholding of weight (lightness) to the assertion of force (strength) (Laban [1950] 1971; Bartenieff with Lewis 1980). The psychological implications of the qualities of touch range from expressions of tenderness to those of violence, while the capacity to choose behaviors within that range, to determine one's impact on the world, constitutes a fundamental confirmation of human agency. Touch is an important and recurring motif in flamenco and bullfighting movement aesthetics; this may be due to Andalusian cultural patterns that sanction and celebrate the tactile sense. Touch (light or strong contact) communicates impact and transmits weight. Flamenco dance is a highly rhythmic dance form; its rhythmic effects are created through movement variations related to both impact (light/strong) and time (fast/slow). In addition to the placement of accents and variations of speed, the practice of flamenco dance entails conscious skill in the gradation of sound dynamics, known as *matiz*. Through rhythmicity individuals have an impact; they assert their agency in relationship to themselves, their physical environment, and the other people in their artistic/social environment.

Eye Contact

In relation to eye contact behaviors, two patterns are particularly notable in the social contexts pertaining to flamenco and bullfighting. The first has to do with the sustaining of eye contact. In Andalusia, as well as other regions of Spain, people are notably willing to maintain and prolong direct eye contact. Behaviors exhibiting general visual interest in the environment often include direct and unabashed visual examination of the people in that environment. Especially having been taught as an Anglo-American that "it is not polite to stare," in Spain I found it quite formidable and unnerving whenever I would experience this phenomenon (direct visual scrutiny or sustained eye contact).

Once, while riding on the subway in Madrid, I spent an uncomfortable fifteen minutes or so while a middle-aged woman, standing only a foot away from me, closely scrutinized me. After enduring this for a while, I stared back at her eye to eye for what was to me quite a long while, hoping to cause

Three. Overlapping Worlds 83

The motif of direct sustained eye contact is reiterated in many flamenco dance performances. Here, two male adversaries face off in a dramatic confrontation as members of the Antonio Gades Company perform *Carmen* for the 2010 Theater, Music and Dance Festival in the Canary Islands, Spain. In the flamenco dance style, strong, sustained eye contact is very often directed toward the audience, creating a sense of an adversarial relationship between performer and audience. Sustaining direct eye contact with one's dance partner is also an essential element in flamenco's social dance, the *sevillanas* (criben/Shutterstock.com).

her to look away. However, she was entirely undeterred and continued her intense examination. I am not alone in recognizing direct and sustained eye contact as a cultural trait in this region of the world. Flamencologist Anselmo González Climent noted that "Andalusia is a culture of an open, luminous eye, lacking in prolonged opening and closing of the eyes. It is a land where they say, 'whoever blinks, loses'" (González Climent 1964, 299).[10]

This intensity of visual engagement is strongly present in both flamenco and bullfighting contexts. The challenges of bullfighting require a matador to have both visual acuity and sustained focus. With great seriousness of purpose, matadors also study the visual perception of the bull. The location of the bull's eyes on the sides of his head affects the bull's behavior, and matadors have a very personal, vested interest in being able to predict a bull's behavior. A matador will want to identify quickly whether a bull favors one eye over the other as this will greatly affect the bull's manner of charging the cape.

The matador must maintain his focus on the bull, and a similarly confrontational quality of eye contact—strong, direct, and unwavering—is often established in the performance of flamenco. Such eye contact may be seen occurring between two dancers or groups of dancers, and between a dancer (or dancers) and the audience. This intense focus may also at times be directed toward various paraphernalia used within performance to extend the body's movement (sword, cape, shawl, fan, cane, or hat), specific areas within the performance space, or particular spatial directions of cultural or personal significance to the performer.

A second phenomenon pertaining to the visual sense emphasized in the cultural practices of both bullfighting and flamenco has to do with the deliberate misdirection of visual attention. In the case of bullfighting, a skilled matador knows well the functional attributes of the bull's visual sense and, like a skilled magician, uses this knowledge to attract the bull's attention to the cape, directing the bull's attention away from the human body that is the bull's true enemy and target. This quality of trickery and misdirection also occurs as a recurring motif in flamenco dance. In the movements of flamenco dance, continuity of action is often interrupted with sudden reversals; trickiness, unpredictability, deceptiveness, and surprise are valued. This sleight-of-hand quality is especially apparent in dance forms such as the *bulerías*, which deliberately employ visual misdirection to create a mood of fun and trickery.

Personal Boundaries

The degree of tension habitually held in the body results in the experience of body boundaries that are contained and rigid (bound flow) or fluid and permeable (free flow) (Laban [1950] 1971; Bartenieff with Lewis 1980). Laban Movement Analysis regards flow as a substrate or basis from which all other expressive movement qualities emerge. A person's attitude of ease or tension, going or stopping, releasing or controlling is expressed through movement qualities described as free flow or bound flow. These flow qualities help the body to regulate blood circulation and the flow of the breath.

Movement phenomena that demonstrate intense levels of flow qualities usually indicate emotional experience and expression as well as the holding/maintaining or releasing/opening of personal boundaries. Intensifying, transgressing, or rupturing boundaries entails emotional release. The quality of flow is determined by the tension between release and containment, between emotional expression and constraint, and is of critical importance in the production of cathartic experience for the individual or for the group. Observing the continuity of flow, its variations, and the patterns of tension and release within flamenco and bullfight performances contributes to understanding how, as ritualized cultural practices, they facilitate catharsis on individual and community levels.

Just as flamenco is intensely interactive, requiring collaborative effort between performers and inviting the direct social participation of audiences, similar attributes are evident in bullfighting despite its more formal hierarchical structure. Both cultural practices seek to create high levels of affect; they embrace emotional intensity and seek to establish human contact and connection through collective affective experience. Flamenco dance and bullfighting nourish, and are nourished by, the sociality that is fundamental to Andalusian life. As traditions, flamenco and bullfighting create opportunities for Andalusians to interact within a context of intense intersubjectivity. An individual's subjective experience is valued for its uniqueness and, by being brought into discourse, is appreciated as an enrichment of the life of the community. Should social conflicts or controversies emerge in the course of performance events, the ensuing drama is generally enjoyed as evidence of individual and community vitality.

Performance Interactions

While social interactivity is general and widespread, specialized interactivity is also at play within performance events. Examining three especially important interactive mechanisms, rhythmic entrainment, music, and vocalization, can provide details of the performance interactions that drive and regulate flamenco and bullfighting practices.

Rhythmic Entrainment

Rhythm constitutes a bond between people; connection is enacted through shared patterns of sound, time, and touch. Rhythm is constructed of both time and force, what Laban Movement Analysis describes as the movement qualities that express a person's attitude toward time and weight. A person's attitude toward time is expressed through movements that appear to expand time, stretch out or prolong it, or movements that appear to condense time, with urgency or haste. A person's attitude toward weight is expressed through movement qualities that appear to withhold weight, becoming light and airy, or movement qualities that appear to intensify weight, creating force and power (Laban [1950] 1971; Bartenieff with Lewis 1980). In the Andalusian context, the weight component of rhythm is affected by enculturated attitudes that place great value on touching, contact, and having an impact, for it is through such phenomena that sociality is invigorated.

"Rhythm may be understood as an essential feature of movement. Rhythm operates at involuntary and unconscious levels, as baseline physiological function, and at volitional and conscious levels, as gesture, song, ritual" (Knox 1992, 77). Thus, while an enculturated experience of rhythm is expressed overtly through flamenco dance and music, the rhythmic patterns typical of flamenco are enmeshed with many other experiences pertaining to the practices of flamenco and bullfighting, including those occurring at an unconscious level. Even when not sounded overtly or heard directly, the rhythmic structure (*compás*) of flamenco music seems to provide the background music accompanying the lifestyle of flamenco and bullfighting. The regular pulse of the *compás* provides temporal stability, a traditional form against which the idiosyncratic and unpredictable aspects of a performer's persona may be noticed and celebrated.

The flamenco *compás* constitutes the rhythmic framework that unites dancers and musicians. *Compás* is the critical underlying rhythmic structure, a number of beats in a measure of music with a repeating pattern of accents, that all performers know and follow. *Compás* is the glue that holds together their performance. It is the common understanding that enables them to take turns, recognize signals, and create artistically; it supports both practiced and improvisational expression. To be "*fuera de compás*" (out of rhythm) is to create chaos or disharmony, to break the mood, to undermine the connection between performers and, at least potentially, to bring everything to a stop.

When the flamenco *compás* is a four-count phrase (such as *rumba gitana*, *tangos*, or *tientos*), its rhythmic patterns are more easily accessible to non–Spaniards. On the other hand, a flamenco *compás* based on a phrase length of twelve counts (such as *soleares*, *siguiriyas*, *alegrías*, or *bulerías*) shifts its rhythmic accents between three-count and two-count emphases, creating patterns that may initially confound newcomers to the art. To a person familiar with the affective culture of flamenco, a particular flamenco *compás* communicates more than rhythm through its metrical structure and pattern of accents. Through musical key (minor or major), tempo (fast or slow), and the placement of accents, the *compás* communicates emotion and mood. A particular musical *compás* may imply a traditional melody line and suggest subject matter appropriate for the song verses (*letras*). Familiarity with traditional flamenco forms results in a population united in their aesthetic expectations after hearing only the first few notes from a flamenco guitar.

Many flamenco audience members have aesthetic expectations that are informed by their knowledge of the temporal/dynamic structure of the *compás* and flamenco song forms. At a fundamental level, their embodied knowledge of flamenco rhythms signifies cultural identity and belonging. As expressed by Knox, "Starting with body, building on the experience of redundant rhythmic interactions, coupled with affective reinforcement and cognitive interpretation, cultural competence can be most accurately understood as body-based, culturally informed knowledge" (1992, 82). Thus, through flamenco dance and bullfighting practices, individuals, either as performers or as audience members, have opportunities to enact living proof of their cultural competence and social belonging.

The phenomenon of rhythmic entrainment also occurs beyond the regulatory function of musical meters such as the flamenco *compás*. Knox addresses these more organic levels of synchronized timing between entities, saying, "We are rhythmic creatures. Rhythm is fundamental to the process of patterning. We cannot help but be patterned and rhythmed by virtue of being embodied: in utero; by birth; feeding, holding; the rhythms of speech and weather; timing" (1992, 47). Movement communicates a sense of time or rhythm, but also a sense of direction or spatial intent. This is true for humans, and primates in general have been found to perceive the intentions of others by observing their movement (de Waal 2005; Wilkerson 1999). An ability to coordinate the timing and direction of our movement so as to match the movements of another is at the root of our ability to bond. Such movement synchronization serves as a mechanism of intraspecies and interspecies bonding, communication, and interaction. The rider synchronizes his or her movements to those of the horse; both human and nonhuman hunters synchronize their movements to those of their prey. These constitute examples of rhythmic entrainment that occur outside of music's metrical system.

Anthropologist Janet Goodridge describes a "tendency towards synchrony in compatible human relationships and in nature—such as are seen in flocks of birds, or schools of fish. Some descriptions of synchrony refer to it as 'entrainment' or 'mutual phase locking'" (1999, 36). The phenomenon of entrainment is basic to establishing empathy and connection in relationships. Cynthia Knox refers to attributes of synchronization as she lists "the fundamentals of interaction, e.g., rhythm, pace, entrainment, empathy, intuition, resonance" (1992, 50). Similarly, creating the quality of entrainment, a matador adjusts the movement of the cape to match the rate of speed of an approaching bull; the goal is to draw the bull into a type of dance.

Daniel Hannan, writing about his experiential learning of bullfighting techniques with Coleman Cooney, director of the California Academy of Tauromaquia, captions a photo with the words, "'Toreo' or bullfighting: 'a kind of ritualized dance, a tragedy with only one correct outcome."' (*Daily Telegraph*; March 8, 2004). Within the bullfight movement vocabulary, the phenomenon of rhythmic entrainment itself may serve as a signifier of dance or dancelike behaviors. The movement qualities experienced during rhythmic entrainment are often purposefully hypnotic and entrancing. Once rhythmic entrainment is achieved, however, "there is no appreciable time quality, the expression becomes what we might call 'spell-like.' The inner attitude towards time rests and the movements radiate a quality of fascination" (Laban [1950] 1971, 88).[11]

Describing the ideal synchronization of timing between the bull and the torero, tauromachy instructor Coleman Cooney notes, "When fighting stock attacks, the animal lowers its head to toss its target. The animal must slow

This photograph, taken May 2008 in Madrid, Spain, shows a professional matador and bull in the final sequence of a bullfight. On charging, a bull lowers his head to come from below to uproot and throw his adversary. The matador's response is to hold his ground while drawing the bull well past his body with the *muleta*, the small red cape supported by a sword. Matadors train intensively to extend the arm long, a movement technique valued for safety and elegance. In this demanding single-arm technique, the farther the arm is extended, the more strength is required to support the weight of both the *muleta* and the sword. Similar configurations of the body occur in the flamenco dance style; often, as one arm is extended, the opposing arm is planted on the hip with elbow wide, the hips are thrust forward, and the dancer's focus is inclined downward (Marcus Obal/WikiCommons).

Three. Overlapping Worlds 89

In this 2008 photograph of a performance of *Carmen* by the Ballet Teatro Español de Rafael Aguilar at the Jichen Theater in Chengdu, China, a flamenco dancer manipulates her skirt so as to create a sense of tension between the center and the edge of her movement sphere, a quality known as peripheral spatial tension. A flamenco skirt should be pulled away from a dancer's center, so that its relationship to the dancer is always dynamic (Jack.Q/Shutterstock.com).

down when its head is lowered. If the target (the cape) is withdrawn at just the right speed this magic moment is prolonged and the torero is in control" (Cooney 2005). The term used to describe this technical skill is *temple* (Cooney 2005), a Spanish word connoting harmony or compromise. A matador seeks to create a sense of congruence between the movement of the cape and the speed of the bull's charge. A sense of entrainment, of being swept along by the majesty of the moment, may also be felt between the matador and the public, or among audience members crowded together into the arena and viewing the same spectacle. Rhythmic entrainment, driven by repetitions of the *compás*, also occurs between flamenco performers, dancer to dancer, dancer to musician, dancer to public, and among witnesses of a flamenco dance event.

Flamencologist Anselmo González Climent points out a quality of intense, empathic compassion supplied by the *palmero* (the flamenco performer who provides the accompaniment of handclapping or *palmas*) to support a flamenco *cantaor* or *cantaora* (male or female singer). He compares it to the support provided to the matador by his assistants in the bullfight arena.

> The soft handclapping symbolizes the intimate companionship with which the *jaleador* [person providing handclaps and/or vocal encouragement] invites the singer, as if assuring him of his authentic participation, moment by moment, break by break [musical], in the unfolding emotions. With it he demonstrates, simply, not to abandon him [the *cantaor*] in the hour of truth, like the assistant to a matador in danger of being gored by the bull. It is to put the hand on the shoulder of the singer, compassionate and encouraging, in order to show him the perfect heartfelt communion [González Climent 1964, 267].[12]

Music

The relationship between music and movement impulse is central to flamenco, as it is to many forms of dance. The relationship between music and dance is so close that Kealiinohomoku asserts "understanding the mechanisms of synaesthesia as a set of simultaneous sensory-transfers that trigger one another is crucial to the understanding of dance" (1976, 196–197). Kealiinohomoku, discussing synesthesia further, notes of the music-dance dyad that "the perception is auditory (an external sense) transferred from sound to kinaesthesia (internal sense), and the response is accomplished in culturally patterned ways" (196). It is common to assume that the music prompts the movement; however, other relationships between music and dance phenomena also occur.

There are three possibilities to consider in constructing an accurate understanding of the music-dance dyad in flamenco performance. The first possibility is that flamenco music leads the dance impulse; this may be an audience member's first impression. However, in some instances the musical stops and starts, tempos, and even melodies are determined or influenced by a dancer's movement choices. Flamenco guitarists and singers regularly take their cue from the rhythms, spatial pathways, postures, and gestures through which a dancer signals or calls for a change. *Llamada*, in Spanish, means "call." Within the flamenco dance vocabulary a *llamada* provides a nonverbal movement signal; its forms are often conventional and therefore easily recognized by performers as well as knowledgeable audience members. A *llamada* signals a shift of activity and leadership among the performers. For instance, a dancer's *llamada* may signal musicians to provide support for a section of footwork or signal a flamenco singer to take the lead at the close of a section of footwork.

A third type of music/dance relationship occurs when neither musician nor dancer is controlling the performance event. At such times, having faith in the formal artistic constructs of the flamenco *compás* and traditions enables performing artists to collaborate freely and creatively. They rely on the abstract rhythmic form, the *compás*, which provides rules for their play; their implicit agreement on the underlying rhythmic structure provides both musicians and dancers a secure base from which to collaboratively explore their artistic potential. All three types of relationships between music and dance can occur within a single performance, artistic control passing easily between the dancers and the musicians numerous times within a single dance. Always, the *compás* provides the rhythmic framework and psychological safety net that allows for and facilitates maximum play and creativity.

Within the practice of the flamenco arts, culturally patterned movement and sound signals enable performers to play flamenco's artistic cultural game. Discussing the importance of signals and symbols within dance practices, Kealiinohomoku notes that "although signals and symbols are both informing devices, signals tend to be denotative while symbols tend to be connotative" (1976, 92).[13] Symbols in flamenco are movements, sounds, or props that help audiences create associations to better appreciate the performance. For example, a flamenco dancer performing with a cane might use it to represent power, domination, a weapon, or violence. Signals in flamenco are movements or sounds that function to directly indicate what needs to happen next within a flamenco performance. For example, dancers perform special movements to signal the guitarist or the guitarist plays a special phrase to signal the singer. Performers are connected through their shared knowledge of flamenco's music and dance traditions. Shared knowledge of performance conventions allows artists to navigate the art form, making instantaneous choices to either conform to traditions or expand them. The strength of flamenco's formal structures allows it to contain high levels of affective expression while facilitating creativity and improvisation.

Knowing what comes next, performers often communicate nonverbally using simple social signals, such as eye contact, gestures, or postural shifts. Within the flamenco tradition there are also some formal mechanisms (particular body movements or rhythmic sound patterns) that constitute signals. Usually what is being communicated is simply that a change is about to occur. Performers know that traditional forms usually begin with an introduction (*entrada* or *salida*),[14] and will alternate between sections that highlight the song, the guitar music, or the sounds of the dancer's footwork. Given their high levels of knowledge, most performers will comprehend (prior to a *llamada*) what is likely to occur next in the performance situation. Change is mutually anticipated; thus these signals fulfill the expectations of flamenco tradition. Due to the pervasive strength of flamenco conventions, even performers who have not rehearsed together are capable of producing an excellent spontaneous performance with improvisational attributes. Whether participants use a rhythmic signal to bring a segment to a close (*remate*) or employ a movement signal (*llamada* or *desplante*),[15] both types of signals constitute intrinsic components within flamenco's music-dance dyad.

In some instances flamenco music accompanies a bullfight; however, it is more common for non-flamenco music traditions to be heard in the bullring.[16] Anthropologist Timothy Mitchell credits Delgado-Iribarren with having "firmly established" the military origin of the music that accompanies bullfighting in Spain's public arenas (1991, 147). Mitchell notes that the *paso doble*,[17] the music most often associated with the bullfight tradition, "is a direct descendent of the military march" (147). Unlike the complexity of flamenco rhythms,[18] musical compositions played in the bullring are noted for "their binary marching rhythm, their allegro movement, their simple melodies, and their facile execution by bands of wind and percussion instruments" (147). The coupling of militaristic musical forms with the male-identified practice of bullfighting significantly reinforces the perception of the bullring as a male domain.

Vocalization

The unique singing style of *cante jondo* (deep song) is known for its rhythmicity and musicality, but also its somatic connection to deep emotions. The *cante jondo* emerges from the body-based experience of lamentation; its vocal techniques are based on crying or wailing. It intensifies the expression of emotion through roughness of the voice (*voz afillá*), sharp catches in the breath, and other emotion-laden sounds. Overtones and resonance in flamenco singing facilitate feelings of intimacy and empathic connection. The play between dissonance (felt as emotional tension or distress) and its resolution (felt as relief or triumph) is a mechanism through which flamenco singers encourage emotional catharsis in their listeners.

Vocalizing, through song or crying out in response to flamenco performances or bullfights, constitutes a social practice that serves the dual needs of catharsis and equilibrium (homeostasis). "It is hypothesized that the primary functions of dance are those of play and ritual, and that the fundamental need served by dance is the achievement of biological, socio-cultural, and psychological homeostasis" (Kealiinohomoku 1976, 50). And so, the vocalizations that accompany the flamenco performance and the bullfight constitute performative mechanisms that facilitate a community's transition through the upset of catharsis and returning to the balance of homeostasis. Each reiteration of the cathartic experience (whether achieved through participation in flamenco or bullfight practices) reinforces an individual's cultural identity, sense of belonging within the cultural group, and the cultural group's customs, beliefs, moral standards, and behavioral expectations. The temporary disruption or stress of the cathartic experience will reenergize, renew, or enhance cultural homeostasis.

In addition to the immediate vocalizations of *cante* and *jaleo*, there is an ongoing social conversation that surrounds the cultural complex of flamenco and bullfighting. A cultural complex involves a notable degree of "focusing of interest" within a group of people (Herskovits 1964, 104). According to anthropologist Herskovits, "the preponderant role of a complex, *for the people who live in the area*, gives point and reason to their ways of life and is a dominating, integrating force in their existence" (1964, 104; Herskovits's italics). Flamenco and bullfighting are deeply integrated into the cultural and social lives of Spaniards, especially Andalusians, affecting even those who demonstrate no overt interest in these practices. While the two cultural practices are not entirely interdependent, neither are they entirely separate; as elements within a cultural complex, they overlap synergistically in significant ways. Their relatedness suggests that each cultural practice will best be understood when insights derived from the other are incorporated, that, in fact, lack of knowledge of one cultural practice may reduce understanding of the other.[19]

Social Goals

Cultural practices such as bullfighting and flamenco dance serve their communities by creating opportunities for courtship and providing cathartic experiences. Courtship serves a community's need for reproductive continuity through couple bonding, and the creation of families and communal cathartic experiences serves the health of a community by raising its energy to a higher state.

Courtship

The practices of both bullfighting and the flamenco arts satisfy an individual's desire to distinguish him or herself through self-defining performative action, and in this way establish status and belonging within the social group. Social bonds related to courtship are also negotiated within these contexts. Traditionally, flamenco dance is a solo dance form that provides individuals with special opportunities to display both personality and personhood in front of their social group. A portion of this display behavior may serve the social goal of courtship. Also, some flamenco dance forms (*rumbas, sevillanas*, and *bulerías*) function as social dances within the community and, when performed as couple dances, more directly facilitate courtship.

As a participant-observer in Jerez de la Frontera, Spain, in the fall of 1999, I had the opportunity to witness firsthand the sociality that surrounds the flamenco practice in the context of a family celebration, a *boda gitana*, a Spanish Gypsy wedding (Landborn 2003). Courtship was part of this context on many levels, the most obvious being the celebration of the consummation of a marriage alliance. *Gitanos* practice endogamy, the strengthening of kinship ties through marriage alliances inside the tribal group. The various family units that make up the tribe may live at some geographical distance from one another and only rarely come together at the same time. A *boda gitana* is one of those rare occasions.[20] And so, a wedding celebration among *gitanos* may also serve as an occasion for other marriage alliances to be arranged (Fraser 1998, 43; Wang 1996, 45–47).

In this instance, the wedding was being celebrated by a well-known Gypsy family that has produced many highly noted flamenco artists. Within this authentic familial context, I was able to observe how the attributes of age, gender, and familial relationships affected participation in flamenco practices. I also saw how differently flamenco was practiced in this context compared to the more formal performance settings I had experienced previously.

In this festive setting the principal party music and dance was the flamenco *bulerías*, a largely improvisational form most often danced by male or female soloists or by a heterosexual pair. Observing flamenco dance practices at this wedding, I became especially aware of their implications in relationship to sociality, gender relations in general, and more specifically the social goal of courtship. My observations led me to consider how the *bulerías*, particularly for females, may sometimes serve as an improvisational form through which a young woman may express herself freely or feel the pressure of social and familial expectations (Landborn 2003).

Gypsy weddings are celebratory occasions during which marriageable young women feel social pressures to be on their best behavior (Fraser 1998, 43; Wang 1996, 45–47). They are also occasions during which male family members may take on the important responsibility of matchmaking in relation to a niece, daughter, or sister. The male marriage-arranging prerogative results in male power, consequence, and importance within the tribe (Wang 1996, 239). This male responsibility is not unrelated to the cattle rancher's responsibility for animal husbandry. A male dancer, during the courtship phase of his life, may experience the *bulerías* social circle as a supportive arena in which to give an uninhibited demonstration of his virility. During their mature years, *gitano* males may participate in the *bulerías* with greater awareness of their family responsibilities. To meet family obligations, they must help the young female family members for whom they are responsible display their vitality, charm, and suitability as wives. Thus, through the social performance of the *bulerías*, male relatives display social controls over female sexuality as they enact a managerial role in relationship to tribal reproduction.

Observing the *bulerías* in this intergenerational context, I saw that a female's behavior, performance, interactions, goals, and emotions were likely to vary visibly within the dance during different periods of her life. As a child she might enjoy complete expressive freedom when dancing the *bulerías*. However, this childlike open expressivity will likely be curtailed by family members during a woman's fertile years. When eventually infertility frees her from the concomitant social constraints and reproductive controls of the cultural group, a woman's freedom of expression may be regained. Her mature dancing may both express an uninhibited freedom and manifest the complexity of her life experiences (Landborn 2003).

When danced by a solo performer, the *bulerías* may serve the function of courtship because it provides individuals the opportunity to display their desirability within the sanctioning attention of the social circle. When danced by a heterosexual duo, the *bulerías* sometimes culminates with the male dancer appearing to dominate, herd, or corral the female dancer, bringing her under male control and removing her from the circle's center. This control of female energy or sexuality appears to be accomplished by the male on behalf of the social group. This dynamic, which is also sometimes reproduced in theatrical flamenco performances, is reminiscent of the dynamics at the end of a *tienta* when the last task is to get a (by then furious) female calf to leave the arena. This is often very difficult to do. Removing the calf from the ring may require the participation of many toreros and the bystanders who love to jump in to help; it includes many opportunities for mishaps; and, being a free-for-all, it is generally very entertaining to watch.

In both contexts, the *tienta* and the dance, the humor that emerges comes from cultural assumptions regarding the dangerousness of females in general and female sexuality in particular, and the resultant male predicament. The dance dynamics between a male and female dancer do not always mirror those enacted between the matador and the bull. The matador's goal is to demonstrate his complete domination of the wild and dangerous bull, including control of the moment of its death. By instinct the bull actively engages in the bullfight in order to defend its territory. The bull is not present in the bullring of its own volition, nor is it complicit in its own defeat. In the flamenco dance context, a male dancer's goal is to demonstrate his (often tenuous) domination of a female whose sexuality is culturally defined as wild and dangerous. These cultural notions about the dangers of female sexuality are likely derived from the Moorish cultural influence of North Africa. Dance constitutes a performative event in which the female dancer is clearly complicit; she collaborates, often by performing a culturally sanctioned sequence that initially demonstrates her (wild) sexual vitality and ends inevitably with her (tamed) acquiescence.

Other types of social control are also enacted through flamenco performance. *Palmas*, *cante*, and the focused attention of the community circle are essential to the dancer of the *bulerías*; the *jaleo* and enthusiasm of the surrounding group serve as the lifeblood of the dance. Any interruption of this support constitutes an instance of social control; it immediately sends a strong, nonverbal message of criticism, disapproval, or censure. Any withdrawal of energy or reduction of support from the circle, however slight, is felt instantly and somatically by the person dancing. This level of social control can be used to discourage, constrain, or ostracize someone whose behavior the group has deemed inappropriate. Flamenco dance practices thus provide both the context and the nonverbal mechanisms through which the social, expressive, and sexual freedom of the women within the group may be limited or controlled (Landborn 2003).

Catharsis

As part of the public ritual life of Spain, and Andalusia in particular, the practices of flamenco and bullfighting elevate the affective intensity experienced by both the individual and the community as a whole. Dance creates homeostasis through the mechanism of catharsis, at both the individual and community level. Functioning as play and ritual, both flamenco dance and bullfighting create opportunities for super-ordinary experiences. Superordinary cultural practices, by "alternately disturbing and resolving sensory perceptions," enable social groups to achieve homeostasis (Kealiinohomoku 1976, 54). Flamenco is more closely aligned with the function of play, and bullfighting with the function of ritual, yet both practices elicit super-ordinary experience to bring about catharsis. Cathartic release of tension occurs when one witnesses the life-and-death drama of the bullfight ritual as well as when one empathizes with the intense emotions expressed through a flamenco performance.

The nature of cathartic release is unpredictable. Tragedy, but also comedy, may be experienced within the release of emotion. Humor, laughter, anxiety, fear, relief, grief, all are possible depending on the happenings and final outcome of the event. Bullfight aficionado Ernest Hemingway pointed to loss of dignity as the element that creates humor in the bullfight arena ([1939] 1994, 5–8). In fact, the comedic effect of unexpected incidents may well be especially effective due to its contrast with the overall seriousness of the *corrida*. In the flamenco *bulerías* as well, the performance of exaggerated personal dignity is the perfect setup for a moment of comic relief. The practices of flamenco and bullfighting embody the Spanish value for living in the moment and for the moment. They create moments of heightened risk and emotion; they draw attention to the precious pleasures of life, while demonstrating that life is precarious and triumph is momentary.

Comprehending the danger they will face in the bullring, toreros and matadors place great value on gaining technical skills and develop their expertise by studying bullfight history, bull breeds, and animal behavior. A performance in the bullring that demonstrates technical ability, personal courage, and artistry is a source of personal pride and contributes to a torero's social status. Matadors often practice alone, sensing their singularity and isolation as they prepare to risk life itself. A matador practices alone to hone his or her tauromachy skills, but matadors are unlikely to fight a bull without an audience to give their actions meaning within the public sphere. Motivations will vary, both between individual toreros and over time within the mind of each matador. Some of the following may motivate a torero's actions in the arena: survival, self-esteem, social standing, career advancement, economic gain, familial well-being, artistic or religious expression, adrenaline addiction, sexual desirability. Although a matador may be self-absorbed, his or her interest in public opinion is also intense. In the bullring, matadors fight to protect themselves from physical harm, but also to protect themselves from social disinterest or even public scorn. Although the physical risks are less than those of matadors, flamenco dancers, too, may practice obsessively to perfect their technique, fear challenging dance steps, and concern themselves with public opinion.

CHAPTER FOUR

Ritual and Performance Events

Flamenco and bullfighting, like other "super-ordinary experiences" that "make up affective culture" (Kealiinohomoku 1976, 56–61), require culturally appropriate institutions, space, and time to bring the super-ordinary into the lives of ordinary Spaniards. They require special spaces to contain them, special people dressed in special clothing with special skills, and special times to be set aside for their performances. There are heightened levels of energy and anticipation before the afternoon bullfight or the evening flamenco show. There are also traditional means for transitioning back to everyday life after attending these super-ordinary events. In Spain, this normalizing is usually accomplished through socializing. In community with other attendees, the qualities of the afternoon's happenings or the evening's entertainment are discussed, absorbed, and laid down as yet another layer in the cumulative social history of the bullfighting and flamenco traditions.

A foreigner attending an afternoon bullfight or an evening flamenco show may not realize how prevalent these practices are in Spanish culture, Spanish life, and the worldview and psyche of many Spaniards. Formal performance events in the *plaza de toros* and the theater are just the tip of a proverbial iceberg; these cultural practices manifest in many less formal situations, and indeed their emergence into the everyday life of Spaniards is part of their magic and power. Whether running with the bulls or enacting the role of the matador encircled by cheering friends, the relative informality of such activities allows each person to choose how much risk they will take as they play. When a flamenco singer begins to sing in an informal situation, he or she is inviting an ineffable passion and mysterious force to break through to enliven everyday life with its power. Experiencing bullfighting and flamenco in formal circumstances adds to a foreigner's understanding of Spanish culture; however, even more enlightening is being present when ordinary Spanish life is interrupted by the sudden appearance of the super-ordinary.

Institutions and Venues

Special institutions and venues, spatial configurations, and time parameters facilitate and organize the cultural practices of flamenco dance and bullfighting, asserting a stabilizing influence. Flamenco and bullfighting are provided the requisite space and time through the support of locations, businesses, and architectural spaces designed specifically to showcase performers and cater to the desires of audiences. Due to the interest of the Spanish population in general, however, flamenco and bullfighting are also supported—given space and time—outside of institutional constraints. These cultural practices should be understood as existing in the people themselves. Flamenco and bullfighting constitute embodied culture and as such they are eminently portable; their first home is in the body, and so, should any informal circumstances provide sufficient encouragement, many Spaniards and Andalusians will take advantage of the opportunity by enacting behaviors related to flamenco or bullfighting.

Their most fundamental spatial form is a social circle that provides witness and encouragement to a performer located in its center. A social circle may emerge—its energies gather and take form—at any time, based on the mood of the people. If someone begins to perform just because they feel like it, a circle will gather around to encourage, bear witness, and enjoy the performer's emotion and energy. Likewise, if a social circle generates sufficient energy, more participants will feel called to the circle's center to take advantage of the performative moment. There are many formal institutions and venues that support flamenco and bullfighting practices, but at times the magic emerges unexpectedly.

BULLFIGHTING

Timothy deWaal Malefyt, discussing the gendered domains of flamenco practice, asserts that "male relations in the public sphere are said to be competitive, where positioning and dominance over another male achieves social status. Masculinity is not a given, but must be proven in actions, hence promoting 'vertical' relationships of competition, display, and inequality with other males" (1998, 53). Although Malefyt's statement originates in the context of flamenco performance, it also elucidates why all bullfight practices are tacitly understood to pertain to the male domain. Whether tauromachy is practiced unceremoniously in informal venues or formally in the public arena, the elements of competition, conflict, and risk taking reside in all forms of bullfighting and are associated with the male domain.

Four. Ritual and Performance Events

This eighteenth-century tapestry, *El Toro del Aguardiente en Carabanchel Alto*, attributed to the renowned Spanish painter Francisco de Goya (1746–1828), is on exhibit at the Real Monasterio de San Lorenzo del Escorial in Madrid. It illustrates Spain's long-standing history of informal bullbaiting practices, such as *capeas*, informal bullfights often held in small municipalities for special celebrations, and *encierros*, like the renowned running with the bulls in Pamplona for the festival of San Fermin. Because interacting with bulls is such a pervasive element in Spanish culture, many Spaniards have some level of actual skill or, at the very least, a well-developed ability to mimic the stylized movements of the bullfight (courtesy Biblioteca Virtual del Patrimonio Bibliográfico).

Flexibility of venue pertains to the practice of bullfighting as it does to the practice of flamenco. Occurring in the professional arena, a *corrida de toros* (public bullfight event) acknowledges Spain's hierarchical social structures through formal ceremony. However, for bullfighting's most informal enactments, a bull is not even necessary; the imagination may suffice. *Toro* means bull and *torear* means to tease, harass, or play with a bull; this enculturated human behavior occurs in a range of situations, from the formal, public bullfighting of the professional matador to the casual play of children taking turns pretending to be the bull by "running the horns" past a matador-playmate (Cooney 2005).

"To become a bullfighter, you become first a bull." For generations the sidewalks and back alleys of Spain's communities have been animated by youngsters putting that simple maxim into action. With noisy shouts, they play at the corrida the way other boys play football or basketball, charging into each other's muletas to learn the basic gestures of the torero's trade [Collins and Lapierre 1968, 130].

The cultural practice of bullfighting is best understood as a collective phenomenon that enables personal risk taking. The elements of play and risk are significant aspects of the activity of *toreando* (the gerund form of *torear*). "Playful curiosity leads us to stick our noses where they've never been before,

El Juego de la Vaquilla, also known as *Niños Jugando al Toro*, a tapestry on display at the Real Monasterio de San Lorenzo del Escorial in Madrid, Spain, was created by the Spanish artist Ramón Bayeu y Subías (1741-1793) in collaboration with his brother-in-law, Francisco de Goya. It shows Spanish boys acting out a bullfight. Known as *toreando*, this childhood game has a long history in the cultural life of Spain. From left to right, the first boy holds a stick in each hand to play the part of the *banderillero*, the second boy wears horns as he plays the bull, the third boy has dangerously fallen beneath the bull, the fourth boy, who is acting the part of the *matador*, wields a lance (*rejon*) and rides on the shoulders of the fifth boy, who plays the matador's horse, while a sixth boy runs away. These boys are acting out what at the time was the most common type of bullfighting from horseback, called *rejoneo* or *toreo de rejones*, practiced by Spanish noblemen. In 1726, a Spanish carpenter's assistant, Francisco Romero, introduced the modern tradition of bullfighting on foot when he leapt into the arena and used his hat to distract the bull and save the life of a nobleman who had fallen and become pinned beneath his horse (Collins and La Pierre, 1968, xi) (courtesy Biblioteca Virtual del Patrimonio Bibliográfico).

or to test just how far we can crawl out on that limb before it breaks. Among humans and other species, play behavior is a frequent cause of injury or death" (Meeker 1997, 18). Play behaviors, such as running the horns or playing the matador, may occur on the street, at the park, with family members or friends; they may also be enacted through dance. The danger implied through such play behaviors becomes actual when risks are taken with bulls at local festivals.

In his book *Blood Sport: A Social History of Spanish Bullfighting* (1991), flamencologist and anthropologist Timothy J. Mitchell catalogs the many occasions in Spanish ritual life in which average Spaniards seek to engage in bullbaiting activities of various kinds. In a public, yet informal, manifestation of the bullfighting tradition known as an *encierro*, a crowd (usually of young men) is chased through blockaded streets by bulls let loose for festival purposes. A well-known example of this practice is the world-famous running of the bulls in Pamplona, Spain. A less notorious component of bullfighting, the *tienta*, occurs in the corrals of Spain's haciendas and provides ranchers with opportunities to assess their animals in action. It also provides opportunities for young torero apprentices to legally practice *toreando* skills in confrontation with an animal.

An opportunity to develop bullfighting skills or test one's luck that is more public than the *tienta* and more contained than the *encierro* is known as the *capea*. Mitchell describes *capeas* as a form of bullbaiting within a designated space. "Unlike an encierro, which is a running of a bull or bulls through town streets, a capea takes place in any enclosed space. The space can be a permanent or portable bullring, but is more often a plaza, square, or intersection that has been barricaded in some way" (1991, 27). The violence of the bullfight, which takes ritualized form in the larger public arenas, manifests as a formless free-for-all in the *capeas*. "Unlike a formal bullfight with its strict time limits and numerous rules, the duration of a capea is only limited by the number or vigor of the bulls and the only rule applied is that of 'anything goes'" (28). The informality of the *capea* is a result also of its changeable personnel. As in the informal practices of flamenco dance, a participant may retreat to safety by shifting into the role of witness, or emerge from the sidelines as an active performer if inspired to join the fray. As a result, like the flamenco social circle, the boundary of the *capea* functions as a place of liminality, a shifting edge between safety and danger.

"The bullfight spectacle is never carried out in private, but in the open glare of the sun and the consensus of the taurine community" (Mitchell 1991, 169). Public arenas provide venues for bullfighting in its most ceremonial, ritualized form as public spectacle; such events are generally sponsored by local municipalities. The dimensions of large arenas direct an intense level of public scrutiny onto the performances of professional toreros and especially the matador. As with the *tienta*, the spatial boundaries of a professional bullfight arena are set, and the protocols of courtesy due the *ganadero* (cattle rancher) at the *tienta* are even more formally expressed to the residing official of a formal *corrida de toros*.[1] The informal protective barricades erected for an *encierro* or *capea* are formalized in the public arena as the *burladero*, "wooden barrier within the ring and next to the ring wall that provides the entry and exit point for the toreros" (Cooney 2005).

The grand architecture of the arena, the formal traditions and protocols that sanction events in the arena, the musical accompaniment and regalia, and the technical and aesthetic values surrounding the encounter between human and bull, all combine in the *corrida de toros* to give stature to the matadors and toreros, the animals and the ranches from which they came, and the cultural event itself. As with flamenco, the media involvement of television, radio, and the Internet signifies wider public interest beyond the immediate attendees in the bullfight arena. Furthermore, bullfighting *peñas*, similar to flamenco *peñas*, are social clubs where aficionados of the bullfighting arts gather for social activities and networking; these are active virtually year-round (Pink 1997, 11).

Flamenco

Flamenco functions as a celebratory practice with family and close friends; in the late night or early morning hours I have heard groups of teenagers walking together down the narrow streets of Jerez de la Frontera celebrating their solidarity with *palmas* and improvisational song and dance. As such spontaneous collections of people gain in energy and momentum, they may manifest as the impromptu flamenco gathering or party known as a *juerga*. A *juerga*, being extemporaneous in nature and often involving the overconsumption of alcoholic beverages, can last through several days and nights with various changes in both its location and personnel. The moods expressed through such informal flamenco performances range from the serious to the celebratory, from the despairing to the euphoric. Open expression of such a broad range of emotions results in a profound sense of intimacy within the social group. Within this richly dynamic experience, participants find personal meaning, establish social relationships, and enact the implicit values of their culture.

Public locations for flamenco range from small, intimate social spaces to large, formal theater spaces, with many variations in between. The *peña flamenca* is a social club that generally caters to the talents of local flamenco artists and provides a gathering place for its members. As performance spaces and social organizations, local *peñas* constitute a fundamental means through which flamenco culture is communicated, enacted, and maintained. "The inner realm of peñas is a highly domestic space, in appearance as well as in social function. The inside is replete with photographs of members, of members with artists, of featured artists, and of awards and plaques of recognition. One might compare the inside to a family den, caught up in the nostalgia of personal memorabilia and clan history" (Malefyt 1998, 58).

On occasion a *peña flamenca* will invite flamenco artists from outside the immediate community to perform in its relaxed social setting. In 1999 I attended a performance of flamenco singer María Vargas at a local *peña flamenca*, the Peña Tío José de Paula in Jerez de la Frontera. The *peña* was very crowded on this occasion, with club members seated in their established places close to the raised performance area and most nonmembers standing in the back; thus, social ranking was embodied, in part, through the seating arrangements. María Vargas sang first from the slightly raised area at one end of the *peña* in a presentational format. After her performance, "the older women put their chairs in a circle and María Vargas (with a great show of deference for the honor being done her) sat in the circle to partake of the Jerez *bulerías*" (Landborn 2003, 14). Spatially, María Vargas was brought down a level; through her placement in the social circle, she was made a witness to local practices.

María Vargas, originally from the town of Sanlúcar de Barrameda, located approximately twenty miles from Jerez de la Frontera, is a mature woman with an international reputation as a flamenco singer. Despite Vargas's professionalism, talent, and regional status as an insider to flamenco, she was an outsider to Jerez de la Frontera, home territory of the *bulerías* form. As the interior space of the *peña* was transformed from the presentational forum to the informal flamenco social circle, Vargas became an honored student of local customs. "It was as if it was obligatory after her performance that she be tutored by this group of older *jerezanas* [women of Jerez]. The professional flamenco artist sat humbly, sitting as witness within the circle to learn the authentic from her elders" (Landborn 2003, 14). Afterwards, writing about the older women who seemed to constitute the core of the *peña*, I noted, "They appear at times to be the power behind the entire event, the architecture of the circle" (2003, 13).

In the *peñas flamencas* the active embodiment of flamenco is profoundly shared. "Within this ambiance everyone is included just from being present and attentive" (Malefyt 1998, 60). Performing inside the social circle, there is no sense of theatrical front; there is instead a sense of being surrounded, enveloped, and viewed from all sides. All directions are equivalent. This human architecture supports performance in the round. The spatial arrangements in the *peñas flamencas* sometimes resemble those used in the flamenco *tablao* (flamenco nightclub). In the *tablao* the spatial parameters of flamenco performance begin to be reconfigured as the inclusiveness of the social circle is blended with the presentational goals of a proscenium theater.

A flamenco *tablao* usually presents professional artists who perform on a small, raised stage with the audience scattered in a semiround formation. This spatial arrangement represents a shift from intimate to public performance and from indigenous practice to professionalism; it also marks the birth of the *cuadro flamenco*. The *cuadro flamenco* is a performance configuration developed during the mid-nineteenth century, the era of the *cafés cantantes*

Left: Flamenco's most indigenous, informal, and traditional spatial form is a social circle of family members, friends, neighbors, or passersby who gather round spontaneously to watch, listen, respond, and participate. Circles are the most ubiquitous spatial forms for human gatherings, with roots in the primordial campfire circle. In the egalitarian formation of the circle, humans of any culture can easily see each other, speak together, and share stories, songs, and dances. *Right*: The *cuadro flamenco* is the spatial formation used in many public flamenco performances in which a semicircle of flamenco performers, musicians, singers, and dancers provides musical and vocal support for a performer who moves forward to perform for the audience. The *cuadro flamenco* opens up the traditional social circle to include the audience as the second half of the performers' social circle, and this informality (even in formal proscenium stage situations) encourages the audience to participate through vocal shouts of appreciation, known as *jaleo*.

Whenever both performers and audience sit in straight lines facing one another, the traditional Western theater conventions of audience passivity will be more strongly felt. Formality, in a stage presentation or in how the audience is seated, inhibits audience participation.

(singing cafés).[2] It consists of a semicircle of flamenco performers who provide support for the dancers or singers whose performance is highlighted when they move forward to perform for an audience. The spatial form of the *cuadro flamenco* maintains the best aspect of the social circle, its enthusiastic and supportive function, while opening that circle to include the audience as the second half of the social circle. As a result, particularly in Spain and Andalusia, flamenco audiences are expected to participate vocally, especially in small, intimate performance venues.

In "Gendering the Authentic in Spanish Flamenco," anthropologist Timothy deWaal Malefyt uses the categories of public versus private to discuss the ideological importance of these contrasting and complementary realms in Spanish society (1998, 51–62). Specifically, Malefyt ties the categories of public and private to Spanish gender norms, noting that "male forms of sociability in public realms are typically based on behavior that is competitive and exploitative, while females in private realms reveal behavior that is cooperative and constructive" (54). He suggests that in private realms, such as the local *peñas flamencas*, the social behavior of men aligns with female norms. "Members of the *peña* flamenco community [male and female] identify themselves in the forms of intimate sociability and private contexts which they articulate to discriminate themselves from others" (60–61). Such identification with female forms of sociality may thereby free males from some of their usual competitive behaviors.

Malefyt's explanation of the gendered sense of domain underlying flamenco performance is insightful, yet performative practice allows people of either sex to participate in both public and private space. When a group of male friends perform for one another informally, their male social circle may enact a type of supportiveness that generates intimacy and is normative within the female domain; conversely, when a female dancer steps to the center of a stage, she enters a male-identified realm wherein she may be temporarily freed from the constraints of female norms that discourage competitive behavior (Landborn 2000).

On large theater stages, with their greater spatial distance between performers and the audience, traditional flamenco performance practices are further altered. As the distance between audience and performer increases, the performers' projection of energy becomes especially unidirectional (toward the proscenium front) in contrast to the multidirectional focus utilized in the social circle or the semiround forms of the *tablao* or *peña flamenca*. For large theater stages, flamenco's traditional emphasis on solo performance may be relinquished in favor of group dances performed in unison. With greater reliance on choreographed movement, the impromptu nature of the flamenco art form is reduced or suspended altogether. Similarly, microphones, video, radio, film, television, and the Internet are media that affect the intimacy, access, and immediacy of flamenco performance conventions.

Spatial Parameters

The circular form, which facilitates both performative phenomena and sociality, is reiterated again and again in the kinesthetic culture of Andalusia and Spain. The circle formation is not unique to Spain; rather, around the world many communities are strengthened and united as they circle around to focus their attention on affective culture events. The circle is a fundamental spatial formation/organization that human beings in any culture may utilize in order to relate to one another and cohere as a group. It is the inherent nature of the circle to enable horizontal sociality; circular forms are generally inclusive and egalitarian in function. Communal eye contact is facilitated; everyone can see everyone else, and no one is left out. The circle also facilitates the focusing of all eyes on the same event, person, or phenomenon in its center. The eyes of witnesses and spectators may remain centered on events at the center of the circle or may rove horizontally within the circle as a function of sociality.

Circular formations have the capacity to contain energy as well as to focus and heighten energy through that containment. The circle's containing power facilitates catharsis; its inherent attributes contribute to the cultural and social cohesiveness experienced within both flamenco and bullfighting practices. Whether viewing events from close proximity or from a distance, within the bullfight arena and flamenco social circle everyone is included through the act of witnessing. Spectatorship is validated as a means of cultural participation through seeing others similarly engaged as witnesses to the event. The spatial and dynamic attributes of flamenco dance and bullfighting

Four. Ritual and Performance Events   109

take place and are contained within circles, the social circle of the flamenco *juerga* or *peña*, and the circle of the public bullfight arena. These circular formations facilitate connections between performers and witnesses and define a territory, space, and time for super-ordinary events.

THE BULLFIGHT ARENA

The architecture of the bullfight arena establishes a fixed, stable circular form that separates insiders from outsiders, providing special status to all those inside the arena, who are made a part of the cultural practice through their participation and witnessing. Thus, the circular architecture of the arena affirms the boundaries of community, and in doing so, binds individuals together in community. Everyone in the arena can see the action in the center. The matador performs in the round. There is no escape from the three-dimensional public exposure of the arena. Sound, energy, and excitement are contained and reverberate within the architectural circle of the arena.

Nor is the visual attention of bullfight witnesses restricted to the action at the center of the arena. Any movement of the eyes away from the action of the

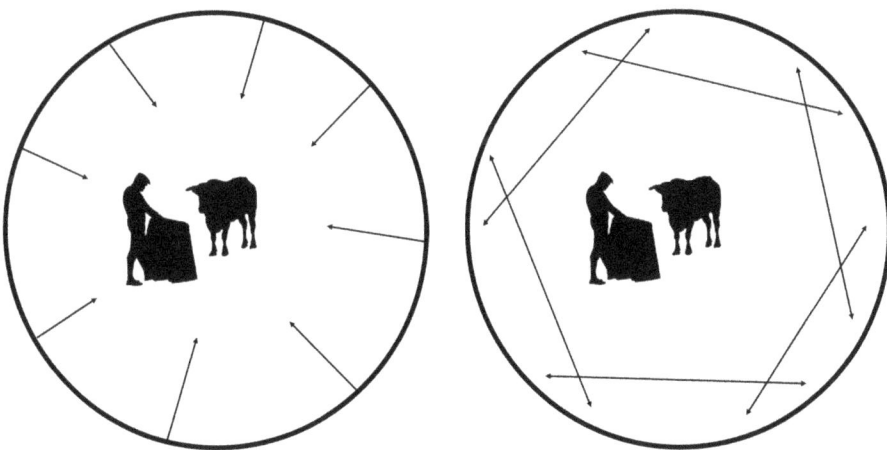

Left: When a matador or matadora confronts a bull at the center of the arena, all eyes are drawn to their interaction. The phrase, *sol o sombra* (sun or shade) refers to bullfight ticket prices and seating. Whether spectators sit in cheap seats in the sun or in the more expensive seats located in the shade, the circular form of the bullfight arena provides a clear view of the bullfight for everyone. *Right*: Bullfight spectators are essentially cheering for the same team. They do not sit on opposite sides of a stadium in support of opposing teams, as they might at a sporting event. Instead, glancing sideways, bullfight spectators are immediately aware of the social possibilities. Looking across the arena, spectators realize the collective nature of the event.

bullfight allows for visual connections that engender sociality. This may include connections ranging from casual eye contact between individuals to recognition of the presence and existence of the social and cultural group as a whole.

The arena provides a definite boundary between observers in the stands and the bullfight spectacle in the center of the arena. This boundary is rarely transgressed, though occasionally a bull will jump the wall into the stands, causing great chaos and concern. Also, in an illegal maneuver known as an *espontaneo*, someone may spontaneously jump into the arena to show off his or her *toreando* skills. In 1957, Manuel Benítez was a poor and desperate *maletilla*, an aspiring matador going from town to town looking for opportunities to fight bulls in small informal *capeas*. *Maletillas* are itinerant toreros, named after the small suitcases (*maletilla*) they carry (Collins and Lapierre 1968). In 1957, Benítez jumped into Madrid's bullfight arena, Las Ventas, in an *espontaneo* that ended with his arrest. Years later he would reenter Las Ventas and become famous as the matador known as "El Cordobés" (Collins and Lapierre 1968, 201).

Mitchell, discussing the psychosexual aspects of the bullfight, notes that "any large gathering that arouses excitement and focuses attention can contribute to social cohesion" (1991, 169). He sees this process as one that can "reinforce group norms" (169), and points out how the somatic nature of the crowd's response to the bullfight, at the basic level of embodied experience, affirms social norms, sanctions the cultural practice of bullfighting, and validates all that the bullfight may mean to those in attendance. "As physiological arousal grows among spectators, so does their reliance on group definitions in order to feel this arousal as appropriate. Awareness that others share the same state of arousal contributes to its intensification, and from there to an 'awareness of supra-individual power,' and from there to an attribution of this pleasing sense of power to one's own commitment to the group's norms" (169). While Mitchell acknowledges the ritualistic aspects of bullfighting, comparing them to the strict formality of the Catholic Mass, he finds bullfighting entirely too unpredictable to be considered a true ritual. "There is always a fair chance that things will turn out sour and anti-climactic, or tragic and ugly, instead of majestic and optimistic" (169). Nevertheless, the bullfight has the power to engage an entire community. "The bullfight need not be a ritual to achieve a *sui generis* sort of *communitas*" (169).

Any discussion of spatial form and its meaning requires consideration also of the fundamental animal-like sense of space that both bulls and humans carry within themselves—territoriality. Two territorial phenomena are notable aspects of a bull's behavior: *querencia* (homing instinct, natural inclination, preference) and *jurisdicción* (jurisdiction, boundary, authority).[3]

Querencia and *jurisdicción* are virtual spaces that may be visualized as circles. They are flexible phenomena; their size and shape are determined by a bull's changing intentions in response to changing conditions.

Querencia

The *querencia* of a bull is any preferred location where the bull has a strong sense of belonging, security, and ownership. The bull identifies the *querencia* as its home territory, and any bull will fight most fiercely when located in its *querencia*. A bull's decision about where in the public arena to locate its *querencia* is arbitrary and idiosyncratic, nor is the bull's *querencia* always a circular form. The matador and his team of toreros will watch the bull's behavior very closely to see where the bull feels most confident and strong. A bull that refuses to leave its *querencia* is difficult and dangerous for a matador to fight. The intelligent bull that establishes *querencia* with its back to the wall is employing a powerful defensive strategy that greatly increases the matador's risk of injury or death.

Querencia, a term used to describe an animal's preferences, often refers to an animal's tendency to become attached to a particular area in the arena that the animal perceives as a home base. It is a location in which the animal feels relatively safe and comfortable. Ernest Hemingway, discussing the phenomenon of *querencia*, noted that

> a querencia is a place the bull naturally wants to go in the ring; a preferred locality. That is a natural querencia and such are well known and fixed, but an accidental querencia is more than that. It is a place which develops in the course of the fight where the bull makes his home. It does not usually show at once, but develops in his brain as the fight goes on. In this place he feels that he has his back against the wall and in his querencia he is inestimably more dangerous and almost impossible to kill. If a bullfighter goes in to kill a bull in his querencia rather than to bring him out of it he is almost certain to be gored" [Hemingway [1939] 1994, 132–133].

The term *querencia* may also be used more generally to describe an animal's preference or tendency to behave or perform in a certain way. Thus it may refer to a particular animal's tendency to hook upward with the right or left horn, or raise the head halfway through a pass, or some other noteworthy movement mannerism.

The matador would prefer to interact with the bull in the center of the arena, where he cannot be caught between the bull's horns and an enclosing wall, and where the bull, having left its *querencia*, is less confident and fierce. Matadors therefore urge the bull to take the offensive and move out of its *querencia* to attack.

Left: The solid line of the outer circle represents the tangible boundary of a bullfight arena, while the dashed line surrounding the bull indicates the bull's *querencia*, the intangible location within the arena that a bull decides is his territory. Toreros watch a bull's behavior carefully to identify where the bull feels most comfortable, and then challenge the bull to leave his *querencia* and charge the matador's cape. *Right:* Here, in addition to the solid line of the arena and the dashed line of the bull's *querencia*, a dashed and dotted line indicates the bull's *jurisdicción*, an invisible line at the outer boundary of the bull's territory that once crossed by a matador impels the bull to charge. As a bull tires, his *jurisdicción* shrinks until a matador may have to approach quite close before instinct compels the bull to charge.

Jurisdicción

In discussing spacing mechanisms in animals, anthropologist Edward T. Hall notes that two distances, "flight distance and critical distance—are used when individuals of *different species meet*" (1969, 10; Hall's italics). Thus, *querencia* and *jurisdicción* serve as examples of what Hall calls an "interspecies spacing mechanism." In relationship to flight distance, Hall asserts that "the larger the animal, the greater the distance it must keep between itself and the enemy" (1969, 11). Thus, in the arena a bull behaves as would any animal that has not been left the option of flight; it turns to face the enemy and fight. Critical distance, according to Hall, "encompasses the narrow zone separating flight distance from attack distance" (12); this corresponds to the bull's *jurisdicción*.

Jurisdicción refers to "a dynamic and invisible boundary around the animal, a line that when crossed causes the animal to attack" (Cooney 2005). As a phenomenon, *jurisdicción* establishes the basic mechanism through which a torero may engage the animal in a fight, i.e., instigate conflict. A torero's working consciousness is often focused on determining the exact boundary

Four. Ritual and Performance Events 113

of the bull's *jurisdicción* and using that knowledge to motivate the bull to charge. "The zone of the bull's jurisdicción is changeable, usually at its greatest extension when the animal first enters the ring and will charge at any movement, from any distance. Generally, the jurisdicción will contract in the course of the lidia [bullfight]" (Cooney 2005).

The bull's sense of its territory or *jurisdicción* has no architecture or fixed form; rather, like *querencia*, it is mutable, based on circumstances and the feelings of the bull. It may not be a precise circle, yet it encompasses, surrounds, or encircles the bull. *Jurisdicción* may be thought of as the outer boundary of the bull's *querencia*. Once the boundary line of the *jurisdicción* is crossed by the matador, the bull (having no way to evade the matador by fleeing the arena) is compelled by instinct to defend itself. This phenomenon, known as critical distance, is a familiar attribute of animal behavior; distance is a determining factor in whether an animal will choose to attack or evade its opponent.

Citing the bull from a close distance using the *muleta*, the matador is face to face with his opponent. In addition to crossing into the bull's territory, a *torero* will often incite the bull to charge by producing the strong vocalization "*¡Éje!*" and simultaneously flicking the *capote* or *muleta* toward the bull. Because the bull tires as the bullfight progresses, the matador will be required to cite the bull from closer and closer distances, which exponentially increases the danger the matador faces. The same dramatic motif of confronting an adversary is also inherent in the flamenco dance style (Juan Pelegrin/Flickr.com).

The bull will charge when it feels that an intruder has crossed the line into its territory or *jurisdicción*. The size of a bull's territory is expansive and undetermined when the bull first enters the arena; the bull takes the offensive and will charge when a torero or matador is still quite far away. During the first *tercio*, the first third of the bullfight, the matador's team of toreros (*equipo*) engages an energetic bull's willingness to attack in any direction and, as the bull begins to tire, will try to lead the bull to establish his *querencia* in a location in the arena that will be advantageous for their matador. The bull's *jurisdicción* contracts in the course of the bullfight, especially when the bull feels unsure of itself, is tired or in pain. Toward the end of the bullfight, during the third *tercio*, a bull often requires the matador to come quite close before it will charge.

Like *querencia*, an animal's sense of *jurisdicción* is flexible over time; it changes depending on the situation, fight conditions, and the animal's past or present experience. A matador's career success and well-being will depend on how quickly and accurately he or she is able to read the behavioral attributes of animals met in the arena. Matadors study *querencia* and *jurisdicción* carefully, noting how these virtual spaces manifest within the particular behavioral patterns of each animal. A primary goal of the matador is to incite the bull to leave its *querencia* and engage offensively in the fight. Being able to judge the bull's spatial *querencia* enables a matador to know when the bull is dangerously on the defensive; being able to judge the bull's spatial *jurisdicción* enables a matador to cite the bull to offensive action.[4]

Flamenco Performance

A performer who dances in the center of the informal (indigenous) social circle is in the center of his or her *querencia*. The social circle helps to define the dancer's territory; the dancer has a sense of security and belonging, of being supported equally from all sides by the attention of the cultural group.

In the informal indigenous flamenco performance everyone in the circle participates; the sociality level is intense. While the social circle creates a boundary that contains the energy of the performance, it is also participatory space from which inspired witnesses may emerge transformed into the next performers. Observers are therefore alert to the presence and potential participation of all who are gathered around the social circle. The boundary and categorical difference between observers and participants is temporary and flexible. Dancers may sit down and join in the *jaleo* and *palmas*, just as observers may move from the social circle to the center of the

Four. Ritual and Performance Events

Left: The lines of interaction in the flamenco social circle emphasize attention to individuals performing in the center of the circle. Indigenous flamenco performance conventions emphasize active participation on the part of observers. Lines in this diagram show the inward-directed vision and *jaleo* of the observers. However, a more complete image would include lines radiating outward to indicate the projection of the dancer's focus and rhythmic sounds. *Right:* The semicircular form of the *cuadro flamenco* enables onstage performers to easily see each other as well as a performer at center stage. Performances at flamenco nightclubs or *tablaos* are typically presented in this formation. A *cuadro flamenco* style performance has the added benefit of opening up flamenco's traditional social circle to include the audience and encourage their vocal participation. While the socializing effect of the *cuadro flamenco* may be felt when an audience is seated in formal rows, seating arrangements with even slightly curved rows will heighten an audience's sense of sociality and inclusion.

performing area to take up the dance. Observers, guitarists, singers, and *palmeros* provide *jaleo* to encourage the dancer, who, like the matador, performs in the round.

People in the flamenco social circle can see the dancer in the center, but they naturally see one another as well. This supports social cohesion. Witnesses to a flamenco performance in the round can see and interact with people to either side of them and see other people across the circle. They experience the performance in the center of the social circle, but also they experience community. They are fully aware of others gathered in the circle with whom they are sharing and experiencing the performance. The performance provides the opportunity to come together to socialize, and in many instances they may be more interested in the sociality than in the performance itself.

The *cuadro flamenco* is the spatial formation that supports the authen-

116   Flamenco and Bullfighting

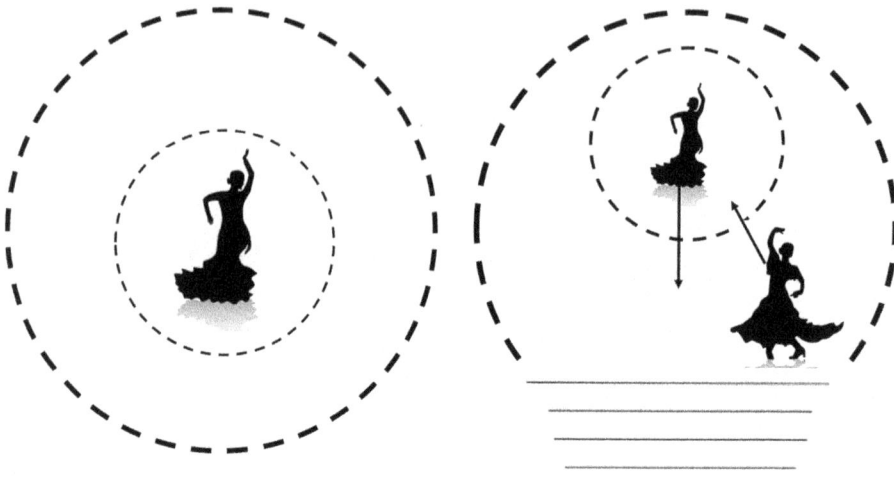

Left: Like a bull in the arena, a dancer may unconsciously develop *querencia*, a particular area of the stage where he or she feels most secure. Having experienced a sense of belonging in the center of an intimate social circle of friends and family, a performer may more easily establish personal territory onstage, radiate stage presence, and revel in the audience's attention. *Right:* Dancers commonly express territoriality, especially during the *marcaje* portion of the dance, by advancing and retreating as if testing an imaginary boundary between themselves and the audience. Alternately advancing and retreating, dancers conjure emotions related to human experiences of transgression, aggression, assertiveness, risk, and defensiveness. After retreating on a diagonal (figure on right), as if surrendering territory, a dancer (figure on left) may suddenly advance forward, as if challenging the audience and reclaiming territory. Both flamenco dancers and audiences enjoy the heightened energy generated as this sometimes playful, sometimes serious, quasi-adversarial relationship is expressed through the dance.

ticity of a flamenco performance by simulating the flamenco social circle and adapting it for theatrical venues. The social circle now includes the guitarists, singers, and *palmeros* arranged in a semicircle behind the dancer, providing *jaleo* and encouragement. Observers are now directly in front of the dancer. The boundary at the edge of the performance area clearly separates performers from the audience. Ideally, the audience completes the social circle of the performers, contributing energy and *jaleo*. The flatter the spatial arrangement of performers and audience members, the less conducive to sociality the performance event will be. Seating at tables or arranged in curved lines better supports the audience's experience of sociality.

In the context of the flamenco social circle, a dancer is in the center of her or his *querencia*. A strong performer appears to claim the territory of the performance space whether it is an informal social gathering of friends, a *cuadro flamenco*, or a formal stage. The energy coming from every direction, musicians, audience, and other dancers, reaffirms the dancer's sense of belonging, rootedness, and strength. Performing with a feeling of *querencia* gives the dancer confidence, self-assurance, and strength in relationship to the movement challenges of the dance performance, and produces a sense of ownership in relation to the performance space.

In the contexts of the *cuadro flamenco* and the formal stage, a dancer will often move forward toward the audience, expressing aggressive energy and displaying the offensive attacking quality of a bull. In contrast, a dancer's retreat to center stage may express a sense of belonging, centeredness, tranquility, insecurity, or a strategic retreat. Retreating movements in the flamenco dance context are similar to the defensive regrouping of a bull returning to its *querencia* or a matador's cautious withdrawal to a safer distance. The social circle of flamenco may appear more permeable than the bullfight arena, more open to transgression; however, this is not necessarily the case. Despite the seeming informality of a flamenco social circle, entering its center to perform requires the approval of the group, because one cannot perform without the continuing energy and support of the group, as expressed through music making, *jaleo*, and *palmas*.

Querencia and *jurisdicción* are invisible, yet are made visible through behavior. As well-known attributes affecting the outcome of the bullfight, they are not only studied by matadors; they are also much studied by *ganaderos*, bullfight aficionados, and the Spanish and Andalusian public in general. They are also part of the cultural knowledge of people who practice the flamenco arts. It is perhaps due to the human capacity for cross-species empathy and mimesis that these phenomena are so influential within the flamenco dance form. A sphere of electrically charged energy appears to emanate from the body of the dancer, a sense of danger, boundaries, and challenge. A dancer's confrontational behaviors create a charged and intense atmosphere and enable the projection and performance of inherent wildness and instinctual power. Like the bull in his *querencia*, a flamenco dancer defends a territorial space. Unlike other dance forms that emphasize traveling through space, ease of motion, or sensations interior to the moving body, flamenco dance presents a human presence in the center of a kinesphere with territorial confrontations at its edge. These attributes of the flamenco dance practice and style are reflections of the bullfight tradition.

Due to the embodied nature of their cultural practice, flamenco and bullfighting are always present within the daily life experience of Andalusians. Whether expressed overtly or subtly, the cultural values these two practices embody are intrinsic to the postures, gestures, and movement patterns of the

Flamenco and Bullfighting

Roger Wood's photograph of the José Greco Company uses a dramatic circle of light to emphasize the solitary, isolated figure of the solo dancer Nila Amparo. Many flamenco dances are traditionally performed as solos, and this is especially true of the flamenco form called the *soleares*, which expresses emotions associated with solitariness, loneliness, and isolation. With her focus cast downward and her feet encircled by the *bata de cola*, the traditional flamenco dress with a long train, Nila Amparo's energy is intense, yet contained (© Roger Wood / Royal Opera House / ArenaPAL; Jerome Robbins Dance Division, The New York Public Library for the Performing Arts, Astor, Lenox and Tilden Foundations).

many Andalusians who accept flamenco and bullfighting as part of their lifestyle.

Temporal Parameters

The ongoing flow of public interest in flamenco and bullfighting is punctuated by periods of time set aside for the heightened experience of special

Four. Ritual and Performance Events 119

events. In addition to providing temporal boundaries, time affects the subtleties of these events at an infinitesimal level through the timing of flamenco interactions, the human-animal interactions of the bullfight, and the empathic responses exchanged between performers and audience. Both the smooth entrainment (*temple*) linking matador and bull and the driving tempo of the *compás* beneath flamenco music and dance provide evidence of time's regulatory function within these practices. Time is also a structural element, governing the beginnings and endings of designated periods. For example, the flamenco dance and music form known as the *alegrías* has distinct sections, like the compositional movements within a concerto: the initial *entrada* (a lively introduction); the *silencio* (a slow section with no *cante*, just guitar accompanying a section of lyrical dance); the *escobilla de pies* (a section of footwork); and the final section, an animated *bulerías* to close the dance with high energy (Morca 1990, 51–53).

The structure of a formal bullfight includes similar timing parameters; a bullfight is divided into three periods or *tercios* (thirds), during which certain actions are expected to occur. During the first period, known as the *tercio de varas*, the bull enters the ring and is maneuvered to the picador, a torero mounted on horseback who stabs the back of the bull's neck with a lance. During the second period, known as the *tercio de banderillas*, the *banderillero* (a torero with specialized skills) runs past the bull, placing *banderillas* (short lances) in the back of the bull's neck. During the third period, the *tercio de matar*, also known as the *faena*, the matador performs with the *muleta* (small red cape) and finally kills the bull with the *espada* (sword).

As in the *alegrías*, different types of interactions are part of the qualitative expectation, the dynamic terrain, of each *tercio*. All the movements in the arena are large and the action is fast during the first *tercio*. The bull, disoriented and angry, charges wildly when he first enters the arena; thus toreros use the larger cape, the *capote*. In the second *tercio*, the bull begins to focus his energy, and the interaction between the matador and bull moves to the center of the arena. The action is further concentrated and intensified during the *faena*, the final *tercio* of the bullfight, as the matador shifts to using the *muleta*. During this final *tercio de matar*, each maneuver with the *muleta* occurs within a relatively small area; the bull and matador now move together within the same small area. The bull is more fatigued now than in the earlier *tercios*, and is also more dangerous. The bull has been learning about his opponent throughout the contest and now concentrates very intently on each attack. Time is short. The sense of urgency increases for two reasons. The matador is racing against the bull's quickly increasing knowledge, and the close spatial proximity of the two antagonists signifies that life-or-death consequences are only seconds away.

Kealiinohomoku identifies two general categories of dance events, "contained" and "extended," that are useful when applied to understanding the temporal and spatial parameters of any super-ordinary event. "The contained dance [event] is often theatrically oriented with a recognizable beginning and conclusion, and although an in-depth study of such an event should include what happens before and after the event, the contained dance event *qua* dance can be studied as an isolate" (1976, 235). Thus, a flamenco dance performance occurring within the defined space-time boundaries provided by the institutions and venues of the *peña flamenca, flamenco tablao*, or theater stage constitutes a contained dance event; a *corrida de toros* might also be considered a type of contained event. A contained event has "three distinguishing features: it is an end in itself, no matter how imbued it is with other functions; it needs a limited number of skilled practitioners; it uses a specific piece of time, and within that limited time it probably does not depend on extreme use of redundancy for its effectiveness" (237).

In contrast, Kealiinohomoku notes that "the extended dance event is enmeshed within a larger context, and it must have a certain fluidity of time" (1976, 237). Thus, the flamenco *juerga* functions as an extended dance event, and in the bullfighting realm, *encierros* or *capeas* might also be considered as types of extended events. The time frame within which these events occur is flexible. *Juergas* may extend over a period of several days and nights, emphasizing the cultural value of spontaneity, of living in the moment and for the moment. During such extended events, dance may suddenly erupt or abruptly subside based on a person's mood, and impromptu *toreando* may take place as either a necessary response to unpredictable behavior of the bulls or as an inevitable succumbing to the temptations of risk, the human urge to play with danger.

Spanish and Andalusian public ritual life often involves experiences that extend time beyond the pattern of circadian rhythm that governs normal life activities. This unusual interruption of daily-life patterns facilitates the experience of catharsis and contributes to the experience of the super-ordinary. "Studies of bio-rhythms would seem to suggest that the lack of sleep can cause sufficient hormonal changes in the dancers so that [they] are not synchronized with their normal circadian rhythms" (Kealiinohomoku 1976, 304). Later, discussing biorhythms and interaction, Kealiinohomoku also notes that "trance and possession dances usually occur in the latter part of the day and at night, and these states of disassociation are surely dictated by biological clocks" (305).

Biological factors clearly contribute to the uncanny and extraordinary experience known as *duende* (spirit) that occurs in both flamenco and bull-

Four. Ritual and Performance Events 121

fighting contexts. The biological effects of sleep deprivation, adrenaline, alcohol, physical exertion, or emotional duress facilitate experiences beyond the ordinary. The extended-event contexts of the *juerga* or *encierro* and the contained-event contexts of the flamenco performance or *corrida de toros* will vary in their biological effects; in any case, biological responses are key to understanding intrapersonal and interpersonal experiences in these contexts and interpreting their meaning.

When the timing of flamenco and bullfighting activities overlap, the practices may begin to merge, resulting in a hybrid type of extended event. Since personnel directly involved with the bullfight (the public, aficionados, *ganaderos*, toreros, and matadors) often celebrate after the *corrida* by attending a flamenco *tablao*, and flamenco aficionados and artists often attend the *corrida* prior to the flamenco performance, each cultural practice contributes substantively to the extraordinariness experienced within the flamenco/bullfight extended event.

The normative scheduling of an Andalusian day accommodates and supports both flamenco and bullfight practices. The Andalusian midafternoon nap, the siesta, provides the population with rest so that they may dine late (10 p.m.) and then partake in social activities, such as those surrounding flamenco, into the predawn hours. However intense the *corrida* and flamenco *juerga* have been, witnesses may continue their own journey toward catharsis by extending their activities into the time period between midnight and dawn, known as the *madrugada*. The *madrugada* has a liminal quality; existing between two days, it is a time associated with the culminating moments of catharsis. The *madrugada* functions as a time out of time, a period of emotional excess during which extreme, unexpected, magical, or uncanny happenings may occur.

The nearness of death fills a matador's consciousness. The emotional significance of the bullfight resonates in the phrase *a las cinco de la tarde* (at five o'clock in the afternoon), which refers to the ending time of the *corrida de toros*. Each day on which a bullfight is scheduled, matadors slated to perform must live with the question of whether they will still be alive at *cinco de la tarde*. In the documentary film, *The Lady Bullfighter* (Bryer 1989), female matador Evelina Fabregas states, "I face death in every fight. But if I think about death, I will not succeed. I don't think about death because just as I was born, so I'll have to die one day. I believe in God, so I have no fear of death." With its repeated intoning of the phrase, *a las cinco de la tarde,* Federico García Lorca's tragic poem *Lament for Ignacio Sánchez Mejías* emphasizes the importance of this defining moment in time both for the bullfighter and for all those who care for the bullfighter's life.

Looking at an even larger time frame, the cyclical nature of a year, the calendar that rules Andalusian public ritual life is based largely on the beliefs and protocols of Spanish Catholicism. The most important ritual of the Spanish Catholic calendar year is the Semana Santa, the week between Palm Sunday and Easter Sunday. Its intense preparations and elaborate processions through the streets lead up to Easter Sunday, which coincides with the first official day of the bullfight season.[5] The forty-day period of Lent (*cuaresma*), beginning Ash Wednesday and lasting until the Saturday before Easter Sunday, is a period of fasting and penitence and a period during which flamenco and bullfight practices are inactive. Being associated with celebration and pleasure, these cultural practices are dormant while the *pasión* (suffering) of Christ is being commemorated. A notable exception to that rule is the religious flamenco-style song form, the mournful *saeta*, which is sung a cappella on the streets in response to the passing religious figures, especially the Virgin Mary.[6] Otherwise, flamenco is not heard during Semana Santa.

Flamencologist Claus Schreiner introduces his volume titled *Flamenco* (1990) with the heading, "Andalusia: Pena and Alegría," thereby drawing attention to the wide range of emotional expression that exemplifies the Andalusian public ritual life to which flamenco dance and bullfighting contribute. The Spanish word *pena* (not to be confused with *peña*, the social club) signifies such things as punishment, penalty, grief, pain, suffering, shame, difficulty, trouble, hardship, and anxiety. *Alegría* signifies joy, gladness, cheerfulness, gaiety, and in its plural form of *alegrías*, it signifies public rejoicings. After the somber mood of Lent and Semana Santa, the tide of public feeling turns swiftly back toward joy. The bullfight season begins the very afternoon of Easter Sunday, and the *feria* (spring fair), celebrated with flamenco-style music and couple dancing (known as the *sevillanas*), follows soon afterwards as the celebratory hedonism of Andalusian life is reestablished. This wide affective range, ritualized through public events, creates a high-intensity emotional life for Andalusians. They seem ready to shift and flow with the inspiration of each moment, their lives an embodied tribute to the belief that "For everything there is a season, and a time for every matter under heaven" (Eccles. 3:1; New Revised Standard Version Catholic Edition).

Chapter Five

An Aesthetic Topography
Gitanismo, Romanticism and *Duende*

A Rubric of Appreciation

To better understand flamenco and bullfighting as art forms, it helps to consider the aesthetic standards and cultural expectations guiding these performance practices and what qualities of performance are most appreciated by their faithful audiences. Aesthetic appreciation has its basis in and is produced by three aspects of experience: sensual, associative, and syntactical (Truitt 1997). Appreciation is deepest when sensory, associative, and syntactical components all contribute to an observer's experience.

The Sensual

The sensual component of aesthetic appreciation is available to all people, though perhaps not to all in equal measure. It comprises any direct experience of sound, visual stimulus, physical sensation, or kinetic response that a person enjoys within a performance context. The sensual component includes what the Spanish call *ambiente* (*ambiance* in French or atmosphere in English). *Ambiente* includes the smells, the temperature, the tastes of food, wine, or kisses, the quality of light, the touch of air, fabric, sunshine, people, or wind against one's skin; *ambiente* is the overall quality of one's surroundings and presumes an exquisite sensitivity to living and being present in the moment.

Performances, whether occurring in the bullring, the flamenco *tablao*, (flamenco nightclub), or flamenco *peñas*, are generally experienced in combination with socializing and consuming refreshments. Socializing with the person next to you, negotiating refreshments, the taste of food or drinks, the smells and flavors of people—sensual experience is by nature multichanneled. While the sensual experiences of performers and witnesses differ, both groups are greatly influenced by sensual experience.

Sensual experience differs greatly depending on whether one is an observer of a performance or an actual performer. A person located in the stands of the bullfight arena may experience: a comfortable sense of anticipation, a commotion of lively social interactions, cool refreshments relieving the heat of the direct afternoon sunshine, or the hardness of the bench. A person inside the bullring itself will have an entirely different set of sensations: the binding formality of the matador's suit of lights, the tactile actualities of handling sword and capes, the nearness of animals, their smell, sounds, and felt presence, sounds from the crowd and arena musicians, awareness of political tensions or rivalries in play, and an inner state of adrenaline-fed anxiety, fear, excitement, and ambition.

The *corrida* constitutes a public spectacle, colorful, noisy; it is both visually and viscerally engaging. From the smell of blood or the slippery feel of sweat on a matador's hands, to the smell of a woman's perfume and the sticky, hot feel of a sweat-dampened shirt in the public stands, the sensual component of appreciation manifests through the actuality of human embodiment and presence. The visual stimulations, the physical privations or comforts, the social import of events and connections with family or friends, direct empathic responses to danger, the energizing sounds of the crowd or music, the unique context of a particular moment in a person's life: all these contribute to the overall appreciation of the drama of life and death being played out in the bullfight arena.

The sensual comprehension of a flamenco event entails similar complexity. As with the bullfight, the observers of flamenco dance performances are surrounded and affected by the sensual attributes of the *ambiente*. The sensual experience of an observer of flamenco dance is a combination of visual perceptions, aural cues, and vibrations of musical and percussive sounds felt by the skin. The colors of costumes, the attractiveness of a dancer, the quickness or unexpectedness of a motion may all draw the eye. Engaging the imagination, an observer may see evidence of relationships among the performers. The interplay between musical sounds and the movement patterns of the dance may be traced aurally and visually, but kinesthetic empathy with the dancer's movement will also play a part.

As a dance form with a great emphasis on a simultaneous multisystem use of the body, flamenco requires dancers to attend to many channels of awareness and action simultaneously. Physical sensations include the sinuous stretch of arms and torso in contrast to the percussive precision of footwork. A dancer's awareness of exerting muscular effort is constantly monitored and adjusted to attain a particular speed, effect, or quality. Muscular strength combines with the dancer's mental concentration to articulate flamenco footwork patterns that correspond to a particular rhythm or attain a particular speed. The technically demanding elements of footwork are felt in relationship to (and are in play with) the other highly articulated, physical motions of eyes, hands, arms, and hips. A dancer's expressive intent fuels each specific movement as she or he strategizes to create the best overall effect. Listening to the musicians, and collaborating with them, a dancer may be driven in equal parts by personal inner emotion, the musical impulse generated outside of the dancer's performing body, and an artistic sense of how best to craft the emotional content of her or his dancing.

A dancer's awareness may also include people in the immediate environment, social relationships with those witnessing the dance, the stretch and pull of muscles on bone, the touch of clothing sliding across skin as a result of movement, the restrictions to movement that clothing may exert due to a too-tight waistband or sleeve, a skirt too long, or the precarious attachment of an earring, hair clip, or hat. The chemistry of hormones, alcohol or drugs, the lateness of the hour, the dragging weight of exhaustion or the high flushed energy of catharsis, all may combine with a personal context, making this a night to be remembered.

The Associative

The associative component of aesthetic appreciation entails an interpretation of immediate experience based on memories of previous experiences or comparisons to cultural ideas, such as stereotypical or iconic cultural images from movies, books, or other performances. It gives immediate experience the power to evoke analogous experiences and metaphoric cultural images. In the case of flamenco dance, the associative appreciation might lead to comparisons with similarly intense, energetic dance forms or contrasting dance forms; it might also lead some observers to see the symbolic power of the bull, the bullfighter, or the bullfight within the dance. The human capacity to associate one idea or experience with another is enjoyable and entertaining; it enlivens poetic sensibilities, giving them a central role in the process of constructing meaning. This construction of meaning in response to a performance experience is pursued both individually and communally. The more ineffable, powerful, or transformative an experience is, the more it will fuel the discourse of bullfight or flamenco aficionados.

The Syntactical

Syntactical appreciation occurs when an observer has a greater degree of knowledge regarding technical attributes of an art form, its performance history, or social context. Such familiarity may give an observer deeper insights into the immediate experience based on more accurate perceptions of the subtleties of a performance. Prior knowledge enables these observers to make informed judgments. Within high-context cultural practices, such as flamenco dance and bullfighting, syntactical knowledge is essential to making aesthetic judgments. Only with sufficient syntactical knowledge can an aficionado reliably discern the unique qualities of performers, compare and contrast the talents of performers in relationship to each other, or assess the relative value of specific performances.

Syntactical knowledge of the technical difficulty entailed in a particular flamenco dance step or a particular maneuver of the matador's *muleta* deepens an observer's appreciation. Being able to compare several performances given by the same flamenco singer or divergent interpretations of the same musical form as performed by two dancers deepens an observer's appreciation. Knowledge of the *compás*, the rhythmic framework for flamenco music and dance, is central to a syntactical appreciation of flamenco, just as knowledge of the animal behaviors pertaining to bulls is central to a syntactical appreciation of a bullfight.

Contextualizing Aesthetics

Geography

Regionalism is strong in Spain; thus, within Spain there exist many subtle geographical associations in relation to these two cultural practices. Flamenco is practiced throughout Spain, yet the southern region of Andalusia is considered the cradle (*cuna*) or birthplace of flamenco. Each of Andalusia's eight provinces has contributed artistic variations and unique song forms. In both large and small towns, Almería, Arco de la Frontera, Badajoz, Cádiz, Córdoba, Granada, Huelva, Jaén, Jerez de la Frontera, Lebrija, Málaga, Morón de la Frontera, Murcia, Sanlúcar, Sevilla, Utrera, and others, geography's influence on the history of flamenco's artistic development is evident (Pohren 1964; Totton 2003; Woodall 1992). The regions of Spain associated with bullfighting are also numerous; they are primarily identified by the locations of important bull ranches and major public bullfight arenas.

Although deeply entrenched in Spanish culture, flamenco and bullfighting are international in their purview and influence. The flamenco arts are popular in Europe as well as in South, Central, and North America, and thrive in such seemingly unrelated places as Japan, South Africa, and Australia. In recent decades, the flamenco arts have expanded globally to reach new audiences in response to the emergence of contemporary musical experimentation involving ethnic-jazz fusion in the genre of world music, improved technologies of the recording industry (both audio and video), increased Internet access and online commerce, and fundamental economic changes (such as Spain joining the European Union in 1986).

In addition to its strong presence in Spain, bullfighting is practiced professionally in Colombia, Ecuador, Mexico, Peru, Portugal, Venezuela, and the south of France, and draws professional matadors from many countries, including Cuba, Great Britain, Puerto Rico, and the United States. As with flamenco, bullfighting has incorporated new developments in global culture and media to expand and strengthen its practice. However far-ranging the influence of these two cultural practices may be, Spain still functions as the central location that institutionalizes elements of form and sets performance standards. Flamenco dance and bullfighting are judged by aesthetic standards specific to their independent traditions, yet there are also significant areas of overlap and sharing of aesthetic attributes and values.

Ethnicity

Historically, the context in which the flamenco arts developed included a mix of cultures and ethnic groups.[1] The Spanish Gypsies, the *gitanos*, are recognized as having asserted a pervasive and substantive influence on the historical development of the performative practices and aesthetic standards of the flamenco arts. Today, the *gitanos* continue to contribute significantly to flamenco's development and sustain its practice in collaboration with the Andalusian people and others. There have always been a significant number of *gitano* families and individual artists actively participating at the core of flamenco's aesthetic and artistic development. Bullfighting, too, has been influenced by the participation of a number of Spaniards who self-identify as *gitano*. However, their number is smaller because bullfighting functions through the actions of Spain's upper classes, particularly the landowning aristocracy. In contrast, the arts of flamenco are the purview of the lower classes, including the subaltern subculture of the *gitanos*.

The term *gitanismo* refers to the particular expressive qualities, stylistic elements, and dramatic intensity associated with the performing talents of the *gitano* people. Such attributes are evident in performance, but also characterize the values and customs that constitute the *gitano* way of life. The Spanish suffix *-ismo* is comparable to *-ism* in English; thus *gitanismo* signifies *gypsyism*, a term used in reference to stylistic vocal patterns or movement mannerisms associated with *gitanos*. The phenomenon of *gitanismo* is inherently connected to the entire set of cultural values that constitutes the *gitano* worldview. Historically, *gitanos* have used flamenco performance as a public forum for their worldview, scattering a subversive set of values, assumptions, and beliefs about personal freedom, spontaneity, and open expressivity into the wider (more conservative) Spanish society. Through embodied performance, *gitano* values of unpredictability, flamboyant risk taking, personal pride, dignity, fatalism, uninhibited emotionality, and volatility are translated into a movement style that continues to influence the direction of flamenco dance's development.

While the term *gitanismo* may imply exaggeration, it also implies authenticity. The term *gitanesco*, on the other hand, signifies that a performance is Gypsy-like; this might constitute a veiled reference to the inauthenticity of a performance. A non–Gypsy flamenco performer or torero may borrow mannerisms associated with the *gitano* movement style in order to add to the appeal of a performance and enhance her or his public image. Such cultural incorporations vary in effectiveness.

On a pragmatic level, efforts to produce a flamenco performance with notably *gitanesco* (Gypsy-like) staging is likely to add to a production's commercial value. While many non–Gypsy performers (Spaniards and foreigners) consciously emulate *gitano* attributes and movement mannerisms to make their own performances more flavorful, exciting, and authentic in appearance, the *gitanos* themselves may also exaggerate and emphasize the *gitanismo* of their performance. Individuality is highly valued and the term *estampa* (literally, stamp) refers to a performer's distinctive style, signature, or trademark that develops over time as a result of a performer's innate personality, artistic sensibility, and creative effort. The more *gitanismos* (Gypsy mannerisms) are quoted within the movement style of a performance, the more an appearance (sometimes an illusion) of authenticity, as well as the reputation of the performers, is reinforced. The association of *gitanismos* (mannerisms) and *gitanismo* (attitude) with cultural authenticity creates social and economic power for the *gitanos*, a community of people who have generally lacked access to such power.

The *gitano* people have been so romanticized as freedom-loving and passionate that their behaviors have garnered value and social currency among particular sets of outside admirers, notably, both foreigners and upper-class Spaniards. *Gitanos*, too, may collude in romanticizing *gitano* culture. As a result, various levels of cultural authenticity, pretense, and performative behaviors may be functioning simultaneously within a flamenco performance. Each performer acts from within a complex set of relationships: to performative participation, to the cultural practice itself, and to the sociality surrounding the cultural practice.

Five. An Aesthetic Topography 129

A flamenco dancer's spiraling posture and adversarial attitude toward a trailing *bata de cola* is similar to the dynamic moment in a bullfight when a matador temporarily ends his engagement with the bull, turns his back, and walks away. In this photograph the author demonstrates a movement known as a *remate*, a type of strong ending that often includes a matador deliberately trailing his *capote* dramatically behind him (photograph by Melissa Lind).

The important role of improvisation within flamenco practice illustrates the *gitano* culture's valuing of spontaneity, individuality, and emotional expression. Improvisation as a performance methodology affects the ways in which flamenco movement vocabularies and stylizations are created and transmitted. The creative richness of improvisation contributes to the transformation of the flamenco arts over time. Improvisational performance is also fundamental to the bullfight; however practiced the matador may be, the unpredictability of the bull ensures spontaneity and provides an improvisational edge to the matador's performance.

Gitanos involved in the flamenco arts have contributed much more than influential mannerisms, *gitanismos*; they have contributed substantively to the development of new musical forms, songs, dance techniques, and traditions. By modeling highly individualistic and idiosyncratic movement styles, personal pride, and passionate intensity in performance, *gitanos* have established an aesthetic expectation for authentic and intense emotional content, flamboyant, full-hearted engagement in the art, and high technical standards. *Gitanos* are often considered to be flamenco's closest inner circle, guardians of its traditions, and inherently authoritative critics of what is and is not authentic, pure flamenco (*flamenco puro*).

Robin Totton in *Song of the Outcasts* writes about "the Gypsies' key role in flamenco," saying that

> it [flamenco] is not exclusive to them. But they are its main torchbearers, and always have been. Their own opinions range from dogged belief that flamenco is theirs alone to the more widespread opinion neatly summed up by the dancer Manuela Carrasco. When asked what was the difference between Gypsy and non–Gypsy flamenco, she said, "None at all," and added, with a smile: "but then again we Gypsies do have a quality all our own" [2003, 187].

Affective Culture and the Super-Ordinary

Flamenco dance and bullfighting are special events that employ specialized movement behaviors and generate high expectations. Unlike the ordinary cultural phenomena of everyday living, flamenco performance and bullfighting activities belong to the category of the super-ordinary.

> Super-ordinary behavior and activities have the quality of attracting attention by their very occurrence. As such, they excite the participants and, far from being automatic in total manifestation, they rivet the conscious attention of the participants and stimulate affective feelings and the need for resolution. In this category are found religious activities, especially those creative and re-creative activities associated with aesthetic values, specialized skills, and intensive prepa-

Five. An Aesthetic Topography 131

Flamenco dancer Manuela Carrasco maintains her statuesque dignity as she dances in the long traditional flamenco dress, the *bata de cola*, in the 1986 performance of *Flamenco Puro* at the Gusman Center for the Performing Arts in Miami, Florida. As she dances, Manuela Carrasco spirals to look back over her shoulder at the trailing form of *bata de cola*. She is not alone in the space, but through her dancing conjures the bull, the *duende*, invisible adversaries, and other ineffable forces (photograph by Ray Fisher/© Ray Fisher; Jerome Robbins Dance Division, The New York Public Library for the Performing Arts, Astor, Lenox and Tilden Foundations).

rations. In short, super-ordinary experiences are the highlights and the punctuations in ongoing existence; they make up affective culture [Kealiinohomku 55–56].

Bullfighting, functioning as a complex combination of ritual, artistic play, and athletic performance event, belongs to the category of the super-ordinary along with flamenco dance. Bullfighting is not considered a sport; rather, it is recognized as an artistic pursuit. Public events featuring flamenco dance or bullfight activities are generally reviewed, often side by side, on the *Cultura* page of Spanish newspapers. Both cultural practices offer performers opportunities to demonstrate creative, artistic, and athletic excellence, and offer audiences opportunities for heightened aesthetic experience, and both function under the influence of the romantic aesthetic (Truitt 1997).

The Romantic Aesthetic

The *Random House Dictionary of the English Language* (1967, s.v. "romantic") states that a romantic literature or art "subordinates form to content, encourages freedom of treatment, emphasizes imagination, emotion, and introspection, and often celebrates nature, the common man, and freedom of the spirit." While form is a significant governing element within flamenco and bullfight practices, its primary function is to create a reliable container for emotion. Adherence to the strictures of traditional form is necessary; the cultural form must be stable and strong enough to withstand the high-intensity affective energy of these cultural practices. Formal elements serve a regulatory role.

The flamenco artist and matador know well the formal limitations within which they function; this clarity of formal traditions, expectations, and rules provides the boundaries within which a dancer or matador exercises freedom of expression.[2] Each performer's expression is valued for its intensity, sincerity, and ability to evoke emotional resonance in others. The performative nature of these practices means that uniqueness in performance is valued as direct evidence of the moral character and personality of the individual. This is not a romanticism of pretense or fantasy. Personhood itself is appreciated; the performing human body is witnessed as a phenomenological event, containing and manifesting raw emotions, creativity, spirit, and, sometimes, an ineffable, transcendent quality known as *duende*.

The romantic aesthetic values innocence and naturalness of expression. The Spanish public has a special fondness for primitive, untutored, or self-taught artists, for flamenco artists and matadors who appear to be naturally

Five. An Aesthetic Topography

gifted. Those performers who appear to have been born with talent, who seem to be led entirely by passion, who display no ulterior motive such as the desire for fame or material gain, will be especially praised and valued. Flamencologist Miriam Phillips notes that "Spanish Gypsy Flamenco dancers today have learned their art form through either formal training in classes in a studio or through 'natural' learning environments, such as among their families or at fiestas" (1990, 267). The near-mythical stature of artistic family lineages, *gitano*, Andalusian, and Spanish families whose flamenco and bullfighting talents are renowned, validates the romantic idea that artistry is innate, a natural phenomenon that is "in the blood."

The concept of talent is different in the aesthetic realm of flamenco and bullfighting. The Spanish word *talante* includes meanings beyond those that an English speaker might expect. *Talante* means talent, mode of execution, and technique, but it also denotes personal appearance, mien, disposition, temperament, wish, and desire. Thus, emotional content, personal character, changeable moods, and passion may all be perceived as intrinsic aspects of an individual, i.e., traits that, in and of themselves, constitute natural talent.

The romantic aesthetic places great emphasis on the value of risk, nobility, courage, and adventure. Risk taking is valued, as are the adrenaline and excitement associated with spontaneity and improvisation. The *gitano* value for freedom of expression and living in the moment produces individuals whose talent for emotional spontaneity is culturally sanctioned. Aficionados of both flamenco and bullfighting value individuals who, by performing improvisationally, demonstrate both mastery of traditions and inspired creativity. Whether a performer is meeting a bull's charge in the public arena or handling artistic challenges on the flamenco stage, the courage to meet challenges head-on is valued in and of itself. The ability to meet challenges directly and unflinchingly demonstrates, through performative enactment, the human capacity for nobility and heroism that the romantic aesthetic champions.

The romantic aesthetic is also evident in the literature of flamenco song, the *cante*. *Letras* are the verses within the *cante*, and flamenco *letras* typically address subjects and cultural values that pertain to the romantic aesthetic. Love and death are common themes; *letras* of the *cante jondo* song forms may convey existential anxiety, angst, and pain, express undying love, or assert religious faith. Songs called *carceleras* express the emotion of hopelessness by recounting experiences of incarceration or captivity. The *mineras* is a work song, a ballad that relates the stories and emotions of tragedies that befell workers in the mines. This is a humanistic romanticism, a romanticism for the proletariat. Flamenco *cante* explores a full range of emotions: humorous stories are shared through the *letras* of the *tanguillos*, happiness in the *alegrías*, loneliness in the *soleares*, and betrayal and bitter sorrow in the *siguiriyas*.

The romance of place and nature, the emotions of nostalgia and regionalism, are also present in the *letras* of ballads, musical renditions of idealized stories about people or historic events. Flamenco singers, *cantaors* or *cantaoras*, are often adept improvisers, able to incorporate the experience of the moment into the *letras* of their song. *Letras* of the *alegrías*, a festive song and dance style that originated in the ocean city of Cádiz, mention boats, waves, ocean breezes, beautiful sunrises, the lovely girls of Cádiz, the various emotions of happiness, and the *alegrías* itself, the song and dance style associated with pleasure, happiness, and joy. Thus traditional flamenco *letras* reflect the *ambiente*, personalities, locations, and cultural values that have surrounded and informed flamenco performance over its long history.

A sense of romantic narrative surrounds both bullfighting and flamenco dance; special events, personalities, and happenings will be commented on, discussed, and perhaps remembered for years. Emotional catharsis is valued as an experience that distinguishes individuals and unites the community as a whole. Technical proficiency is an important aspect; it keeps the matador alive and forms the basis for much of the competition within the flamenco arts. Yet it is emotion that is the aesthetic touchstone of bullfighting and flamenco: emotional content, display, resonance, and catharsis. One of the most derogatory comments one can make regarding a flamenco performance is to say "*no dice nada*," i.e., "it doesn't communicate anything." Likewise, if witnesses to a bullfight remain unmoved, the matador, despite his or her technical skill, did not meet the aesthetic requirements of success in the bullring. Success, for both flamenco and bullfighting, requires that emotional resonance be created between performer and audience and that, together, both are transported beyond the ordinary.

Aesthetics and Aesthemics

All assessments are formulated relative to the enculturation of the person making the assessment (i.e., assessments are subject to the principle of cultural relativity). Emic perceptions and perspectives are key to understanding the aesthetic standards by which flamenco dance and bullfighting are evaluated. Emic expectations affect the performer-witness dyad, performativity itself, and aesthetic discourse within both flamenco dance and bullfight contexts. I use the term *aesthemics* to signify emic perspectives and an enculturated sense of pleasure; aesthemics also involve a perceived right to make assessments and judgments, a sense of entitlement that is rooted in cultural identity and social belonging.[3]

Anthropologist Edward T. Hall, discussing degrees of cultural complexity, notes the differences between cultures that he defines as *high-context* and *low-context* (1976, 113). Due to the historical, performative, and cultural complexities of flamenco dance and bullfighting, they exemplify the type of high-context culture in which witnesses are expected to understand much about what is hidden and occurring below the surface. In contrast, Hall describes the low-context culture prevalent in the United States, noting such things as our reliance on technology, our penchant for logical reductionism, and the simplistic adversarial conventions of our judicial system.

Hall asserts that "high-context cultures make greater distinctions between insiders and outsiders than low-context cultures do. People raised in high-context systems expect more of others than do the participants in low-context systems" (1976, 113). The identification of insider/outsider status in relationship to the various groups that make up Spanish culture is an ongoing aspect of Spain's social life; this is evident, too, in relationship to flamenco, bullfighting, and the *gitano* subculture. In the high-context culture of Andalusia, it is expected that one should be adept at reading the subtleties of mannerism, dress, speech, and movement style that distinguish a person's regional, ethnic, or political affiliations as well as personal attributes of character, economic status, or level of education. In contrast, the value of inclusiveness championed by the cultural mainstream in the United States may result in a people who habitually pay less attention to the distinctions of dress, speech, and movement style that signal cultural diversity.

Differences in the cultural identity of audience members will affect whether their responses to flamenco and bullfighting events are purely aesthetic or include aesthemic values. Most bullfight events and flamenco performances will be witnessed by a mix of cultural insiders and outsiders, and as a result foreigners are likely to be exposed to the spontaneous responses of cultural insiders and begin to absorb emic perspectives. Hypothetically, there would be a significant contrast between the experience and response of a foreign audience made up of cultural outsiders with little or no direct social ties to the performers and an indigenous (local) audience made up of cultural insiders (perhaps even family members or contacts from a performer's immediate social circle).

Foreign Audiences

Foreign witnesses to a bullfight or a flamenco performance will have many sensory impressions, yet may lack the requisite associative and syntactical understanding that would help them to organize the complexity of their experience into meaningful form. Foreign observers have few ways to categorize their sensory impressions and distinguish which elements within a complex array of phenomena are actually significant. Lacking sustained experience with these cultural practices, they are unfamiliar with the reiterative value of the formulaic cultural behaviors of each performance form. If they lack knowledge of the social and performative conventions that govern audience participation, cultural outsiders may also experience fewer embodied responses and be unable to form empathic feelings for the performers. Though they may be emotionally affected, the investment of cultural outsiders in the event is relatively temporary and impersonal in nature.

For the uninitiated, or for people enculturated within a low-context culture, flamenco dance and bullfighting may be experienced as exotic cultural oddities. A taste for these practices must be acquired; one either appreciates them or one does not. Some foreign observers will be aware of their own lack of cultural preparation. They may realize that "a significant number of dance features and details are to be appreciated relative to their culture" (Kealiinohomoku 1976, 135), and make an effort to gain additional cultural knowledge and develop syntactical perspectives. Others may have more ethnocentric responses, blaming the perceived foreignness of Spanish/Andalusian customs for their own lack of understanding or aesthetic appreciation.

The negative responses of outsiders may include horror at the cruelty of bullfighting or boredom at the perceived sameness (redundancy) of flamenco dances.[4] Most people are unaware of the critical function of redundancy within their own cultural practices. "Formulae and redundancy patterns are satisfying to participants and respondents alike because they promote feelings of effectiveness and confidence" (Kealiinohomoku 1976, 107). In the context of flamenco dance and bullfighting, formulae and redundancy patterns promote and affirm feelings of social belonging. "The addition of innovative interpretations and the use of dramatic devices keep the patterns exciting and stimulating" (107–108); and redundancy supplies the requisite background that makes such artistic innovations enjoyable. In the highly social context of flamenco dance and bullfight practices, these innovations also serve to enhance the social standing of the innovator within the social group.

Acquiring an appreciation for either flamenco dance or bullfighting is dependent on various factors, including access to direct experience, exposure over time (redundancy), achieving a degree of syntactical knowledge, and enjoying a personal sense of comfort or inclusion within the social scene surrounding these practices. Foreigners newly introduced to the flamenco arts

Five. An Aesthetic Topography

With multiple bodies, man, horse, and bull, all engaged in the dynamic swirling chase of the *toreo de rejones*, the spatial form of a double helix may emerge as their postural inclinations and full-bodied efforts swirl around the dangerous vortex between them (Juan Pelegrino/Flickr.com).

or to the bullfight have much to learn before they can begin to decipher the complexities of these high-context cultural practices. As stated by an American bullfighting critic for a national newspaper in the documentary film, *The Lady Bullfighter* (Bryer 1989), "There is probably no spectacle that offers less to the uninitiated observer than bullfighting." Nevertheless, with time, access, and interest, it is possible for cultural outsiders to acquire an appreciation for flamenco dance and bullfighting.

Indigenous Audiences

For the people whose lives are surrounded by these two cultural practices, their socialization, enculturation, familiarity, and the direct encouragement they receive make participation in flamenco dance or bullfighting entirely natural and, in some cases, virtually inevitable. Many *gitanos* and Andalusians are actively involved in flamenco or bullfight practices as participants and/or witnesses. For them, these activities enact deeply held cultural values and represent a way of life that provides them pleasure and in which they take pride. Flamenco dance and bullfighting practices provide a significant source of vivid lived experience from which cultural insiders draw meaning and purpose.

As members of an audience, cultural insiders will have a different sense of responsibility and proprietary connection to the performance of culture. When their own culture is being enacted through ritual or dance, cultural insiders serve as active witnesses to the performance of community. They rely on redundancy while monitoring innovations within their cultural tradition. Cultural insiders are generally more adept at interpreting events and experiences; they have the requisite experience to distinguish unusual qualities manifested within the performance event and sufficient syntactical knowledge regarding cultural traditions and artistic standards to make informed aesthetic/aesthemic judgments. Because of their personal connections to the cultural traditions, the artistic standards, and the performing artists themselves, and because of their direct concern with the performative outcome of these events, such witnesses are able to construct significant meaning from their experience. Their experience of a performance is of immediate interest to them; it is pertinent. It will also have ongoing value because it provides subject matter for social discourse within their community.

Aesthemic appreciation is not based on a single type of judgment; it is instead a deeply enculturated amalgam of different types of judgment. This judgmental mixture is rich and nuanced; it combines moral, formal, and aesthetic judgment. Judgment and assessment are important means through which people participate in both flamenco and bullfighting. Judgment of a matador's performance may include assessments of personal style, technical proficiency, and knowledge of bulls, but also judgment of the matador's character and courage. Flamenco artists participate within a similarly charged social context in which judgment of a performer's authenticity, compliance to flamenco traditions, appropriate social conduct, proper adherence to musical forms, personal style, and individual character is constant.

Judgment, both having and expressing opinions, is intrinsic to the cultural realms of flamenco dance and bullfighting. Thus, discussions after the performance event constitute a significant component of participation; the volatile nature of these cultural practices adds intensity to the post-performance discourse. As both competition and art, flamenco and bullfighting open many a conversation and maintain the attention of the public. Each day (afternoon or evening) there are new occurrences in the realms of flamenco and bullfighting; and so, the cultural conversation is perpetually renewed.

Within this discourse, the judgment of some people is more highly valued. The opinions of *gitanos*, particularly regarding the flamenco arts, are highly valued because they reflect a unique expertise, authenticity, and adherence to traditions that result from the *gitano* way of life. Ethnicity in this instance constitutes an acknowledged level of expertise. The opinions of others (Andalusians, Spaniards, aficionados, toreros, and flamenco artists) are also valued, particularly when expressed by someone with a significant degree of syntactical knowledge.[5] Such expertise may be gained through performance, scholarship, or continuous cultural experience.

The Spanish phrase *los cabales* refers to those few individuals who, through their knowledge, sense of perfection, and unerring sense of judgment, function as the voices of aesthetic authority, establishing performance standards and maintaining the cultural values of flamenco and bullfighting. These may be members of Spain's upper classes, personages experienced in the traditions of bullfighting, or patrons of the flamenco arts; *gitanos* may also wield this level of authority in the aesthetic realm of flamenco.

> *El cabal* exercises an important and prominent function, especially in the profound and changeable artistic world of flamenco appreciation (bullfighting, song, and dance). They are the faithful guardians of the purity and legitimacy of the art of the people. They are of a rank that exerts watchful jurisprudence. Nothing escapes them. *El cabal* personifies, if you like, a frustrated flamenco, the flamenco singer without possibilities, the potential bullfighter, the unexpressed dancer. He is the great witness [González Climent 1964, 227].[6]

Los cabales are high-level aesthetic arbiters, valued for their expertise within these high-context arts. *Los cabales* know the history, formal and technical elements, and aesthetic values, as well as the personalities of artists and the lineages that constitute the flamenco and bullfighting traditions. González Climent's reference to *el cabal* as the great witness is significant. Performers naturally concern themselves with the opinions of the general public, members of their social circle, and people with whom they are intimate. However, many performers perform with *los cabales* (i.e., the critics) in mind. *Los cabales* are the experts who will ultimately determine careers, reputations, and the historical record of the flamenco and bullfighting traditions.

Highly contextualized practices function through the human ability to recognize patterns in movement, sound, and relationship. That humans experience pleasure as a result of pattern recognition is a propitious fact, favorable to the continuation of these cultural practices. *Los cabales* of flamenco and bullfighting, being expert in pattern recognition within these high-context cultural practices, are the most valued of witnesses; their participation in the roles of witness, judge, and contributor to public discourse supports the survival of these traditions.

As movement practices, both flamenco and bullfighting enact the tenuous psychological balance between an artist's dual needs to master the form and to expand artistic possibilities. A tension between technical discipline and risk taking is manifest in the arts of both tauromachy and flamenco. Flamenco performances generally require musicians and dancers to forge an artistic event collaboratively; intense concentration is required as the urge toward artistic innovation and personal risk taking is balanced against the necessity of remaining in sync with fellow performers and adhering to the strict traditions of form that rule the art. The musicians, *palmeros* (musicians who maintain the rhythm through flamenco's signature handclapping, *palmas*), singers, guitarists, and dancers perform as a team; the need of individuals to distinguish themselves is balanced against the need to coordinate and excel as a group.

In bullfighting a similar tension exists between a matador's desire to perform with dignity, technique, and style, and the inherently unpredictable nature of the bullfight encounter. In the public arena, a matador's years of technical practice in pursuit of controlled artistry and elegant physical form may come to fruition in a glorious performance or be challenged, disrupted, and laid waste through the actions of an enraged and unpredictable bull. As stated by Manolo Escudero, a distinguished teacher of bullfighting, in the documentary film *The Lady Bullfighter* (Bryer 1989), "The bull doesn't obey any rules; he's a complicated beast. A hundred bulls will charge in a hundred different ways. No bull will let you do what you want."

The matador's desire to survive the instinctual raging power of the bull plays against a desire to perform excellently certain well-practiced lines and maneuvers. At times a bullfight performance may embody some of the same aesthetic principles that govern the practice of flamenco dance, just as flamenco dance often enacts a deeply embedded cultural knowledge and appreciation of the art of bullfighting.

Aesthemic Expectation and the Experience of Duende

Aesthemic expectations often focus on *duende*, a key emic concept affecting appreciation of both flamenco dance and bullfighting. *Duende* constitutes the ultimate aesthemic expectation, namely, that the cultural events of flamenco dance and bullfighting entail emotional transformation and transcendent experience. The role of expectation is significant in the formulation of conscious and unconscious aesthetic judgments. "Disgust, disappointment, boredom, pleasure, excitement, and delight are all points on a continuum of responses to expectancy patterns" (Kealiinohomoku 1976, 137). Expectancy patterns exist in relation to sensory, associative, and syntactical appreciation, and "in order for expectation to be rewarded beyond expectation three levels of evaluation are probably universally operative. The first is that cultural norms are appropriately realized. The second is that special standards are fulfilled. The third is that the object or behavior transcends those special standards so that something is at one and the same time both consonant and unique" (139).

When a performance satisfies the expectations of cultural norms, it is judged to be "culturally acceptable," and when an event satisfies special performance standards it is judged "aesthetically acceptable" (Kealiinohomoku 1976, 139). When a flamenco or bullfighting performance satisfies the third level of expectation, it exceeds those special standards and thus "transcends verbal analysis" (139). The first level of expectation is satisfied when performers conform to the codification of formal elements within the flamenco and bullfighting traditions, the rituals of behavior in the arena, and the rhythmic structures that rule flamenco performance. The second level of expectation may be satisfied through colorful costumes, the play of talent and energy, or the physical appeal and personality of performers. The third level of expectation, the expectation of a transcendent experience, is always operative and constitutes a powerful expectation within these two cultural practices.

The expectancy patterns of the flamenco and bullfighting public are informed by the Andalusian concept of *duende*. This transcendent experience, *duende*, is an emergence of dark spirit; discussing flamenco's *cante jondo*, Federico García Lorca alludes to flamencologist Manuel Tortes' statement that "whatever has black sounds, has *duende*" (García Lorca 1955, 154). *Duende* signifies the super-ordinary and transcendent; it is the ultimate aesthemic requirement that drives the bullfight and flamenco traditions.

The cultural practices of flamenco and bullfighting provide opportunities for an intense and dynamic expression of emotion by individuals; they also sanction the experience of emotional catharsis within the wider community. Flamenco and bullfighting practices invoke a full range of human dynamics, from the emotions of conflict and struggle—fear, grief, and anger— to the sublime emotions through which humans celebrate life and survival— peace, harmony, humor, and joy. Sharing aesthetic expectations, including expectation of the super-ordinary manifestation of *duende*, both performers and audience members are prepared for a transcendent experience that spans disruption and resolution. Through the reiterative cycle of rupture and resolution, the dynamic strength of a culture is enacted and reaffirmed.

The ultimate arbitration of value within the romantic aesthetic of flamenco and bullfighting is based on the ineffable experience of emotional depth and struggle, on *duende* rather than technical prowess. The emotional palette of flamenco is wide, colorful, deep, and complex; bullfighting, too, in order to be effective in its super-ordinary function, must be emotionally affecting. Individual and collective emotional catharsis is an expectation upon which an ultimate aesthetic judgment is based. Through joy and anguish, despair and euphoria, the cultural rites of flamenco and bullfighting strive to deliver transcendence and transformation, and the demon/god that rules this process goes by the name of *duende*.

Describing *duende* as a "Spanish term for daemonic inspiration," Lorca scholar Arturo Barea notes that

> While to the rest of Spain the *duende* is nothing but a hobgoblin, to Andalusia it is an obscure power which can speak through every form of human art, including the art of personality. A performer can infuse an insipid piece of hackneyed music with his or her *duende*, and turn it into truth and beauty. A dancer can give stirring power to a ritual gesture. A bullfighter can transform the mathematical rules of space and the feats of masculine courage which belong to the stylized play with death in the bullring, so that he creates beauty and emotion charged with knowledge of human limits transgressed [1958, 132–133].

Drawing from the depths of his own cultural experience, the renowned Spanish poet Federico García Lorca (1898–1936) makes full use of his poetic license to provide a richly evocative discussion and description of *duende* in his essay, "The Duende: Theory and Divertissement" (García Lorca 1955, 154).[7] Contrasting *duende* with the angels and muses that inspire and assist artists of all kinds, Lorca notes, "Angel and Muse approach from without; the Angel sheds light and the Muse gives form." Lorca asserts that "the *Duende*, on the other hand, must come to life in the nethermost recesses of the blood." Lorca associates *duende* with the artist's inner spiritual struggle. "To seek out the *Duende*, however, neither map nor discipline is required. Enough to know that he kindles the blood like an irritant, that he exhausts, that he repulses, all the bland, geometrical assurances, that he smashes the styles" (García Lorca 1955, 156–157).

This destructive/creative force is the inspiring spirit that informs and inspires the flamenco arts and rules the artistry of bullfighting.

> In the bullfight, the *Duende* achieves his most impressive advantage, for he must fight then with death who can destroy him, on the one hand, and with geometry, with measure, the fundamental basis of the bullfight on the other.
> The bull has his orbit, and the bullfighter has his, and between orbit and orbit is the point of risk where falls the vertex of the terrible byplay....
> The bullfighter who moves the public to terror in the plaza by his audacity does not *fight* the bull—that would be ludicrous in any case—but, within the

Five. An Aesthetic Topography 143

reach of each man, puts his life at stake; on the contrary, the fighter bitten by the *Duende* gives a lesson in Pythagorean music and induces all to forget how he constantly hurls his heart against the horns [García Lorca 1955, 164].

The connection between the ritual arts of flamenco and bullfighting thus has to do with the acknowledgment of death and the darkest of spiritual and emotional possibilities. "Flamenco, at its very best, enacts an a-religious, non-rational expression of tragic awareness, which 'understands' death.... But what is especially peculiar is the unfettered joy and exhilaration that come with it; the proximity of death to celebration in much of the singing and dancing is a feature unique to this musical culture, and is why it is inimitable" (Woodall 1992, 60). Paradoxically, it is the presence of death that elucidates life's value—that inspires life's celebration.

According to Lorca, the *duende*

will not approach at all if he does not see the possibility of death, if he is not convinced he will circle death's house, if there is not every assurance he can rustle the branches borne aloft by us all, that neither have, nor may ever have, the power to console.

With idea, with sound, or with gesture, the *Duende* chooses the brim of the well for his open struggle with the creator. Angel and Muse escape in the violin or in musical measure, but the *Duende* draws blood, and in the healing of the wound that never quite closes, all that is unprecedented and invented in a man's work has its origin [García Lorca 1955, 162].

Here Lorca identifies *duende* as the creative force itself. This quality of creativity is both irrepressible and illusive; it may burst through unexpectedly to electrify a performance or evade a performer for years. Artists actively seek it—attempt to court and elicit it from within—yet *duende* occurs when the artist surrenders or is overcome. Lorca ends his essay by saying, "But the *Duende*—where is the *Duende*? Through the empty arch enters a mental air blowing insistently over the heads of the dead, seeking new landscapes and unfamiliar accents; an air bearing the odor of child's spittle, crushed grass, and the veil of a Medusa announcing the unending baptism of all newly-created things" (García Lorca 1955, 166).

Duende is the harsh ruling spirit of both flamenco and bullfight aesthetics. For, as Lorca notes, "the great artists of southern Spain, both gypsies and flamenco, whether singing or dancing or playing on instruments, know that no emotion is possible without the mediation of the *Duende*" (García Lorca 1955, 157). *Duende* opens into the deepest and darkest emotions; performances touched by the uncanny spirit of *duende* are thereby made unforgettable to witnesses.

Emotional catharsis, transformation, and transcendent experience are the core values sought within the flamenco circle and the bullfight arena. The true value of *duende* resides in its very ineffableness; its inexpressible nature provides a cognitive challenge that energizes social and aesthetic discourse. An occurrence of *duende* within a performance lifts social discourse from prosaic matters to poetic heights. People, having shared an experience of the super-ordinary, are eager to discuss impressions and engage cultural metaphors in a shared search for meaning.

The following summarizes the primary aesthetic attributes that function within both flamenco dance and bullfighting practices. This list is meant to be indicative and evocative rather than exhaustive.

Excitement
Adrenaline
Risk taking
Unpredictability
Surprises
Danger
Fear
Spontaneity
Impulsivity

Drama
Intensity
Heightened emotional life
Life and death
Fatalism
Passionate intensity
Pride
Tragedy/comedy
Ambition

Fighting Energy
Dynamic tensions between protagonists
Struggle
Competition
Duress
Courage
Strength
Laban's "fighting qualities" (strong, direct, quick, and controlled movement qualities)
Fierceness

Connecting Energy
Emotional resonance
Empathy
Rhythmic entrainment
Sensuality
Physical (body) awareness
Sociality
Pleasure
Sensibilities
Jaleo, encouragement

Innovation
Creativity
Improvisation
Idiosyncrasy
Individualism
Personality
Style
Estampa
Flamboyance
Llamativo, calling attention
Exaggeration

Continuity
Specialized skills
Traditions
Requisite proficiency
Ritualized, codified frameworks of behavior
Artistic forms
Conformity
Highly patterned
Authenticity

Event
Super-ordinary

Duende
Transformation

Five. An Aesthetic Topography   145

Event (cont.)
Ritual
Play
Spectacle
High-context
Performative

Duende *(cont.)*
Transcendence
Uncanny
Ineffable
Catharsis
Poetry, metaphor

CHAPTER SIX

Movement Repatterning and Culture

Enculturation and Acculturation

Culture is the living/learning context through which we become human. We learn to be human from other humans; without each other and the many generations who lived and learned before us, we would not be able to achieve humanness. The first process through which we learn to be human, known as enculturation, enables us to become culturally competent in relationship to our own cultural group. It is "a process of conscious or unconscious conditioning, exercised within the limits sanctioned by a given body of custom" (Herskovits 1964, 24). Enculturative learning results in emic understanding of the worldview, social values, historical perspectives, and manners of living of our culture of origin, and an appreciation for our own place within the lineage of a cultural tradition.

While culture is the conscious focus of enculturative learning, much learning about culture is achieved unconsciously through movement. Emic perspectives root us in exoteric knowledge, in what our culture group considers common knowledge. Emic perspectives may also entail highly nuanced esoteric knowledge of some obscure or secret aspect of our culture. Emic perspectives will always be flavored by kinesthetic culture, the movement environments and learning processes through which we absorbed our first lessons in being human.

Cynthia Knox, speaking to the fundamental role of movement phenomena in these cultural processes, notes that "all movement is culturally patterned. Though our movements may be based on underlying human developmental patterns, evidence of innate movement potentialities, the actuality of movement involves human contact and humanness and therefore is liberally inundated with the cultural" (1992, 50).

Culture provides the parameters within which human behaviors develop

Six. Movement Repatterning and Culture 147

"¡Olé!" These children are engaged in the cultural game of *toreando*. Taking turns to embody the matador and the bull, they incorporate the dynamics, movement forms, and psychology of the bullfight into their way of understanding and dealing with the world around them. Many generations of Spaniards have played this game (see Goya tapestry in Chapter Four), and *toreando* still goes on today (Everett Collection/Shutterstock.com).

and function. Knox notes that eventually "the infant becomes capable of more variation within the cultural parameters, more capable of elaboration within a narrowing frame" (84). Thus, children who learn how to be human in the context of flamenco dance and bullfighting will, through mimesis, instruction, and verbal, aural, tactile, and rhythmic awareness, quickly develop skills and emic knowledge of these two cultural practices.[1] They will unconsciously allow the tacit rules of cultural performance to influence their embodied expression and creativity.

Adaptation to circumstances and environmental factors, including culture, is inherent to the human experience. "Human movement is informed by, indeed shaped within, culture. Culture is our pressing environmental demand, the requisite heritage of our species" (Knox 1992, 31). We meet the demands of living through the malleability and flexibility of our learning selves. We have the capacity to repattern our movements, adjusting our habituated movement patterns in order to accommodate vocational requirements, compensate for disabilities caused by age, illness, or injury, and respond to changing social or cultural circumstances. Most such movement repatterning occurs below the threshold of consciousness; it is a natural function, allowing us to respond more or less automatically to the demands of living.

Acculturation, learning how to be human through contact with another culture, entails the gaining of new layers of cultural knowledge that conflict or complement our own culture's worldview and manner of living. Acculturative learning can be thought of as a type of repatterning. Acculturation can happen through intense experiences of cultural immersion, travel to foreign lands, or casual contact with people of other cultures that we meet in our daily lives. When acculturative learning is undertaken as an academic enterprise, it often uses etic perspectives (objective methods) for the purpose of cross-cultural comparison. Through acculturation, human beings gain a degree of cultural competence in relation to the culture of another group, and it is through acculturative learning that cultural attributes or behaviors are transmitted between cultural groups.

Over time, a process of cultural sharing between groups may result in new cultural forms that reflect multiple cultural influences; the result is cultural hybridity, which is neither a new nor a rare phenomenon. In fact, flamenco dance and music are examples of cultural hybridity; their formal structures, aesthetics, and style elements share features with a variety of cultures that passed through the southern region of the Iberian Peninsula throughout its long history. Flamencologist James Woodall, author of *In Search of the Firedance*, describes the unique sound of flamenco song as "something that owes its provenance to non–European culture, Africa (Arabic, not black) … with interjections from two great wandering peoples of the earth: the Jews and the Gypsies" (1992, 3). Flamenco is a cultural hybrid form that incubated and evolved for centuries before it emerged as a definitive cultural practice.

Classifying flamenco dance and bullfighting as cultural practices implies that each cultural practice functions as what anthropologist Paul Connerton refers to as an "incorporating practice" or "bodily practice" through which the memory of a culture group is preserved. In *How Societies Remember*, Connerton describes the particular actions within incorporating practices as "messages that a sender or senders impart by means of their own current bodily activity, the transmission occurring only during the time that their bodies are present to sustain that particular activity" (1989, 72). Thus, flamenco and bullfighting practices entail in-the-moment actualities and real consequences. Connerton asserts that through incorporating practices, a cultural behavior "re-enacts the past in our present conduct"; he also affirms the significance of the somatic realm, concluding that, "in habitual memory the past is, as it were, sedimented in the body" (72). Thus, our dancing carries not only our own in-the-moment expressive content, but also reflects the performative history of a people.

Embodied cultural practices serve as a means of maintaining social memory and protecting cultural continuity. The transmission of such incorporating practices as flamenco dance and bullfighting between generations is often achieved through direct, pedagogical interventions that provide students with formal training in codified movement techniques. Formal training has a stabilizing effect on the cultural practices themselves. The transmission of flamenco dance and bullfighting practices also occurs in informal contexts that allow for much greater variation and innovation in their movement practices. It is often through the medium of an informal social and performative context that individual or collective innovations are brought forward to enrich and revitalize the embodied cultural practice. Continuity and change function collaboratively in relation to cultural practices and movement forms. Redundancy, a word which in many contexts has negative connotations, is a phenomenon of tremendous value in the context of culture. "Although structure, *per se*, does not have meaning, it operates to promote communication of meaning since it is composed, in part, of patterns of redundant features and redundancy promotes communication" (Kealiinohomoku 1976, 100). The reiteration, repetition, and redundancy of movement behaviors and forms in flamenco dance and bullfighting are fundamentally necessary; they provide the requisite foundation of habituated behaviors and artistic forms, the matrix out of which creative impulses and cultural innovations emerge.

Somatic phenomena, such as sensation, action, expressivity, and emotional content, are important subjects in the study of culture; they are active ingredients that nourish the roots of cultural learning (both enculturative and acculturative) as well as culture itself. Bodily presence is not a tangential attribute of flamenco dance and bullfighting; rather, bodily presence is central to their practice. The

The semicircular form of the traditional *cuadro flamenco* tends to flatten out in proscenium stage situations. As seen in this 2008 photograph of the Ballet Teatro Español de Rafael Aguilar performing *Carmen* at the Jichen Theater in Chengdu, China, proscenium stage productions are also more likely to entail uniformity of phenotype (matching body types) and movements performed in unison. The result is a less individualistic presentation of flamenco culture that values symmetry of form above individual expression (Jack.Q/Shutterstock.com).

dancer's body is on view while experiencing the stresses, constraints, heightened energy, and expressive risks of the dance, and the matador's body and actual life are risked in the public spotlight of the bullfight. The details of a performer's body, bodily presence, and body movements receive great attention in the pedagogical and aesthetic discourses of flamenco dance and bullfighting.

The learning that infants and children achieve through movement processes in the early years of human development is truly phenomenal, and this capacity for experiential learning through conscious exploration of embodiment and movement phenomena is also a potentiality in adulthood. The same neuromuscular patterning that coordinates such early developmental actions as an infant lifting its head, sitting up, manipulating objects, speaking, or walking for the first time, also supports our human capacity to bond and communicate. We are endowed at birth with the potential to be human, but with no guarantee of achieving our full human potential. We depend on other humans to show us the way; we learn our humanity and fulfill our potential through embodied contact and the direct nurture of other human beings. Being fully human is an individual achievement accomplished through community.

This understanding has great relevance in relationship to the highly social practices of flamenco dance and bullfighting. Encouragement is both an ongoing attribute of normative cultural participation and a requirement in the enculturation process as a child learns its own culture or in the acculturation process as an adult attempts to learn the ways of another culture. *Jaleo*, shouted encouragement from onlookers, reaffirms cultural values even as it supports individual performers. The cultural practices of flamenco dance and bullfighting provide opportunities for performers to assert their individuality before a gathered community of witnesses. The assertion of humanity, individuality, and social belonging through such public performances satisfies basic human needs for integrity, self-respect, purpose, authenticity, mental stimulation, self-expression, mastery, meaning, creativity, order, aesthetic experience, choice, freedom, self-empowerment, social validation, appreciation, respect, admiration, acknowledgment, aliveness, intensity, and excitement. Basic human needs of the public are met through the act of witnessing flamenco or bullfighting events, and by engaging in the many social activities before, during, and after these public events.

Continuity and Change

According to Connerton, incorporating practices (bodily practices) may be generally categorized along a continuum between formal and informal practices. Connerton points out the tendency for incorporating practices occurring in more formal contexts to exhibit a high degree of invariance, while in informal contexts, a high degree of variance is exhibited (1989, 79). Thus, in the context of the formal stage one is likely to see flamenco dancers of matching body types performing choreographed dances in unison, whereas in informal performance settings one sees solo dancers within a wide range of body types performing more improvisationally. Both flamenco dance and bullfighting occur in formal and informal settings, affirming their culture group's value for the stability of tradition and the collective and individual creative impulses that contribute to its further development.

In both practices, performers study and practice fixed movement forms, choreographed dances or traditional techniques and styles of movements with a cape (*capote* or *muleta*). And yet, although dancers face significantly less risk than toreros, matadors and dancers both know that performance often includes encounters with the unexpected. How do performers prepare for a rendezvous with the unexpected? Practice, practice, and more practice—whether a flamenco dancer or matador, the performer is focused on attaining mastery.

A performer's relationship to mastery changes over time. A young flamenco dancer may focus on technique, creating a personal style or *estampa*, or mastering different dances within the extensive flamenco repertory. Having mastered those elements, the same dancer later in her or his career may focus on refining the expressive nuances within their performance style or using mastery in the service of more creative and ambitious projects. And here I am thinking of some of the remarkable contemporary innovators in the flamenco dance tradition, such as Sara Barras, Joaquín Cortés, Israel Galvan, Pastora Galvan, Belén Maya, Eva La Yerbabuena, and others. Through performative acts individuals engage directly with the cultural tension between continuity and innovation, between the traditional and the new. The first requisite cultural task of flamenco dancers and bullfighters is to prove that they know the rules of the game. Once basic mastery is established, the game may be played with verve and passion, with the ultimate goal of enhancing the tradition through creative innovation.

Discussing the contrasting cultural mechanisms of conservatism and change, Herskovits notes that "in our earliest years we are being continually conditioned to conformity" (1964, 25). With maturity, the demands of enculturation become less insistent and more sporadic; also mature adults are exposed to greater possibilities and are afforded more opportunities to select and choose between different types of behavior. "The enculturation of the individual in the early years of his [her] life is the prime mechanism making for cultural stability, while the process, as it operates on more mature folk, is highly important in inducing change" (25). And so, although it may seem counterintuitive, when we view the generational dynamic of cultural change, youth function as the conservators of cultural traditions while adults influence the direction and rate of cultural change. In other words, gaining mastery of the essential skills and knowledge of flamenco dance or bullfighting traditions is more than sufficient challenge to keep young people busy, while with maturity, many older performers expand their artistic scope by playing more freely within the form and experimenting within the cultural practice.

The performative practices of flamenco dance and bullfighting express the fundamental tension between the innovative potential of individual expression and the constraining rules of the game. What Knox refers to as the "capacity to elaborate within a narrow frame" constitutes a primary cultural task in the context of flamenco dance and bullfighting, tantalizing children, youth, and adults with its continual challenge to prove cultural competency through artistic mastery.

Mature members of the culture group determine the direction and rate of innovation in traditions such as flamenco and bullfighting through the mechanism of judgment, which they exercise in various contexts, both formal and informal. The pedagogical context offers very direct opportunities for adults in their role as teachers to slow the rate of cultural change by enforcing traditional forms and performance standards. Teachers are also positioned to sanction technical innovations or aesthetic shifts that emerge from within the practice by either encouraging or limiting student creativity. Interestingly, male flamenco dance teachers often serve as effective arbiters of female dance styling, while female flamenco dancer Pilar Lopez was known for greatly influencing male dance styles due to her "ability to train, coach, and help create superb male dancers" (Morca 1990, 92). Mature experts are also called upon to serve as judges in formal competitions; this places them in a position to determine which young people will be given professional performance opportunities in the bullring or onstage. Discussing flamenco experts and critics, flamencologist González Climent noted that often "retired flamenco artists or bullfighters later become *cabales*" (1964, 202).[2] Thus, after retiring or withdrawing from direct participation as performers, older artists may gain additional recognition and status by actively employing their aesthetic judgment and expertise.

Creativity in these arts emerges both in the process of devising new fixed forms, such as choreography or techniques, and in inspired moments of improvisational experimentation. In both instances, redundancy is a key feature of the creative process. "Like his [her] counterparts in other formal affective situations, the dancer is protected by his [her] habituation.... The formulaic nature of dance makes it possible to survive stressful and prolonged situations, and contributes to [cultural] homeostasis" (Kealiinohomoku 1976, 102). In other words, the fixed artistic structures and rules that constrain flamenco dance performance also strengthen its creative practice by providing a stable framework for interpretive or improvisational elaborations. "Improvising, like choreographing, is a rule-based activity and although it might be argued that, theoretically, the entire range of possible movements is at the disposal of a person moving at any given moment, the actions chosen usually reflect the individual's exposure to certain specific sets of actions that are the result of training—formal or informal—whether as a dancer, acrobat, martial artist, or musician [or matador]" (Puri and Hart-Johnson 1995, 168).

These understandings apply also in the bullfighting context. Entering the bullring on a Mexican ranch with my brand-new, untried skills, I was a beginner with unhabituated movements. In that circumstance it was appropriate that I assert little creative agency. Any improvisational aspects of my performance in the informal bullring in Mexico were actions taken in response to the whims and choices of the animal with which I interacted; they did not reflect intentional artistic choices on my part. More established or professional matadors, in contrast, are highly habituated to the standard movements of tauromachy and enhance their performances by drawing from a well-practiced set of innovative *pases* (movements of the cape). Creative matadors develop entirely unique *pases*, choreographing and practicing these actions in preparation for their performance in the bullring (Ramón 1998). To be actively creative *while* engaged in a bullfight demonstrates the highest degree of mastery.

My movement habituation in the flamenco dance style is well established, and so I can more easily create through improvisational or choreographic means while staying true to the conventions of the flamenco art form. Within the flamenco dance genre, I find choreographing easier than improvising. When choreographing, I can be thoughtful, I can take my time; no time pressure or sense of immediacy complicates my creative process. When improvising in the flamenco dance style, I notice my lack of the necessary base (habituation, redundancy, and enculturation) for the improvisation of flamenco footwork. There appears to be a categorical difference between the physical habituation of movement and the ability to play improvisationally within that skill set. Formal training habituates flamenco footwork patterns deeply into the body's neuro-muscular system until they can be performed as automatisms. However, even with well-developed flamenco footwork skills, improvising presents a significant challenge for those of us who gained our

Six. Movement Repatterning and Culture

skills through acculturative learning. I identify this gap as the gap between enculturation and acculturation; for me, narrowing that gap represents mastery.

Another acculturative learning challenge is emic knowledge of the tacit rules of flamenco dance and bullfighting practices. This is challenging because of the high-context nature of each practice as well as the fact that each practice is intensely difficult—physically, mentally, and emotionally—even for cultural insiders. It is especially difficult for foreigners to obtain the specific syntactical knowledge of flamenco structures that is needed for improvisational performance. This may be because so much acculturative learning is carried out in the formal contexts of classrooms and dance studios. In addition, most pedagogical approaches only address improvisational forms later, after a student has developed and mastered basic movement skills. Non-Spaniards learning flamenco dance through formal training may have only limited access to the informal contexts where improvisational performance skills are developed. This is another reason that non–Spaniards are less likely to be adept at improvisational performance than those who gained improvisational skills early and informally. The ability to wield a complex movement vocabulary with the creative agency of a choreographer or improvisational performer is a significant accomplishment, one that is most often demonstrated by people enculturated in the flamenco dance practice.

Redundancy also plays a key role in the aesthetic appreciation of flamenco dance and bullfighting. In the flamenco dance practice, redundancy produces a matrix of consistent formal elements and reiterative patterns of behavior. Innovations in form, interpretation, or behavior are recognized through their contrast to this culturally patterned background. And so, observers unfamiliar with the culturally patterned movements of flamenco dance may notice only the phenomenon of redundancy and be entirely unable to discern any artistic innovations that might occur; to them it may "all look the same." In the bullfight arena, the ritual formalities and protocols observed are also reiterative and redundant, as are many of the basic movement techniques of bullfighting. Observers of flamenco dance or bullfight events with extensive experience and syntactical knowledge of the cultural practice know what to look for and will better discern and appreciate the uniqueness of each performance.

Cultural continuity is served through the formality, invariance, and redundancy in a performance practice. Fixity of artistic form may not only reflect but actually support social stability, order, an inflexible social hierarchy, or the socialized, civilized, and tamed individual, i.e., the citizen who conforms to and supports the social norms established by the culture group. Cul-

In the Antonio Gades Company's performance of *Carmen* for the 2010 Theater, Music and Dance Festival in the Canary Islands, Spain, a staged version of flamenco culture conveys authenticity by showing that everyone and every body type is invited to participate in the informal game of flamenco. Nonmatching phenotypes abound in the traditional flamenco social circle, where individualism, eccentricity, uniqueness of style, and vivid personalities are highly valued (criben/Shutterstock.com).

tural innovation is served through informality, variance, and impulsive or deliberate resistance to the state of redundancy. Fluidity of form may encourage or lend its support to historical moments of change, social instability or revolution, a flexible social hierarchy, egalitarian social order, and the rebellious, anarchic, or wild individual, i.e., the nonconformist who resists the established norms of the culture group. As flamenco dance and bullfighting enact and reenact cultural values through their incorporating practices, they provide evidence of a fundamental cultural game played out between the stabilizing influence of reiterative acceptance and the destabilizing influence of creative instigation.

The Flexible Self

For me, dance and movement phenomena have long been not only subjects of study but also my most profound life teachers. After years of physical training in Western theater dance styles (modern contemporary dance, ballet, and jazz), I had, through my body, also received a significant degree of cultural indoctrination. Dance training impresses upon one's mind and body the culturally nuanced particulars of how to be a human being: how to be female or male, how to thrive, hunt, propitiate the gods, call down the rains, have a good time, increase one's social standing, find a mate, etc. After years of unconsciously absorbing Western cultural values through its dance forms, I had the opportunity to study the developmental repatterning techniques of Bartenieff Movement Fundamentals™. This movement repatterning process cleared away some of the cultural debris I had unconsciously absorbed through my dance training and returned my movement function to a more natural state, aligned with human developmental patterns.

This movement repatterning process produced immediate personal revelations, and significantly influenced my thinking about the relationship between culture and movement. I came to understand that (1) my movement had been culturally patterned prior to the development of conscious choice; that (2) this is true of all human beings; that (3) the human experience of embodiment is both limited and diversified as a result of many factors, one of which is culture; that (4) it is possible to embody a greater range of the human potential through movement repatterning; that (5) repatterning movement in order to embody the practices of another culture provides somatic and kinetic clues to the lived experience of people from that other culture; that (6) through such a repatterning of the cultural attributes of my movement, I might be able to exercise those portions of my human potential that my own culture inhibited or failed to develop; and that (7) through this process I might attain some degree of freedom from the limitations of my cultural background and develop a sense of the full range of human cultural diversity as it manifests at the level of embodied experience. I credit my training in Bartenieff Movement Fundamentals with cleansing my kinetic/somatic palate and alerting me to the possibilities of cultural exploration through movement.

And so I began a conscious and deliberate movement repatterning process, a somatic journey of exploration in the context of culture and meaning that began with some initial flamenco dance classes and led to deeper learning about how flamenco functions as a cultural practice (not just a formal dance class), and eventually led into an all-out investigation of bullfighting nuances within the style. I did not study Spanish culture from an objectifying distance, but took on the deeply subjective experience of becoming acculturated to the movement vocabularies, aesthetic values, and performative outcomes of both cultural practices. In my experience, acculturation entailed immersion; it also required humility. While enculturation provides one's first experiences of learning how to be human, acculturation requires that one let go of precisely those deeply fixed ideas. Initially, acculturation stimulates the ethnocentric impulse; given sufficient time, acculturation may transform or annihilate it altogether.

This learning process included interrogating my tauromachy and flamenco dance teachers, who were my teachers not only in relation to movement techniques but also in relation to the cultural values of flamenco and bullfighting. I followed the dictum that "rather than *studying people*, ethnography means *learning from people*" (Spradley 1980, 3; Spradley's italics); in my role as a student I was learning from people "in order to discover the hidden principles of another way of life" (4). I lived in Madrid from 1991 to 1992, traveling to other areas of Spain (including Andalusia) during that time. In subsequent years I visited Spain on other occasions seeking insight into flamenco dance and its cultural roots.

My goal was to gain emic perspectives into flamenco dance; interestingly, one of my best learning tools was the etic perspectives of Laban Movement Analysis. While living in Madrid and taking daily dance classes, I developed a method using Language of Dance motif symbols to notate flamenco dance, and created footwork symbols and notated each of the eight choreographed flamenco dances I learned during that period.[3] This application of etic perspectives in the collection and analysis of movement material resulted in a significant increase of my understanding of flamenco dance rhythms and forms.

Much of what I have come to know is the result of the living choices I made while in Spain. My understanding sometimes increased as a result of happenstance. Often I learned while I was caught up in immediate concerns, coping in the midst of living a cross-cultural life in culturally unfamiliar circumstances. But there is great power in unconscious learning; the imprint of such lessons can go quite deep. It seems that the actual synthesis of knowledge often occurs just beyond the reach of conscious thought, behind the scenes, while one is sleeping, off camera, in a moment of negotiation, in the middle of a meal, or running errands. Although new information and lived experience usually weave into coherent form only gradually, knowledge often becomes conscious through a sudden revelation—the "Aha!" moments that punctuated my learning process.

One such revelation occurred in 1989 when I first traveled to Spain and studied with flamenco dancer Mariano Torres at the Paco Peña Festival Internacional de la Guitarra in Córdoba. I already knew that flamenco's rhythmic cadence, the *compás*, functioned as a foundational structure for improvisa-

Six. Movement Repatterning and Culture   159

tional performance. However, being relatively new to flamenco, flamenco music was like a barely decipherable foreign language, the logic of its rhythms difficult to discern. Within the flamenco arts, dance has an interpretive function in relation to the musical forms, so I knew that I needed to imprint flamenco's musical patterns deeply in my bodily senses and unconscious expectations. I studied flamenco dance during the daylight hours, and all through the late evening hours I heard the sounds of the practicing flamenco guitar students with whom I shared lodgings. This immersion in flamenco music (nearly twenty-four hours per day) prepared me for a breakthrough in my comprehension of flamenco's deep patterning. Late one night, I rode for an hour with a friend in one of the horse-drawn carriages in Córdoba, a tourist outing that provided us an experience of another culture as well as another historical era. As we rode through the streets I heard flamenco's *compás* within the

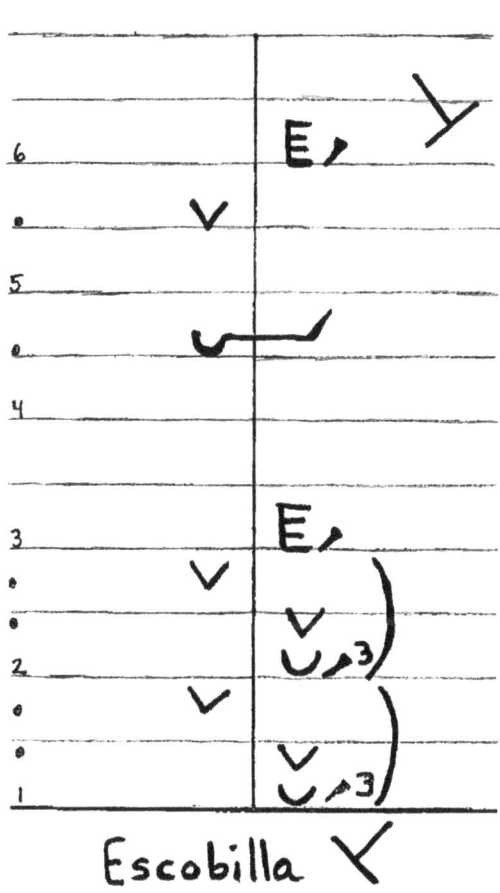

This example shows the first six counts of the footwork section (*escobilla*) of a dance called the *alegrías*. With counts on the left, the placement of footwork symbols to the right or left of a central footwork line indicates whether the right or left foot performs each action. Reading from the bottom to the top, you begin facing the right forward diagonal. Using the right foot, the sequence ball (*planta*), heel (*tacon*), and left heel (*tacon*) is performed twice, ending with a full-foot strike (*plano*) of the right foot on count 3. Then crossing in front of the right foot, the ball of the left foot (*planta*) lands on the "and" after count 4, and the left heel (*tacon*) drops on the "and" after count 5. The 6-count phrase ends facing the left forward diagonal with a full-foot strike of the right foot (*plano*) on count 6. With just five primary flamenco footwork actions, it is actually much easier to write or read the notation of this movement sequence than it is to describe it in words.

driving, repetitive sound of the horses' hooves. In my travel journal I wrote that "one of the best parts of the trip for me was the sound of the horses' hooves against the stone street—an even beat that invited *palmas*, the clapping of the rhythms we'd been dancing to all day!" (Landborn 1989–99).

I now recognize in this early experience the phenomenon that in the flamenco tradition is known as *soniquete*. *Soniquete* is essential to the flamenco arts and is understood and explained differently by different people. For me, *soniquete* is a person's inner containment of the musical experience, so that a dancer is dancing to an inner experience of music, or a singer is hearing the song internally even as he or she sings it. *Soniquete* is a pattern of musical experience laid down in the interior imaginative space of a person's mind, and aesthetic pleasure results when an externalized expression matches this internal memory or pattern. *Soniquete* is experienced when, after a day of intensive flamenco practice, the musical sounds of flamenco are still resounding so strongly inside one's mind that one involuntarily hears flamenco's musical patterns in the most innocuous, banal music being played at the mall.

Early the next morning, across the street from the famous Mezquita,[4] I walked by carriage drivers who were grooming and singing directly to their horses, improvising humorous flamenco songs, verses of affection and praise for being such a fine horse. Through this experience of cultural immersion I realized that flamenco dance was not just an interesting and challenging new dance style for me to explore. Rather, it was an integral part of a larger cultural context, embodying an aesthetic sensibility that permeates an entire way of living. These breakthrough experiences, "Aha!" moments, occurred as a result of a confluence of motion, rhythm, music, song, and words, and explain why so many flamencologists describe flamenco as a way of life.[5]

Similar moments of discovery revealed the intrinsic importance of bullfighting within the Spanish worldview and as a way of life. A note from my travel journal recorded one such experience I had in 1999 while visiting Madrid:

> Came out of my *hostal* on a very rainy, cold (5 degrees centigrade), miserable afternoon and began walking down Atocha. Within just a few blocks there was some commotion. There were about 6 or 7 street cleaners, wearing bright yellow rain jackets and pushing green handcarts, producing a very visual effect. They were engaged via *jaleo* with an older rough-looking character, who, despite the cold and wet, had taken off his jacket to use it as a cape as he demonstrated his *toreando* skills for their entertainment. This went on for quite a while and he seemed pretty good, *verónicas* [basic two-handed passes] and behind-the-back passes of the cape, with lots of vocalizations, the street cleaners encouraging him, while he encouraged the invisible bull. Passersby seemed to ignore or side-

step him as if he were drunk. He was definitely making a spectacle out of himself, but didn't seem drunk exactly—drunk on the moment perhaps, and the attention [Landborn 1989-99].

Absorbing this unexpected scene, I gained new perspectives regarding the competitive play behaviors of working-class Spanish men. I saw that bullfighting, as a male-identified activity, brought Spanish males together in both competition and encouragement. I saw the influence of rural values being exerted within the modern, cosmopolitan context of Madrid. I saw that the qualities of emotional catharsis and participation were not always limited to the hours between midnight and dawn. That period of the night, the *madrugada*, is a temporal construct in the flamenco way of life that invites self-expression and excess. But the expansive spirit of the *madrugada* extends beyond the flamenco *juerga*, affecting all kinds of performative practices, including this duel between a would-be bullfighter and his imaginary bull.

In Spain, I was seeking esoteric knowledge regarding the role of bullfighting movements within the flamenco dance practice, but whether knowledge is considered esoteric or exoteric depends in part on one's relationship to the cultural context. "The principle that, to understand a culture, exoteric information is as important as esoteric—that what is of common knowledge is as significant as what is held secret—was enunciated many years ago. But the challenge to uncover what is secret is hard to resist, and the value of the commonplace has only recently come to be recognized" (Herskovits 1964, 75). Flamenco dance functions within a high-context system consisting of all the flamenco arts: singing, dancing, guitar playing, and other activities that directly support a flamenco performance. To gain sufficient knowledge to perform, choreograph, and teach flamenco dance, I needed to experience flamenco dance as a cultural practice; I needed direct contact with the sociocultural surround of Andalusian Spain, home to flamenco's more indigenous performers. After living in Madrid, and visiting Andalusia where flamenco and bullfighting exert their influence on everyday life, the information I sought no longer seemed esoteric. In Jerez de la Frontera, I found that what other Anglo-Americans back home considered to be my odd esoteric interest in bullfighting and flamenco dance was actually a common subject of conversation for local residents.

Repatterning my movement in order to embody the flamenco dance style entailed much more than changing habitual neuromuscular patterns; embodying the dance of another culture changed my somatic reality. Over a lifetime of experience I have woven a deep somatic reality that is my familiar home base. Multiple strands contribute to the weaving of this deep reality, each strand reflecting some aspect of the cultural assumptions, values, and motivations I absorbed on the way to adulthood. Culture has woven my body over time—and my body's next somatic transformation as I learn the movement patterns of bullfighting promises to be a complex process, dense with cultural significance.

Chapter Seven

Gaining the Emic Edge

Arriving in Madrid, Spain, in 1991, I took flamenco dance classes daily in order to learn to perform flamenco style movements more authentically. However, to perform flamenco dance with credible technique and style wasn't enough; I wanted to improve my accent within the flamenco genre. I call this acculturative learning process "gaining the emic edge." Kealiinohomoku points out that "dance languages, in analogy with spoken languages, display dialects, ideolects, and code switching" (1976, 330).[1] I needed to learn more about the indigenous roots of flamenco in order to better understand certain elusive movement patterns in the flamenco dance vocabulary. Some culturally patterned movements have their kinetic roots in the real-life concerns and lived realities of the agricultural lifestyle concerned with breeding and cultivating Spain's fighting bulls. Seeing that this was an important influence within the flamenco arts, I decided to develop a more authentic flamenco dance dialect by learning more about the movement vocabulary of bullfighting and the cultural dynamics surrounding its practice.

I was delighted when an opportunity arose for me to study bullfighting movement with Jaime, a professional matador from Colombia.[2] Jaime and I would meet once a week for bullfight movement training and practice with the *capote*, the large, stiff canvas cape (fuchsia on one side and bright yellow on the other) that is used by toreros during the initial stages of a bullfight. To the park where we met, Jaime would bring the horns of a bull that had been specially mounted for use during practice sessions for simulating the behavior and movements of a charging bull.

I was surprised when my first movement training session in bullfighting techniques began with an extensive introduction to the mental preoccupations of the matador, namely, bulls and their movement behavior. That was a good lesson. In the end, the glamour, public acclaim, high fees, and elegant suit of lights[3] that a matador wears are superficial accouterments; the primary focus of the matador is always the bull. Bullfighting motivates human beings to understand the sensory perceptions, motivations, and behaviors of a nonhuman animal, the bull. In Spanish and Andalusian culture, knowledge of bulls is highly valued; children play together by taking turns being the bull and the matador. Imagery of conflict is implicit within the playful *toreando* of childhood, although the lighthearted dynamic of play can quickly transform into the serious dynamic of violent conflict in response to situation and circumstance (Joseph Meeker, pers. comm. 2005). A child's early mimetic adventuring into the terrain of bullfighting may remain innocent. The elements of conflict, risk, and violence become more overt when bullfighting play behavior continues into adulthood and involves actual interaction with bulls. Eventually, at the professional level, *toreando* displays discipline, technical proficiency, and aesthetic judgment. The matador's aim is domination of the bull and mastery of the art.

My practice sessions with Jaime often involved learning highly formulated (choreographed) technical maneuvers, yet he always acknowledged the fundamental improvisational nature of the bullfight. Despite the efforts of matadors to understand bull behaviors, the fact remains that bulls are fundamentally unpredictable. Matadors make every effort to note each animal's behavioral habits, yet it is widely understood that any patterns noticed through such observations are subject to change without notice based on the whim of each individual bull or its response to changing conditions.

The tension between predictable and unpredictable behavior is thus fundamental to bullfighting, and is also a key aesthetic value that plays out within all of the flamenco arts. The unpredictable behavior of the bull and the situational uncertainties of the bullfight are prototypes of the unpredictability of flamenco artists and the improvisational opportunities that open up in performance situations. A fundamental tension exists in flamenco performance between two contradictory imperatives, performing within the constraints of the tradition's formal patterns (the civilizing influence of human society) and the improvisational impulse (the wildness of the bull).

Spain

At my first lesson, Jaime was immediately delighted by those postural and stylistic attributes of my movement that I knew had come from my training in flamenco dance. The strongly held upright posture in a flamenco dancer's torso, the Laban term for which is *vertical stress*, gives physical expression to Spanish cultural values of innate human nobility and pride of self. The chest is held high in flamenco dance and this posture is also valued in bullfighting. The term *contoneo* signifies a proud manner of walking often seen in flamenco dance that is also performed by toreros as they parade or circle the bullfight arena in triumph after a successful bullfight.

While a dictionary definition of *contoneo* might reduce its meaning to a strut or a parade, the fact is that any act of walking embodies distinct culturally patterned meanings and associations. The "undulating, graceful walk of the Balinese ... is not just a distinctive trait: it incorporates values and assumptions about how the world functions; it embodies a coherent complex of knowing and being" (Knox 1992, 120). A similarly rich and distinctive quality imbues the habituated vertical posture and *contoneo* of the matador and the flamenco dancer. In performance, flamenco dancers often circle the stage performing a *contoneo*-like walk with chests held high and a strong focus toward the audience. In bullfighting, the vertical uprightness of the torso is in direct conflict with a pragmatic need to focus the eyes downward in order to keep one's eyes on the bull as it passes by. As a result of these two contradictory movement patterns, matadors often maintain an upright posture and lifted chest while the chin is tucked downward; this posture, which is emblematic of bullfighting, is a posture seen in many photos of matadors. However, the posture is also easily spotted in the flamenco dance style.

Flamenco dance patterns often employ a dramatic stylization that creates a sense of maintained tension between the center of the body (especially the pelvis) and an area at the very edge of a dancer's range of movement. Laban Movement Analysis identifies this phenomenon as *peripheral spatial tension*. As a term, *spatial tension* refers to the body's organization of muscular tensions in relationship to the volume of space around the body known as the *kinesphere* (movement sphere). "The normal reach of our limbs, when they stretch away from our body without changing stance, determines the natural boundaries of the personal space or 'kinesphere' in which we move. This kinesphere remains constant in relation to the body even when we move away from the original stance; it travels with the body in the general space" (Laban [1950] 1971, 38). Peripheral spatial tension occurs when *countertensions* (opposing tensions) within the body and its movement are organized to draw attention to the distance between the center and edge of a person's kinesphere.[4]

Flamenco dance training prepared me, as a matter of habituated response, to stylize my movements with peripheral spatial tension. And this was an aspect of my movement that seemed to coincide with Jaime's idea of how a matador should move. As I practiced the movements of bullfighting I realized that what I had thought was simply a flamenco dance stylization, peripheral spatial tension, was actually intrinsic to the matador's motivations in the bullfight. Those who *torear*, who play with bulls, are always highly aware of the precise distance between the core of their own body and the sharp horns of the bull passing through their kinesphere. Being able to assess that distance accurately in the midst of the action of a bullfight is vital to a matador's well-being. After all, the safest way to share one's kinesphere with a bull, even momentarily, is to maintain a certain distance as the bull passes by.

In many ways peripheral spatial tension is deeply emblematic of the matador's overall predicament. To publicly demonstrate courage, a matador must lead the bull to pass close by the body's center; yet to survive the *corrida*, a matador must not allow the bull to entirely bridge that short distance and make contact with the body's vulnerable core. The matador is caught between the aesthetic exigencies of pleasing the public (by drawing the bull near) and the dire necessity of evading death (by maintaining distance). It is within those bounds that matadors strive to craft an aesthetically admirable performance. Thus, the movement theme of distance between the body's center and edge is created, noticed, established, maintained, guarded, and asserted as a function of artistry, technical mastery, and as a matter of life and death. Both functional and aesthetic in the bullring, this theme is reiterated within the flamenco style as a dancer holds her flamenco skirt tautly away from her body. Without the quality of peripheral spatial tension, the movements of her skirt will fall short of flamenco's aesthetic expectations. Many flamenco dance arm gestures are also performed with peripheral spatial tension and are often combined with a lean of the pelvis and eye focused downward in mimetic tribute to the matador's ritualized dance with the bull.

The *capote* swirls around the upright, ver-

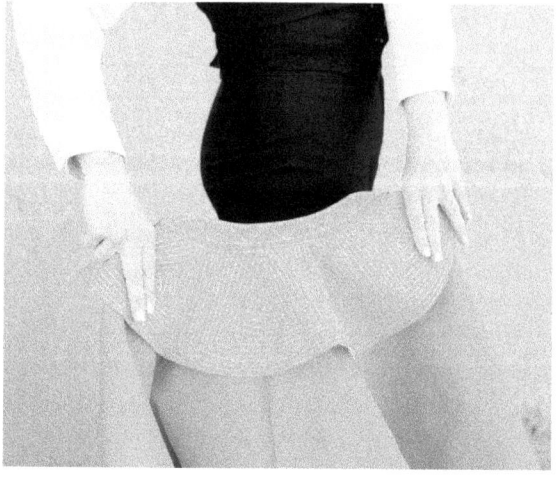

A matador initially grasps the *capote* by pinching its stiff, heavy canvas fabric between two fingers, the index and middle finger, and his thumb. His next action (seen in the next two photographs) is an outward rotation of the wrists, which further strengthens and stabilizes his grasp. Controlling the movement of the *capote* and *muleta* is of vital concern for *toreros*, and they aim for both technical and aesthetic perfection as they practice these skills (photograph by Melissa Lind).

tical line of the matador's body, creating a spiraling movement. Given the size and weight (about ten pounds) of the *capote*, learning to maneuver it reliably requires both dexterity and strength, especially in the forearms and wrists. The key to controlling the movements of the *capote* begins with the unique way in which the matador grips the center of the *capote* on either side of the collar. Gripping with the fingers on the fuchsia side and the thumbs on the yellow side of the *capote*, both hands rotate outward, which creates tension between the two hands and a straight line through the collar of the *capote*. Maintaining the tension of that straight line is key to maintaining control over the movements of the *capote*—and maintaining control over the movements of the *capote* is a first step toward gaining control over the bull.

Learning to hold the *capote* with this technique, I recognized that I had performed similar movements during my flamenco dance class. My teacher, Carmela Greco, taught an arm exercise in which the arms moved in tandem, circling in the vertical plane while maintaining a set distance between the hands. Each time the arms reversed direction, the hands pinched as if taking hold of the *capote* and the wrists rotated outwardly; it was as if Carmela Greco's arm exercise had been designed to reinforce that key movement pattern on which the matador's life depends. This arm exercise was performed with peripheral spatial tension, vertical stress in the torso, and with one's focus tracking the hands as they circled. The entire constellation of movements was performed with dramatic intensity, as if a bull were passing close by.

Once I felt the direct connection between flamenco and bullfighting demonstrated in this arm exercise, I began to notice many similar phenomena in the movement vocabulary of flamenco dance, particularly a recurring movement pattern in which both arms move through space, simultaneously and in tandem, the distance between the hands never varying. This unusual movement pattern occurs quite often in the flamenco dance vocabulary and correlates to the maintained distance between the torero's arms as they move the *capote* through the torero's kinesphere.[5]

The torero maintains a strong grip on the *capote* using a simultaneous outward rotation of his wrists. Wrist rotations in the flamenco dance style generally emphasize symmetrical outward or inward motions; it is less common, for instance, for a flamenco dancer to simultaneously rotate one wrist outward as the other wrist rotates inward. While the pattern of both arms moving in tandem is highly dynamic and destabilizing, this simultaneous, symmetrical outward or inward rotation of the wrists has a stabilizing effect on a dancer's body. These types of movement correlations between flamenco dance and bullfighting are numerous, and while sometimes they are deliberate and overt, at other times they occur as subtle revelations of a deeper innate correspondence between the two forms.

The manipulation of a dancer's costume and performance props is a common element in many world dance forms. Manipulation of fabric (*capote* or *muleta* by the matador or a skirt or *manton* [shawl] by a dancer) or per-

Author (left) teaches student Rachel Varela (right) proper technique for holding the *capote*; the outward turn of the wrists reinforces one's grasp, providing better control over the movement of the *capote*. As the *capote* moves, the two hands maintain a fixed relationship to one another. By experiencing this action with a *capote*, students acquire kinetic patterning for the common flamenco dance motif of moving both arms in tandem and parallel to one another, and for controlling a flamenco skirt or *manton* (shawl) (photograph by Melissa Lind).

formance props (swords, canes, fans, etc.) constitutes another notable similarity between flamenco dance and bullfighting. When used in dance these items are referred to as body extenders and they become an intrinsic part of the movement phenomenon; in regard to body extenders, "it is difficult simply to restrict embodiment to the living human body" (Strathern 2004, 197). Movement patterns using body extensions are neurologically mapped in the brain, becoming part of the moving person's body image. Props or costumes used in this way have the effect of extending the body's spatial range and increasing the impression of size or dynamic vitality that a body produces when moving. "A person's body image is transformed when he [or she] adds a body extender, because it affects the way the person moves and behaves, despite habituated body postures and movements. Body extenders also tell the other members of the culture something about the person who has added a body extender, and this feeds back to the person's own self image" (Kealiinohomoku 1976, 215).

In bullfighting, the *muleta, capote,* and *espada* (sword) function as body extenders. A spiraling movement in the matador's torso is extended, amplified, and broadcast through the fabric medium of the *capote* or the *muleta,* directing the bull's movement. As a matador prepares to kill the bull, the reach of the matador's arm is extended several feet with the addition of the sword. In flamenco dance, as in many other styles of Spanish dance, body extenders amplify the body's movement through space for dramatic effect and are often manipulated in stylized ways that make reference to the bullfighting practice.

The Bata de Cola

A notable body extender in the female flamenco dance tradition is the long, trailing flamenco dress, the *bata de cola* (dress with a long train; *cola* literally means "tail"). I have performed in a *bata de cola* dress and have taken several flamenco dance technique courses focused on its manipulation, from Adela Clara of San Francisco, California, U.S.A., and Yolanda Heredia of Madrid, Spain. Through these experiences, I became aware of the transformation of self and body image to which Kealiinohomoku refers. The size and weight of the *bata de cola* dress required me to learn new ways of moving. The dress transformed my sense of my own movement limitations and possibilities and added a sense of female power and dignity to my self-image. The experience was paradoxical; the length of the trailing *bata de cola* functioned as an extension, lending a sense of grandeur, drama, weightedness, reserve, importance, dignity, and an expanded sense of presence; and yet the *bata de cola* also created unique restrictions and difficulties. My own *bata de cola* is a very traditional one made in Seville, Spain. Although it is shorter than a full-length *bata de cola*, it weighs about ten pounds (as does my *capote*); weight and trailing length constitute two elements that make dancing in any *bata de cola* a significant technical challenge.

Dancing while wearing the *bata de cola* signifies the female domain[6]; it calls upon a unique range of movement qualities and performer sensibilities associated with femininity and female presence. In performance, one focuses on body movements taking place interior to the dress; this produces an introverted quality that on the cultural level connotes the mysterious interiority of female being. The intimacy of the movement, its subtle and contained character, requires the dancer to be calm, centered, and relaxed. However, within this aura of tranquility, the dancer must be very alert, plan ahead, and think strategically; each artistic movement is also technical and calculated. Reducing one's range of movement and carefully aligning one's center of gravity facilitates the spatial maneuvering of the *bata de cola*, adding to performance effectiveness as well as performer safety. Safety? Yes. Dancers performing in a *bata de cola* risk serious injury. Yolanda Heredia, teaching *bata de cola* techniques, pointed out many hazards; she herself stopped dancing for two years to recover from a bad fall. An improperly performed movement can easily whip the long skirt beneath a dancer with sufficient force to cause a fall; accidentally stepping on the skirt in the midst of a complicated maneuver can produce similarly unfortunate results. Technical prowess and artistry are required in order to perform well in the *bata de cola*; these same abilities are required in the bullring.

CITING, PASSING, AND *REMATE*

Three aspects of dancing with the *bata de cola* that drew my attention were later clarified in the process of studying bullfight movements and manipulating the *muleta* and *capote*. These aspects, also referenced generally within the flamenco dance vocabulary, relate to three phases of a matador's interaction with a bull: (1) citing, or *citación*, meaning to challenge or incite the animal with a simultaneous shout and a quick, strong movement that crosses the boundary, the *jurisdicción* (by infringing upon the animal's territory, this causes the bull to charge); (2) passing, or *pases*, movements of the *capote* or *muleta* during the passing of the bull; and (3) the finish, or *remate*, a technical term used in both the flamenco dance and bullfighting practices, which brings an end to a series of *pases* (Cooney 2005). These three phases typically occur

Seven. Gaining the Emic Edge

(and are reiterated) in a dynamic sequence: citing, a number of passing movements, with a *remate* to bring closure to the sequence.

Practicing the citing action with a *muleta*, I was reminded of flamenco dance movements in which (with quickness, strength, and directness) one moves the *bata de cola* forward. Such an accented movement of fabric, whether of a skirt or a cape, is eye-catching; the fabric demands the attention of the audience. If done with force, it conveys a sense of challenge, an invitation to conflict and confrontation. The adversarial challenge of citing is effective in both bullfighting and flamenco dance. The fabric, whether of the *muleta*, *capote*, or the *bata de cola*, lands with emphasis on territory that is charged with meaning. The cape crosses over into the bull's jurisdiction, inciting him to charge. The *bata de cola* potentially transgresses a similarly invisible virtual boundary between the performer and the audience. The fabric's forward movement may constitute an assertion of the dancer's territory or a challenge or infringement on the audience's territory; either intention may incite audience response.

The second phase of the sequence involves movements with the *muleta* or *capote* called *pases*, with which the matador demonstrates multiple ways of guiding a bull past his body. The swirling weight of the *capote* and the careful attention to angles required for manipulating the *muleta* focus the performer's attention on movements occurring away from the body's center. Performing with the *bata de cola*, I experienced similarly decentering sensations. Wearing a *bata de cola* requires that one dance with constant awareness of the *bata de cola*. One is not dancing alone; instead, there is a sense of another entity within one's kinesphere and one's relationship to this other entity is very often adversarial in quality. While practicing and performing in the *bata de cola* I have often felt as if I were engaged in the passing phase of a sequence of bullfighting movements. Alternately teasing and avoiding, chasing and being chased, such dancing with the *bata de cola* creates and celebrates close calls and the coexistence of danger and artistry.

My technique improved when I experimented with moving as if the *bata de cola* was a bull; the image reinforced several of the key aesthetic attributes within both flamenco dance and bullfighting: tension and countertension, direct sustained focus of the eyes, and spiraling. Dodging the *bata de cola* as if it were the bull, the interior core of my torso moved in a counter direction to evade the dangerous quality sensed at the periphery of my kinesphere. For me, the *bata de cola* represents the presence of a bull, of danger, inside the dancer's territory. These reflections are based on personal experience of dancing while wearing a *bata de cola*, yet such impressions are also observable in the performance of other dancers wearing a *bata de cola*. The image of a bull does not always occur as an overt, conscious, or literal representation in a dance performance. Rather, such a movement reference is often simply implicit at the somatic level of experience. Implicit referencing to the bull locates flamenco dance as a cultural practice within a broad category of play behaviors, mimesis, and the bullfighting ritual itself. Through a performer's imagination and artistic conjuring, and through the empathic comprehension of the audience, the *bata de cola* intermittently transforms into the dynamic presence of a passing bull.

In practice sessions with the *muleta* and *capote*, I gave my attention to the third element of the bullfighting sequence, the *remate*. In flamenco dance, the term *remate* refers to an ending; its performance dynamics can be conclusively abrupt or tantalizingly extended. At the end of a phrase, the *bata de cola*, serving as an extension of the dancer's body, may be the last portion of her form to arrive at an ending position. The *bata de cola* may close a dynamic phrase with a final punctuation, providing the ultimate moment of the *remate*. Similarly, in the bullfight a dynamic last flourish of a cape may provide a sharp *remate* after an exciting series of *pases*.

However, a dancer may also end a phrase by performing a *remate* with slow, smooth, gliding qualities. These qualities draw attention to the clearly defined visual line of fabric trailing against the ground. In the dance, this often occurs with a *bata de cola*. This sustained type of *remate* also occurs in the bullfight when a matador, having judged that a bull is not going to charge again (due to the bull's tiredness after a series of successful *pases* or due to a safe distance between the matador's body and the edge of the bull's territory), safely walks away with a cape trailing dramatically behind him or her. During a *remate*, the cape, especially the larger *capote*, is often maneuvered so as to trail behind the matador in a spiraling form. This theme of sustained trailing and spiraling is commonly performed in flamenco dances that use the *bata de cola* as a body extender.

In a performance, a dancer may designate the audience as the bull and cite them by moving the *bata de cola* toward them in a challenging manner, or a dancer may let the *bata de cola* trail behind with arrogant disdain as a *remate* that ends a dance sequence. A dancer may appear to chase and be chased by a bull passing close to the body's core as the *bata de cola* spirals around her. A dancer's ability to both cite and evade often assumes a seductive quality that is eminently feminine within the Spanish cultural context. As a dancer ends a phrase of movement or an entire dance, the *remate* suggests triumph over adversaries or perhaps the audience. Audience response to the dancer's performance is a result of their enjoyment of the dancer's personal qualities as a performer, but also an indication of their unconscious response to the reiterative enactment through dance of the cultural values inherent in the ritual of the Spanish bullfight.

Signals and Symbols

Within the flamenco practice, many signals are used by performers to indicate shifts or changes in the flow of the performance. These signals may be obvious or barely perceptible nonverbal movements, such as eye contact or a slight nod of the head. Overt signals (such as *llamadas*, "calls," or *desplantes*, calling for a change) form part of the performance vocabulary; they constitute traditional dance movements that both performers and indigenous audience members recognize and interpret as formal signals. A guitarist's rhythmic cadence or a singer's dynamic emphasis within flamenco's traditional musical structures can also constitute recognizable signals.

Teaching at the Amor de Dios dance studio in Madrid in 1985, Merche Esmeralda (right) shows student Rika Hamada (left) the proper technique for holding a *manton*. Holding it as a matador holds a *capote*, a dancer manipulates the fabric of the *manton* to bring the space around her body to life while maintaining strong core support for her arms as they carve through a full range of movement. Holding her skirt the same way, a dancer maintains control over the skirt while using her hands for expressive movement (*maneo*). Functioning as partner or dramatic adversary within the dance, the *manton* creates a sense of volume around a dancer's dynamic moving form (photograph by Elke Stolzenberg).

Symbolic meaning is synthesized through the associative level and elicits an immediate and culturally conditioned response (Campbell 1943, 122). Symbolism within the flamenco dance is less pragmatic and overt (compared to signals); its presence is often a matter of personal interpretation. Such interpretations often reflect a tacit understanding of the symbolism of the bullfight ritual.[7] The performative context is by nature a liminal space of creative imaginings and dark dreams; it is flexible, allowing for many varying interpretations of the symbolic meaning of any bullfight or flamenco dance performance.

A female flamenco dancer's bullfight-like interactions with her *bata de cola* evoke the presence of the bull at a symbolic level. Through the movement qualities and organization of tensions and countertensions within her kinesphere, she uses the *bata de cola* to symbolize the danger and power of the bull. With a slight inclination of the torso or movement of her eyes, the bull's essential presence may be summoned; the bull, as a symbolic entity, is then both expressed and conjured through the act of dancing. Through the symbolic nature of such performances, dancers may assert cultural identity and

Cited by the author (left), student Rachel Varela (right) summons her aggressive bull energy and charges the *capote*. Once having kinetically experimented with the dynamics of passing, students can use that experience to refine their style and incorporate greater strength, speed, playfulness, and dramatic intensity into their performance of flamenco dance movements (photograph by Melissa Lind).

affirm social belonging. Through movement's symbolic power a dancer has not only summoned the bull of the audience's imagination, she has summoned all that the bull, as a cultural icon, may symbolize.

California

Based on his assessment of my natural coordination and flamenco styling, Jaime was immediately eager to have me try my skills with an animal. He earnestly assured me I could do it, explaining it would only be a *tienta*, an informal testing of the bravery of young female calves.[8] Just as earnestly, I assured him that I was only interested in learning the movement, that I had no desire to actually face off with an animal.

On leaving Spain, I began incorporating my first lessons in bullfighting movements into my practice as a teacher and performer in the flamenco dance style. As my somatic and kinesthetic perspectives deepened and stabilized, I began to investigate the topic further. While in Madrid I had focused on learning how to move with the larger cape, the *capote*. Now I began to wonder what new perspectives would emerge from moving with the smaller, red felt cape, the *muleta*. I began to wonder how my perspectives might change if I actually followed Jaime's suggestion to test my abilities by *toreando* with an animal. In 2005 I took the opportunity to find out when I attended a weekend course offered by bullfight aficionado and tauromachy instructor Coleman Cooney at the California Academy of Tauromaquia in San Diego.

The Training

The plan was to practice movement techniques with the *muleta* Friday evening, and then cross the Mexican border on Saturday to attend and participate in a *tienta* being hosted at a Mexican hacienda, a local working ranch. Friday night constituted my first experience training with the *muleta*; about half of the *muleta* is supported by the *palillo* (a wooden dowel-like stick) while the remaining fabric hangs freely. I learned immediately that it takes a great deal of wrist and forearm strength (also dexterity, coordination, and finesse) to control the movements of the *muleta*. One's wrist must rotate in a very specific way to maintain the cape's proper position in relation to the animal as it passes by. Subtle angles of the wrist greatly affect the movement of the body extender, the *muleta*. The slightest change can make a significant difference, resulting in a pass that is successful, problematic, dangerous, or even deadly.

Basic *Pases*

I learned two basic *pases* from Coleman Cooney, the *natural* (natural) and the *redondo* (rounded). The *natural* was simplest to learn; it consists of a simple pass of the hand holding the *muleta* in a forehand position. Using the *natural*, the matador[9] causes the animal to travel a back-and-forth pathway that remains on the same side of the matador. This is performed with either the left or right hand in either forehand or backhand position. The same hand completes both passes, alternating forehand and backhand passes successively, without any need to change one's basic stance or grip on the *muleta*. Each time the animal turns to charge again, its opposite horn will be closest to the matador. Therefore matadors commonly begin by using the *natural* because it allows the matador to note any asymmetry in an individual animal's behavior.

The *redondo* or *toreo en redondo* is a pass that provokes the animal to charge with the same horn toward the matador several times, causing the animal to travel an oval pathway around the matador. Using this technique, the matador must add a pivoting movement with the feet to smoothly turn to face the animal; this is followed by a full rotation at the wrist to repeat the same pass, i.e., a forehand pass several times in a row or backhand pass several times in a row. In performing these movements great value is placed on the technique whereby the arm "runs long," meaning that the arm reaches far beyond a comfortable extension to lead the bull well past the matador's body. This results in a tilt of the entire torso at the hip joints. This technique provides a striking example of the characteristic peripheral spatial tension discussed earlier. Supporting the weight of the *muleta* at this furthest extension creates significant dynamic stress in the body's core.[10]

In order to manipulate the *muleta* appropriately, the *palillo* is held horizontally, level and parallel to the ground. No visible gap should appear between the matador's body and the *muleta* because the animal will sometimes see that gap as a potential target to charge. If there is too large a gap between the matador and the *muleta*, the animal's attention can shift from the cape to the matador. The *palillo* is cocked at an angle that brings the outside edge (the edge farthest from the matador) closer to the animal. This means that it is the outside edge of the *muleta* that first crosses into the animal's territory. This is very important, because the animal is most likely to see and charge whatever first crosses the boundary of its territory. Once the animal's attention is drawn to the outer edge of the cape, its attention must be maintained there for the duration of the pass. This is the basis of a technique that involves the wrist in precise degrees of rotation (gradated throughout the arc of the arm's movement) in order to maintain the proper (and safest) spatial relationship between the *muleta*, animal, and matador.

The *muleta* is also manipulated using the *ayuda* (literally, help), which is a wooden or aluminum sword.[11] The *ayuda* helps support the weight of the *muleta*, which (to the matador) becomes heavier in proportion to the distance it is held away from the body. The *ayuda* is also used to spread the *muleta* out, creating a larger target for the animal and a larger shield for the body of the torero. While the left hand supports the *muleta*, the right hand is free to use the *ayuda*, and a two-handed action results. The *ayuda* is always held in the right hand, so when using the right hand to manipulate the *muleta*, the right hand must support both the *palillo* and the *ayuda*. Stylistic and technical differences therefore apply, depending on whether the *muleta* is being manipulated with the right or left hand.

Applying Techniques with the Animal

When the *muleta* cites to the animal's right side, the animal's left horn will pass closest to the matador, and vice versa. Citing involves a quick, strong, direct action of the *muleta* that crosses into the animal's territory or *jurisdicción*. It is an attention-getting action of the far edge of the *muleta* into the territory of the animal, often accompanied by a verbal challenge to goad the animal to charge the *muleta*. At the same time, the matador widens his or her stance to make a small but important forward weight shift. This step allows the matador to better support the *muleta* away from the body's center of gravity. The animal will charge toward the cape's leading edge and the most visible or *llamativo* (attention-grabbing) movement. So it is important that the *muleta* move quite dramatically. If the weight shift of the matador is too visible or pronounced, the animal could find that quick shift of weight *llamativo* and charge toward the person, not the cape.

Mexico and the Tienta

The scene was remote, a beautiful, mountainous, desert region south of the border town of Tecate, Mexico. We crossed through the town and continued beyond it on a very rough road of dirt and rock. There seemed to be a lot of open dumping of trash beside the roadway, tremendous amounts of garbage and small packs of stray dogs. When we left the hacienda eight hours later, driving on the dirt road as evening fell, we passed about five garbage trucks coming into the area. Poverty. It is always distressing, its scope often overwhelming. Yet I suppose the border town of Tecate may in actuality be considered relatively prosperous; it was certainly bustling with people and commercial enterprise.

During the *tienta*, the *ganadero* (cattle rancher) watched carefully, assessing the performance of his animals in the arena; for breeding purposes, he took notes on the behavioral attributes of his young female calves (*vaquillas*). These notes help him make decisions about the overall fate of these animals. If a *vaquilla* performs bravely, she will be bred to strengthen his herd; if she performs badly, she may be raised and sold for beef. So, as active participants in the *tienta*, we had a responsibility to help each *vaquilla* show her courage and strength to best advantage. I found it fascinating that cattle ranchers make breeding decisions based not only on the animal's character, physical conformation, or demonstration of bravery, but also based on the movement preferences and characteristics of each animal. This implies that, at least in the opinion of the ranchers, movement patterns are genetically transmitted.

In the course of the *tienta*, I counted eighteen men, including about four ranch workers who moved the animals from pen to pen and finally into the arena, and watched the *tienta* proceedings.[12] Until the last moment, I was not sure if I would actually go into the arena to face off with a *vaquilla*. Friday night Coleman Cooney had taught me only the *natural* and *redondo* passes with the *muleta*. Then, on the day of the *tienta*, as we were practicing in the arena before the *vaquillas* were brought in, he began teaching me how to use the *ayuda*. Then, right before I was to go into the arena with the animal, he suggested I switch back to using the *muleta* with one hand. At that, I rebelled. My wrists and forearms were tired and sore, and I felt I needed the extra help of the *ayuda*. Also the detailed and technical nature of the coordination required in the wrists and arms meant that, ideally, the movements would be much practiced and as close to second nature as possible. I didn't want my concern with technical issues to interfere with keeping my attention focused on the *vaquilla*, and Coleman agreed that it might not be best to switch techniques.

Animal Behaviors

These are herd animals. Coleman explained that the cruelest part of the *tienta* occurs when the animal is first separated from the herd, which is very distressing for them. We saw the animals in the corral beforehand. Already frightened as a result of having been brought in from the field and contained in the corral, their response to this fear, since they could not stampede and run away, was to pack themselves together very tightly. They were in constant motion, swarming and repositioning themselves as a group in relationship to perceived threats in the environment. Observing this behavior clarified for me what Coleman had meant about the distress each animal would later feel on finding itself alone in the arena. When an animal charges, it is due to fear and instincts of self-defense. In the arena they can't escape; so they must turn, face, and charge the human beings that enter their territory. Separated from the herd, taunted and harassed, when an animal's *jurisdicción* is infringed upon, its boundaries broken, it will attack.

Beginning from a position near the wall of the arena, I was instructed to incite a *vaquilla* to charge. The animal, seeing a wall, will predictably charge to the side of the matador away from the wall. Later, once the animal is tired and discouraged, it may put its own back to the wall as a defensive strategy. That type of defensive positioning is a strategy that serves the animal well, and matadors generally try to keep the bull/*vaquilla* in the center of the arena and engaged offensively in the conflict. The *ganadero* mentioned that although the three animals that afternoon had never before been in the arena, each quickly recognized as a likely exit a wide, but closed, blue gateway. He shared that his animals often choose to put their backs to the wall right at that blue gateway. This reminded me of the times I have seen the last moments of a bullfight being played out near the inside wall of a bullfight arena.

When an animal first enters the arena, it is angry, upset, and disoriented, and will charge anything that moves. Within a relatively short time the animal settles down and is more selective about charging. Eventually, an animal will tire and may decide not to participate any more. At the *tienta* it was fascinating to witness these two individual animals of different species, the herd animal and the primate, locked in a battle of wills. It was sometimes humorous to witness amateur matadors struggling to get a recalcitrant little calf to charge them.

Observing the *tienta*, some attributes of the social and performative dynamics that affect the behaviors of professional matadors were clarified for me. Matadors enter the public arena seeking to emerge again, alive, triumphant, and with their dignity intact. If a matador does not succeed in exiting the arena alive, the result is tragic; if a matador loses not life itself, but merely dignity, the result may well be comedic. Laughter is a somatic release of tension caused by elements of surprise or incongruity, and situations may occur unexpectedly in either the *tienta* or *corrida* that have significant comic potential. The matador, whether amateur or professional, is attempting to project a dignified, brave demeanor; if the matador has to chase the bull around the arena trying to get it to turn and fight, he or she ends up feeling frustrated and looking pretty foolish.

The *tienta* provides an advantageous context for observing the practice of bullfighting; it clarifies both the actual level of difficulty of tauromachy and the reality of the risks involved. Often professional matadors are so highly skilled that, like professional dancers, they make difficult maneuvers look deceptively easy. The remarkable skill level of professionals is very evident once one observes the contrasting performance of relatively inexperienced matadors. Also, in witnessing the dangers posed to student matadors even by small female calves, one is implicitly reminded of just how dangerous, powerful, and deadly an angry mature bull can be.

The large bull of five to eight years of age in the professional arena is quick to respond to any infringement of his *jurisdicción* and slow to tire. A matador studies each animal for predictable traits and tendencies, but must remain very alert to the animal's potential for unpredictable behavior. In contrast, the *vaquillas* are very brave and will charge fiercely, but, overall, are less sure of themselves. Sometimes a young calf's *jurisdicción* must be crossed several times or crossed very close to her before she will charge. When a *vaquilla* will no longer charge, if a new person comes in to take up the taunting, she will (as if suddenly refreshed) begin to charge again. This was a surprising energy shift to witness. One would think the animal was exhausted, only to see it respond with high energy all over again. Apparently a *vaquilla*, having become mentally tired of a repetitious interaction or frustrated by being unable to connect with her antagonist, is enlivened to fresh effort by the novelty of a new antagonist. The bullfight constitutes a mental and emotional contest based on psychological dynamics between human and animal. Ultimately, a matador dominates the animal by encouraging it to stay on the offensive and offering it fresh opportunities to succeed.

The *Tienta*

During our afternoon experience, two *vaquillas* were tested and approximately ten student matadors took turns testing their skills in the small, informal arena of the hacienda. The *ganadero* is paid by student or apprentice matadors for the opportunity to work with his cattle.[13] One young bull also appeared in the arena with an amateur matador who was preparing for an upcoming public bullfight festival in Tijuana, Mexico. He had paid the *ganadero* to practice the full complement of his skills that day by killing the bull at the end of his engagement with it. This was a longer session, and the other participants served as his *cuadrilla* or *equipo* (his support team of toreros).

We mainly worked with *vaquillas*, but the same basic animal behavior is operative for the older bulls with their greater maturity and power. The informal *tienta* with young animals serves as a prototype of the formal *corrida* with its full-grown bulls. Throughout the afternoon, I was consciously and unconsciously involved in a process of comparing my immediate experience of the *tienta* to my remembered experiences as a witness of professional bullfights in Spain.

I was reminded of the magician's classic technique of misdirection. The animal is made to focus on and charge the *muleta* and, seduced by the movements of the *muleta*, remains blind to the presence of the matador. If for any reason—and this happened repeatedly at the *tienta*—a matador touches the animal, that touch provides the animal with direct tactile knowledge of where its true enemy is located. It is therefore important to avoid direct contact as much as possible. Any touch between human and animal serves as a signal that communicates to the animal exactly where its target is: "Here I am ... right here!" Several times during the *tienta* an animal was able to get the *muleta* away from a student matador. At such a moment a matador is very exposed and vulnerable to attack. However, these young animals generally maintain their attention on the cloth that has been harassing them, often continuing to attack with their horns a *muleta* that has been abandoned on the floor of the arena. Mature bulls (the smart ones) don't do that.

Besides having the opportunity to face a *vaquilla* and try out the two types of passes I had learned, I learned a great deal by watching from behind the barrier, called a *burladero*, a wooden barrier within the arena behind which matadors take shelter from the animal. Members of a matador's *equipo* also emerge quickly from behind the *burladero* if it becomes necessary to distract an animal away from a fallen matador. From my vantage point behind the *burladero*, I could easily see the action and hear the communications taking place between the students of tauromachy and our mentors. From the *burladero* I was coached to identify the movement patterns of the animals. I also observed from the *burladero* the support that toreros provided one another, both through verbal coaching and through their quick action whenever a torero was in danger. Fundamentally, the *tienta* was a competitive situation for aspiring matadors; so it came as no surprise that behind the *burladero* I also heard a few mildly derogatory comments on the knowledge, skill, or performance of other matadors.

There was one *vaquilla* that would pass by the torero nice and straight when her left horn was closest to the matador, but she would consistently lean in close and come up early to catch the matador off guard when she led the attack with her right horn. There was one *vaquilla* that would pass twice, nice and close around the matador, but then, after every third pass she would go in a straight line right past the matador, as if to say, "Enough of that. I'm going somewhere else!" To keep the rhythm of the interaction going the matador had to run after her and try to keep her interested in the contest. Otherwise, he had to reestablish the adversarial connection between matador and animal at each new location in the arena.

There was an eleven-year-old boy who participated very actively in the *tienta*. His father was tutoring him and urging him on. It was quite impressive to see him face off with a female calf because he was very short, even for an eleven-year-old. He was so small that the *vaquilla* constituted a very large adversary for him. However, he clearly had been practicing tauromachy for some time; he performed the movement techniques easily and with style. I was impressed that he seemed so accustomed to the weight of the *muleta*; it didn't seem too heavy for him despite his small size. This young matador demonstrated considerable courage by coming back into the arena despite having been knocked down by a female calf earlier that afternoon.

Language and Gender

My prior experience in flamenco dance contexts made clear that language and gendered behavior patterns can present difficulties in any acculturative learning process, and this was borne out in the context of the *tienta* in Mexico. Language idiom (English or Spanish) affected the extent and efficacy of communication as well as the lines of communication between participants. Although under most circumstances a *tienta* would be conducted in Spanish, this scene was essentially bilingual. The shift to bilingual communication occurred automatically because the primary language of the paying clients was English. To some extent the language used was an indicator of social status. Speaking English well was likely to be interpreted as a sign of education and higher social class; the Mexican men who were the more adept English speakers took the opportunity to demonstrate their bilingual abilities.

My Spanish-language ability was not immediately obvious or known to others. Some, hearing Coleman and others speaking to me in English, probably assumed that I spoke little or no Spanish. This may have reduced their inhibitions around me when speaking Spanish. On the other hand, some men may have been deliberately gaining status with their peers by speaking English with the American woman. My being female surely affected my experience, but I don't know whether I would have been spoken to more often or less often had I been a beginning-level male student.

My videographer, who remained in the viewing stand, is fluent in Spanish and overheard and understood comments made by the observers, the *ganadero* and his friends. Later, she reported to me what they had discussed. I was pleased to hear that they thought I performed well. However, after conceding that there were many very good female matadors, they dismissed the subject, saying, "But they don't count." This perhaps provides insight into the difficulty any woman will have in achieving status within the male-identified domain of bullfighting. Essentially, any bullfight by female *matadora* Cristina Sánchez is automatically discounted; because of her sex, even her most brilliant performance will be seen as occurring outside of the male competition. It therefore does not count.

In her book, *Women and Bullfighting: Gender, Sex, and the Consumption of Tradition*, Sarah Pink discusses many of the attitudes that present difficulties for women aspiring to be professional matadors. The history of early female matadors is limited primarily to the *señoritas toreras*, women whose bullfighting skills gained attention as novelty acts; female participation in bullfighting was then "prohibited in the mid 1930s until 1974" (Pink 1997, 145). Controversy has surrounded the career of Cristina Sánchez, whose goal was to compete professionally on the same level as male matadors. Pink discusses the discourse surrounding the controversy, pointing out that "arguments against women performers tend to concentrate on female physiology and to naturalize gender difference" (57). Traditionalists are likely to see femaleness as innately inappropriate for bullfighting. Pink reviews these arguments, noting that "the female body has been considered unsuitable for bullfighting in terms of the composition, 'functions' and 'experience' of a woman's body" (57).

Cristina Sánchez has had a remarkable career. She won "the 'best student' competition at the Madrid Bullfighting School, which by implication proved her superiority to her male contemporaries" (Pink 1997, 118). Prior to attaining the rank of a *matador de toros*, Sánchez fought professionally as a *novillera*, and "maintained her position amongst the top ten *novilleros*" (120).[14] Despite her talents, she encountered much resistance. Pink describes Sánchez' response to one such difficulty.

> Some men oppose the incorporation of women into mainstream bullfighting and in 1993 several leading novilleros refused to perform with Cristina Sánchez. Subsequent to Pedrito de Portugal's publicized rejection of a contract to perform with Cristina, it was announced that she would undertake a single-handed performance to kill all six bulls herself. Some informants complimented Cristina's bravery. Not only did she defy her competitor's scorn, but two hours of continuous performance with six bulls is a tiring and difficult feat, which was taken by some informants as evidence that Cristina was more than worthy of sharing the ring with a man performer [146].

Pink outlines many of the critiques and dismissive responses that Sánchez continued to encounter throughout her career. "Reviews of Cristina were positive. Some traditionalist informants shrugged off this detail, remarking that it would be too unkind to print the cruel truth about the low quality of a woman's performance" (1997, 118–119). Describing a response similar to the one that my videographer had reported to me, Pink mentions that "it was conceded that she [Sánchez] displayed bravery of different types, but often the granting of such a quality was tempered by the qualification that it still was not 'the same' as seeing a male bullfighter perform" (119).

An outstanding performance by a female within the male domain of bullfighting intensifies the stakes for male matadors. It increases the potential for social humiliation and professional or economic loss. A male matador

Spanish female matador Cristina Sánchez de Pablos is seen here engaging with a bull in the *faena de muleta* (the final act of the bullfight). Cristina Sánchez was born in 1972, debuted as a professional matador in Madrid in 1993, and retired in 1999. She was one of the first professional female matadors to gain significant fame and recognition. The bull follows the movement of the *muleta*, lowering its head while passing. This is due to the bull's instinctual fighting strategy, which is to come from underneath with its horns and use its powerful neck muscles to completely upend and throw its adversary (Raúl Gordon Blasini/ WikiCommons).

would not want to risk public exposure or ridicule should his own performance fall short of the performance given by a female *matadora* in the same arena on the same afternoon. Thus, the more talented the female *matadora* is, the fewer men will want to risk appearing in the arena with her.

By way of contrast, I was not perceived as a serious competitor in relation to the male competition at the *tienta*. In fact, my role as a beginner signaled to other participants that I would welcome any sharing of their expertise and experience. As an outsider, a beginner, and an American woman, I was in an advantageous position at the *tienta*; I understood most of what was being said, whether in English or Spanish, and was in a good position to observe the social dynamics and relationships between the participating male matadors.

Human Interactions

Relationships between the men participating in the *tienta* were ambiguous. The toreros served a supportive role as members of the amateur matador's *cuadrilla*, but most were also aspiring matadors themselves. They were in competition with each other. Thus, more than once, a man would provide encouragement, praise, or advice to another student matador, later making disparaging remarks outside his hearing. While this dynamic of competition is intrinsic at the nonprofessional level, it could occur between a professional matador and his or her *cuadrilla*. However, the team that a matador works with professionally is made up of individuals that the matador has chosen, is paying well, and is trusting with his or her life. Members of the *cuadrilla*, the picador, *banderillero*, and other assistants, are professional specialists.[15] They may also serve the matador as advisors, bringing with them many years of experience and knowledge of animal behavior and tauromachy techniques.

From my position as an active participant-researcher, I came to understand movement technique, the dynamics of confrontation between animals and human beings, and the spatial relationships and movement attributes that are key to a matador's strategizing. As a beginning student I was offered a great deal of advice and information throughout the afternoon. This support came not just from my instructor, Coleman Cooney, but from nearly all of the participants. Standing in the *burladero*, I was able to observe the animal-human interactions of the bullfight from the ground level and up close for the first time. Prior to this *tienta*, I had only observed bullfights and *tientas* from the safer distance of the viewing stands. Now, I was watching with a sense of immediacy and heightened attention, knowing that my turn would come next.

My Experience in the Arena

I was probably in the arena *toreando* with a *vaquilla* for only about fifteen to twenty minutes. That is my best estimate, because my sense of time was affected by the intensity of attention required. Despite the brevity of the experience, I did learn several key things. I learned that if I did the simple techniques I had practiced, they were remarkably effective. I remember being a little surprised that the tauromachy techniques actually worked, that the *vaquilla* did (on the whole) follow the *muleta* as promised. But the *vaquilla* was not completely predictable in her response either. I was glad not to be tossed or tumbled by her. But, even in that short session, I had the experience of being launched into improvisation and raggedly trying to find my way back to the technique of the *muleta*, which for me was still a barely known movement vocabulary.

At the *tienta* I saw that improvisational practice itself constitutes another correlation between flamenco dance and bullfighting, affecting both practices at the levels of technique, aesthetics, and philosophy. I gained a tactile sense of the calf's force and power during a few moments when she made contact with me. Although the contact was minor and fleeting, I found it significant as somatic information. When the *vaquilla* did not follow the motion of my *muleta* as expected, there seemed to be time enough to question my technique, to self-assess, and reassess, even in the midst of responding to out-of-control events. This aspect of performance, the play and tension between the known and unknown, between technique and improvisation, constitutes an important similarity between flamenco dance and bullfighting practices.

When I faced off with the *vaquilla* I seemed to perceive her differently than the male students did. They seemed to perceive the *vaquilla* as an inferior bull, a step down from the real thing. More than once I heard a student matador refer to the female calf as "he," as if in the male student's mind the *vaquilla* was a stand-in for the bull, a mock bull, a symbol of what the male student matador was preparing to fight someday. They seemed afraid of the *vaquilla*. Strangely, I was afraid of physical injury, but somehow I was not afraid of the calf herself. I admired and appreciated her; I was proud of her for protecting herself by charging us humans when we crossed into her *jurisdicción*. I felt a sense of solidarity with the *vaquilla*, even as I deliberately challenged her to charge toward me.

Even my short interaction with the *vaquilla* was energetically and emotionally draining. I felt we both performed well. The *vaquilla* bravely charged me again and again. I met her face-to-face, extending the *muleta* into her *jurisdicción* and inviting her charges. I was not knocked down by her; neither was I harmed or humiliated. As a result of this embodied learning, I have greater appreciation of the intense challenges that professional matadors face in the bullring when engaged in conflict with a full-sized bull.

The embodied experiences that I gained by participating in the context of actual conflict drew my attention to the contrast between planned and impromptu actions. Both occur in the bullfight context, but are equally important in the flamenco dance context. The improvisational mode is synonymous with creativity; it results in innovations that enrich movement traditions. Improvisation engages a performer deeply in the performative moment where performance entails real consequences. Balancing between practiced techniques and improvisational responses presents challenges in both performance contexts.

Human and Animal Interactions

One human-animal interaction I witnessed that afternoon especially drew my attention. An experienced young Mexican torero was there with his *capote*. He had come to help out with the *tienta* in general, and especially with the amateur matador fighting the young bull. He was quite adept, at home in the arena and around the animals. I never had occasion to speak to him directly, but I heard others speaking about him. They said that he was quite good, but that "unfortunately" he didn't like dealing with the larger animals. By saying that he did not like to fight full-sized animals, they meant he would not use his skill to fight or kill a bull. This was accepted, but it seemed to reflect poorly on his courage or lower his status.

At one point, a *vaquilla* had her back to the wall; she was left in that position while a student matador recovered by getting advice, resting, and drinking some water. Meanwhile, I observed the young Mexican torero's interaction with the *vaquilla*. He squatted, leaning against the wall of the arena about ten feet from her. She looked at him, assessing him as a threat. His presence kept her from running to the other side of the arena; he was purposefully keeping her in position until the return of the student matador. The young Mexican torero spoke to the *vaquilla* calmly and encouragingly; his tranquil affect and actions expressed kindness and appreciation of her predicament and distress. The sense of empathy he demonstrated is an important aspect of the indigenous realities of the ranching business. Despite the fact that the bullfight is a bloodsport, a love of animals is often present for many of those who participate in these practices. This signifies a level of ambivalence, complexity, and ambiguity that a casual observer of a public bullfight might not suspect.

After the *Tienta*

Wrist strength is fundamental to the ability to manipulate the *muleta*, and after the physical exertions of participating in the *tienta*, my forearms were very sore. Technical form is important, but timing is also a significant factor. The matador coordinates the movement of the *muleta*, responding to the movement and speed of the charging animal. The line that the body creates when extending the arm (Coleman Cooney called it "running the arm long") has acquired aesthetic value for matadors themselves as well as for the bullfighting public. It challenges a matador's postural strength and placement, producing an exaggerated tension and distance between the arm and the pelvis, producing the peripheral spatial tension and arc-like configuration of the body that are iconic of bullfighting.

Studio Work

I took my *tienta* experiences into the dance studio for further practice, examination, and reflection. In the studio I could choose between bullfighting and flamenco dance movements, examining and comparing them and using a mirror for visual feedback. I examined movement phenomena in greater detail, using etic perspectives from Laban Movement Analysis. New information emerged as I performed movements at slower speeds, repeated movements many times, and could simultaneously perform and observe movements from various angles using dance studio mirrors. Using Laban Movement Analysis, I could identify specific combinations of shape, dynamics, and spatial forms that constitute correlations between the two movement vocabularies.

I practiced each action sequence of the tauromachy techniques I had learned, seeking to reproduce the sought-after quality of smoothness that constitutes an aesthetic value in bullfighting. Emic witnesses interpret this quality of smoothness (in Laban's etic system this would be called sustained flow) as an expression of the control, courage, and unhurried calm of the matador; to them it indicates a matador's self-assurance and ability to dominate the bull. The smoothness of a matador's movement performance with the *muleta* or *capote* has significant pragmatic value in helping to assure the trajectory of the bull's path past the matador. A cape's continuity of motion through space establishes and communicates a spatial direction to the eye of the bull, leading the bull safely past the matador's body. In the hands of an accomplished matador, the *capote* or *muleta* functions as does a prop that manifests a master magician's talent for misdirection and deception; the smoothness of the cape's motion is key.

In the context of bullfighting, synchronization occurs as an interspecies phenomenon. With smoothness, the matador induces the bull to follow the cape's motion exactly. If successful, *temple* (the perfect synchronization of bull and cape) will be achieved, enabling the matador to control the bull. The matador must take his or her timing from the bull, adjusting each tauromachy technique to meet the bull, directly, being to being. Such a heightened sense of attunement to the bull may affect both the artistic success and longevity of a matador.

With studio practice, these patterns became easier and more fluid. Once the newness of a movement pattern wears off, it begins to speak a new language; it begins to speak in a more poetic modality, speaking of human desire and motivation. In the learning phase, my mind's inner dialogue spoke to me in technical directives; it reminded me to hold the *palillo* level, to rotate the wrist gradually throughout the *pase* of the *muleta*, or to "go long" with the arm at the end of the *natural*. Later on, my imagination was activated and my inner dialogue shifted to respond more poetically to my dancing interactions with an imaginary bull.

My movements conjured the bull's presence; he joined me in each studio practice session as the quintessential antagonist, the perfect match for my protagonist self. Whatever fear is mine in life to conquer, whatever battles I need to fight, whatever conflicts in my life are in need of resolution, through my imagination give me the essence and energy of a bull, give me my ideal adversary. Within the performative acts of a dancer, the bull does not function as a generic cultural archetype. The bull's symbolic meaning is fluid: nature, power, threat, fertility, sexuality, the untamable, death. His symbolic resonance is personally constructed and reconstructed in each moment, not only by the performing protagonist, but also in the individual and collective minds of witnesses.

I walk forward slowly, envisioning the bull before me. When, in my imagination, I judge myself to be approaching near the bull's *jurisdicción*, I turn sideways preparing to incite his attack. This quarter turn represents a highly charged moment of decision; it is an action of great import and consequence. While practicing this movement sequence repeatedly in the dance studio, I realized that this very simple movement occurs often and in various forms within the flamenco dance vocabulary. It is simple; facing the audience and maintaining eye contact, a dancer makes a quarter turn so that his or her body now faces to the side. This movement corresponds to that critical moment when the matador decides to cite the bull. It is an invitation to conflict, danger, and the unknown. It is both an outward-directed challenge and an inner acceptance of risk.

The movements of bullfighting and flamenco dance express specific movement ideals that performers try to embody while facing intense challenges. Each movement is a blend of deliberate technique and a performer's response to the lived moment with all of its unknowns, dangers, and surprises. The impromptu, the unexpected, the sporadic dip into poor technique occasioned by the necessity of conflict and danger, are apparent in the bullfight, and similar qualities appear in flamenco dance. A performer's quick response to the exigencies of lived experience within each performance event is highly valued in Spanish and Andalusian culture. Audiences attend flamenco dance performances and bullfights to participate in their performative traditions by bearing witness to a unique human being, both at risk and at play, mastering extreme challenges with artistry.

Chapter Eight

Movement Analysis

Enactments

There are many ways bullfighting movements function in flamenco dance, from direct enactment in theatrical productions to the subtlest of gestures in casual settings. Sometimes openly represented, sometimes deeply buried, bullfighting resonates within flamenco dance, and my analysis of this phenomenon employs a variety of approaches.

Cultural Scripts

Because bullfighting has long been an important aspect of Spanish cultural life, it has been portrayed in many Spanish stage productions. In the contexts of the *zarzuela* (Spanish light opera), classical Spanish dance performances such as those of the Ballet Nacional de España, and other theatrical productions that use flamenco as part of their dance vocabulary, scenes reflecting Spanish cultural life often reiterate a familiar narrative, a cultural script with plot, characters, and outcomes that satisfy cultural expectations. The values of romance and tragedy are united in the bullfight, making it prime material for theatrical reiteration and artistic interpretations. The heroic matador and flamenco femme fatale are basic to the cultural script and normative within Spanish dance narratives.

Sarah Pink points out that "the iconography of the bullfight is centered on the *torero* figure: the individual triumphant masculine hero" (1997, 17). This cultural script strongly reinforces gendered roles. The male protagonist, the matador, is scripted as a tragic hero led into a disastrous or deadly situation by the alluring beauty of a dangerous woman (fiery, exotic, sexually potent).[1] A famous teacher of tauromachy, Manolo Escudero, in the documentary film *The Lady Bullfighter* (Bryer 1989), links the death of bullfighters to their relationships with women, saying, "If you want to know what significance a woman has in bullfighting, I'll tell you.... She's the ruin of the bullfighter." However, the cultural script commonly calls for the negative effects of the femme fatale to be countered by the actions of a good woman. This role of idealized womanhood usually belongs to the matador's saintly mother, long-suffering sister, or faithful sweetheart. Thus, the cultural script facilitates a performative reiteration of Spanish moral values and gender roles.

Bullfighting movements are most overtly present when the theatrical story line entails the enactment of a bullfight scene. The inclusion of bullfight enactments within Spanish and flamenco dance performances has a long history, beginning with the *cafés cantantes* of the nineteenth century and extending into present-day dance theater productions. Álvarez Caballero states that the female dancer Manuela Valle performed the first known example of *mimetismo taurino* (mimed bullfighting) in 1874 at the theater Bretón de Cádiz (1997, 88). Since then numerous male and female dancers have developed successful performances based on this popular cultural theme: Trinidad Huertas ("La Cuenca"), Salud Rodriguez ("Hija del Ciego"), Juan Sánchez ("El Estampío"), Vicente Escudero, and many others (Álvarez Caballero 1998; Puig Claramunt 1977). Over time such performances have provided opportunities for bullfighting movements to influence the flamenco dance style and become codified within Spanish classical dance traditions.

In 1910 Antonia Mercé, "La Argentina," first danced a solo work titled *La corrida* which became a popular standard in her repertory. In her biography of La Argentina, dance historian Ninotchka Bennahum writes that in *La corrida*, "Argentina dressed as a woman while playing the dual male roles of the matador and the bull: the conqueror and the victim of her own kill" (2000, 114). *La corrida* was considered a signature work of La Argentina, who was still performing this solo in 1934 (111). While *La corrida* was a short solo work, only about five minutes in length (113), the cultural script of the bullfight has also inspired full-length dance productions.

Through all such performances the links between flamenco and bullfighting are impressed upon the public imagination, and the trope of flamenco and bullfighting as a cultural complex is reinforced in Spanish popular culture. One modern example is provided by dancer/choreographer Antonio Canales, who in 1993 premiered his full-length story ballet in the flamenco dance style titled *Torero*. This work followed the Spanish cultural script faithfully; its cast included the matador (a role danced by Canales himself), the matador's assistants, toreros and picadors (who support the matador in the bullfight arena), the matador's mother and girlfriend (who worry and pray for him), a female crowd of admirers (who celebrate his successes with amoral abandon), and, last but not least, the matador's fierce antagonist in the arena, the bull. *Torero*, listed in my audiovisual references, provides numerous exam-

Eight. Movement Analysis 193

The renowned flamenco dance teacher Ciro Diezhandino Nieto, known as Ciro, is shown (second figure from the left) in rehearsal at the dance studio Nachos in Madrid, Spain. In 1982, Ciro mounted his ballet, *Torero*, which was based on the García Lorca poem *Llanto para la muerte de Ignacio Sánchez Mejías*, for Dalia Low. Dancers for the production of *Torero* were: Dalia Low, Joaquín Ruíz, Javier Barón, and Miguel Ángel. The dancers, seen rehearsing (identities unknown), follow Ciro closely as he demonstrates how a torero holds the *capote* as a shield that hides his body from the bull. Whether functioning as a body extender that expands a dancer or matador's kinesphere or as a transitional object to turn aside the threat of a real or imaginary bull, the dynamic movement of a *capote* adds visual drama both onstage and in the arena (photograph by Elke Stolzenberg).

ples of direct referencing and overlap between flamenco dance and bullfighting practices (Canales 2002).[2]

MOVEMENT QUOTATIONS

The public's recognition and appreciation of bullfighting movements influence choreographers and performers to incorporate movement quotations and gestures into dance sequences even when the theatrical narrative does not directly call for it. As a result, like a spice, the flavor of the bullfight is peppered throughout many flamenco dance performances. Formal and informal acts of *toreando* are pervasive within Spanish and Andalusian culture, and were even more prevalent in past eras. Choreographic and other theatrical productions reiterate *toreando* and bullfighting as normative behaviors, and by doing so satisfy the Spanish audience's appetite for nostalgia, romance, and drama. Over time, many stylized dance movements incorporating bullfighting movements have been codified into the repertory and pedagogy of the Spanish classical dance tradition and the *zarzuela* (Spanish light opera).

In *The Language of Spanish Dance*, dance scholar Matteo Marcellus Vittucci (known as "Matteo") describes the *paso de muleta*, a step from the ending of a woman's solo performed in the late 1800s (Matteo with Goya 1990, 165). The *paso de muleta* used an actual *muleta* and sword as props to enact the bullfight within a dance. Through its use of the *muleta*, the dance established the *faena*, the last and most dangerous portion of the bullfight, as its context. Matteo credits a particular dance, *El vito*, as having included the *paso de muleta* (165). The *paso de muleta* was likely performed by early *cafés cantantes* performers, such as Manuela Valle, Trinidad Huertas, and Salud Rodriguez.

Other examples of dance movements directly associated with the bullfight are forceful lunging movements known as *estocadas* (Matteo with Goya 1990, 83). An *estocada* in the context of bullfighting is the final sword thrust that kills the bull. This type of dance movement is associated with a particularly intense moment in the drama of the *corrida*, a moment when the matador's skill and courage are supremely tested and the matador's life is at greatest risk. When performed as a dance step, lunging in the forward direction, an *estocada* is called a *paso de caida* (falling step). In the *paso de caida*, a dancer lunges forward dramatically, touching one knee down to the floor. Matteo points out that this step is "typical of a farruca," a dance form traditionally performed by male dancers (158). When performed to the side, an *estocada* is called a *careo*; the term comes from *cara* (face) and signifies a side-lunging pattern that allows partners to pass close by one another face-to-face while maintaining eye contact (51).

The *vuelta torera* (bullfighter turn) is a flamenco turn generally performed by male dancers. Both the name and shape of this dance step constitute direct references to the art of the bullfight. The *vuelta torera* is a simple turn employing a parallel position of the feet. Simultaneous with the turn, the upper body spirals and the arms move as if manipulating a cape. It is this upper body elaboration combined with the lower body's position of stability that gives the turn its bullfighting flavor (Matteo with Goya 1990, 263–264).

These dance examples quote directly from the bullfight movement

Eight. Movement Analysis 195

Ciro (second figure from the left), in rehearsal at the dance studio Nachos in Madrid, Spain, is preparing dancers (identities unknown) for a performance of his ballet *Torero*. Looking diagonally back and down over his shoulder at the trailing *capote*, Ciro evokes the moment in the bullfight known as a *remate*. A *remate* occurs when a matador ends a dynamic series of passes of the cape, assesses the aggressive energy of the bull, and then deliberately walks away from the bull with the *capote* trailing behind him. The matador's torso spirals and the feeling is one of dramatic suspense, as no one, including the matador, knows if the bull will charge unexpectedly (photograph by Elke Stolzenberg).

vocabulary, providing evidence of movement correlations between flamenco dance and bullfighting. However, flamenco dance does not only mimic bullfighting or borrow the matador's vocabulary for dramatic effect. Rather, a deeper source of movement intentions, impulses, and responses connect the cultural practices of bullfighting and flamenco dance. These movement correlations are rooted in a deeper layer of somatic experience and culture. Movement provides evidence of the culture that shapes it. Culturally inscribed attitudes, habits, and beliefs are expressed, both consciously and unconsciously, through human movement phenomena. The resultant movement patterns expose the interface between the actual behaviors of a cultural group and their shared cultural ethos, worldview, or cosmology.

The adrenaline-filled fighting context in which a matador attempts to dominate the phenomenal natural power of a bull is deeply understood and appreciated in the flamenco community and the wider Spanish culture. The life-and-death intensity that is integral to the bullfight is celebrated through flamenco dance and comes to imbue it with a similar intensity. The metaphors flow both ways between these two arts: *toreo* is valued for its dancelike beauty, and flamenco dance is appreciated for its *toreo*-like sensibilities and moments of *toreando*. Evelina Fabregas addresses this point in a film documenting her own bullfighting career, *The Lady Bullfighter*, saying, "A bullfight is a battle between the strength of the animal and the intelligence of the man [or woman]. They become a pair, and fighting together they perform a dance." Similar thoughts are expressed by flamencologist González Climent, who notes that there are moments when bullfight movements inspire handclapping in the flamenco style and "make us question the distinction between dances that appear to fight bulls and bullfighting that dances" (1964, 268).[3]

Theoretical Perspectives

Metonymy

The function of metonymy in language provides a useful analogy for considering the unconscious communication of cultural meaning through dance and movement phenomena. A *metonym* is the signifying word used in a figure of speech that, though it is only an attribute of something, is used to stand in for the thing itself, as, for example, when the word *brass*, a reference to brass buttons, is used to signify an entire group of people, military officers. Through association the word *brass* may then also come to signify an authoritarian power structure, rigid hierarchy, admirable discipline, arrogant behavior, higher social class, or educational status. Thus, when the part stands in for and signifies the whole, there may be a great disproportion between the subtlety of the single attribute and the immensity of its signification.

This is an important point in relationship to how dance vocabulary functions in the flamenco genre. At a flamenco dance theater performance in Madrid, I witnessed a large crowd respond with immediate, overwhelming enthusiasm when, at the end of a dance sequence, a dancer made a slight gesture of proudly adjusting his vest (exactly in time with the musical phrasing, the *compás*). Similarly, even quite subtle movement references to bullfighting performed in a flamenco dance can significantly affect an audience's appreciation, judgment, and interpretation of a performance. As a metonym, even a small movement reference to the bullfight may invite the audience to see the dancer as noble, courageous, daring, and able to exert masculine power and domination.

That bullfighting movements function as metonyms within the flamenco dance vocabulary reinforces the importance of Edward T. Hall's distinction between high-context and low-context cultures. Flamenco dance and bullfighting are related cultural practices functioning within a high-context culture. Hall suggests that "greater pattern-recognition capacity" is required for functioning within a high-context culture (1976, 120). Attributes of bullfighting movement techniques and vocabulary performed in dances serve as metonyms for the culture, practices, and significance of the bullfight, and their communicative effectiveness depends on the observer's ability to recognize movement patterns and give them their intended meaning. This need not entail overt consciousness of the meaning-making process itself. A movement reference to bullfighting occurring within the flamenco dance vocabulary can be subtle or incomplete and still communicate effectively on the cultural level. It need not consist of a direct movement quotation, literal enactment, or pantomime. Rather, a single movement attribute or combination of attributes drawn from the context of bullfighting can stand in for the entire cultural practice of bullfighting and any or all of its unique attributes, values, and experiences.

Bullfighting practices are competitive in nature; each public bullfight performance highlights interactions that test the power differentials between human and animal protagonists. Within the bullring, the overwhelming physical power of the bull is matched and met by the matador's courage, intelligence, greater mobility, and acquired skill. While the outcome of the bullfight in nearly all instances entails the death of the bull,[4] the risk of injury, permanent disability, or death for the matador is also quite real. Bullfight aficionados attend the bullfight to see human beings (generally male) triumph over the bull and all that the bull represents—untamed nature, instinctive knowledge, death, sexuality, and fertility. Bullfight interactions reiterate a cultural script that asserts the dominion of human beings over the animal kingdom. To the degree that the bull is certain to be dominated and killed, the ritual performance of the bullfight reiterates and affirms the anthropocentric tendency of the cultural group.

Flamenco dance practices also often enact less overtly violent competitive interactions through movements that test the power differentials between dance protagonists. Generally this is theatricalized as either two males vying for dominance or a heterosexual couple in the initial, fiery stages of a courtship. When a female flamenco dancer appears to acquiesce to male power within the dance, the androcentric tendency of the cultural group is publicly reiterated. For the female dancer, the performing of acquiescence may constitute a performative act that signifies her actual acquiescence to male authority and patriarchal power. However, such a performance may only signify a temporary willingness to comply with traditional dance forms or the will of a male or female choreographer. In any case, the metonymic meaning of social conformity to gendered rules is conveyed through the dance form.

Even a subtle metonymic occurrence of bullfighting movement within the flamenco dance vocabulary constitutes a significant reference to the male-identified domain of the bullfight and public ritual acts that affirm human domination of animals. Human domination of animals and male domination of females are understood as parallel cases, perhaps modeled on the Catholic Church's doctrine that "just as the church is subject to Christ, so also wives ought to be, in everything, to their husbands" (Eph. 5: 22–24; NRSV Catholic Edition). Bullfighting movements in the flamenco dance context function as metonyms that reaffirm the generally accepted Andalusian and Spanish social patterns of male entitlement and dominance in relationship to females and animals.[5]

Transitional Phenomena

Bullfighting metonyms in flamenco dance performances communicate directly with audiences; yet another significant source of evidence of the bullfighting-flamenco cultural complex exists in the deeper realm of the somatic and kinetic experience of the performers themselves. As a flamenco dancer evokes the fierceness of the bullfight in her or his dancing, and as the bullfighter evokes the grace of the dance in his or her confrontation with the bull, their actions extend into a liminal area of human experience, a transitional space of ritual and play wherein the boundary between reality and illusion is tested.

Discussing human psychological development in his book *Playing and Reality*, D. W. Winnicott asserts that developed individuals are aware of the contrast between external reality and their own inner reality, but that in order to comprehend human nature a "third part of the life of a human being" must be considered, namely, the transitional phenomena through which individuals integrate their inner and outer realities (1971, 2). Winnicott explains that transitional phenomena occur in "an intermediate area of *experiencing*, to which inner reality and external life both contribute" (2; Winnicott's italics).

He describes this transitional space as "a resting-place for the individual engaged in the perpetual human task of keeping inner and outer reality separate yet interrelated" (2). Performers actively engaged in flamenco dance or bullfighting are balancing a variety of immediate realities and idealized dreams, and on a deeply personal performative level are seeking integration of the two.

Winnicott's examination of transitional phenomena and objects in relationship to the psychological development of human infants reveals human play as a critical mechanism within the processes of enculturation, one that continues to serve the social and cultural needs of adults. A child's teddy bear serves as a transitional object; by signifying safety and security it assists the child to integrate inner needs with actual or imaginary dangers in his or her outer reality. Similarly, in the liminal space of the performance, objects (fans, skirts, shawls, *capotes*, swords, etc.) take on meaning and function as transitional objects through which performers attempt to integrate their actual human limitations and the idealized matador or dancer of their imagination. Their creative manipulation and play with these transitional objects may hold an actual bull at bay or control an audience's attention. In either case, the transitional object protects the performer, enabling him or her to negotiate between a harsh reality and an elusive ideal. Noting that "in any cultural field *it is not possible to be original except on a basis of tradition*" (99; Winnicott's italics), he views play as an activity involving transitional phenomena that is integral to the functioning of culture.

The use of transitional objects in the movement vocabularies of flamenco dance and bullfighting is pervasive. Matadors wield the cape, whether *muleta* or *capote*, as a lure for the bull. Matadors also value the cape as a protective shield; it provides a deceptive target, misdirecting the bull's attention and screening their own bodies from view. The cape is mere cloth; its protective power is more transitory and illusory than actual. Its efficacy as a defense is entirely contingent upon whether the bull is tricked by the matador's movements of illusion and misdirection. For the matador, the cape functions as a vitally important extension of self; it functions as a transitional object. The matador depends upon it for security, yet when circumstances demand, a matador will drop it, because the safety it represents to the matador is conditional, not absolute. The bullfight public is witness to a ritualized performance of interspecies play based on illusion and trickery. That the consequences of this ritual play potentially include the matador's death intensifies the experience.

A flamenco dancer who, even momentarily, wields a skirt as if it were a cape has, by referencing the bullfight, transposed the elements of illusion, play, and ritual into the dance context. Take out the causative factor—the bull—and the remaining movement phenomena that constitute the dance have the quality and function of play. Play in the flamenco genre includes the play of serious emotions, known in flamenco as *jondo* (deep, profound). Emotions are accepted and appreciated as transitory phenomena. However deeply experienced and vehemently expressed emotions may be, as performative beings we know that emotions can be summoned, created, falsified, and transformed. In performance, emotions function as transitional phenomena enabling performers to integrate inner and outer realities.

INTERACTION

Interactions occurring in the practices of flamenco dance and bullfighting are innumerable, complex, and varied; however, they are generally characterized by the presence of conflict. The people of Spain and Andalusia generally feel secure about their own physical and personal boundaries, pressing forward to make contact with one another and finding satisfaction in encounters that involve conflict. This cultural attribute—appreciation for the energy generated through conflict—colors the practices of both flamenco dance and bullfighting. The performative practices of flamenco dance and bullfighting reiterate scenarios of conflict in order to satisfy an Andalusian and Spanish need for intensity, continuity, interconnectedness, and sociality. Conflict provides performative opportunities through which the energizing effects of dissonance are exploited and enjoyed as a means of strengthening cultural homeostasis and social belonging.

The interspecies conflict ritualized through the bullfight sets the matador in opposition to the bull; in flamenco dance interactions of conflict or competition occur between performers or are visible in a dancer's attitude toward the audience. The enactment of competition and conflict generates energy and excitement at a fundamental level. If the competition enacted focuses on a contest between persons of the opposite sex, it becomes a performative opportunity for both challenging and affirming the androcentric worldview of the cultural group. A defiant and strong female is much appreciated for the energy she brings to the competition; nevertheless, her initial performance of defiance is often formulaic and will be balanced later by her performance of compliance to the normative behaviors of the group. Thus, her performance of rebelliousness energizes male-female dynamics; it does not disrupt them.

Nor must a male and female dance together in order for sexual dynamics to be operative. Dance is super-ordinary and liminal; therefore flamenco dance interactions may consist of actual or illusory exchanges between real or imagined entities that entail actual or figurative outcomes. Just as no actual bull need appear for a movement reference to convey danger or triumph over fear, so dance soloists may make reference to sexuality through dance whether or not a dance partner of the opposite sex is actually present. In the performative context of flamenco dance, sexual expression is commonly sanctioned, as are anger, defiance, and despair. Performative practices provide opportunities for safely channeling potentially disruptive behaviors and emotions into culturally acceptable directions. In addition to male-female interactions of conflict, flamenco dance often features a rivalry between two members of the same sex, a feud between two opposing groups, or a single individual who acts defiantly toward a partner or a group, or whose conflict is internal.

A large portion of these dance interactions, however fiery or dramatic they may appear, can be interpreted as simply providing a baseline for the continuation of cultural traditions. Communication researcher Ray Birdwhistell believed "that at least 90 percent of the exchange along all of the channels in any moment of human interconnectedness consists of signals that maintain the communication context and secure the baseline of the conversation" (Lomax ed. 1968, 173). Flamenco dance and bullfighting are self-engendering practices that function primarily to secure their own continuance, the types of infinite play James P. Carse writes about in his book *Finite and Infinite Games: A Vision of Life as Play and Possibility*. "A finite game is played for the purpose of winning, an infinite game for the purpose of continuing the play" (1987, 3). Individual flamenco dances and bullfights generally function as finite games; individual dances have clearly defined endings and the *corrida* ends when the last bull is killed. However, as performative practices flamenco dance and bullfight also function as infinite games. They ensure the continuation of their respective cultural traditions through reiteration of movement patterns and the powerful effect of redundancy.

Movement Analysis

Laban Movement Analysis

Laban Movement Analysis provides etic frameworks for the analysis of collections of movement data, based on the categories of body, space, shape and dynamics.[6] It has been used in various cross-cultural dance research contexts,[7] and in this book is applied to intracultural movement phenomena and data gathered through embodied learning procedures.

Significant patterns and shared movement principles operative within the movement vocabularies of flamenco and bullfighting emerge when the two practices are examined and compared through etic analysis. While Laban's concepts facilitate study of isolated movement features, his theories also express a sophisticated understanding of the integrated nature of movement phenomena; Laban concepts of body, shape, space, and Effort (i.e., expressive movement qualities) are understood to function in conjunction with each other. "It is not just the physical movement of the body that gives the [movement] statement communicating power. The communication of the move is expressed by combined spatial and Effort patterns" (Bartenieff with Lewis 1980, 87).[8] To comprehend the role of movement phenomena in the expression of culture, etic analyses must be reintegrated with emic perspectives.

Image as Gestalt

Body, space, and expressive movement qualities (Effort) may be analyzed as separate components of a movement event, but the intrinsic unity of movement expression is undeniable. Movement arises from the inner life, imagination, and feeling state of a person, and attains somatic integrity through poetic metaphor and image. Image often serves as the gestalt that tacitly influences each movement's form, the ultimate test of a movement's value for both the performer and the audience. A simple flamenco dance movement can resonate with meaning. The chest fills and lifts. Widening to the side of the body, the elbows initiate and lead the action of arms lifting forward and high. The index and middle fingers are held together, pointing downward sharply, elbows high. The movement is slow, smooth, and powerful; it is ominous and threatening. Through this movement of a dancer's arms, the bull is summoned; he raises his head, the arc of his horns outlined against the sky. Whether or not he will charge is uncertain; all is suspense.

Thus, within a simple dance movement the image of the bull is embodied and employed as a metaphor of power and danger. This simple movement of the arms also evokes the presence and expressive qualities of the *banderillero*, the member of the matador's *cuadrilla* whose arms lift high, his *banderillas* pointing downward, in preparation for his run toward the bull. With no cape to shield his body, the daring *banderillero* relies on speed, agility, and accuracy. His arms must curve up and over to reach past the bull's horns to place the colorful *banderillas* into the back of the bull's neck.

This stylized movement of a flamenco dancer's arms constitutes a movement motif, a metonym for the bull and/or the *banderillero*, for conflict between matador and bull, or for all that the bullfight represents within Span-

Eight. Movement Analysis

This 2005 photograph of José Pedro Prados, "El Fundi," taken at the Plaza de Toros de Las Ventas in Madrid, Spain, clearly shows the typical posture and attitude of the *banderillero*, the *torero* whose job is to place the *banderillas* (decorative barbs) in the back of the bull's neck in the second act of the bullfight. With chest high, hips pressed forward, full body arcing, vertical head, and arms lifting from elbows with fingers pointing downward, the *banderillero* prepares to meet the bull's charge and reach over the bull's horns with the *banderillas*. Similar styling of the arms is often used in flamenco dance (Manuel González Olaechea y Franco/WikiCommons).

ish culture. Such ambiguity of meaning does not dilute the gesture's power; rather, its ambiguity may increase the motif's expressive power within the dance. For both the general Spanish and regional Andalusian audiences there is immediate, holistic comprehension of the significance of such movements. Movement, image, and significance are bound together; even subtle movement gestures may contain a wealth of cultural reference.

Body

In suggesting "embodiment as a paradigm for anthropology," Csordas wrote that "the body is a productive starting point for analyzing culture and self" (2002, 87). The body serves as a source of both sensory experience and personal agency for performers, and serves as a medium through which the

Italian American flamenco dancer José Greco performs a flamenco dance version of the typical *banderillero* stance. As he maintains the position of his feet, with his hips pressed forward, his lifted arms arcing sideways, and his focus inclined downward, José Greco's entire body is drawn into a dynamic tensile arc. This prototypical posture is seen in many flamenco dance photographs (©Roger Wood / Royal Opera House / ArenaPAL; Jerome Robbins Dance Division, The New York Public Library for the Performing Arts, Astor, Lenox and Tilden Foundations).

shared cultural values of flamenco and bullfighting are manifest and made explicit within the community. To better understand the body's participation in movement phenomena, the following categories are useful: phenotypes, posture, gesture, gender, body extensions, and self-awareness.

Phenotypes

Kealiinohomoku points out that most dance practices include cultural expectations in relationship to the phenotype and body type of performers, and that the performer's phenotype constitutes a significant factor in both aesthetic and aesthemic assessments (1976, 141–142).[9] Whether phenotype and body type expectations are met determines whether a dancer's performance will create for audience members a feeling of cognitive consonance or dissonance (140–141). In the flamenco dance genre a wide range of possible body types are considered acceptable. Acceptance is conditioned, however, by various factors such as age, gender, ethnicity, social status, and professionalism. The more restrictive expectations in relationship to phenotype and body type are applied in the professional theatrical context, while the least restrictive expectations pertain to the informal practices of the *gitano* community. These two highly contrasting performance contexts demonstrate the extent to which different social contexts, personnel, and aesthetic standards affect how the body is perceived and judged.

In the professional context of Spanish classical dance, flamenco theatrical productions, or *zarzuelas*, the phenotype deemed most acceptable is relatively tall and slim; it is comparable to the phenotype expected in Western theater dance or ballet productions.[10] Performers in this context are expected to be young, attractive, and flawless. In addition, a dancer's visual appearance is expected to match or blend well with the other performers; any obvious idiosyncrasy of physical form would be grounds for a performer's exclusion. A few older dancers do perform in these contexts, usually as soloists, and usually because they are well-known dance artists, i.e., historic figures.

In contrast, the informal flamenco dance context provides performative opportunities for a much wider range of body types. In the *gitano* community, flamenco dance typically functions as an intergenerational practice revered for its social inclusivity. An impressive example of intergenerational dance is seen in the 1997 Carlos Saura film, *Flamenco*, as the late, renowned *bailaor* (male flamenco dancer) "El Farruco" shares the dance stage with his young grandson, "El Farruquito." In authentic flamenco dance contexts, performances by older adults are particularly valued, and any physical imperfections or limitations a dancer has are accepted as part of the uniqueness of their performance and character.

Dance performances by older *gitana* women, with their matronly figures, bowed legs, and inelegant shoes, are valued for their authenticity, uninhibited expression, and demonstration of traditional values. Neither is a performer's excess weight seen as a contraindication to his or her participation in dancing activities. The flamenco dance circle signifies family, tribe, and community, and its purpose is inclusion. A dancer's personal attributes, flaws, and idiosyncrasies may, in fact, provide a basis for his or her *estampa*. The career of the dancer Enrique Jiménez Mendoza (1912–1985), "El Cojo" (literally, "the lame one"), serves as an example. Lamed as a child, El Cojo nevertheless developed a unique style of his own, performed, and was an influential flamenco dance teacher (Álvarez Caballero 1998, 312–314, 316).

Posture

The expressivity of posture, whether cultural or individual, is a widely recognized phenomenon. Posture denotes particular tensions that are habituated in the body as a means of maintaining verticality. Movement researchers, such as Laban, Birdwhistell, and Lomax, note that postures are culturally distinctive. "The particular stance normal to a group of people becomes a cultural statement so that at a distance a person may be identified as a member of a certain tribe merely from his [her] silhouette or his [her] stride" (Lomax, Bartenieff, and Paulay 1968, 236). The torso (from the base of the pelvis to the top of the head) in flamenco dance has distinctive attributes in common with the use of the torso in bullfighting. An exaggeratedly erect posture is valued in both movement practices, yet torso mobility is also essential. There are three interrelated attributes of posture that are distinctive to the cultural context of flamenco dance and bullfighting: (1) verticality is stressed; (2) the upper body (head and thorax) and lower body (pelvis) often move in isolation or in contradiction to one another; and (3) the mobility of the pelvis is facilitated by the lift, control, and stability of the upper body.

The cultural values of nobility and dignity are expressed in the held verticality of a flamenco dancer or matador, though this posture may also be interpreted as individual self-confidence, self-respect, arrogance, or pride. As a habituated postural response, the vertical posture serves as a performer's somatic model of equilibrium or homeostasis. If a performer's verticality is significantly challenged or disrupted in performance due to being tossed by the bull or physically falling, he or she will immediately try to reestablish an erect vertical posture and all that it connotes: control, dignity, self-mastery, and competence.

Contrast between the movements of the upper and lower body is a notable feature of the flamenco dance style. Technically these movement differentiations are accomplished by a slight bend of the knees combined with strong lift and support from the upper body. This increases lower body mobility, freeing the pelvis to swing side to side and the feet to perform footwork. This striking separation between the upper and lower body in the movements of flamenco dance expresses Spanish and Andalusian cultural attitudes and beliefs. The cosmology of Spanish Catholicism has traditionally conceived of human beings' place on earth as a location halfway between heaven and hell. With uplifted chests human beings aspire to be closer to God and heaven, while the mobility of the pelvis and lower body proves that they are also subject to low, earthly temptations.

These cultural beliefs are performed and made habitual through bodily practice. Such beliefs create emotional and moral tension; they establish as normative a polarization between upper space and lower space that is expressed through the artistic metaphor of the body. In contrast to flamenco dance, the differentiation between upper and lower body in the bullfight strives to ground and stabilize the lower body, while lifting and mobilizing the upper body to move through a significant range of space with strength. Torsion and countertension, which are created by the contrasting movements of a performer's upper and lower body, are important attributes of both flamenco and bullfighting, and evidence of the value Andalusian culture places on excitement, drama, and conflict.

Gesture

The gestural movements of flamenco dance are highly articulate and complex; they involve an ornamentation of the upper portion of the kinesphere with curvilinear movements of the arms, wrists, hands, and fingers, and an elaboration of rhythms in the lower portion of the kinesphere.[11] These rhythms are achieved through the use of highly articulated percussive footwork patterns that also constitute a gestural component of the flamenco dance vocabulary. The exaggerated lift and support of the upper body enables the speed, mobility, and strength of flamenco footwork, and creates the somatic sensation of being suspended above the footwork while directing percussive gestures downward with the lower legs and feet.

This contrast of upper and lower body usage manifests differently in the movements of bullfighting. In bullfighting, the lower body strives for stability and rootedness, while the upper body actively gestures in space, with arm movements reaching to the farthest edge of the kinesphere. In both flamenco dance and bullfighting movement vocabularies, the torso must be strong to withstand the contrasting dynamics and contradictory spatial intentions between the upper and lower body. The functional demands that torsion and twisting movements place on the integrity of the body's core are significant. For the matador, these demands are exacerbated by the use of far-reach space and the extra weight of body extensions (sword, *muleta*, or *capote*) that are an intrinsic part of the tauromachy practice.[12] For the flamenco dancer, the physical demands of torsion are exacerbated by the speed of movements performed by the lower body in combination with extensive use of far-reach space by the upper body.

The separate articulations and contrasting intentions expressed through the upper and lower body greatly complicate the analysis of the qualitative aspects of flamenco dance movements. Often within the flamenco dance form, the attitude of the performer toward time, weight, space, and flow is expressed in entirely opposing ways by the upper and lower body. In fact, a signature of the flamenco dance style is its combination of sustained, controlled, and curvilinear movements of the arms simultaneous with direct, quick, and strong percussive movements of the feet. Both of these expressive components make significant demands on the core strength of the dancer. Intense demands of articulation, strength, and endurance are also made of the forearms, wrists, and hands of both flamenco dancers and matadors.

Gender

Like flamenco dance, the bullfight has aesthetic expectations in relationship to phenotypes. Although a less than ideal body does not preclude success, having an ideal body type is a professional asset for a matador. In the documentary film *The Lady Bullfighter* (Bryer 1989), tauromachy teacher Manolo Escudero defines the matador's ideal phenotype, saying, "A bullfighter has to have shoulders wider than his hips." Continuing, he points out "a woman has hips wider than her shoulders." Aesthetic expectations in relationship to the ideal phenotype of a matador are the basis for Escudero's rejection of female matadors; and he concludes that the reason "a woman can't be a bullfighter is because her body isn't right for it. For a woman to look right, she wouldn't have a woman's body."

Beyond phenotypes, other gendered movement attributes are significant factors in the performance of flamenco dance. In 1996, American female flamenco dance students attending the annual dance workshop of the Festival Flamenco Internacional in Albuquerque, New Mexico, were discussing their concerns about gender and performance style. They wanted to know how to perform in a more feminine way. As American females, they were not culturally habituated to the movements of flamenco dance that assert strength, directness, and quickness, and feared that by performing these movement qualities they would appear masculine. They asked a female member of the Antonio Canales dance company, Patricia Torrero, for her thoughts about how to maintain female qualities and appearance in their performance. She clearly did not share their concern, responding somewhat impatiently, "Everyone is going to know you are a woman." In Torrero's view, a woman is free to dance however she wishes precisely because her sex is entirely obvious onstage and her sex is understood to constitute an immutable and inescapable aspect of her being.[13]

Torrero's comment signals the modernity of her perspectives in relation to the history of the flamenco arts. During the era of the *cafés cantantes*, which occurred "between 1847 and 1920" (Grut 2002, 87–88), flamenco dance was stylized very differently depending on the sex of the performer. The *macho* (male) and *hembra* (female) movement styles were sharply defined; the men presented the strong footwork and unrelenting straight lines that characterized *macho* movement qualities, and the women asserted their female charm through a more curvilinear, delicate, sensuous, and expressive use of torso, hips, shoulders, and head inclinations. At that time, male dancers emphasized footwork, maintained strict upright postures, and performed hand movements (*maneo*) in a more limited, reserved fashion, while female dancers emphasized *braceo* (arm movements) and performed a softer style of footwork and ornate, fully articulated *flores* (hand movements). Today both female and male flamenco dancers are accorded far greater expressive range. The movement style of current-day male flamenco dancers includes greater emotional expressivity and sensuality, and today's female flamenco dancers may dance with power and overt passion without having their femininity questioned.

Body Extensions

Patricia Torrero's comment draws attention to the importance of body shape as a signifier of sex and the function of costumes as extensions used to emphasize an ideal phenotype, body type, or shape. The matador's "suit of lights" emphasizes an ideal body shape for the bullring, wide shoulders and narrow hips. Similarly, a flamenco dance dress is constructed to emphasize an ideal body shape for female dancers. In 1992, I attended the *feria del caballo* (horse fair) in Jerez de la Frontera, where the streets were full of women, all of them wearing the *sevillanas*-style dress traditionally worn during the *feria*. This dress so exaggerates shoulders with an abundance of ruffles and hips with a ruffled bell-shaped skirt that every woman, no matter her actual waistline, walked along the public streets displaying and enjoying the classic female hourglass figure. This phenomenon correlates with Kealiinohomoku's theories asserting that the "dancers' culturally distinctive use of space and shape" constitutes an "identifying signature" of a dance and dance culture (Kealiinohomoku 2001, 35). *Sevillanas* dresses immediately communicate information about region (Andalusia), gender (female), celebratory purpose (*feria*), and the season when they are most often worn (springtime).

In addition to signifying gender, a flamenco dance skirt provides dancers with a prop that, as a body extension, facilitates movement references to bullfighting. Andrew J. Strathern, in discussing embodiment as an aspect of anthropological study, points to the importance of understanding extensions as part of the performer.

> The body may be a symbol among other symbols. Notable here also is the fact that *embodiment* is being used to refer to human beings only, and not to material artifacts. Yet we know also that such artifacts may carry powerful meanings as extensions of the human body or in being modeled on the human body (or vice versa) [2004, 197; Strathern's italics].

These comments acknowledge a fundamental ambiguity between person and body extension that is indicative of transitional objects and phenomena. In the performative context of flamenco dance, this pertains to the use of the cane, sword, cape, skirt, fan, or shawl. How performers and observers relate to these objects often reveals underlying cultural attitudes and aesthemic perspectives.

In the daily lives of Andalusians and in the performance contexts of flamenco dance and bullfighting, male and female experience are generally distinct from one another. Many of the differences between male and female behaviors and experience are created and maintained through movement habituation. Despite clear gender-based distinctions, both matadors and female flamenco dancers focus a great deal of their attention on acquiring skill in the manipulation of fabric. A matador will practice long hours with the *capote* and *muleta* because being skilled in their manipulation is a matter of life and death. For a female flamenco dancer being skilled in manipulating a skirt, shawl, or *bata de cola* is a style essential with social and perhaps professional ramifications. The spiraling patterns practiced with all these fabrics also have similar attributes, technical challenges, and use of space.

Matadors develop exceptional dexterity and strength in their upper body, arms, wrists, and hands as they practice manipulating the sword, *capote*, and *muleta* with technique, skill, and style. Matadors practice the movements of the *capote* and *muleta* assiduously to develop smoothness of flow until the ability to control the cape's moving form is second nature. Slow technical practice assures that the cape will maintain the integrity of shape and direction that allow the matador to catch and control the bull's attention. The matador's manipulation of fabric constitutes a significant movement motif, is varied to produce unique movement patterns, and is practiced with a discipline near obsession.

The volume of material in a flamenco dancer's skirt is sometimes similar to the weight and shape of a matador's cape; as she moves, a female dancer's skirt takes on spiraling forms similar to those of the *capote*. A flamenco skirt is a visually decorative aspect of a dance performance; however, at its root in the life of an Andalusian woman, the skirt is also an intimate extension of her being.[14] Wrapping about her like a second skin, it signifies her sexual identity, and serves as a useful tool in her everyday life. She may use her skirt to hold olives, oranges, tomatoes, or grapes that she has gathered, to wipe her children's faces or her own hands, or to chase away a dog or chicken. She may also be adept at manipulating a shawl or fan flirtatiously.

Holding her skirt as a matador holds his *capote*, a woman evokes the art of bullfighting directly in her dancing. Flamenco dancers often practice long hours to perfect their technique in manipulating the flamenco skirt, shawl, or the long trailing skirt of the traditional *bata de cola*. The beautiful spiraling line of the *bata de cola* follows the same aesthetic principle as the matador's *capote* as he circles it behind his back, around his waist and hips, and then allows it to trail behind him as he walks away from the bull. Through manipulations of her skirt, a female dancer may easily enact either male or female behavioral patterns; thus the flamenco skirt, functioning as a transitional object, provides opportunities for androgynous expression.[15]

Self-awareness

In *Gypsies in Madrid: Sex, Gender, and the Performance of Identity*, Paloma Gay y Blasco notes attitudes toward body and identity that distinguish the *gitano* culture. "Gitanos do not make a conceptual separation between individuals, their bodies, and their actions. Together, the three make up the Gitano concept of the person, with the body working as a sign indicating the kind of person an individual person is—not only a man or a woman, but a more or less morally acceptable man or woman" (Gay y Blasco 1999, 177). It is notable then that the performance contexts of flamenco dance and bullfighting often involve moral as well as aesthetic judgment. Performative opportunities exist in both ordinary and super-ordinary situations; most Andalusians are habituated to the dramatic potential of daily life and to playing the central role in their own life story. In Andalusia, going for a walk may be undertaken as exercise for the good of one's health; however, it also constitutes a significant social and performative opportunity. Going for a walk in Andalusia provides opportunities for seeing and being seen within one's community; it is a performative promenade of self in a social/moral context.[16]

The Andalusian custom of public display heightens the consciousness of self that pervades both daily life and performative events. The following observation by dance scholar La Meri suggests that this heightened sense of oneself as an embodied presence with visual impact heightens the performance abilities of average Andalusians.

But the Sevillanas [dance] can be viewed from any angle, and the spectator will encounter a beauty of line and counter-line as perfect as the most perfect line planned by the greatest choreographer. It is possible that the unconscious creation of air design is due to the Iberian subconscious self-consciousness. He [she] has a sixth sense which stands away and views him [her] as others see him [her]; and no less an artist than Elenora Duse claimed that this sense is what makes genius [La Meri 1967, 97].

This heightened awareness of and public presentation of self is utilized in both flamenco dance and bullfighting contexts. While the promenade is a normative activity in Spanish life, on the dance stage or in the bullfight arena this quality is exaggerated; the normative vertical posture becomes *contoneo*, a proud, strutting walk expressive of personal pride, confidence, and triumph.

SPACE

Kinesphere and General Space

Laban's theories about space as an expressive factor in human movement are comprehensive and complex. When examining movement in relationship to space, Laban differentiates between the kinesphere, a personal sphere of movement immediately surrounding a person, and the general space through which a person may travel. Laban defined twenty-seven directions in which the whole body, or any part of the body, may move, and developed additional concepts to describe how a person shapes movement effectively in relationship to a spatial intention.[17] Laban describes the three dimensions of space as comprising the vertical, horizontal, and sagittal dimensions.[18]

Verticality is primary in the movement practices of both bullfighting and flamenco dance. In the context of the bullfight, matadors must maintain their uprightness for reasons of both aesthetics and safety; in the context of flamenco dance, the dancer exaggerates vertical uprightness to assert dominion over the stage space. In the flamenco dance style few movements are performed using low areas of the kinesphere; such movements as kneeling are generally performed only as special accents that provide dramatic effect. Neither does the flamenco dance vocabulary rely on use of high areas of the kinesphere; jumping movements are rarely performed nor is the height of any jump emphasized.

The body's vertical posture, generally maintained in flamenco dance and the bullfight, functions as a hub from which the performer moves in relationship to the space around the body. In flamenco dance and bullfighting, verticality itself functions as a metonym signifying the nobility of the human race. The arms of the flamenco dancer are expressive of voluminous, curvilinear space, often emphasizing presence and presentation by moving cyclically in the vertical plane.[19] Movements that reiterate the intersection of the three dimensions at the body's center are stabilizing in their effect, while mobility often occurs through the destabilizing effects of movements that range outside of this three-dimensional intersection.[20]

Movements that travel through general space are not emphasized in the flamenco dance tradition; footwork is often performed in place, and those movements that do travel through space often circle around, returning the dancer to his or her original position. Flamenco dance and bullfighting are often practiced in the round performance spaces of the arena or the social circle, the semiround space of the *cuadro flamenco*, or the rectangular space of the proscenium theater. These external spatial contexts influence a performer's expressive use of both the kinesphere and general space.

Spatial Tension

The term *spatial tension*, as used by Laban, refers to the ways that tensions and countertensions within the body are organized in relation to three

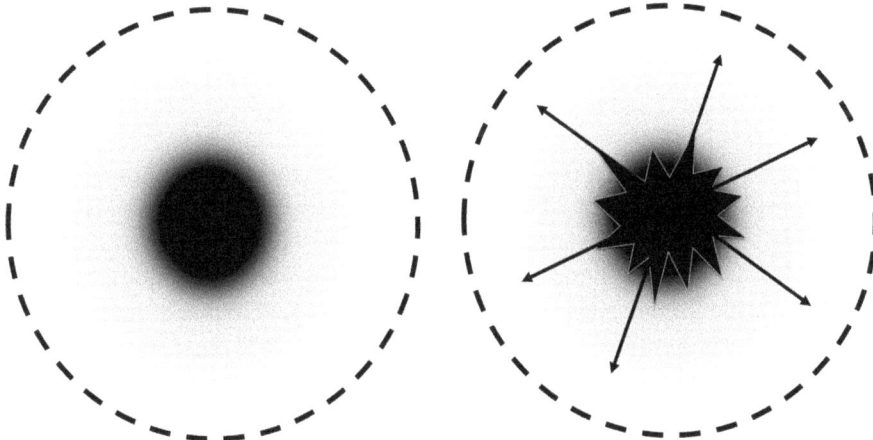

Left: Kinesphere is Laban's term for the bubble of space immediately around the body through which our limbs and torso move (in contrast to the "general space" through which we travel). It may help to visualize the kinesphere as an egg: the yoke is like the center of the kinesphere; the egg's shell is like the outer edge or periphery of the kinesphere; and the egg white is the volume between the edge and center of the kinesphere. *Right:* Moving with central spatial tension, one's energy appears to radiate outward from or inward toward the body's core. In the flamenco dance style, the motif of central spatial tension occurs often, both in the subtle radiating expansion of a dancer's posture and in dynamic gestures or whole-body actions that add an explosive quality to the dance.

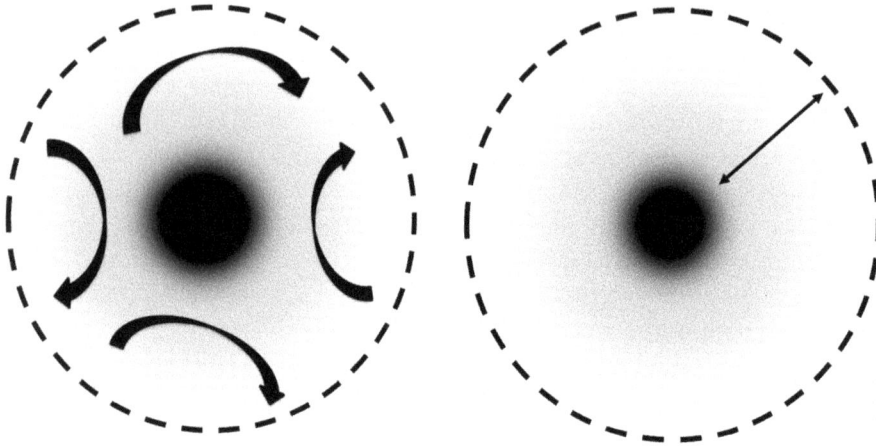

Left: Moving with transverse spatial tension, one may appear *off-balance* while moving dynamically through the volume of the kinesphere. When dodging, swooping, or carving through the space around the body, a flamenco dancer may seem to actively engage and interact with unseen forces in the volume of his or her kinesphere. *Right:* Moving with peripheral spatial tension, one asserts and maintains distance between the center and the edge of one's kinesphere. In flamenco dance, this is often seen in gestures that exert a tensile pull or countertension between the core of the body and the outer boundary of the dancer's kinesphere. Manipulations of a skirt, *manton*, or other props may also be used to draw attention to the distance between the center and the edge of a dancer's kinesphere.

areas of the kinesphere: (1) the center of the kinesphere, (2) the kinesphere's inner volume, and (3) the edge or periphery of the kinesphere. Spatial tension comprises three subcategories: (1) central spatial tension, (2) transverse spatial tension, and (3) peripheral spatial tension. These concepts provide a framework for identifying how a person organizes a range of muscular tensions to express his or her spatial intentions and attitudes toward the kinesphere and general space.

In the context of bullfighting, energies are polarized between bull and matador and between the crowd and the bullfighter. Tension is intrinsic to the bullfighting event; the outcome is uncertain and the bullfighter is at risk. In the context of flamenco dance, energies are often polarized between dancer and musicians or between the audience and the flamenco performer. In the flamenco dance style, the natural counterbalancing movements of the body are often exaggerated for dramatic and dynamic effect. Thus, the body's organization of tensions and countertensions is expressive, and can be used to dramatically embody a dancer's responses to various polarities, male-female, social isolation–connection, or personal risk–safety.

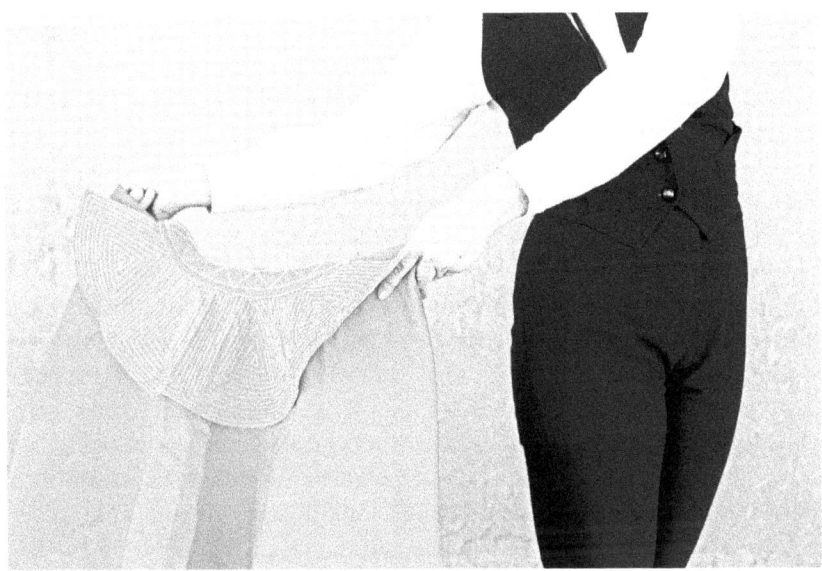

Peripheral spatial tension is shown here as the author demonstrates a basic maneuver with the *capote*. Skillful manipulation of the *capote* helps a matador to maintain a safe distance between his body and the horns of the bull (photograph by Melissa Lind).

When a performer's tension patterns are organized to demonstrate or express energy that radiates inward or outward in relation to the center of the kinesphere, the movement phenomenon is called *central spatial tension*. Central spatial tension occurs in such flamenco dance movements as the extroverted, outward burst of energy seen at the climactic end of a phrase. In contrast, central spatial tension may also be observed in the dancer who heightens the dramatic effect of his or her outburst by first drawing energy toward the center of the body, emphasizing introversion or emotional containment. Central spatial tension is expressed when the body's center is the locus through which spatial intent and muscular tensions are organized.

When tension patterns of movement are organized to demonstrate the aliveness and instability of the inner volume of the kinesphere, the phenomenon is called *transverse spatial tension*. The body's center is no longer the locus of attention for the person moving; transverse spatial tension signifies that attention is focused on the space between the center and the edge of the kinesphere. Transverse spatial tension is seen in the unplanned movements of the bullfight such as the impulsive dodging and evasive torso inclinations of the matador known as *quiebros*. Flamenco dance movement traditions incorporate these off-balance, dynamic actions, and individual dancers use them to add excitement and dynamic energy to their style. Movements employing transverse spatial tension add a contrasting sense of danger and precariousness to a flamenco dancer's usual attitude of dignity and self-control.

When tension patterns of movement are organized to create a heightened awareness of the distance between the center of the kinesphere and its edge, the phenomenon is called *peripheral spatial tension*. A matador survives in the bullring through an intense kinesthetic commitment to organizing his or her movements so as to monitor, control, and maintain the distance between the center and the periphery of the kinesphere. A critical distance must be maintained between the vital center of a human torso and the bull's trajectory along the edge or through the volume of a matador's kinesphere. The excitement of the audience increases as the matador brings the bull closer on each pass. Peripheral spatial tension focuses the audience's attention on the distance between human being and bull; it is key to compelling their emotional involvement in the bullfight. Its constant reiteration in the flamenco dance style is also significant, and is particularly noticeable when attention is drawn to the distance between core and periphery as the dancers' pelvis moves in the opposite direction from his or her gesturing arm.

Movement Dynamics

Laban's system includes methods for analyzing movement dynamics—the expressive qualities of movement—technically referred to as *Effort qualities*. The analysis of expressive qualities provides evidence of the intentions and attitudes that influence human movement. The expressive movement qualities outlined in Laban's system of movement analysis convey a performer's attitude toward four factors: flow, weight, time, and space. These attitudes are described as either condensing or expanding in relation to each factor.

Condensing and Expanding Effort Qualities

The condensing movement qualities, sometimes called the *fighting Efforts*, are especially prevalent in both flamenco dance and bullfighting. They are (1) bound flow—movement is controlled and emotions are contained; (2) strength—the body's weight is actively used to create power and manifest force; (3) quickness—time is cut short or there is a sense of urgency; and (4) directness—attention to space is unidirectional and honed. The expanding movement qualities, sometimes called the *indulging Efforts*, are (1) free flow—the body relaxes and emotions are released; (2) lightness—expressing weightlessness, the body appears to float; (3) sustainment—time extends endlessly; and (4) indirectness—attention to space is multidirectional and flexible.

In flamenco dance the condensing Efforts produce accents and climaxes, while the expanding Efforts generally occur as recuperative moments and moments of dynamic rebound. The most striking demonstration of lightness/sustainment that I ever witnessed in any dance form occurred in a flamenco dance class taught by Manolete (Manuel Santiago Maya).[21] He demonstrated dynamic rebound from condensing to expanding Efforts, that is, from the fighting to the indulging range of movement expression, repeatedly within a set movement phrase. Qualities of lightness and sustainment suffused his entire body immediately after a very strong, quick, direct accent of footwork.

Effort Combinations

When movement qualities express a performer's attitude in relation to two movement factors simultaneously, the combination is known as an *Effort state*. Laban points out that "these attitudes [Effort states] appear very often as transitions between essential actions, and frequently have a recovery function" (87). Movements that combine quickness and strength (*rhythm state*) occur in the footwork of flamenco dance and in many of the full-bodied responses of matadors. Movements that combine directness and control (*remote state*) occur as dancers and matadors orient themselves, focusing on an antagonist, whether real or imagined, within the performance space.

Movements that combine strength and tension (*dream state*) occur in the flamenco dancer's controlled weight shift and deliberate arm gestures and in the matador's controlled support of the cape from a wide stance. Movements that combine directness and quickness (*awake state*) are prevalent in the flamenco dancer's sharp changes of focus (often combined with gestures); similarly, the matador's dexterity with *muleta* and sword is made effective through his alertness to the movement factors of space and time. Movements that combine strength and directness (*stable state*) occur as the flamenco dancer lunges with eyes straight ahead in preparation for a turn and as the matador prepares to meet the bull's charge. Movements that combine tension and quickness (*mobile state*) are expressive of emotion and urgency. A fallen, disoriented matador quickly protecting his body or a flamenco dancer caught up in the immediacy of an emotion might display this combination of Effort qualities.[22]

When movement qualities express a performer's attitude in relationship to three movement factors simultaneously, the combination is known as an *Effort drive*. Laban identifies four Effort drives. *Action drive* occurs as a performer attends to weight, time, and space, and disregards flow, the emotion motivating the movement. *Vision drive* occurs as a performer attends to time, space, and flow, disregarding weight; Laban notes "the drive becomes 'vision-like,' because it is now not supported by active weight Effort and is therefore reduced in bodily import" ([1950] 1971, 88). Describing the *spell drive*, which occurs as a performer attends to weight, flow, and space, and disregards time,

This 1948 photograph of Teresa and Luisillo Ballets Espagnol shows the movement motif near-to-but-not-touching. One can also see the motif of direct eye contact and the *banderillero*-like stylization of flamenco arms, with elbows back and fingers pointing downward. On the Spanish Dance Society website, Dame Marina Keet (Grut) wrote that Luisillo (1927–2007) wanted to become a bullfighter until he saw Carmen Amaya dance and decided to dedicate his life to flamenco dance. Luisillo is seen here with his dance partner Teresa Viera Romero, whom he met when both were dancing with Carmen Amaya's company and married in 1950 (©Roger Wood / Royal Opera House / ArenaPAL; Jerome Robbins Dance Division, The New York Public Library for the Performing Arts, Astor, Lenox and Tilden Foundations).

Laban notes that "the inner attitude toward time rests and the movements radiate a quality of fascination" (88). A fourth Effort drive, *passion drive*, occurs as a performer attends to flow, time, and weight, and disregards space; Laban points out that "when spatial qualities are dormant, bodily actions are particularly expressive of emotion and feeling" (88).

The English word *passion*, often used in relationship to flamenco dance, requires clarification in relationship to both its Spanish-language cognate and Laban's definition of passion drive. The Spanish word for passion, *pasión*, connotes suffering and is associated primarily with the suffering of Christ on the cross. Sexual desire is its second meaning, and such desire is understood to carry with it the potential for the torment of body and soul. In Laban's Effort analysis terms, however, passion drive suggests that a person has completely invested his or her energy in the qualities of flow (feeling), weight (self), and time (an attitude toward the present moment). A person whose energy is invested in passion drive may be visually unaware and inattentive to the actual space in which he or she is moving. Thus passion drive is suggestive of a tantrum, swoon, or paroxysm of emotion. The intense emotions flamenco dancers express or matadors experience while performing are not the same as the passion drive defined by Laban.

Flamenco dance and bullfighting may cause some observers to experience a state of emotional catharsis during which their awareness of space may be reduced or eradicated. The manifestation of opposing qualities in the upper and lower body of flamenco dancers further complicates the impression of passionate excess that observers often report. The flamenco dancer's upper body often utilizes the Effort qualities of vision drive: bound flow, sustained, indirect or direct; or of the spell drive: bound flow, strong, indirect. The expressive upper body may seem to float above the action drive of the lower body's footwork, which shows quick, direct, and strong Effort qualities. However, though observers receive an impression that passionate emotions are being expressed, a performer is not likely to embody the Effort qualities as defined by Laban's passion drive. Flamenco dancers and matadors are very unlikely to be inattentive to the space (the stage or arena) that constitutes their immediate reality; in fact, strong direct focus or eye contact is a significant motif in both movement vocabularies. Any matador whose attentiveness to space becomes dormant is at very great risk. Flamenco dancers have spatial concerns regarding their performance environment and other performers, and the dance style itself emphasizes direct eye contact. In the context of flamenco dance and bullfighting, the movements of flamenco and bullfight performers use Effort factors that define the action drive: weight, time, and space, rather than the qualities Laban attributes to the passion drive.

Effort Phrasing

The manner in which movement dynamics occur, their sequencing and intensity, is known as *Effort phrasing*. There are four types of Effort phrasing: (1) *explosive phrasing*, which begins suddenly with an emphasis or accent, then gradually subsides; (2) *impactive phrasing*, which begins quietly, then builds energy gradually to culminate with an emphasis or accent; (3) *breath phrasing*, which gradually builds up to an emphatic accent in the middle of the phrase before again subsiding; and (4) *swing phrasing*, which begins and ends with emphatic accents.

Of these four types of phrases, impactive phrasing is most typical of flamenco dance dynamics. *Matiz* is the gradation of sound quality and volume that creates dynamic contrasts in flamenco footwork. By developing *matiz*, flamenco dancers are able to respond to the music more artistically and expressively. Flamenco movement phrases often begin slowly, gradually accelerate, and end with a strongly accented movement. The Laban Movement

Left: A Labananalysis symbol similar to the musical symbol for *decrescendo* is used, beginning with a sounded accent symbol, to indicate the dynamics of an explosive phrase. This signifies that after an emphatic beginning a dancer is becoming quieter, moving away from the initial dynamic moment, reducing energy gradually and ending quietly. *Right:* A Labananalysis symbol similar to the musical symbol for *crescendo* is used, ending with a sounded accent symbol to indicate the dynamics of an impactive phrase. This signifies that a dancer is becoming louder, moving toward a maximum dynamic, and ending with a strong accent. Impactive phrasing occurs often in flamenco dance.

Left: Labananalysis symbols similar to the musical symbols for *crescendo* and *decrescendo*, along with a sounded accent symbol in the center, are used to indicate the dynamics of a breath phrase. This signifies that, similar to the inhalation and exhalation sequence of a single breath, a dancer begins quietly, becomes louder, and moves toward a maximum accented moment, after which the movement dynamics gradually fade and come to a soft ending. *Right:* To indicate the dynamics of a swing phrase, a sounded accent symbol initiates the phrase followed by a *decrescendo* in dynamic intensity, and then a *crescendo* indicates increasing intensity to end the phrase with a final strong accent.

Analysis term for this type of phrasing, *impactive phrasing*, is defined by Marion North as "a phrase which builds up to a definite movement at its end" (1971).[23] Flamenco dance often produces a crescendo of sound leading to an accented ending in movement patterns, and uses acceleration to further emphasize the sense of immediacy, excitement, and impact. In flamenco, such movement sequences usually comprise more than one musical phrase (*compás*), providing the overall dynamic form with its emphasis coming at the end (Hackney 2002, 239). A *compás* with a phrase length of twelve beats is traditionally cut short to end with an accent on the tenth count of the final phrase. This strengthens the feeling of unpredictability or abruptness that typifies the emphatic endings of flamenco phrases.

The relationship of flamenco dance footwork to bullfighting resides primarily in the expressive dynamics, specifically the reiteration of impactive phrasing. While impactive phrasing in flamenco footwork produces an impression of acceleration, this is not always the case from the dancer's point of view. Often impressions of acceleration are not created through any actual increase of musical tempo, but are created by the dancer's use of progressively smaller rhythmic subdivisions in relationship to a constant tempo. Such rhythmic subdivisions add to the effectiveness of flamenco's impactive phrasing. Flamenco footwork may also evoke the dynamics produced during the passing of the bull, with the highest dynamic intensity of the dancer's sound correlating to the moment of the bull's closest spatial relationship to the matador. In the bullfight arena, a bull passing by a matador constitutes the central element of the performance. The psychological tension and physical danger of the moment cause a rush of adrenaline in both the matador and the observing crowd. The bullfighter's phrasing of movement shifts from concentrated preparation and anticipation before the bull charges, to an intense climax of dynamic action and heightened risk as the bull passes, and ends with relief and satisfaction as the bullfighter recuperates and prepares for the next pass. Anticipation, intensifying danger, climax, and immediate relief are reiterated as a phrase. Over and over this dynamic phrasing is experienced directly by the matador and vicariously by the public. In the context of the *corrida*, as in the context of flamenco dance, impactive phrasing constitutes a movement motif that is important, reiterated, and varied creatively.

The dynamics of flamenco dance footwork often mirror this rush of energy that is so iconic of the bullfight, beginning at lower dynamic levels, building through a gradual crescendo, ending as an emphatic finale with strongly accented movements or sounds. The predominance of impactive phrasing in flamenco dance generates energy and excitement. Originally generated and perceived through the body, the adrenaline rush experience has become stylized and acquired aesthetic value in the flamenco dance form. Though all types of dynamic phrases are used to produce expressive footwork, impactive phrasing is especially evocative of the bullfight. On an aesthetic level, impactive phrasing locates flamenco dance in relationship to the dangerous bullfight arena, and its reiteration in the dance serves as a somatic metonym for the emotions associated with the bullfight arena: fear, courage, and triumph.

Chapter Nine

Movement Parallels
From Structures to Motifs

> The corrida itself is the most tragic and beautiful ballet that was ever staged: the torero creating consciously with his [her] own slim glowing body and his [her] plastic capa [cape], balancing spiral lines to the unconscious curves of the charging black bull. It is this magnificent creation of beauty in counterline in the face of death that the Spaniard cheers, not the danger and death itself.[1]
> —La Meri, *Spanish Dancing*

Movement Structures of Tauromachy

In tauromachy, artistry is an ideal. Creative innovation and individual expressivity are highly valued within the performance tradition; however, a matador's priority is to survive his or her encounter with the bull. To that end, the bullfight movement vocabulary is fundamentally pragmatic; it is disciplined, limited, defined, focused, technical, and restricted, especially in comparison to the more generative, free-form, and emotionally demonstrative flamenco dance vocabulary. A matador's success in the bullring depends upon his or her ability to survive the bull while demonstrating courage, strength, artistry, and personal style in a manner pleasing to the crowd. In bullfighting, two intrinsic rules help a matador succeed. These two directives cause specific movement configurations to occur that are reiterated, important, and open to variation, i.e., they constitute movement motifs. Being of great pragmatic value, they are followed assiduously as part of the technical preparation of a matador. They are communicated both implicitly and explicitly through pedagogical and other means. Originating in the context of bullfighting, they also constitute underlying rules, movement principles, or intrinsic coding that guide the movement forms and expressivity of flamenco dance, structuring the dance both as it is practiced and as it is newly created through choreographic, improvisational, or other means.

First Movement Directive: "Don't move your feet."

The first movement directive is "Don't move your feet," which reflects the cultural value placed on courage. Courage and strength are values being tested implicitly and explicitly throughout bullfight practices.[2] Confronted by a bull's overwhelming power and fierceness, most humans experience an instinctual fleeing response. Therefore, the simple act of holding one's ground and facing the bull constitutes a heroic act. This first directive, "Don't move your feet," although counterintuitive, actually has significant pragmatic value. Like most animals, a bull sees movement and responds.[3] Therefore, if there is no movement, a bull will not be provoked to charge. We have more human instinctual responses to danger than "fight or flight." A third physiological response to stress situations, used particularly by females (human and non-

In this 2012 photograph of matador Alejandro Talavante performing at Madrid's Plaza de Toros de Las Ventas, the first rule, "Don't move your feet," is evident in the relative motion of the bull passing by at tremendous speed while the matador maintains a fixed, stable position (Juan Pelegrin/Flickr.com).

human), is "tend and befriend," a strategy that attempts to deescalate conflict by creating bonds between potential adversaries (Taylor et al. 2000). And a fourth behavioral response to danger is to "freeze"; by not moving, a person may avoid confrontation with (some kinds of) dangerous animals.

In the case of bullfighting, the directive "Don't move your feet" protects the matador by applying knowledge of a bull's behavior based on how a bull sees. In fact, there is a bullfighting stunt based on the fact that a bull will only charge a moving target. Named after its inventor, it is called a "Don Tancredo" and is described by matador Juan Belmonte as "a trick sometimes performed in the bullring, in which a bullfighter stands on a box in the middle of the arena when the bull is first let out. If he remains absolutely motionless the bull is supposed to sniff all around him and go away without attacking him" (1937, 86). In general however, a matador's control and domination of the bull depend on the ability to keep the bull's eyes, attention, and fierceness focused on the movement of the cape. Extraneous movements of the feet can draw the bull's attention to the person holding the cape, especially the center of weight, the vulnerable torso, increasing risk and interrupting the matador's control over the bull. A wide base of support facilitates the upper body's manipulation of the cape through an extensive range of space. In general, movements of the lower body, such as lunges, wide stances, or deliberate, smooth weight shifts serve the matador technically by providing stability. The most traditional stance during the passing of the bull employs a narrow parallel position of the feet, conveying performative proof to an audience of a matador's courage.[4]

While the fast footwork of flamenco dance seems to contradict this bullfighting movement directive, movements of the lower body in the flamenco dance tradition are not limited to footwork patterns. Stable lunges, wide stances, and deliberate, smooth weight shifts are also prevalent in the flamenco dance style. Stabilizing the lower body facilitates greater mobility in the spine and upper body. The expansive range of movement and expressivity of a flamenco dancer's upper body is a significant feature of the flamenco dance style, particularly in dance movements (called *marcaje*) that are performed to interpret the *cante*. Such movements, lunges, and wide stances are well grounded and so also serve as stabilizing movements preparatory to the performance of flamenco dance turns. Also, when performing fast, dynamic flamenco footwork patterns, dancers strive, as a matter of technique, to maintain a stable location, to not drift or travel away from their *sitio* (place). Flamenco footwork may express the high energy of "flight," but they do not "run away"; in this sense, the flamenco dancer's feet follow the bullfighting directive "Don't move your feet."

Second Movement Directive: "Keep Your Eyes on the Bull."

The second directive affecting the form of a matador's movement is "Keep your eyes on the bull." Because the matador is participating in a life-threatening improvisation with an unpredictable adversary, this rule is of critical importance. The matador engages with intense concentration and a sense of immediacy. "Keep your eyes on the ball" serves as the athlete's mantra in many sports; for a matador, following the directive to "Keep your eyes on the bull" is even more vital. Bulls are individuals, unpredictable and unique

This 2012 photograph of matador Lopez-Chaves at Madrid's Plaza de Toros de Las Ventas captures the inherent dramatic tension as a matador turns his back to walk away from a bull. Similarly, a flamenco dancer's back turned toward an audience can convey a variety of expressive qualities: mystery, suspense, denial, isolation, anger, or danger (Juan Pelegrin/Flickr.com).

in their behavioral patterns. Matadors study the movement behavior patterns of bulls; their ability to predict a bull's behavior may enable them to survive and triumph over the bull. Matadors do occasionally look away from the bull as a dramatic stunt, but only when their knowledge of the bull's condition and behavior suggests that it is fairly safe to do so. They have also been known to come to grief as the result of taking such risks.

Movement Motifs

The underlying rules and purposes of the bullfight tradition, and the movement configurations that result when those rules are followed, are easily transferred, both consciously and unconsciously, into the flamenco dance practice and can be identified as movement motifs.[5] A movement motif is a movement design, shape, or dynamic that (1) is recognized as important, (2) is reiterated, and (3) serves as a pattern or template for the creation of movement variations.[6] The movement principles underlying the practice of bullfighting result in movement motifs that fulfill all three of these conditions.

THE MOTIF OF ARCING

Arcing the whole body with hips pressed forward is one such motif. This movement motif is the result of two opposing movement intentions. One movement intention is to follow the first bullfighting directive, "Don't move your feet"; the opposing movement impulse is to move the pelvis and center of the body so as to evade the horns of the bull. The dynamic shape that results involves the entire frame of the body, which bows to form a unified arc. I call this "arcing" to describe movements in which a tensile stress unifies the entire length of the body, and to distinguish it from movements or postures that curve only a portion of the spine. In arcing, the pelvis is often pressed forward, creating tensile force within the entire body, much like an archery bow creates potential energy for an arrow. Arcing movement patterns can occur in a variety of spatial directions, depending on the direction that a matador's body faces and the trajectory of the bull.

Sometimes in flamenco dance, although the back is curved, the pelvis may have actually retreated, creating a sway back or hyperextended lower back in a posture or movement that I call "arching." Dancers with arched backs can be seen performing in both the flamenco dance and Spanish classical dance styles.[7] However, as a matter of dance technique, the arched back involves a more localized curvature of the back and is often accomplished

In this photograph, the author demonstrates the potential drama of back space in combination with other bullfighting movement motifs, such as near-to-but-not-touching, arcing the whole body with hips forward, and focusing down and to the side (photograph by Melissa Lind).

through the upper body's proud lift. This generally dysfunctional spinal curvature may become habituated in a performer's posture, but it represents a low-intensity or incomplete reference to bullfighting compared to the more dynamic, integrated, and demanding movement motif of arcing. Because the motif of arcing produces tension throughout the entire body, it communicates "bullfighting" completely and with more intensity than does the movement motif of arching the back. When transposed and performed within the flamenco dance vocabulary, arcing is stylized and exaggerated. Because it provides excellent photographic opportunities, the motif of arcing is often represented in books on flamenco dance.[8]

Peripheral Spatial Tension as a Motif

The movement motif of arcing sometimes organizes the entire body in a pattern of tension that draws attention to the distance between the center and the edge of a performer's kinesphere. Positioned at the center of the matador's kinesphere are the pelvis and torso, the vulnerable core of the body that needs to evade danger. At the kinesphere's edge is the matador's counterbalancing gesture, the cape extended away from center to redirect the bull's attention away from the matador's body. A matador is always intensely aware of the distance between the vulnerable center of his or her body and the bull, and attempts to maintain distance at all times. The more closely a matador draws the bull toward the body during the bullfight, the more courage and skill is displayed. Though *toreando* closer to the bull is considered better aesthetically, too close may prove deadly.

As if an electric charge exists between the center and the edge of his or her kinesphere, a matador is hyperconscious of this crucial distance at all times; this results in a specific type of countertension that Laban identifies as *peripheral spatial tension*. As a movement motif, peripheral spatial tension is reiterated in many variations within the flamenco dance style. If performed without peripheral spatial tension, some flamenco dance movements will be judged deficient; they will neither look right nor satisfy flamenco aesthetic standards. On the other hand, almost any movement performed with peripheral spatial tension may be suggestive of the flamenco movement style and/or bullfighting. Recurring often within the flamenco dance vocabulary, peripheral spatial tension thus serves as a movement signature of the flamenco dance style. It is an aspect of the flamenco dance technique to be practiced and refined, and is a movement motif open to creative interpretation and elaboration.

The movement forms of different cultures express discernible preferences in the relative use of three types of spatial tension (central, transverse, and peripheral); these preferences are salient in relationship to cultural activities, beliefs, or patterns. Peripheral spatial tension dramatizes the space immediately around the body and is often used to portray emotionally charged relationships or polarized situations or conflict. Within flamenco dance performances, peripheral spatial tension is reiterated, is important, and serves as a movement motif that can be used variously as a metonym for the contrasting dualities of life and death, heaven and hell, dominance and submission, fight and flight, male and female, human and animal, pain and pleasure, or love and hate.

Peripheral spatial tension is endemic and pervasive in flamenco dance and is valued for its dramatic contributions and engendering of energy for the dance. It create a sense of distance and an electric charge between protagonists, between performers and audience, between performers and transitional objects. Peripheral spatial tension complicates movements with an aura of tension, creating dynamic relationships in the space around the dancer's body such that invisible entities appear to be involved in the dance. The overall sense of tension is a quality to be played with artistically and is a movement element that reflects the Spanish cultural value of conflict. The presence of conflict presents opportunities for the artistic resolution of conflict as well. Although peripheral spatial tension constitutes a significant style element, movements expressive of central and transverse spatial tension are also present in flamenco dance. Central spatial tension is seen in dynamic movements that appear to burst with energy radiating outward from a dancer's core, and transverse spatial tension is seen in dynamic movements when a dancer moves through the volume of her or his kinesphere, appearing to evade, fall, or dodge.

NEARNESS AS A MOTIF

In the bullfighting interaction, one protagonist, the matador, seeks to avoid touch while encouraging closeness, while his adversary, the bull, seeks to assert his power by achieving contact, goring or throwing the matador.[9] The matador's goal is have the bull pass closely by without making actual contact; the bull's effort to achieve contact with the matador is generally frustrated, but occasionally rewarded. Thus, a game of proximity, like dodgeball or tag, is played through the movements of the two protagonists of the bullfight. Being of different species, their movement capacities differ. Once a heavy bull has begun to charge, its momentum reduces its ability to adjust the trajectory of its charge. By contrast, the lighter-bodied matador has greater agility and ability to adjust in response to the bull's charge. Not moving one's feet is an artistic ideal, but all matadors must be ready to dodge if necessary.

The matador's goal is to control the bull's charge so that it passes through a range of space "near to, but not touching" the matador; in Laban terms this quality is described as *nearness* or *closeness*. In discussing the dramatic potential of this quality, dance notation specialist Ann Hutchinson Guest notes that "nearness may register as a suggestion" (1983, 137–138). In the bullfight context, nearness signals that physical disaster or death may ensue if the matador's skilled evasions are ineffective, whereas in the dance context the motif of nearness is only suggestive of danger.

As a spatial relationship, "near to, but not touching" is culturally charged with meaning. In the context of the bullfight, the consummation or avoidance of touch is central to the event, its participants, and its witnesses. Life and death are in the offing; the space between the bull and bullfighter is culturally measured. The distance maintained between protagonists is of vital importance; it is perceived as a space charged with energy. This motif is mirrored in the flamenco dance style, which limits contact between dancers while using peripheral spatial tension to direct attention to the distance between them. Dancing in near-reach space but without touching is a motif borrowed from tauromachy that dramatizes sexual allure, danger, and power play between the sexes.[10] The dance becomes a contest between two bodies, played like a game of tag; the adrenaline of the near miss and the chase increases the energy of the dance.

The following quote from matador Juan Belmonte's autobiography, describing his experience of an ideal bullfight, further illustrates this point.

> What I was doing was a graceful game, an amusing recreation of body and spirit, rather than a heroic and terrible exercise. I had that day more than on any other the feeling of playing which a torero has when he is really fighting well. I called the bull and drew it toward my body, making it pass so that it brushed against me, as if that trembling, furiously turning bulk which shook the arena with the thunder of its hooves and slashed the air with its sharp horns were something soft and harmless. To convert the powerful and perilous reality of the animal into something impalpable as a veil held in the hands of a dancer is the great marvel of bullfighting [1937, 224].

The Motif of Spiraling

Hips shifting out of harm's way, the matador's body arcs. With lower body stabilizing, the matador's upper body turns to visually track the path of the bull. Simultaneously conforming to both movement directives, "Don't

Matteo Vittucci (1919–2011) was the Italian American dance partner (and husband) of Spanish dancer Carola Goya. Matteo was a teacher, choreographer, scholar, and author of *The Language of Spanish Dance: A Dictionary and Reference Manual* as well as a reference book on castanets, *Woods That Dance*. In this photograph, Matteo takes on the classic bullfighter's posture for his performance of *Bolero Goyesco*. Performance footage of Carola Goya and Matteo can be viewed online at Jacob's Pillow Dance Interactive site: http://danceinteractive.jacobspillow.org/dance/carola-goya-matteo?ref=artist (John Lindquist Photograph. ©Harvard Theatre Collection, Houghton Library, Harvard University; Jerome Robbins Dance Division, The New York Public Library for the Performing Arts, Astor, Lenox and Tilden Foundations).

move your feet" and "Keep your eyes on the bull," the matador's body spirals. These movement motifs are reiterated as the matador responds to each charge of the bull. Practicing these movement motifs, the matador's lower body maintains the position of the feet while his or her upper body tracks the bull's movement past the body's core and a spiraling movement passes through the entire body. A clockwise spiral initiated by the upper body occurs as the bull passes on the right side of the matador and a counterclockwise spiral results as the bull passes on the matador's left. For aesthetic and practical purposes, the integrity of the spiral would be lost if either the matador's feet were to falter in their stability or the matador's focus were to shift away from the bull as it passes by.

This movement motif, which Spanish dance scholar Matteo describes as "probably the most dominant characteristic of Andalusian and flamenco dancing," is known as *torcido*, meaning spiraled or twisted (Matteo with Goya 1990, 242).[11] Noting the important role of the upper body in creating this movement motif, Matteo asserts that *torcido* actions result from "the torque or spiraling action of the chest and upper torso against the pelvis."

> This twist (*torcido*) is even further amplified by arm movements (*braceos*), which seem to flow in nonstop circles and curves, reaching away from but always returning toward the body. This oppositional play of movements (*oposiciones*),[12] although basic and essential, is one of the most difficult techniques for the classically trained ballet dancer to acquire. Without *torcido*, Andalusian and especially flamenco dances have a wooden look. Without it all the steps (*pasos*) may be there, but the movement says nothing ("no dice nada") [Matteo with Goya 1990, 242].

The bull and bullfighter appear to collaborate in the creation of spiraling forms, the bull trying to toss the matador with its horns and the matador turning his body to avoid the bull's trajectory. As the spiraling form of the matador's body mirrors the curving trajectory of the bull, one sees a double helix. In the case of *rejoneo*, this double helix is especially notable, manifesting through the spatial interactions between the bull and the *rejoneador*'s highly trained horse.

Use of the Eyes and Confrontational Facings as Motifs

Eye movements influence the coordination of the entire body of the matador or flamenco dancer and are an integral component of many movement patterns. In human movement patterns generally, eye movements are integrated with the movements of the arms through basic patterns of eye-hand coordination; they also facilitate movement articulations of the spine (Cohen 2003; Feldenkrais 1990; Myers 2003; Todd [1937] 1972). These patterns assert a controlling influence in the flamenco dance style, in which the focused intensity of the eyes is notably sustained.

Flamenco dancers generally maintain an aggressive focus, projecting a challenge that is often directed toward the audience. Even when this quality of direct, sustained eye contact is not maintained throughout a flamenco dance, it is reiterated; it is important; and it is varied for artistic effect. Thus, eye contact constitutes a motif in both bullfighting and flamenco dance movement vocabularies. A flamenco dancer establishes adversarial relationships by maintaining a strong, direct focus toward the audience or toward another dancer or dance partner. Generally, the eyes look straight ahead, so the dancer turns her or his head to address different directions in the space. Dramatically, performers may project upon "the other," the audience or their dance partner, the adversarial role of "the bull." Sustained eye contact charges the space between performers, dramatizing adversarial relationships and assigning importance to the distance between them.

The direction that a person faces is indicative of relationship and intention; similar significance applies to the direction a person addresses with her or his eyes. Human behaviors in relationship to eye contact and body facings function in response to both situational needs and cultural norms; the significance of these behaviors is generally interpreted on the same basis. Facings and eye contact are of great importance in the bullfight and play a significant role in the artistry of flamenco dance. Direct face-to-face interactions with maintained eye contact are generally indicative of intimacy, but occur in confrontational interactions as well. Thus, sustained staring may be interpreted as inviting social contact or sexual engagement, or it could constitute a territorial challenge with roots in animal behavior.

While participating in the *tienta* in Mexico, I realized firsthand how very significant a simple shift of facing with maintained eye contact can be. When first approaching the female calf, I walked directly toward her, facing her directly and maintaining my focus. While approaching, my task was to judge her *jurisdicción* and establish myself at an appropriate distance. My intent was to encroach on her territory enough that when cited, she would charge.

The moment I felt I was in position to cite her, I maintained the focus of my eyes, but made a quarter turn to the right or left with my body. This movement, a quarter turn while maintaining my focus, was very simple, yet its portent was tremendous. In the tauromachy context, it signaled my choice of personal territory and a decision to initiate the conflict from that location. This movement surely contains even greater emotional meaning for a matador who faces the dangers of a full-sized bull. Maintaining the forward focus of the eyes and head, the body may turn or pivot from side to side while the head's position in space is perfectly still. (In Labanotation this is known as a

Nine. Movement Parallels 235

"space hold" or "body hold" [Preston-Dunlop 1995, 237].) This action occurs repeatedly in the flamenco dance vocabulary. Each time that a flamenco dancer focuses on a dance partner or the audience using the same configurations of body facings and eye contact that a matador employs in relating to the bull, the significance of that decisive moment in the bullfight is reiterated through the dance.

As the author practices movements with the *capote*, her torso arcs and spirals simultaneously. Flamenco performances are especially convincing when the qualities of challenging an adversary, of facing danger, or of having a near escape create a sense of urgency and passion in the dance (photograph by Melissa Lind).

MARCAJE AND THE PERFORMANCE OF TERRITORY AS MOTIFS

Querencia and *jurisdicción* are territorial realities that govern interactions between human and animal antagonists in the bullring. It is common, especially for the people of rural Spain, to have a practical understanding and fine appreciation of how these phenomena function; in Andalusia, this does not constitute esoteric knowledge. *Querencia*, an animal's sense of security at the center of its own territory, and *jurisdicción*, a bull's defense of territorial boundaries, are understood as natural phenomena that apply to the behavioral patterns of the human animal as well. These territorial phenomena also inform and influence flamenco dance movements.

A highly valued aspect of traditional form in flamenco dance is the quality of maintaining one's territory and the dancer's ability to communicate his or her sense of *querencia* to an audience. *Querencia* is visible in the spatial forms of many flamenco dance steps, especially *marcando*, the (generally nonpercussive) stepping patterns employed to mark the rhythm, or *compás*, of the music. These *marcando* steps, also called *marcaje*, generally travel diagonally, upstage and downstage, crossing in some variation on a figure-eight design while the performer's eyes remain focused forward toward the audience. The expressive result of these pathways through space is that the dancer establishes and maintains territory.

The spatial forms and movement timing of many *marcaje* patterns evoke the dynamics of interactions between a bullfighter and bull. While maintaining a forward focus, a dancer edges slowly back on a diagonal, as would a bull retreating toward the safety of its *querencia* while keeping a close eye on an adversary, then charging forward to reassert its territorial rights. The dancer, moving as the bullfighter, cites or challenges an imaginary bull to attack, evades the bull's horns as it rushes by, and recuperates after a close call. The dancer's role is changeable, fluid, and liminal; sometimes the dancer moves as the bull, sometimes as the bullfighter. Often all of this dramatic potential and dynamic range occurs within a single *compás*, and without those emergent qualities of danger and risk a movement phrase will not deliver its full cultural message. It is in this instance that an observer may say "*No dice nada*" (it says nothing).

Marcaje expresses territorial feelings. The dancer returns again and again to the same location, as though defending an instinctual attachment to a *querencia* at the center of the stage space. Flamenco dancers create many variations on this movement motif, using it to portray their ever-changing emotional territory. As an act of aggression or provocation, dancers may move

Nine. Movement Parallels 237

Bullfight movement motifs are deeply integral to the flamenco dance form. Flamenco dancers often use them when posing for still photographs, but action photographs of flamenco dance also reveal the influence of the bullfight. In this in-motion photograph of the author, you can see a combination of bullfight movement motifs: dynamic use of the skirt, arcing the entire body with pelvis thrust forward, and focusing down and to the side (photograph by Melissa Lind).

forward toward the audience, pushing outward to defend or expand their *jurisdicción*. Having defended their territory, they then return to their *querencia*, occupying the space at center stage with a sense of natural entitlement.

Quiebros and the Improvisational Impulse as Motifs

A successful matador, aided by circumstance, character, skill, and luck, asserts control over the nature of the contact that occurs in the bullring. The immediacy of the conflict and play between human and bull requires both planned and unplanned movements on the part of the matador. Planned movements performed by the matador are likely to include much-rehearsed movements, such as lunging in preparation for the matador's final sword thrust, the *estocada*. The unplanned spontaneous movements performed by the matador include impulsive or responsive actions taken to evade the bull's horns; these abrupt twisting, dodging, or torso inclinations are known as *quiebros*. Planned movements constitute movement techniques integral to tauromachy and are deliberate efforts to wrest artistry from the conflict situation, whereas the matador's unplanned movements are reflexive actions connected directly to human survival instincts.

In the context of a bullfight *quiebros* are essential movements born of necessity that manifest in moments of immediate, extreme danger. In the flamenco dance context, *quiebros* occur in stylized form and constitute a movement motif. A *quiebro* occurring in the flamenco dance context functions as a metonym for danger or risk, but it also signifies surprise, fun, and play. A *quiebro* is a dodge, an evasive lunge; a common action occurring in the *bulerías* dance form (usually performed with the quality of a *quiebro*) is a *recoje* in which a dancer lunges back toward the diagonal as if to regather or re-collect his or her energy before returning to again face the front.

Participation in the cultural practices of flamenco dance and bullfighting is voluntary, and risk and voluntary participation are both attributes of play behavior. As a metonym, the performance of a *quiebro* within a dance affirms the play ethos. By suggesting a close call or surprise, a *quiebro* may contribute humorous qualities to the dance. This is corroborated by the fact that *quiebros* often occur in flamenco dances that express the lighter emotions: *alegrías*, *bulerías*, or *rumba*. Performed in the bullfight, a *quiebro* is a response to the unexpected; as a dance motif, too, one of the key attributes of a *quiebro* is its unpredictability. When *quiebros* are incorporated into the flamenco dance style, they enliven the dance aesthetic through their implicit reminder of danger, play, and surprise.

Practicing movements with the *capote*, the author performs a *quiebro*, a quick dodge or evasion of a bull. Most often initiated from the body's core, *quiebros* launch the whole body into action with transverse spatial tension. When dodging, one naturally lowers one's center of gravity and retreats back and sideways to escape danger. In this photograph, the resulting lunge (toward the back diagonal with a tilt of the whole torso) closely resembles the flamenco dance movement of a *recoje* (photograph by Melissa Lind).

Embodying the Spanish and Andalusian philosophy of living in the moment, the uncertainty of survival is at the heart of the bullfighting practice. Despite its highly technical techniques, the bullfight is fundamentally improvisational in nature. However often a matador may practice his movement patterns beforehand, the moment of truth in the bullring is also a moment of spontaneity, publicly enacted. The flamenco dancer's psychological terrain shares some qualities with that of the matador. Like the matador, a dancer

Recoje comes from the Spanish verb *recoger*, to collect or gather. Flamenco dances alternate between sections of slower, quieter movements, called *marcaje*, in which a dancer maintains the rhythmic *compás* and interprets the *cante* while a singer sings, and sections of dynamic footwork, called *escobillas*. *Recoje* is a vernacular term for a common movement within the *marcaje* occurring in the second half of a twelve-count phrase. Similar to the *quiebro*, a *recoje* entails a lunge toward the back diagonal with a counterbalancing tilt of the dancer's whole torso (photograph by Melissa Lind).

experiences fear, nervousness, and determination during a period of intense preparation. And like the matador, the flamenco dancer gives a high-energy performance in a public arena, coping with a profoundly unpredictable and improvisational event, unexpected actions by other performers, and the possible game-changing emergence of *duende*.

Interacting with the unknown requires improvisational skills and creates the adventure and excitement of the *corrida* and the flamenco dance performance. Part of a matador's desire to be tested in the bullring is a desire for confrontation and intensity. Similarly, a flamenco dancer seeks to be tested by the challenges inherent to performance. Both dancers and matadors strive to push beyond the commonplace, physically and artistically; through their daring acts of participation, cultural stagnation is averted and the superordinary is made possible.

Dynamic Motifs

Three actions, citing, passing, and the dramatic ending flourishes known as *remates*, are basic components in the interaction between the matador and the bull. As movement motifs, these three actions are incorporated, reiterated, and elaborated within the flamenco dance vocabulary, contributing important dynamics, namely accents and impactive phrasing. Further, these motifs—citing, passing, and *remate*—are often reiterated in sequence; thus, many flamenco dance phrases have a compositional structure that implicitly conveys the drama of the bullfight.

Citing

The matador's act of citing instigates the bull's charge. Often performed with a simultaneous shout of *"¡Éje!"* citing is a sharp, aggressive movement whereby the matador gains the bull's attention, simultaneously crossing into the bull's *jurisdicción*. In the flamenco dance context, citing occurs as a dynamic motif within the interactions of dancers, musicians, and audience. Although the actual shape of the dance movement may vary, the dynamics of directness, quickness, and strength are typical and are consistent with the performer's intention to demand attention. Outsiders to the flamenco dance context and Andalusian culture may interpret the aggressiveness of such movements as signs of anger. However, emic perspectives that take into account the influence of the practices of bullfighting and appreciate conflict as a positive cultural value reveal that such accented movement motifs serve the positive purpose of incitement. The movement motif of citing issues a challenge that demands response and enjoins the participation of a potential adversary, whether a bull, fellow dancer, musician, or the audience itself.

The motif of citing happens often as an element within a *llamada*, the signal between performers that calls for a change, such as for the singer to begin, or indicating that the dancer is about to perform footwork. Flamenco dance and bullfighting both use the term *desplante*; in flamenco dance it refers to an extra long *llamada*, one that is extra showy or *llamativo*.[13] In the bullfight, *desplante* refers to a highly stylized manner of citing that is daring and emphatic. Such terms often are used loosely and their meaning can shift depending on the context.

Passing

The act of passing has great significance in the bullfighter's movement experience and is an important movement motif in the flamenco dance tradition. Two adversaries are united by their mutual participation, as the image and intention of passing take spatial form repeatedly within the bullfight or the dance. As a motif, passing may be referenced in many ways within the dance just as it is performed in many variations in the bullfight itself.[14] In flamenco dance, the motif of passing is enacted both spatially and dynamically through the movement motifs of arcing, peripheral spatial tension, nearness, spiraling, the impactive phrases, and maintained eye contact.

Within the flamenco dance vocabulary, the best-known example of the motif of passing is called *careo*. In Spanish, *careo* (derived from the word *cara*, meaning face) signifies the action or effect of facing off to settle a dispute. The *careo* is basically an *estocada* (lunging movement named and fashioned after the final sword thrust of the matador) as it is performed to either the right or left side. Traditionally, the *careo* is a face-to-face passing of partners that is performed in couple dances. A well-known example of the *careo* is reiterated at the end of the fourth *copla* (short dance or verse) of the *sevillanas* (Matteo with Goya 1990, 51). As they pass one another, dancers maintain a strong, direct, and sustained eye contact that is analogous to the matador who keeps his eyes on the bull as it passes by.

Dancers often perform the movement form and dynamics of the *careo* so as to emphasize the dance step's association with the bullfight. Spanish dance scholar Marina Grut refers to this connection in her description of *careos* (as performed in the fourth *copla* of the *sevillanas*). She describes *careos* as having "the character of a bullfighter avoiding a bull" and mentions a modern-day male dancer who "swivels with his feet together following his partner with his arm, like a bullfighter with his cape" (2002, 40).

Variations of this motif occur also in duet forms of flamenco dance other than the *sevillanas*. The pleasure of sparring with an adversary, whether in play or in all seriousness, is a recognized value within the flamenco dance practice, and the bull is a central symbol of that adversarial spirit. In performing the movement motif of passing, the flamenco dancer, as described by Grut above, consciously draws upon this known cultural metonym. In doing so he summons all that the bull represents and opens the dance to the power of metaphor. Even if a dancer is not fully aware of the implications, cultural meaning is inherent within the motif of passing itself and will tacitly communicate the cultural values of bullfighting to many observers.

Remate

A *remate* is a movement flourish occurring at the end of a series of *pases* and serves as an artistic statement that demonstrates the individual creativity and unique flair (signature or *estampa*) of the matador. Through the brilliance of the *remate* a matador declares domination and triumph over the bull. Also called an *adorno* (adornment), the *remate* demands attention and congratulations from the audience; it is *llamativo*, or showy. Flamenco dance phrases, or long sequences of dance phrases, often end with a *remate* as well. Just as a successful matador will circle the bullring to receive praise from the crowd, a flamenco dancer often enacts triumph at the end of a dance through similar performative actions such as *contoneo*, the arrogant, stylized walking motif that is common to both movement vocabularies.

These three phases of the bullfighter's interaction with the bull—citing, passing, and *remates*—serve a combination of pragmatic and aesthetic purposes within the *corrida*. As dance motifs they serve the flamenco tradition in similar ways. Pragmatically, they constitute clear signals of intention that facilitate communication between dancers and musicians. Aesthetically, they provide a culturally familiar sequence to be varied creatively within the dance. As a set of actions, the most typical order of their sequencing is: citing, several passes, ending with a final *remate*. They often occur in combination with the other movement motifs: arcing, peripheral spatial tension, nearness, spiraling, sustained direct eye contact, confrontational facings, *marcando*, and *quiebros*. The reiteration of these motifs serves the flamenco dance tradition's need for both continuity and innovation, and reinforces Spanish and Andalusian cultural values at the level of somatic experience in the context of both ordinary and super-ordinary events.

Chapter Ten

Kinesthetic Culture

Kinesthetic Culture: A Four-Dimensional Model in Three Spheres

The kinesphere is the sphere of space within which we each live and move, and comprises all three dimensions of space (vertical, horizontal, and sagittal).[1] In addition, Laban coined the term *dynamosphere* to acknowledge the presence of the fourth dimension, time, and so more fully describe the expressive dynamics that we use in our movements within the kinesphere ([1966] 1974, 27–36).

I think of kinesthetic culture as consisting of three realms of phenomena through which the connections between movement and culture take place. I picture these realms as three concentric spheres, nested within one another and sharing freely across highly flexible boundaries. The innermost sphere is an area of somatic and kinetic interplay occurring within the person. Highly subjective and sensate, the inner sphere entails kinesis, which is movement occurring at the cellular level, and is ultimately the root source of our human agency. It is within this sphere that a person absorbs, adapts, resists, or conforms to the processes of enculturation and acculturation. This sphere contains our biological functions, all our movements, and our deepest physiological adaptations to culture; it comprises our innate capacities, our human potential.

Surrounding this somatic center, I envision an intermediate second sphere, a sphere of contact, interaction with others and the environment, learning, and cultural patterning. The phenomena that occur in this second sphere comprise all forms of interplay between the person and his or her cultural environment. This is the sphere of active enculturation and acculturation, of human adaptation, resistance, and self-assertion in relationship to all that a person experiences outside of his or her personal boundaries.

Surrounding both these two inner spheres, and providing them both broader context and special opportunities, I envision the outermost third sphere of kinetic culture, which comprises affective culture itself. In this third sphere, culture's role is not only evident, it appears as a central organizing focus of the person. Here cultural traditions have weight and power, and cultural abstractions have consequence. The inner sphere of somatic and kinetic interplay and the intermediate sphere of cultural patterning are ongoing as the person enters the third sphere of cultural performance, to embody, participate, and perform in the public realm of affective culture. Through dance movements and ritual acts, the individual makes actual and visible the concepts, values, beliefs, or emotions that are central to the culture.

Sphere One: Somatic and Kinetic Interplay

At the core of kinesthetic culture, its innermost sphere, is the body, breathing, sensing, responding, seeking, and taking action. The neurological structure that facilitates kinesthetic experience is known as the sensory-motor system, which connects our sensory experiences with our physical responses and actions. Thomas Hanna notes that "the sensory-motor system is a mechanism fundamental to all human experience and behavior," and describes its importance, saying:

> Everything we sense in the world outside our bodies and everything we sense inside our bodies comes into our brain by way of the sensory nerves. Everything that we do in the world and every movement we make flows out from our brain down the spine by way of the motor nerves. The sensory nerves control our perceptions of the world and of ourselves. The motor nerves control our movements in the world and inside ourselves by means of their attachments to the muscles of the skeleton and the smooth muscles of the viscera [1986, 6].[2]

The sensory-motor system is complexly reciprocal and phenomenally fast in its functioning. It provides us immediate agency in the world through motor function in response to sensory input. However, our motor patterns also affect our perceptions. Movement patterning specialist Bonnie Bainbridge Cohen discusses this complexity, noting that "our perception of movement, i.e., our interpretation of movement, is dependent upon all of our previous experiences of movement, as it is for every other sense. We develop preconceived expectations based upon how we have perceived similar information in our past experiences." Cohen points out that there is a "motor component of perception," that we engage our motor abilities in order "to choose which aspects of incoming stimuli we will absorb or attend to." This capacity "to direct or focus our sense organs" is another aspect of our kinesthetic life that is patterned by culture (B. Cohen 2003, 199).

Somatic knowledge is constructed through a person's inner evaluation of sensual experience and physical action, the continuous cycling of awareness between bodily sensations, emotional content, cognitive functioning, and kinetic responses. In the literature of flamencology and tauromachy, a performer's ability to respond fluidly to the demands of performance is often described as a quality of *plasticidad* (plasticity). Plasticity is a quality that is specifically valued within the flamenco aesthetic. Plasticity is the physical fluidity and adaptive capacity of a performer's body, within which the mutable nature of emotion itself is always implicit. Plasticity refers to the mutability of the person, his or her ability to adapt, accommodate to changing circumstances, and employ a range of movement options; it implies a quality of mobility and change at the cellular level.

Physical plasticity enables a matador to shift weight slightly so as to accommodate the passing of the bull with just inches to spare, evading a bull's unpredictable horn thrust with subtle fluidity. Mental plasticity allows the flamenco dancer to shift tempos, rhythmic accents, or movement qualities improvisationally in response to musical changes and the emotions of the moment. Mental plasticity supports a dancer's instant adaptation of choreographed sequences in response to such variables as spatial limitations, audience interactions, or lighting conditions. Emotion is the root of the flamenco arts; it is the nature of emotions to change, and this is a fundamental understanding in flamenco. Emotional plasticity is the first requisite for emotional volatility. "Plasticity" implies changeability, that emotional qualities are capable of fluctuating, that a performer may transform one emotional state into another with no loss of integrity. "Volatility" implies that emotions vary greatly in their intensity and may change erratically, their timing unpredictable. Emotional plasticity and volatility are highly valued in flamenco dance; they manifest in quick changes of mood and expression. They enliven the flamenco *juerga* by allowing a performer to shift between serious and festive emotions, fluidly, moment-by-moment, in response to outer events and inner experience.

A performer's capacity to both initiate action and react constitutes a dynamic factor in flamenco and bullfighting practices. Proactivity occurs when a person takes action in order to fulfill needs, while reactivity occurs when a person responds to a need deficit, such as an affront to safety, integrity, or values. At the physiological level, proactive and reactive movement impulses manifest in the deep interplay between sensory experience and motor response. The ability of a flamenco dancer or matador to be proactive is critical to her or his personal sense of empowerment and the effectiveness of her or his public performance. A flamenco dancer or matador's reactivity, whether emotional, cognitive, or kinetic, completes the dynamic cycle by acknowledging human vulnerability and risk.

In *Playing and Reality*, psychiatrist D. W. Winnicott (1971) discusses cultural experience as a transitional phenomenon that functions in the space between a person's inner experience and the external environment, the same space wherein a child's transitional object functions.[3] He links cultural experience with the phenomenon of human play, asserting that "the place where cultural experience is located is in the *potential space* between the individual and the environment. The same can be said of playing. Cultural experience begins with creative living first manifested in play" (100; Winnicott's italics). Discussing enculturation he says. "For every individual the use of this space is determined by *life experiences* that take place at the early stages of the individual's existence" (100; Winnicott's italics).

Sphere Two: Cultural Patterning

The processes of enculturation and acculturation function in relationship to the two categories identified by Kealiinohomoku as the ordinary and the super-ordinary (1976, 55). The second and third spheres of kinesthetic culture comprise the actions, responses, and cultural learning experienced through ordinary and super-ordinary events. The kinesthetic culture of Spain comprises movement patterns that function in the context of the ordinary activities of Spanish life, as well as specialized movement patterns, such as those found in the movement vocabularies of flamenco dance and bullfighting, that function in the context of the super-ordinary events of Spanish public ritual life. Knowledge of the culture-specific baseline of movement patterns that occur within the category of ordinary behavior enables movement researchers to properly identify and appropriately interpret behaviors, such as dance, ritual, or play, which belong to the category of the super-ordinary.

Cultural patterning in the second sphere of kinesthetic culture comprises the enculturation and acculturation of movement patterns and habits associated with ordinary daily activities of living. Knowledge of these normative behavioral patterns, pervasive movement patterns, and typical affective patterns of a particular culture contributes to a holistic understanding of the culture. In fact, understanding this realm of ordinary movement behavior provides a culture-specific baseline from which to evaluate specialized cultural behaviors such as flamenco and bullfighting.

Perceptual Inference Patterns

The way that a people perceive and interpret their life experiences is determined by their enculturation. Patterns of perception, sometimes referred to as "perceptual inference habits," are an important aspect of cultural patterning (Segall, Campbell, and Herskovits 1966, 214).[4] Spanish perceptual inference habits focus on emotion and sociality. Within the kinesthetic culture of Spain, meaning is sought through contact and energy exchanges with others in the cultural environment. In daily life, people notice emotional content and intensity, and they interpret and value these qualities as proof of an individual's authenticity. In performance situations, the personality expressed through a performer's movement style or *estampa* is interpreted and valued as a sign of integrity, presence, and uniqueness. As a result of their enculturation, Andalusians require emotional stimulation; they seek it through ordinary patterns of sociality as well as through super-ordinary events such as flamenco dance and bullfighting that support the more intense sharing of emotional catharsis.

Behavioral Patterns and Cultural Relativity

People living in Spain generally enjoy well-defined personal boundaries,[5] and this is evident in the social norms of Spanish culture that encourage public display and performative behaviors. As a result, rather than avoiding or defusing potential conflict situations, Spanish people often enjoy the heightened energy that conflict situations create. They enjoy dramatic events and celebrate life through their participation in super-ordinary events, such as the cultural practices of flamenco dance and bullfighting that involve emotional intensity and situations of risk and conflict. However, this enjoyment of conflict also occurs in ordinary life situations.

As an example of how this may play out in daily life, I once went for an afternoon walk in downtown Madrid arm in arm with my *dueña* (landlady) Encarnación. A delivery truck had double-parked along the street and the truck driver was in the process of getting a ticket from a policeman. As a conflict-avoiding Anglo-American, a person enculturated with a less well defined personal boundary, I felt that the appropriate behavior was to ignore the situation and walk on by; after all, in my view, it was the truck driver's business and the policeman was already doing his job. However, Encarnación was a Madrileña and a señora of a certain age, with a well-defined personal boundary as a result of her Spanish enculturation. So, although she was probably less than five feet tall, Encarnación enthusiastically launched herself into the middle of the situation, scolding the truck driver and arguing with the policeman.

Finally, the policeman convinced Encarnación that he was taking care of the situation and that she should continue on down the sidewalk. I sensed patient acceptance in the policeman's manner; he seemed to understand that she was really just having a good time on her afternoon walk and happy to come across an opportunity to boost her energy and spark up her day by participating in a little conflict. It boosted her ego, strengthened her sense of self, exercised her sense of agency, demonstrated her character and right to assert herself publicly in relation to her broader community, the city of Madrid, and she had the opportunity to do all this with me, her foreign friend from America, as witness. She was having a great time.

In situations such as this it is useful to remember the theory of cultural relativity, that the observations and evaluations one might make in relation to the behaviors of people from another culture are based on one's own early enculturation. Anglo-Americans unaware of the effects of cultural relativity may distrust open emotionality, considering Spanish expressive behaviors excessive, exotic, and overly passionate. They might judge behaviors as "lacking self control" and therefore the Spanish as "less than," uncivilized, primitive, and childlike. By Anglo-American standards of adult behavior, Spaniards seem to lack the ability to contain, inhibit, repress, or sublimate their feelings. In contrast, the norms of Anglo-America cultural patterns result in self-restricting behaviors and inhibited or cautious emotional display. Lacking awareness of cultural relativity, Spaniards may consider such Anglo behaviors to be uptight, cold, and passionless; the ethnocentrism of Spaniards may lead to evaluations of the Anglo-Americans as "less than," machinelike, passionless, and rigid. We only see other cultures through the lens of our own.

High-Context Culture Patterns

The Spanish kinesthetic culture also functions as what anthropologist Edward T. Hall would describe as a high-context culture, a complexly layered culture in which tacit knowledge and implied meanings are critical (1976, 105–116). Within the daily lives of Andalusians (the cultural group most closely tied to the practices of flamenco dance and bullfighting), the social rules are both complex and tacit in nature. Andalusian movement behaviors respond to social pressures toward conformity that are sometimes quite intense; however, this is countered by an equal drive toward individual expression within socially proscribed boundaries. This combination of contrasting drives—toward social conformity and toward individual distinction—results in a people accustomed to both monitoring the details of their own behavior and watching each other carefully. The constant social monitoring of Andalusian life requires that people be very adept at reading subtle signals conveyed through movement behaviors, clothing choices, eye contact, and vocal patterns.

Because of the high-context nature of Spanish Andalusian culture, the complex cultural practices of flamenco dance and bullfighting require high levels of syntactical knowledge in order to be practiced or fully appreciated in performance. This high-context complexity places demands on both participants and observers to recognize cultural signals and know a great deal about the events they observe. These demands contribute to the intense enthusiasm aficionados feel for flamenco dance and bullfighting; those aficionados who are most familiar with and alert to contextual cues and who have the highest degree of syntactical knowledge of these art forms are best equipped to fully appreciate and evaluate performance events.

Interspecies Movement Patterns

Traveling through life in the company of other human beings, we interact with one another in a wide range of contexts. This provides diverse experiences, a diversity compounded when one considers that human beings also interact in a variety of ways with nonhuman animals. Generally, human beings, as a species, are associated with the phenomenon of culture; in contrast, it is generally felt that nonhuman species do not display true cultural behavior. The degree to which nonhuman animals have been found to demonstrate rudimentary levels of culture is an expanding area of study with interesting implications for cultural research generally.

In *The Evolution of Culture in Animals*, evolutionary biologist John Tyler Bonner defines culture as "the transmission of information by behavioral means" and discusses teaching and learning as the behaviors through which culture is transmitted in animals (1980, 10). Interspecies teaching and learning of movement patterns is of particular interest in relationship to the kinesthetic culture of flamenco and bullfighting practices. Spaniards who live in rural areas often live in symbiotic relationship with animals, caring for them, training them, and relying on animals for their sustenance and livelihood. The lifestyle of Andalusian ranchers and agricultural workers entails a degree of learning, teaching, and mutual adaptation across species. Does the proud lifted chest of the flamenco dancer or matador reflect the performer's self-identification or emulation of the elegance of Spanish horses, or have Spanish horses been trained to posture in ways expressive of human ideals of elegance and pride? In either case, the resemblance is striking and is part of Spanish kinesthetic culture. Inevitably, Spanish horses and bulls are woven into the meaning-making project of Spanish affective culture in a very wide range of contexts, from the formality of the professional bullrings and the less public practice sessions of the *tienta*, to the more chaotic public forms such as the *capeas* and *encierros* (running with the bulls).[6]

Considering the question of interspecies communications, Cynthia Knox notes that "the duck cannot tell us much about duck-ness. Nor can we tell the porpoise much about human-ness—at least, not with words. But we sense a connectedness—which we attribute, rightly, I believe, to our common sentience" (Knox 1992, 56). Much of cross-species communication occurs through nonverbal communication, through touch, sounds, interactions, felt presence, and eye contact. In the documentary film *The Lady Bullfighter*, the female matador Evelina Fabregas speaks about her experiences and feelings about killing bulls. Asked by an interviewer, "Have you ever felt sad when you killed a bull?" Fabregas responds by saying,

> Yes. Once I was fighting a bull and when it came to killing him at that moment he gave me a look of affection. A bull had never looked at me like that before. It was the moment of death and the tears almost came down my face. He had such a penetrating stare. He looked at me with such warmth. It was very difficult to deal with [Bryer 1989].

Interactions with bulls in the context of the *corrida* (or with female calves in the context of the *tienta*) involve humans in movement patterns that entail high degrees of empathic awareness and rhythmic entrainment in relation to the animal. Andalusians are also intensely involved in the movement patterns of their horses through the activities of training, riding, and caretaking.[7] Given that movement patterning and repatterning occurs between human beings through the processes of enculturation and acculturation, it is reasonable to assume that some degree of movement patterning and repatterning also occurs between species.

Sphere Three: Cultural Performance

In the third and outermost sphere of kinesthetic culture, enculturative and acculturative learning and movement patterning take place in the context of super-ordinary events, the performances and rituals of affective culture. In the context of super-ordinary events such as flamenco performance and bullfighting, one often sees that all three spheres of kinesthetic culture are active: (1) the somatic/kinetic body is present, thus moving, sensing, and responding to the event, (2) the ordinary movements of interaction and sociality are occurring, and (3) super-ordinary events present opportunities for heightened movement experience and performative activity, including the possibility of emotional catharsis for individuals or the group as a whole.

Movement as an Integrative Factor in Culture

Through embodiment we are present and able to experience events. Through movement we acquire agency, and are able to take action and participate in events. Herskovits states that "the integrative factor gives to a cultural complex its unity, no matter what fortuitous traits seemingly comprise it" (1964, 91). It is clear that the social worlds of flamenco dance and bullfighting overlap; focusing on embodiment and movement patterns, one can also see that they overlap within bodies, particularly within those individuals that participate in both practices. The body of an individual that participates in super-ordinary events of flamenco and bullfighting and the ordinary life that surrounds and connects the two practices will resonate with their values, emotions, movement patterns, and cultural attitudes. I see movement as a key integrative factor giving unity to the cultural complex of flamenco dance and bullfighting.

The performative behaviors and kinesthetic phenomena of flamenco and bullfighting play out, from an inner sphere of intimate somatic and kinetic complexity, through the interactive sphere of culturally inscribed actions, reactions, and interactions, and emerge into the external sphere of cultural performance with its outwardly directed expression and publicly performed affective culture. They also play out as individuals make gradual transitions between their ordinary life to super-ordinary events and back again to the ordinary.

In dividing affective culture into the ordinary and the super-ordinary, Kealiinohomoku provides a useful contrasting pair; however, these two realms are not opposites separated by rigid boundaries. In fact, a great deal of human cultural activity occurs in the transition from the ordinary to super-ordinary through anticipation, preparation, planning, training, and rehearsing activities prior to super-ordinary events, and in the transition back to the ordinary through rest, recovery, reflection, review, and cleanup activities afterwards. Super-ordinary events also slip into ordinary daily life as people watch bullfights on television, read newspaper reviews of dance performances, or review and discuss events in informal conversations. Also, when aspiring dancers and matadors prepare to participate in super-ordinary events, part of their daily routine will be training, disciplined practice, and rehearsals that flavor their ordinary life with the spice and adrenaline-heightened experience of the super-ordinary.

Thomas J. Csordas proposes "embodiment as a paradigm or methodological orientation" for anthropology, suggesting that "embodied experience is the starting point for analyzing human participation in a cultural world"

(2002, 241). He distinguishes between body and embodiment, saying, "The body is a biological, material entity, while embodiment can be understood as an indeterminate methodological field defined by perceptual experience and the mode of presence and engagement in the world" (2002, 241). Thus, within Csordas' concept of embodiment the person, subjective and self-aware, is present, and the human somatic perspective, which includes experience, intentionality, and agency, is acknowledged. It is important that the words *embodiment* and *somatic* not be used in ways that suggest the body as a sensate, but largely passive, entity. The concept of kinesthetic culture both acknowledges the effects of culture on sensory awareness and recognizes the central role of human agency and personhood in the life of a culture.

Both sensory awareness and active agency are inherently interconnected and function together as neurological partners through a refined sequence of sensory output, perceptual interpretation, motor planning, motor response, sensory feedback, and perceptual interpretation. Investigating this sequence closely, Bonnie Cohen describes a more complex sequence, adding "preconceived expectations" and "active focusing" to the work of the sensorimotor loop (2003, 199–203). These additional elements reconfirm my understanding of how aesthetic and aesthemic appreciation of super-ordinary events is constructed. Arriving with preconceived expectations, audience members actively focus on a performance event in order to see if it will meet those expectations; they actively seek to see what they are culturally prepared to see. Thus, the cultural expectations and syntactical knowledge of individual audience members actively contribute to their experience, perhaps as much as does the flamenco performance or bullfight itself.

In examining the similarities between flamenco and bullfighting practices, both broadly in terms of their formal and informal structures, and in the minutiae of the movement motifs that illustrate their connection, my thoughts often return to the 1968 Choreometrics Project of Alan Lomax and Kealiinohomoku's critiques of it. Kealiinohomoku and Lomax appear to agree on the importance of redundancy in facilitating communication (Lomax 1967; Kealiinohomoku 1976). However, in discussing the communicative effectiveness of dance, Kealiinohomoku describes both redundancy and affect as important elements. She notes that both dance and music compositions "depend primarily upon redundancy and affect as their major devices of communication" (1976, 103).

Affect or emotion is a vital element that Lomax did not adequately consider in his study; affect and emotion may be exactly the elements that are carried in an individual's body as he or she transitions between ordinary and super-ordinary realms. Both flamenco dance and bullfighting constitute super-ordinary occasions in the cultural life of Andalusia and Spain, and the important attribute of redundancy is evident in their performance, as is the reinvigorating effect of innovation. Also clearly evident is the importance of emotional affect. Despite any successful reiteration of cultural form, a performance will have failed utterly if it elicits no emotional response. If afterwards one can say "*No dice nada*" (it says nothing), then a performance event will have failed the primary test of its culture.

Implicit within discussions of redundancy and affect is an underlying epistemological issue. While redundancy can be measured quantitatively, and thus provide objective data that satisfy the methodologies of "hard" science, affect or emotion require qualitative evaluation, provided through subjective data that report on felt experience, the type of research that constitutes "soft" science. In regard to these contrasting ways of knowing, Csordas, in a footnote to his essay "Embodiment as a Paradigm for Anthropology," makes the following point:

> The very distinction between hard and soft is imbued with machismo, for there is no doubt about its cultural connotation that hard data are more tough-minded and hence better. To the extent that our attitudes are shaped by conventional metaphors, and as someone who has worked in both modes, I would propose that we experiment with replacing "soft and hard" data by "flexible and brittle" data [2002, 291, n23].

Alan Lomax and his research collaborators in the Choreometrics Project, Irmgard Bartenieff and Forrestine Paulay, attempted to accomplish both cross-cultural and intracultural research aims. They focused on redundancy as a measure of the movement connections between ordinary and super-ordinary movement patterns by adopting "the strategy of searching for the redundant patterns discoverable in the everyday activity of a culture that resembled the stylized forms of its dances" (Lomax, Bartenieff, and Paulay 1968, 223). Choreometrics was devised as a means of using "dance as a measure of culture" (223). It emphasized etic research approaches, seeking to reduce a highly complex array of movement phenomena to data that could answer specific questions. Accessing emic knowledge, employing expansionist rather than reductionist approaches, or acknowledging the fundamental indeterminacy of movement phenomena was contrary to Lomax's vision for the research project.

Emotion was not of immediate interest to the Choreometrics Project researchers, who "considered dance first as a representation and reinforcement of cultural pattern and only secondarily as an expression of individual emotion" (Lomax, Bartenieff, and Paulay 1968, 223). By focusing on movement pattern redundancy and quantitative data, Lomax amassed "brittle" data to confirm his intracultural hypothesis that the movement patterns of work and everyday activity influence the movement patterns of dance. Lomax, Barteneiff, and Paulay write that within the Choreometrics Project dance and movement were rated "in extremely general qualitative terms" (1968, 223). However, their observations of qualitative phenomena were collected, collated, and analyzed as quantitative data.

To largely discount the role of affect and emotion may have initially increased the respect afforded the Choreometrics Projects by a scientific community accustomed to "hard" data. Lomax sought to link movement phenomena that occur in the contrasting realms of the ordinary and super-ordinary. However, given the importance of emotion, particularly in the realm of the super-ordinary, choosing to largely discount the role of affect was ultimately counterproductive. Since its completion, the Choreometrics Project has had many critics in the anthropology of dance field, such as J. Hanna (1979a), Kealiinohomoku (1979), and Williams (1972). Emotional content and its relative intensity remain key components (along with redundancy) in the study of affective culture generally, and certainly any discussion of the relatedness of bullfighting and flamenco dance that relied on quantitative evidence alone would provide, at most, only half of the information.

Employing embodiment as a paradigm for anthropology, as suggested by Csordas (2002, 58–87), necessarily entails using somatic perspectives. As defined by Thomas Hanna,

> somatics is the field which studies the *soma*: namely the body as perceived from within by first-person perception. When a human being is observed from the outside—i.e., from the third-person viewpoint—the phenomenon of a human body is perceived. But when this same human being is observed from the first-person viewpoint of his [her] own proprioceptive senses, a categorically different phenomenon is perceived: the human soma [1986, 341].

It is conceivable that the somatic effects in the body in response to the emotions and actions of the bullfight and flamenco dance (changes in heart rate, breathing rate and depth, adrenaline, brain chemistry, muscle tone, etc.) could be measured to produce brittle data. However, such data could report only phenomena of the biological body and would run the risk of being senseless from emic perspectives (*no dice nada*). Where understanding of persons and their culture is sought, a need for brittle quantitative data reporting on the phenomena of the body is limited. Instead, it is somatic evidence, which extends validation to the first-person perception of the body and interrogates emic perspectives of movement phenomena, that proves most useful. Emotion constitutes the basis for aesthetic experience in both flamenco dance and bullfighting, making the understanding of human emotion critical and requisite to any analysis of these practices. The value that academic endeavors often place on researcher objectivity and emotional detachment do not suffice when physical sensuality, risk taking, and emotional catharsis are at the heart of what is being examined and understood.

Kinesthetic Culture in Conflict and Celebration

Flamenco dance and bullfighting practices celebrate life through the stimulation of poetic sensibilities and the adrenaline-producing excitement of risk and conflict. The poetic sensibilities and passionate spirit that are central to flamenco dance and bullfighting are kept alive and function by cycling and recycling through the emotions of conflict, risk, play, catharsis, and celebration. The intrinsic relatedness of flamenco and bullfighting stems from the values of control, elegance, and power idealized through the dance and the play between danger, unpredictability, and technique characterized by the bullfight. The flamenco dancer is free to move within a broad range of emotions, including the type of emotions engendered through the experience of the bullfight; the matador aspires to the experience of the dance while constrained by the reality of the bull's dangerous presence. The aesthemic concept of *duende* is a significant organizing principle, but the contrasting elements of comedy, play, surprise, and spontaneity are also important within both practices. Comedic elements occur in the lighthearted dances of the flamenco tradition and constitute emergent qualities in the bullring, where they are inherent in the unpredictable nature of the interspecies encounter.

Conflict and Risk

Within Spain's kinesthetic culture, conflict functions as a strategy for making contact. Within social interactions, conflict functions as a strategy to satisfy the basic human needs of contact, intensity, belonging, and self-knowledge, for being known as well as knowing others deeply. Conflict is valued as an opportunity to bond with others and as a source of dynamic energy worthy of celebration. Conflict provides opportunities for passionate interactions that result in revelations of the character, integrity, or mettle of an individual. Deep sorrow, anger, or struggles of the soul are shared and celebrated through flamenco song and dance; in the Spanish worldview, all of life's emotions are valued.

The performance of a matador or flamenco dancer reveals the interplay between embodiment and cultural meaning. The ritual of the *corrida* may express reverence and admiration for the nobility of the bull, a deep appreciation for the natural instincts of the animals with which some Andalusian and Spanish people share a symbiotic relationship. Within the bullfighting arena, risk, danger, and conflict are essential elements that draw public attention; dynamic tensions fueled by conflict are also notable in flamenco performance. In either case, a performing protagonist engages antagonistic forces while encircled by a community of witnesses. In the bullfight arena a matador demonstrates his or her courage by meeting the bull, being to being, to engage in a ritual of conflict. In a flamenco performance, the conflict enacted may be internal as the dancer strives to master artistic territory. It may be abstract as a dancer strives to conform to the structural forms of music and rhythm, or it may be emotional or spiritual as the dancer participates in the art form with transcendent passion or *duende*.

The tradition of bullfighting intentionally creates risk; it creates a context of danger or crisis. Participation is freely chosen. In this way, bullfighting is similar to other cultural traditions that provoke crisis or induce catharsis as a means of demonstrating human endurance or courage. Viewing conflict, crisis, and catharsis as strategies, it becomes apparent that bullfighting may serve a wide array of human needs: self-empowerment, individuality, self-worth, self-respect, purpose, honesty, mental stimulation, heightened awareness, beauty, grace, inspiration, creativity, mastery, admiration, appreciation, acknowledgment, recognition, validation, intensity, excitement, passion, or communion.

Strathern notes that "what is embodied is always some set of meanings, values, tendencies, orientations, that derive from the sociocultural realm" (2004, 197). However, the embodiment of culture is not only a derivative of culture; the embodiment of culture through dance, play, and ritual also creates, asserts, and reinforces cultural values. The psychological element of conflict residing at the center of bullfighting and flamenco practices is embodied in their movement styles through expressive qualities of quickness, strength, directness, and tension, and the use of extreme countertensions (*oposiciones*). Flamenco dance and bullfighting aesthetics emerge from the experience of an embodied human being facing, respectively, the challenge of the music/audience or the danger of the bull.

Emotion, Catharsis, and Transcendence

As for the public, the cultural practices of flamenco dance and bullfighting serve a unique and culture-specific need for a communal and shared emotional resonance. Bullfighting and flamenco communities celebrate life through the cathartic emotions released when, through the act of witnessing, they participate in the dynamic tensions of conflict. The repeated shared experience of dynamic tension followed by emotional release forms a basis for deep knowledge and shared cultural values. Having all witnessed the same bullfight, a crowd achieves an emotional and energetic resonance that then carries over into the socializing activities that follow immediately after the bullfight. Such experiences often continue to hold meaning long after the event, as in the instance of particularly dramatic happenings, unique performances, or history-making outcomes. In the flamenco tradition, also, a notably successful performance event will achieve notoriety, elicit commentaries, and heighten the sociality of the group's cultural life.

Celebration and Play

Both flamenco dance and bullfighting are art forms and may therefore be thought of as high forms of play. "Art, like play, sometimes takes risks that threaten the tidiness that civilization values so highly. Art and play are sources of new experience and they encourage change, so they worry people who like things to stay put and be obedient. They are not the kinds of activities that fit into neat categories, and they are both full of surprises" (Meeker 1997, 19). Valuing transformative art traditions, Joseph Meeker is perhaps assuming that the arts in question stress innovation and creativity. However, art traditions may also assert and maintain a social or cultural status quo through reiteration and redundancy.

Whether bullfighting and flamenco dance are practiced as cultural games or performative events, whether they occur in communion with intimate friends or as a public spectacle, they contain the energy dynamics of both fighting and play. Bullfighting is most associated with the energy dynamics of the fight. Bullfighting is a ritual event with formal protocol, and its traditions remain primarily conservative. Play is its leavening element. Flamenco dance is associated with the energy dynamics of play. Although the artistic rule of flamenco's rhythmic form, the *compás*, stabilizes the tradition over time, the flamenco dance practice often loosens social constraints through informal and spontaneous performance. The element of conflict gives the flamenco dance practice its social significance; it roots the practice in the hard realities of life.

The arts are the epitome of cultural play. "The play of great art calls for high skills and imagination, and reminds us that the world itself can be our gigantic playground" (Meeker 1997, 19). The bullfight practice provides opportunities for a type of play—a deep play between animal and human, between life and death—just as the flamenco dance practice provides opportunities for the enactment of conflict and life's darker moods. Creativity, a transcendent quality valued in both the bullfighting arena and the dance performance space, meets basic human needs for novelty, spontaneity, self-expression, self-empowerment, freedom, play, and celebration. Flamenco and bullfighting aficionados anticipate and require the emergence of creativity; thus, from contexts of dynamic conflict there emerge life-affirming qualities of hope, surprise, survival, courage, passion, and the miraculous. "Most play involves risks of some kind" (18).

In both the intimate social circle of flamenco performance and the public bullfight arena, human courage is proved through a combination of artistry and risk. Risk and passion are the crucibles of both flamenco and bullfighting, giving them their performative power within the kinesthetic culture of Spain. Whether their results are tragic, comic, or sublime, flamenco and bullfighting events occur in the realm of the super-ordinary and signal an uplifting revitalization of a cultural community.

Siguiriyas. *Sitting in anticipation, tall, proud, full of self. Glowing. Belonging here, I sit beside* peña *friends, around us the smells of food, sounds of laughter and voices raised, colors and motion swirling. Suddenly, the first dark chords of the* siguiriyas *strike the room. The sounds of the guitar searing the air with memories and loss. Siguiriyas, its rhythm relentless and mean. Its vortex streams upward even as I rush deep, down, into the interior space of the music and my body. Fierce energy rises to meet the challenge of those piercing chords. I rise to my feet, each step forward a commitment to the coming dance. Stepping forward, trembling and unshielded, I stand before my community, friends, and strangers. Seeking good ground, I stand firm in this* querencia *from which I take strength and can grow. Dance of risk, of conflict, of struggle. With resolve I begin; arms weaving, chest straining. Entranced by a darkening vision, I turn inward and face the demons. For my community, I dance each demon down, one by one. This shared catharsis is for them, friends and strangers alike. I dance with the ocean of our grief, our fear, our sorrow, our anger. Summoning my dear familiar partners to the dance. Come grief, dance with me. Come sorrow, come fear, come anger, come betrayal, dance with me. No bull rushes to annihilate me, only demons and the unknown, only the sharpest cutting blade of love. The guitar resounds with pain, the practiced singer's voice breaks, undefined feelings stir, and in my body arises the portent of movements crafted by all that is not holy.*

Spinning down, inward into the depths, seeking power for the struggle, life force rising. I will not be denied. I summon from within powers I had thought lost. Dance, help me drive back grief, overcome sorrow. Dance, help me give birth to courage, rare like a white lion, keening like a river on fire, real like the blackest bull covered in dust and blood. Siguiriyas, its imperative rhythm, life force rising. I will not be defeated. I fight to overcome death's power, to overcome all that which strives to defeat me. Whatever demons next appear, I am present, I am here, spirit honed and ready to meet life's cruelest lies. My feet resist, punishing the floor with determined force. Arms grasping, space thick with sorrow, evasive torso arcing, stinging gestures of hope and despair, still my fighting spirit dances on, past hope and despair, into the new territory of a willful faith. Eyes forward, challenging my community to see me dance among them, fierce and proud, to see in my dancing a battle won. Triumph over tragedy, loss, difficulty. Until, by bearing witness, in them too a spirit stirs. Welling upward come resourcefulness and energy for their own struggles. Uplifted, a catharsis of striving and triumph for all. **Siguiriyas.**

Appendix 1

Laban Movement Analysis Overview

The theories and symbol systems known as Laban Movement Analysis (LMA) emerged as Rudolph von Laban (1879–1953), with his colleagues and students, worked to develop an effective system for the notation of dance and other movement phenomena. Their work produced three interrelated theoretical systems, Labanotation, Effort-Shape, and Choreutics (also referred to as Space Harmony) (Bartenieff 1970). The LMA system is multifaceted and complex; its most basic theoretical concepts are summarized below.

Labanotation is a symbol system that facilitates a descriptive written notation of dance and other movement phenomena. "Making use of geometry, dynamics and anatomical concepts," Laban defined "the phenomena of movement for the first time in kinetic terms … abstracting them into pictorial symbols" (Bartenieff 1970, 14).

Effort-Shape theories and symbols facilitate research through descriptive notation of the qualitative attributes of movement phenomena. A mover's expressive dynamics are identified in relation to four Effort factors: flow, weight, time, and space. Effort-Shape facilitates the notation of movement qualities as they occur in combinations, and their sequential distribution in time, i.e., dynamic phrasing.

Choreutics/Space Harmony theories and symbols define the dynamic space through which all movement passes. This system enables the notation of movements occurring in single dimensions, two-dimensional planes, and many three-dimensional forms.

While LMA concepts and symbol systems provide research tools for the study of isolated movement features, Laban's theories also express a deeply sophisticated understanding of the integrated nature of movement phenomena. Concepts of body, shape, space, and effort are understood to function in conjunction with each other. "The whole framework represents a kind of phenomenology of movement elements" (Bartenieff 1970, 13).

Through developing researchers' skills in observation, performance, and notation, LMA enables them to recognize combinations of dynamics, body shaping, and spatial use within movement sequences. The scientific values and etic methods of LMA make it a reliable data-gathering methodology for the identification and categorization of movement elements for cross-cultural dance and movement research. LMA has been used in various cross-cultural dance research contexts, most notably perhaps the Choreometrics Project designed by Alan Lomax (1968). See audiovisual materials listed in the bibliography: Lomax (1977); Lomax and Choreometrics Project of Columbia University Dept. of Anthropology (1976); Lomax and Paulay (1977); Lomax, Paulay, and Choreometrics Project of Columbia University Dept. of Anthropology (1984).

In this book LMA concepts are used primarily to identify movement attributes. For readers interested in learning more about the LMA system, useful texts are listed in the bibliography under: Bartenieff, B. Cohen, Daly, Davis, Dell, Guest, Hackney, Jablonko and Kagan, Laban, Lomax, Matteo, Maletic, Moore, North, Sossin, Van Zile, and Winter.

Appendix 2

Notes on Language Use

Translations

Much of the research for this book was pursued using Spanish-language texts. Unless otherwise noted, all translations are my own. I used the following dictionaries:

Diccionario de la lengua española. Edited by Real Academia Española. Decimoctava Edición (18th ed.). Madrid: Editorial Espasa-Calpe, 1956.
Raventós, Margaret Hambleton. *Spanish-English, English-Spanish Dictionary*. 2d ed., New York: Random House, 1999.

For the convenience of English-speaking readers, when material from a Spanish-language text is quoted, it is translated into the English language. For the convenience of Spanish-speaking readers, the original text in Spanish is provided in a chapter note. For works written in Spanish, the titles are shown in English in parentheses. The first time a Spanish word is used, a brief definition is provided in the text and again in a glossary of flamenco and bullfighting terms, and other Spanish words. Spanish words unfamiliar to most English speakers are italicized. Spanish words such as aficionado, fiesta, hacienda, matador, etc., that have been incorporated into English usage are not italicized, but are listed in the glossary.

In using my reference list, it will be helpful to those who do not speak Spanish to know that Spanish surnames often consist of a double family name, with the father's family name preceding the mother's family or birth name. Such compound names are alphabetized under the first element of the double name. For example, Alfonso Puig Claramunt is listed under Puig Claramunt, and Federico García Lorca is listed under García Lorca.

Terminology

For readers who may not be familiar with the more technical terminology in this book, an overview of Laban Movement Analysis is provided in Appendix 1. Technical terms related to Rudolph von Laban's system of movement analysis are italicized when they are first presented, accompanied by a brief definition in the text or in a chapter note.

Gender Representation

My goal has been to write about the hierarchical social structures and dichotomized beliefs of bullfighting and flamenco dance without necessarily reinforcing the cultural values or political perspectives they empower. The issue of sexual identity, sexual behavior, and gender norms is a case in point, and I certainly do not want my language use to add to cultural biases against female matadors or male flamenco dancers.

The language I use will, however, accurately represent the facts, namely, that matadors are predominantly male, and female flamenco dancers outnumber male flamenco dancers. Despite being fewer in number, male flamenco dancers are often highly rewarded and may exert a significant influence within this female domain, as teachers, choreographers, performing artists, or directors of professional dance companies. The same cannot be said of female matadors, who are fewer in number and are significantly disenfranchised in the male-dominated field of bullfighting. I have chosen to use gendered pronouns in a manner that reflects, at least in part, these disparities. I use "he and she" when referring to matadors and "she and he" when referring to flamenco dancers; thus in relationship to each cultural practice I refer first to the predominant sex followed by the underrepresented sex.

When quoting materials that use male-specific words as generics, my strategy has been as follows: when I believe that the author's intentions were to describe a phenomenon that applies equally to all sexes, I have added to the quoted material the appropriate corresponding female or generic language in brackets. Additionally, though it sometimes seems to me that an author should have known better than to use male-specific words as generics, I prefer to avoid the censorious and have therefore provided publication dates, letting the reader consider and interpret each case individually.

The issues of gender and language are further complicated by the contrasting rules of the Spanish language regarding gender. For instance, in Spanish any group of people that includes both males and females is referred to using the masculine form. Therefore, in the case of the word torero (meaning bullfighter), the word toreros is the plural form and refers to male bullfighters and bullfighters generally. Thus toreros includes females, while rendering them invisible. The feminine word form *torera* and its plural form, *toreras*, refer to females only. In other words, if there were twenty female *toreras* and one male torero, as a group they would be referred to using the masculine form, toreros. Since the words matador and aficionado are recognized in the English language, I use them as English words. I also use the word performer as a generic form; this allows me to discuss flamenco dancers and matadors together in one category.

The topic of bullfighting also brings up issues of gender and language use related to bovine animals. There are two primary distinctions to be made in this regard: *toro*, which means bull, a mature uncastrated male bovine animal; and *vaquilla*, which means a female calf. In some instances, such as descriptions of movement interactions between a bull and a male matador, the use of male pronouns for both becomes problematic. For clarity's sake, I often use the pronoun "it" when referring to the bull; when interactions involved a female calf and male matador this problem did not arise.

Glossary of Spanish Terms

adorno   An adornment. In a bullfight, the culminating movement at the end of a series of passes of the cape. Similar to terms *desplante* and *remate*.
aficionado/aficionada   Aficionado; a fan, enthusiast, scholar, or expert.
alegría   Joy.
alegrías   Lighthearted twelve-count flamenco rhythm, music, and dance form, upbeat and in a major key.
alternativa   The ceremony in which a *novillero* or *novillera* becomes a *matador de toros*.
ambiente   Ambiance or atmosphere, the sensual context.
amor propio   Self-love.
ayuda   Literally, help. A wooden or aluminum sword used to help support the *muleta*.
bailaora/bailaor   Indigenously trained flamenco dancer, capable of serious dance expression.
bailarina/bailarin   Classically trained dancer, with a light emotional palette.
baile   Dance.
banderilla   Colorful barb or short lance used in bullfighting.
banderillero   Member of the matador's *cuadrilla*. A *torero* with specialized skills who thrusts the *banderilla* into the bull's neck during the bullfight.
bata de cola   Dress with a long train; *cola* literally means "tail."
boda gitana   Gypsy wedding.
braceo   Arm and hand movements in flamenco. Flamenco hand movements are called *maneo*, *flores*, or *filigrana*.
bulerías   A quick-tempo improvisational form of flamenco music and dance based on a twelve-count phrase.
burladero   Wooden barrier inside of the bullfight arena.
cabal   An expert, an artistic authority, critic.
cafés cantantes   Singing cafés.
caló   Language spoken by the *gitano* people, a blend of Romany and Spanish.
cantaor/cantaora   Flamenco singer.
cante   Song, flamenco song, the flamenco song tradition.
capa   Cape.

capea   Rural fiesta. Small-town, informal bullbaiting.
capote   Large fuchsia and yellow cape used during the early portions of the bullfight.
cara   Face.
carceleras   Songs that express the emotion of hopelessness by recounting experiences of incarceration or captivity.
careo   A flamenco side-lunging pattern that allows dance partners to pass close by one another. Derived from the word *cara*, meaning face. The verb form *carear* signifies the action or effect of facing off to settle a dispute, to confront.
cinco   Five.
citación   Citing, which means to challenge or incite a bull. A simultaneous verbal shout and a quick, strong movement that infringes upon a bull's territory, causing it to charge.
cojo   Lame.
compás   The rhythmic structure of flamenco music and dance. Identified by length of phrase, placement of accents within the phrase, and the beginning and ending points within that pattern.
contoneo   A proud manner of walking, with the chest held high, seen in both flamenco dance and bullfighting. Strutting.
copla   Short verse of *cante*, or the short dance form that it accompanies.
corrida   Commonly used short form of *corrida de toros*.
corrida de toros   Public bullfight event.
cuadrilla   The matador's support team. Also known as *equipo*.
cuadro flamenco   The half circle of musicians and *palmeros* onstage providing support to a flamenco dancer.
cuaresma   Lent.
cuna   Cradle or birthplace.
danza   Dance.
desplante   The culminating movement at the end of a series of *pases* of the cape. Often the term *remate* or *adorno* is used instead.
duende   Sprite, spirit; ineffable quality eliciting awe, anguish, angst.
encierro   The running of a bull or bulls through town streets.
ensayo   Rehearsal or practice session. Also, a written essay.
entrada   Entrance, introduction.
equipo   The matador's support team. Also known as *cuadrilla*.
espada   The matador's sword. Also known as *estoque*.
espontaneo   The act of entering the bullring to *torear* without permission.
estampa   A performer's search for (or creation of) a uniquely identifiable personal style, his or her distinctive way of doing things that gives each performance a special stamp or imprint.
estocada   Lunging movement named after the sword thrust of the matador. The final contact of the matador's sword thrust, stab. Forceful lunging movements.

estoque The matador's sword. Also known as *espada*.
faena The last, most dangerous portion of the bullfight.
farruca Solo dance form traditionally performed by males to a slow four-count rhythm.
feria A fair.
feria del caballo Horse fair.
fiesta Party, festival, or celebration.
flamenco The distinctive song, dance, and performance practice originating from Andalusia, southern region of Spain.
flamenco puro Authentic, pure flamenco.
flamencología Flamencology; scholarship focused on the culture, social history, and aesthetics of flamenco performance.
ganadero Cattle rancher.
gitanesco Gypsy-like.
gitanismo The particular expressive qualities, stylistic elements, and affective intensity associated with the performing talents of the *gitano* people.
gitano/gitana Gypsy.
hacienda Cattle ranch.
hembra Female.
hostal Lodging, with rooms for rent.
incitar To incite. To provoke or goad into action.
jaleador A person providing handclaps and vocal encouragement in flamenco.
jaleo Handclapping and vocalization in support of flamenco performers. Literally, ruckus or uproar. Term comes from the practice of hunting from horseback with dogs.
jondo Deep, profound, serious emotions in flamenco.
juerga An informal flamenco gathering.
jurisdicción A bull's sense of the boundaries of its own space; literally, jurisdiction. If someone crosses into the bull's jurisdiction, he will charge to defend his territorial boundaries.
letras Verses of flamenco song.
lidia Bullfight.
llamada Literally, call. In flamenco generally, a nonverbal movement signal.
llamativo Showy. Loud, in the sense of calling attention to itself.
los seises Literally, the sixes. A dance performed by young boys in the Cathedral of Seville.
macho Male.
madrugada Period between midnight and dawn.
maletillas Literally, suitcases. Young, poor, itinerant men and boys seeking to break into the bullfighting business and become matadors; named after their suitcases.
marcando Literally, marking, as in marking time. In flamenco, simple,

weighted stepping patterns employed to mark the basic rhythm of the music. Usually occurs as the singer is singing.

matador   Literally, killer. The torero who performs with the *muleta* and ends by killing the bull.

matiz   Gradation of dynamics. A dancer's ability to control the sound qualities of her or his footwork.

mimetismo taurino   Mimed bullfighting.

mineras   *Cante jondo* whose *letras* deal with the dangers or tragedies of mining.

minué   Eighteenth-century couple dance. The minuet.

minuetta   Short minuet.

morisca   Moorish-style dance.

muleta   The small red felt cape used by the matador in the last *tercio* (third) or *faena* of the bullfight.

natural   Natural. In bullfighting, a basic pass using the *muleta*.

no dice nada   A derogatory comment conveying that a performance has left one unmoved. Literally, "It communicates nothing."

novillero/novillera   Professional bullfighter who has not taken the *alternativa*, i.e., has not received recognition as a *matador de toros*.

olé   Comes from Moorish expression calling on Allah, or God.

oposiciones   Oppositional movements.

orgullo   Pride; could be personal, familial, or regional.

palillo   A wooden dowel-like stick, part of the *muleta*.

palmas   Flamenco handclapping.

palmero/palmera   A person who is expert at performing flamenco handclapping.

pases   Movements of the cape during the passing of the bull.

pasión   Suffering, especially the suffering of Christ.

paso   Step.

paso de caida   Falling step. Dance step with deep lunge performed in forward direction.

paso de muleta   A sequence of dance steps that mimic the matador's movements with the *muleta*.

paso doble   Traditional marching music played in the bullfight arena.

patrones   Financial patrons of the flamenco or bullfighting arts.

pena   Pain, suffering.

peña   Private social club; member activities are based on shared enthusiasm for flamenco or bullfighting.

picador   Member of the matador's *cuadrilla* who rides a well-padded horse and, during the first third of the bullfight, draws the bull's attack, then uses a single long lance to weaken the bull's neck muscles.

pitos   Flamenco finger snaps.

plasticidad   Plasticity; a performer's ability to respond fluidly to the demands of performance.

plaza   Town square.
puro   Pure, authentic.
querencia   An animal's sense of security at the center of its own territory.
quiebros   Impulsive dodging and evasive torso inclinations of the bullfighter.
raza   Race; a people.
redondo   Rounded.
rejoneador   One who practices bullfighting from horseback.
rejoneo   Bullfighting from horseback.
remate   The finish, which brings an end to a series of passes in a bullfight. Sometimes referred to as the *desplante* or *adorno*. This term is also used in the technical vocabulary of flamenco dance for the culminating movement at the end of a series of movements.
rito   Rite. The film series titles, Rito y geografía del cante and Rito y geografía del baile, are translated as Rite and Geography of the Song, and Rite and Geography of the Dance.
rumba   A popular Latin American music and dance form.
rumba gitana   A popular flamenco-style rumba; music and dance based on the Latin American rumba.
saeta   Religious flamenco song; a solo sung a cappella during Semana Santa processions.
salida   Exit, or music that accompanies the ending of a dance.
sarao   Soirée, evening party.
seguidilla   A traditional Spanish classical dance form.
seis   Literally, six. See **los seises.**
Semana Santa   Week between Palm Sunday and Easter Sunday.
señoritas toreras   Women whose bullfighting skills gained them attention as novelty acts.
sevillanas   A flamenco-style folk dance form and social dance for couples.
siesta   A midafternoon nap.
siguiriyas   A *cante jondo* form of music and dance with themes of death, hate, persecution, or sorrow, based on a twelve-count *compás*.
silencio   A beautiful, slow instrumental section of the *alegrías* music and dance.
sitio   Place, location.
soleares   A *cante jondo* form of music and dance with an emotional theme of loneliness, based on a twelve-count *compás*.
sueño   Dream.
suertes   Passes of the cape.
tablao   Flamenco nightclub.
talante   Talent, mode of execution, and technique; also denotes personal appearance, mien, disposition, temperament, wish, and desire.
tangos   A four-count flamenco rhythm, song, and dance form, expressing a wide range of emotions.

tanguillos   An emotionally light song and dance in the popular flamenco style with mischievous *letras*.
tarde   Afternoon.
tauromaquia   Tauromachy; the art, pedagogy, and scholarship of bullfighting.
temple   The in-sync timing between the matador and the bull. Entrainment.
tercio de banderillas   The second period of a bullfight, in which *banderillas* are used.
tercio de matar   The third and last period of a bullfight, during which the bull is killed.
tercio de varas   The first period of a bullfight. Includes the actions of the picadors.
tienta   The informal testing of the bravery of female calves.
tientos   A slow four-count flamenco rhythm, song, and dance form, similar to a slow *tangos*.
toque   Literally, touch; in flamenco, playing the flamenco guitar.
torcido   Twisted; spiral form, especially of the torso.
toreando   Gerund form of verb *torear*. Messing around with bulls, playing with bulls, or acting as if one is fighting a bull.
torear   To tease, harass, or play with a bull.
toreo   The action of bullfighting.
toreo en redondo   A series of at least two *pases* that cause the bull to circle the matador.
torero/torera   Bullfighter; any person that performs an active function in the course of a bullfight. Includes picadors, *peons*, *banderilleros*, and matadors.
toro/toros   A bull/bulls.
vaquilla   Yearling heifer.
verónicas   Basic *pases* with the *capote*.
voz afillá   Rough-voiced flamenco singing.
vuelta torera   A flamenco turn; literally, the bullfighter turn.
zarzuela   Spanish light opera.

Chapter Notes

Introduction

1. See also in audiovisual reference list Lomax (1977); Lomax and Choreometrics Project of Columbia University Dept. of Anthropology (1976); Lomax and Paulay (1977); Lomax, Paulay, and Choreometrics Project of Columbia University Dept. of Anthropology (1984).

2. Entrainment occurs when two or more beings move in sync with one another. This phenomenon is discussed further as "rhythmic entrainment" in Chapter 3, "Overlapping Worlds."

3. Keillor, founder and host of the American Public Media show *A Prairie Home Companion*, based the fictional Lake Wobegon on his own Minnesota small-town upbringing.

4. The theory of ethnocentrism requires that we question any suggestion that a research language or system of thought might seriously be considered "culture-free," i.e., free of the effects of culture.

5. Labanotation is the primary notation system developed through the work of Laban and his associates, and later codified by Ann Hutchinson Guest; the notation systems of Motif Writing and Language of Dance were also derived from Laban's research (Guest 1983, 1998).

6. Readers wishing further information on the scientific reliability of Laban Movement Analysis–based observational systems may begin by referring to the studies of Martha Davis (1987), Martha Davis and Dean Hadiks (1987), K. Mark Sossin (1987), and Deborah Du Nann Winter (1987).

7. Female participation in bullfighting was illegal from the mid–1930s until 1974 (Pink 1997, 145).

8. See "Fashioning Masculinity in Flamenco Dance" by William Washabaugh and "Gendering the Authentic in Spanish Flamenco" by Timothy deWaal Malefyt (Washabaugh, ed. 1998).

9. See Sarah Pink (1997).

10. In using the hyphenated term Anglo-American my intention is to explicitly acknowledge the influence of British [Anglo] cultural attitudes on many U.S. American behaviors and perceptions.

11. Rating high on the "Barrier score," referred to as "high Barrier," indicates a well-established, separate, stabilized identity. Rating low on the "Barrier score," referred to as "low Barrier," indicates a lack of those characteristics.

12. Discussed in Kealiinohomoku 1976, 204–205.

13. See Adrienne L. Kaeppler (1972) and Drid Williams (1996) for taxonomic use of linguistic concepts; Judith Hanna (1979b) for semantic analysis; also Eliot D. Chapple and Martha Davis (1988) for cautions against the assumption that linguistics can provide an adequate theoretical model for understanding nonverbal communications.

Chapter One

1. The Fundación de Flamenco (Flamenco Foundation) is the library archive of the Centro Andaluz de Flamenco (Andalusian Flamenco Center) (http://caf.cica.es) that collects and makes available to scholars and others a wide selection of cultural materials pertaining to the flamenco arts. The Biblioteca Municipal de Jerez de la Frontera is the local library in Jerez de la Frontera. La Biblioteca Nacional de España is Spain's national library.

2. See Matteo with Goya 1990; Landborn 2002.

3. Spanish classical dance often uses flamenco styling as one of many regional variations of Spanish folk dance forms. However, in general, Spanish classical dance is performed on the proscenium stage accompanied by classical Spanish music (usually orchestra); it presents highly choreographed dances; and its dancers employ ballet-like styling, often while playing the castanets.

4. "una cierta afinidad entre ambos artes, sobre todo en lo que se refiere a los ambientes en que se producen, a la calidad de sus personajes y a unas singulares posibilidades de comparación, especialmente por lo que al baile se refiere" (Álvarez Caballero 1998, 87).

5. Readers may refer to my essay published in 2000 in the journal *Visual Anthropology*, titled, "Cultural relativity: Views on passion in music and dance," in which I review Washabaugh's book.

6. General works about the challenges of ethnographic writing are also informative: *Writing Culture: The Poetics and Politics of Ethnography* edited by James Clifford and George E. Marcus (1986), which included the essay "Ethnography as Narrative" by Edward M. Bruner (1986), *Liberating Scholarly Writing: The Power of Personal Narrative* by Robert J. Nash (2004), "Ethnography and The Book That Was Lost" by Ruth Behar (2003), and "Writing: A Method of Inquiry" by Laurel Richardson (1994).

Chapter Two

1. Anthropologist Joann Kealiinohomoku asserts that "a given dance culture is a microcosm of the culture and the study of the microcosm requires that the macrocosm be delineated" (1976, 233).

2. In Chapter 7, I refer to this cultural repatterning of movement as "gaining the emic edge."

Chapter Three

1. Edward T. Hall differentiates between *high-context* and *low-context* cultures as a means of describing the complexity and penetrability of a culture, and the degree of tacit knowledge a culture assumes (1976, 105–116).

2. The processes and maneuvers of the *tienta* are similar to the bullfight, although the context of the *tienta* is less formal. The female calves are "yearling heifers (*vaquillas*) approximately 12 to 18 month old animals" (Cooney 2005). Because they constitute valuable livestock for the *ganadero* (rancher), the female calves are not killed or harmed materially in the *tienta* process. The *tienta* traditionally offers opportunities for young toreros to develop their tauromachy skills.

3. This is notably dissimilar from the more passive role generally assigned to audience members in the Western theater traditions.

4. This applies to public rituals with religious or civic significance. I have witnessed both in Jerez de la Frontera: the religious processions of Semana Santa (Easter Week) and a festive parade celebrating a successful grape harvest. (*Jerez* means sherry; grape harvests constitute a major economic indicator for the city.)

5. The term *jaleo* originates in the baying of hounds and encouraging shouts that accompany a hunt. In a performance context, *jaleo* refers to the mix of sounds that urge performers to excel.

6. "Después de presenciar una corrida de toros, es tradicional que los buenos aficionados se reúnan y comenten que hay que rematar la noche acudiendo a algún Tablao Flamenco" (Palencia, quoted in Arrebola, 1991, 13).

7. Testing the bravery of cattle is a normal part of a rancher's work. The type of testing mentioned here indicates skills drawn from the aristocratic practice of bullfighting from horseback, known as *rejoneo*.

8. "El campo, montar a caballo y, sobre todo, el cante y el baile flamenco: eso me vuelve loco; no en teatro ni entre público, sino en pequeña reunión de amigos" (González Climent 1964, 233).

9. Moorish influence on Spanish culture lasted more than seven centuries, from 711 to AD 1492 (Fletcher 1992, 8).

10. "Andalucía es una cultura de ojo abierto y luminoso, carente de pestañeos prolongados. Es ésta la tierra donde se dice 'quien pestañea, pierde'" (González Climent 1964, 299).

11. Heightened attention to timing will likely be employed in order to achieve rhyth-

mic entrainment; however, once the synchronization of timing is achieved a performer's attention may shift to the other movement qualities of space, flow, and weight.

12. "Las palmas sordas simbolizan la íntima compaña que le brinda el jaleador al cantaor, como asegurándole su auténtica participación, punto a punto, quiebro por quiebro, en el despliegue sentimientos. Con ello demuestra, sencillamente, no abandonarle a la hora de la verdad, como el peón al matador en trance de estocada. Es poner la mano en el hombro del cantaor, comprensivo y alentadora, para manifestarle la perfecta communion de lo entrañal" (González Climent 1964, 267).

13. Interest in the function of signs, signals, and symbols within dance and other forms of movement communication is shared by many anthropologists and dance scholars, Drid Williams, Brenda Farnell, Ray Birdwhistell, Edward T. Hall, and others.

14. *Entrada* means entrance and *salida* means exit; however, in practice these words are often used interchangeably. This is because the terms also refer to conventional music forms that support a variety of actions within the performance, such as entering, exiting, transitions, and the passing off of leadership between performers. This depends too on one's perspective. The actual action would be the same whether a dancer thinks of leaving the cuadro flamenco behind (*salida*) or entering the performance space (*entrada*).

15. A *llamada* is a single *compás* in length, while a *desplante* is a type of *llamada* that is two or more *compás* in length.

16. Example of flamenco performed by singer María Toledo at a bullfight: https://www.youtube.com/watch?v=Q8e7EwSOCKI—t=17.

17. The *paso doble*, literally the double step, is also known as a ballroom dance performed to Latin American rhythms.

18. While some flamenco rhythms are evenly accented, the most characteristic flamenco rhythms distribute accents unevenly within a twelve-beat phrase.

19. Further visual evidence of the ties between flamenco and bullfighting personnel and cultural activities are at http://www.europhoto.eu.com. Search term: Carmen Amaya. Image 71 shows wax figure of Carmen Amaya at the Barcelona Wax Museum with bullfight exhibit to her right. Image 96 shows Carmen Amaya dancing at the Plaza de Toros in Barcelona, Spain. Search term: Merche Esmeralda. Images #2–8 show flamenco dancer Merche Esmeralda posing at Plaza de Toros, Madrid's main bullfight arena. Search term: La Chunga. Images 60–64 show La Chunga *toreando* (trying her skills with a heifer) with bullfighter Luis Miguel Dominguín. Search term: flamenco party. Image 7 shows flamenco party at wedding celebration of bullfighter Vitoriano Cuevas Roger "Vitoriano Valencia" and Paloma Díaz.

20. For an outsider to have an opportunity to attend this type of event is quite rare.

Chapter Four

1. This official, known as the *juez de la plaza* or *presidente* (the judge or president of the bullring), signals for the trumpeter to call for the beginning and ending of each of three sections (*tercios*) of the bullfight ritual (Frontain 1966, 112).

2. The height of the *cafés cantantes* era, the golden age of flamenco, occurred from approximately 1860 to 1910 (Schreiner 1990, 171).

3. Animal behaviors related to *querencia* and *jurisdicción* apply to all cattle, both male and female.

4. The English verb *incite* is comparable to the Spanish verb *incitar*, meaning to provoke; however, in actual practice English-speaking toreros use the English words *cite* or *citing* to indicate the torero's action of provoking an animal to charge the cape (Cooney 2005). I use the English verb *to cite* which corresponds to the Spanish verb *citar*, one definition of which (specific to the *corrida de toros*) is the torero's act of inciting the bull to charge. It is also compatible with a less commonly used definition of the English words *cite* and *citation* that signifies the act of summoning, calling, or rousing to action.

5. The official Spanish bullfight season ends on October 12 (Wheaton 1988, 281).

6. Another more anomalous cultural tradition sanctions dance in the Cathedral of Seville. The centuries-old tradition occurs three times per year. Known as *los seises de Sevilla*, today it is performed by ten young

boys in formal costume dancing with castanets. Their dances involve formal dance figures with "some elements of the *seguidilla*, of the *minué* or *minuetto*, of the *danza de espadas*, of the *sarao*, of the *morisca*" (González Barrionuevo 1992, 229).

Chapter Five

1. The Moors of North Africa and the Indo-Pakistani Gypsies are generally recognized as having made significant cultural contributions to the early development of flamenco music and dance (Wheaton 1988).

2. This corresponds with the combination of social containment and freedom of expression described by Fisher and Cleveland (1958) as producing the *high Barrier* personality type with the well-defined personal boundaries and uninhibited behavior patterns often associated with Spanish culture.

3. Kealiinohomoku credits art historian Robert Plant Armstrong with coining the term "aesthemics" (Kealiinohomoku, pers. comm.; for definition see Armstrong 1971, 47).

4. The word *redundancy* is used throughout this discussion as a technical term that signifies the formulaic reiteration of cultural patterns.

5. In flamenco and tauromachy contexts the term aficionado means more than enthusiast or fan; it generally implies serious study of the bullfight or flamenco arts.

6. "El cabal ejerce una función de importancia resaltable, sobre todo en el mundo artístico vario y profundo del flamenquismo (toreo, cante, y danza). Son los fieles vigías de la pureza y de la legitimidad del arte del pueblo. Están en un rango de alerta y jurisprudencia. Nada se les escapa. El cabal personifica si se quiere, un flamenco fallido, el cantaor sin posibilidades, el torero en potencia, el bailaor tácito. Es el gran testigo" (González Climent 1964, 227).

7. Originally written and delivered as a speech in Havana, Cuba, in 1934 (appended in García Lorca 1955).

Chapter Six

1. An online video shows modern-day children being taught the skills of toreando by a matador from Badajoz, Spain, Miguel Ángel Perera at: www.larioja.com/videos/riojanizate/informe-rioja/1826900259001-miguel-angel-perera-ensena-torear-ninos.html.

2. El flamenco o el torero retirados se convierten en cabales (González Climent 1964, 202).

3. Language of Dance provides a method of recording movement; it is closely related to Labanotation, but provides a method of notation that can be adapted for various purposes (Guest 1983). For those interested in learning more, a book outlining my method for the notation of flamenco dance is available at www.adairlandborn.com.

4. The Mezquita in Córdoba is a huge mosque; its construction began in AD 785. In 1523, construction of a Catholic cathedral, the Church of the Virgin of the Assumption, was begun inside the mosque. As a result, the Mezquita is "both a product and a symbol of the grafting of Christianity onto Muslim Spain" (Wheaton 1988, 165).

5. For example, D.E. Pohren's *A Way of Life*, published in 1980 by the Society of Spanish Studies, Madrid.

Chapter Seven

1. The similarities and dissimilarities between language and dance have been noted and utilized as a basis of theory in the study of dance and other human movement behaviors by many anthropologists, including Drid Williams, Brenda Farnell, Adrienne Kaeppler, Judith L. Hanna, Anya Peterson Royce, and others.

2. I knew my first tauromachy teacher only as Jaime and probably never knew his last name. Nevertheless, we worked together intensely on an informal basis over a period of months.

3. The matador's suit of lights is the formal, highly ornate costume worn in the bullfight; it includes pants that fit tightly and a jacket that emphasizes the width of the matador's shoulders.

4. *Countertension* is a technical term for opposing tensions or spatial pulls in the body; in the context of dynamic movements, countertensions often assist the mover to stabilize or maintain equilibrium.

5. "Torero" is a broad category that includes all bullfight personnel whose work involves them directly in the action of the bullfight. The use of the *capote* is less specialized, while the use of the *muleta* is restricted in the bullring to the actual matador.

6. An impression of female domain remained for me even in the rare case of a classically styled flamenco dance, *Suspiran* (choreographed and performed by Marco Berriel), which features a male soloist wearing a *bata de cola*–like costume (Cortés 1997).

7. Interpretations of the symbolism of the bullfight vary greatly; see Mitchell 1991, 36–44.

8. The *tienta* involves similar tauromachy skills and activities, but is less formal and less dangerous than the professional *corrida*. The *tienta* tests the bravery of young female calves, "yearling heifers (vaquillas) approximately 12 to 18 month old animals" (Cooney 2005). The female calves are not killed in the *tienta* process. In fact, because they constitute valuable livestock for the *ganadero* (rancher), efforts are made to limit any injury a *vaquilla* might incur during the *tienta*.

9. Although in the following discussion I am writing primarily about neophytes, amateurs, and students of tauromachy, I use the word matador, rather than torero, as a generic term. My choice is predicated upon the fact that the training I describe pertained to the use of the *muleta*, which is used only by matadors.

10. The *muleta* is held with a grip and positioning of the hand and arm similar to that used to perform a tennis stroke. Using this comparison, it is useful to distinguish between the movement of preparation and the primary action. In tennis, the racket moves back in preparation for its primary action, an active stroke forward to meet the ball. In tauromachy, the *muleta* is extended forward to incite the bull, preparatory to its primary action of moving backward to draw the animal past the matador's body.

11. The *ayuda* is used during the *faena* prior to the matador's receiving official permission to kill the bull. Once the matador receives permission from the bullfight officials, the *ayuda* is replaced with an actual sword.

12. Except for the five-year-old daughter of one of the *tienta* observers, my videographer and I were the only females present.

13. At the *tienta*, bull ranchers charge an average of $200 to $300 per female calf; this is for the "bravery" of the animal, which is where its primary value lies. Professionals usually do not pay to participate in the *tienta*. Sometimes *ganaderos* give young bulls to professionals to train with, but most often they charge for them. In Mexico, the *ganadero* charges from $800 to $1,500 to kill one of his young bulls. This price varies worldwide, with the top ranches in Spain charging as much as $40,000 for a bull. An average price in Spain would be about $8,000 (Coleman Cooney, pers. comm. These prices were originally quoted in 2006).

14. The *novillero* or *novillera* is defined as a "professional bullfighter who has not taken the *alternativa*" (Greenfield 1961, 101). The *alternativa* is the "ceremony in which a *novillero* [or *novillera*] becomes a *matador de toros* (sometimes referred to as taking the doctorate of tauromachy)" (106).

15. The picador rides a horse and, during the first third of the bullfight, draws the bull's attack, then uses a single long lance to weaken the bull's neck muscles. The job of the *banderillero* is also to weaken the bull's neck muscles. He accomplishes this by running on foot to place several short lances called *banderillas* in the neck of the bull.

Chapter Eight

1. The 1941 film *Blood and Sand* follows this cultural script. It includes a dance duet between a matador, Anthony Quinn, and a femme fatale, Rita Hayworth. Although the duet does not constitute traditional flamenco dance, it employs many of the movement motifs discussed in this chapter.

2. *Torero* was performed live in 1996 at Popejoy Hall in Albuquerque, New Mexico, as part of the Festival Flamenco Internacional. I watched the performance from the lighting booth where I was contributing commentary on the confluence of flamenco and bullfighting in the ballet's performance for a radio program, "La Raza" (KUNM, Albuquerque, New Mexico).

3. Full quotation provided: "Hay momentos—¿por qué ocultarlo?—en que dan ganas

de acompañar con un medido jaleo de palmas la precisión rítmica de ciertas pases, de ciertas verónicas, chicuelinas, en fin, de ciertos ramalazos sonoros que a veces nos hacen dudar la definición entre danza taurina o taurinismo danzable" (González Climent 1964, 267–268).

4. In very rare instances the bull may, in recognition of its remarkable performance, be spared and returned to the ranch as a breeding bull. Also, bullfighting practices in Portugal differ in that bulls are not killed in the public arena. This reprieve is brief, however, as bulls in Portugal are usually killed after the bullfight. Generally, once having learned in the arena how to fight human beings, bulls are considered too dangerous to be released.

5. The roots of these cultural attitudes toward gender may reside in traditional patterns that assign responsibility for management of the fertility of agricultural communities to males. Men are traditionally responsible for both the work of animal husbandry, upon which the well-being of their community depends, and the negotiation of marriage alliances, upon which the well-being of their family depends.

6. Theoretical perspectives for my research utilize Rudolph von Laban's system for analysis of movement phenomena, which uses the primary categories of body, space, shape, and dynamics Laban [1950] 1971), [1966] 1974). A brief overview of Laban's analytical system is included in the back matter of this book; interested readers may access additional information by consulting texts provided in the reference list (Bartenieff with Lewis 1980; Dell 1977; Hackney 2002; Laban [1948] 1968, [1950] 1971, [1966] 1974; Maletic 1987, 1998). To allow for a more expansive treatment of the movement parallels between flamenco and bullfighting, discussion of the category of shape is subsumed within the other three Laban categories, and I incorporate non–Laban concepts in my analyses of body (phenotypes) and movement significance (metonyms and transitional objects).

7. Most notably perhaps the Choreometrics Project designed by Alan Lomax (1968). See also in audiovisual reference list Lomax (1977); Lomax and Choreometrics Project of Columbia University Dept. of Anthropology (1976); Lomax and Paulay (1977); Lomax, Paulay, and Choreometrics Project of Columbia University Dept. of Anthropology (1984).

8. Authors of the original text capitalized the word Effort to clarify that it was being used as a technical term for expressive movement qualities as they are analyzed within the framework of Laban Movement Analysis. I follow this convention to avoid confusion with standard usage of the English word "effort" in reference to exertion in general.

9. The term *phenotype* refers to that portion of a person's physical appearance and body type that is a result of the interaction between their genotype and environment. Aesthemic assessments are judgments based on emic perspectives and whether the artistic expectations of the particular cultural form have been met.

10. Spaniards present a range of phenotypes. The younger generation of Spaniards is generally taller than their elders. Flamenco dancers Manolete and Antonio el Pipa would probably be considered too short and too tall, respectively, for the classical Spanish dance genre.

11. Movement gestures are those movements, particularly of the limbs, that do not involve supporting the body's weight. They may be performed with or without postural involvement. Locomotion through space does not preclude the use of gestures.

12. Laban delineates the range of the kinesphere into which a gesture may reach as: near-reach, mid-reach, or far-reach space.

13. Male identity may be more contested in the flamenco dance context. See "Fashioning Masculinity in Dance" by William Washabaugh (1998) and "Gendering the Authentic in Spanish Dance" by Timothy deWaal Malefyt (1998).

14. As modern Andalusian and Spanish women wear pants and less voluminous skirts, these movement patterns are changing; however, these patterns may still apply to the many women in the *gitano* community who continue to wear full skirts.

15. William Washabaugh describes an ironic gender-bending mannerism employed by many male flamenco dancers of "grabbing his vest and lifting its hem" in a movement "similar to, and reminiscent of the movement of *bailaoras* as they grab the hem of their dresses, hoisting them up to reveal their fancy footwork" (1998, 47).

16. Walking as a social activity is generally supported by the spatial design of Spanish cities and architecture. In Andalusia, social promenading occurs regularly in the late afternoon or early evening hours. Weekends and special public events also elicit this socializing behavior.

17. Watching a slow-motion sports replay, one may easily observe how an athlete's body continuously shapes and reshapes itself in response to his or her movement intentions in relation to an important spatial boundary or the movement trajectory through space of an object or another person.

18. The vertical dimension expresses up-down spatial pulls, the horizontal dimension expresses right-left spatial pulls, and the sagittal dimension expresses forward-backward spatial pulls.

19. Movements in the vertical plane combine up-down and side-to-side spatial possibilities. With no movements forward or back, movements in the vertical plane are flat and presentational. The vertical plane is sometimes called the "door plane."

20. The spatial form created by the intersection of the three spatial dimensions is called the dimensional cross of axes. It has stabilizing and orienting properties that make it a significant spatial component of many dance forms.

21. This well-known flamenco dancer's stage name matches that of the famous matador Manolete, who was fatally gored in 1947 (Mitchell 1991, 94).

22. All examples given in this paragraph are condensing Efforts, the fighting qualities of strong, direct, bound flow, and directness.

23. Also referred to as emphatic phrasing; such phrases "end with a bang" (Ness 1988, 143).

Chapter Nine

1. The phrase "plastic capa" refers to the flexible, sculptural qualities of the matador's cape. *Plasticidad* is a Spanish term used in aesthetic discussions to praise the vocal mobility of flamenco singers or physical flexibility of dancers or matadors. It is also used in reference to the ephemeral nature of performative or expressive phenomena in general.

2. Bullfighting practices include: the *tienta*, which tests the bravery of female calves; the *capea*, which provides informal opportunities for human beings, particularly young males, to demonstrate *toreando* skills and courage; the *encierros*, running with the bulls, which offer similar opportunities; the *corrida*, which tests the bravery and skill of professional toreros, matadors (male and female), and a mature bull, the strength and courage of the picador's horse and, in the case of *rejoneo*, bullfighting from horseback, the superbly trained matador's horse. Another bullfight practice involves testing the courage of young cows and bulls in the open countryside. Referred to as "tilting," this practice uses the skills of *rejoneo* to chase down and knock over the animals. Here the courage of an animal is tested in unenclosed circumstances.

3. Bulls are virtually colorblind. They respond to the movement rather than the color of the matador's *muleta* or *capote*.

4. In the film *A Matador's Mistress*, Manolete is challenged as a young matador to step into a pair of shoes that are nailed onto a board (in a parallel position) and manages to demonstrate his skills with a cape and his courage in facing a bull. Unlike a sprinter's low crouch position that facilitates a quick burst of speed, a matador's narrow foot positioning during a pass is a difficult stance from which to quickly escape from a bull.

5. This term is sometimes spelled "motive." The terms *motif* and *motifs* are used here to avoid confusion with another concept important to discussions of dance and movement phenomena, namely, motive as it pertains to the reasons or purposes of moving, i.e., motivation.

6. I am not using the term *motif* as it is used in producing a detailed ethnochoreological analysis of dance movement structures.

7. For further visual examples of arching, see Puig Claramunt 1977, pages 45–151, photographs 44, 94, 108, 131, and 162.

8. For further visual examples demonstrating variations on the movement motif of arcing, see Puig Claramunt 1977, pages 99–189, photographs 102, 132, 133, 148, 164, 170, 187, and 204.

9. Though illegal and considered a fraudulent practice, a bull's horns are sometimes shaved before a bullfight. This reduces the acute tactile sensitivity of the bull's horns,

hindering its ability to make contact with the matador.

10. *Near-reach space* is that portion of a person's kinesphere that is near the body; thus it may imply a degree of intimacy.

11. For further visual examples demonstrating variations on the movement motif of spiraling, see Puig Claramunt 1977, pages 79–211, photographs 89, 132, 143, 145, 159, 187, 204, and 259.

12. *Opociciones* is essentially the Spanish language equivalent of Laban's term countertensions.

13. Teo Morca defines *desplante* as "a climactic point in the dance, consisting of two or more *compás*" (Morca 1990, 117). Matteo Vittucci states that *desplante* is "the dancer's signal to the guitarist to indicate a rhythmic break, change, or link in a dance and is performed with a series of foot stomps (*golpes de pies*)" (Matteo with Goya 1990, 71).

14. In *Todas las suertes por sus maestros (All of the Cape Passes from the Masters)*, José Luis Ramón describes 123 variations on the passing motif, attributing each variation to the matador who developed it (1998).

Chapter Ten

1. This is not to deny discoveries in the field of theoretical physics of additional dimensions. http://www.pbs.org/wgbh/nova/physics/imagining-other-dimensions.html.

2. Although Hanna emphasizes the experience of the human sensory-motor system, it is a basic feature in most life forms. Even the microscopic movement potential that enables single-cell life forms to move, known as *kinesis*, functions in response to stimulation or sensation.

3. Winnicott is primarily interested in the paradoxical nature of experience in the psychology of the baby, child, or person who relates to the transitional object (such as a teddy bear or fetish) as being both of their body and not of their body, or who flexibly alternates between those two attitudes.

4. This was discussed previously in Chapter 3. It also is related to B. Cohen's "motor component of perception" (2003, 199).

5. As discussed in greater depth in the Introduction, people enculturated by Spanish kinesthetic culture (rating a high Barrier score) will tend to "press forward and stimulate one another in their search for human contact" (Fisher and Cleveland 1958, 216).

6. For a survey of Spanish cultural events involving bulls, see Mitchell (1991, 13–24).

7. See audiovisual reference: Real Escuela Andaluza del Arte Ecuestre. 1989. *Un Caballo Jerezano*.

Bibliography

Abella, Carlos. 1996. *Derecho al toro! El lenguaje de los toros y su influencia en lo cotidiano*. Madrid: Anaya y Mario Muchnik.

Aix Gracia, Francisco. 2002. El arte flamenco como campo produccíon cultural: Aproximación a sus aspectos sociales. *Anduli: Revista Andaluza de Ciencias Sociales* 1:109–125.

Alarcón Sánchez-Manjavaras, Enrique. n.d. *Romance del torero eterno ballet*. A ballet scenario; available in Biblioteca Nacional de España, Madrid.

Álvarez Caballero, Ángel. 1998. *El baile flamenco*. Madrid: Alianza Editorial.

———. Photos by Elke Stolzenberg. 1992. *Las Máscaras de lo Jondo*. Madrid, Spain: Ediciones del Prado.

Aposhyan, Susan. 1999. *Natural intelligence: Body-mind integration and human development*. Baltimore: Williams & Wilkins.

Armstrong, Robert P. 1971. *The affecting presence: An essay in humanistic anthropology*. Urbana: University of Illinois Press.

Arranz del Barrio, Ángeles. 1996. *El baile flamenco*. Madrid: Librerías Deportivas Esteban Sanz.

Arrebola, Alfredo. 1991. *Cante y toros: Un ensayo de aproximación*. Málaga, Spain: Universidad de Málaga, Gráficas Dialar.

Barea, Arturo. 1958. *Lorca: The poet and his people*. New York: Grove Press.

Bartenieff, Irmgard. 1970. The root of Laban theory: Aesthetics and beyond. In Bartenieff, Davis, and Paulay, 1970.

———, Martha Davis, and Forrestine Paulay. 1970. *Four adaptations of effort theory in research and teaching*. New York: Dance Notation Bureau Press.

———, with Dori Lewis. 1980. *Body movement: Coping with the environment*. New York: Gordon & Breach Science Publishers

———, and Forrestine Paulay. 1968. Choreometric profiles. In Lomax, ed. 1968, 248–261.

Behar, Ruth. 2003. Ethnography and the book that was lost. *Ethnography* 4 (1): 15–39.

Belmonte, Juan. 1937. *Juan Belmonte, killer of bulls: The autobiography of a matador*. Garden City, NY: Doubleday, Doran.

Bennahum, Ninotchka D. 2000. *Antonia Mercé, "La Argentina": Flamenco and the Spanish avant garde*. Hanover, NH: Wesleyan University Press.

Berman, Morris. 1989. *Coming to our senses: Body and spirit in the hidden history of the west*. New York: Simon & Schuster.

Birdwhistell, Ray L. 1970. *Kinesics and context: Essays on body motion communication*. Conduct and Communication. Philadelphia: University of Pennsylvania Press.

Blacking, John, ed. 1977. *The anthropology of the body*. London: Academic Press.

Blas Vega, José, and Manuel Rios Ruiz. 1990. *Diccionario enciclopédico ilustrado del flamenco*. Madrid: Editorial Cinterco.

Boas, Franz. 1951. *Primitive art*. Irvington-on-Hudson, NY: Capitol Publishing.

Bonner, John T. 1980. *The evolution of culture in animals*. Princeton, NJ: Princeton University Press.

Borrull, Trini. 1982. *La danza española*. Barcelona: Manuales Meseguer.

Bowlby, John. 1969. *Attachment*. New York: Basic Books.

Bright, Roderic. 1961. *Toros without tears: A simple explanation of what you will see at a bull-fight*. Mexico: Ediciones Luna.

Browner, Tara. 2002. *Heartbeat of the people: Music and dance of the northern pow-wow*. Urbana and Chicago: University of Illinois.

Bruner, Edward M. (1986). Ethnography as narrative. In *The anthropology of experience*, eds. Victor W. Turner and Edward M. Bruner. Urbana and Chicago: University of Illinois Press. Also in Clifford and Marcus, eds. 1986.

Buckland, Teresa J., ed. 1999. *Dance in the field: Theory, methods, and issues in dance ethnography*. Houndmills, UK: Macmillan.

_____. 2001. Dance, authenticity and cultural memory: The politics of embodiment. *Yearbook for Traditional Music* 33:1–16.

Caballero Bonald, José Manuel. 1997. *Luces y sombras del flamenco*. Barcelona: Editorial Lumen.

Campbell, Douglas G. 1943. Neuropsychiatric foundations and clinical applications of general semantics. In *Papers from the Second American Congress on General Semantics*, Marjorie M. Kendig, ed., 117–134. Chicago: Institute of General Semantics.

Cannon, Walter B. 1927. The James-Lange theory of emotion: A critical examination and an alternative theory. *American Journal of Psychology* 39:10–124. Summarized on http://changingminds.org/explanations/theories/cannon_bard_emotion.htm (accessed November 4, 2005).

Carretero, Concepción. 1981. *El baile*. Seville: Grupo Andaluz de Ediciones-Repiso Lorenzo.

Carrithers, Michael. 1992. *Why humans have cultures: Explaining anthropology and social diversity*. Oxford: Oxford University Press.

Carse, James P. 1987. *Finite and infinite games: A vision of life as play and possibility*. New York: Ballantine Books.

Carter, Alexandra, ed. 1998. *The Routledge dance studies reader*. London: Routledge.

Chapple, Eliot D. and Martha Davis. 1988. Expressive movement and performance: Toward a unifying theory. *The Drama Review* 32 (4) (Winter): 53–79.

Charnon-Deutsch, Lou. 2004. *The Spanish Gypsy: The history of a European obsession*. University Park: Pennsylvania State University Press.

Clébert, Jean-Paul. 1963. *The Gypsies*. Harmondsworth, Middlesex, England: Penguin Books Ltd.

Clifford, James. 1988. *The predicament of culture: Twentieth-century ethnography, literature, and art*. Cambridge, MA: Harvard University Press.

_____, and George E. Marcus, eds. 1986. *Writing culture: The poetics and politics of ethnography*. Berkeley: University of California Press.

Cohen, Bonnie B. 2003. *Sensing, feeling, and action: The experiential anatomy of body-mind centering*. Northampton, MA: Contact Editions.

Cohen, Ronald D., ed. 2003. *Alan Lomax: Selected writings 1934–1997*. New York: Routledge.

Collins, Larry, and Dominique Lapierre. 1968. *Or I'll dress you in mourning*. New York: New American Library.

Committee on Research in Dance. 1967. *Research in dance: Problems and possibilities*. Riverdale, NY: Committee on Research in Dance.

Connerton, Paul. 1989. *How societies remember*. Cambridge: Cambridge University Press.

Cooney, Coleman. 2005. Unpaginated course handouts. Weekend intensive: 12 hours of instruction in *toreo* and *tienta* protocols. California Academy of Tauromaquia, San Diego.

CORD. *See* Committee on Research in Dance (renamed Congress on Research in Dance in 1978).

Cossío, José María de. 1960. *Los toros: Tratado técnico e histórico*. 11 vols. Madrid: Espasa-Calpe.

Csordas, Thomas J. 2002. *Body/meaning/healing*. New York: Palgrave Macmillan.

Daly, Ann. 1988. Movement analysis: Piecing together the puzzle. *The Drama Review* 32 (4): 40–52.

Davis, Martha, ed. 1975. *Anthropological perspectives of movement. Body Movement: Perspectives in Research*. New York: Arno Press.

———. 1987. Steps to achieving observer agreement: The LIMS Reliability Project. *Movement Studies: Observer Agreement* 2:7–19.

———, and Dean Hadiks. 1987. The Davis nonverbal states scales for psychotherapy research: Reliability of LMA-based coding. *Movement Studies: Observer Agreement* 2:29–34.

Dell, Cecily. 1977. *A primer for movement description: Using effort-shape and supplementary concepts*. New York: Dance Notation Bureau Press.

———, Aileen Crow, and Irmgard Bartenieff. 1977. *Space harmony: Basic terms*. New York: Dance Notation Bureau Press.

Desmond, Jane C., ed. 1997. *Meaning in motion: New cultural studies of dance*. Durham, NC: Duke University Press.

de Waal, Frans. 2005. *Our inner ape: A leading primatologist explains why we are who we are*. New York: Riverhead Books.

Dils, Ann, and Jill Flanders Crosby. 2001. Dialogue in dance studies research. *Dance Research Journal* 33 (1) (Summer): 62–81.

Durand, Jacques, and Claude Viallat. 2001. *Toros bravos*. Paris: Jannink.

Emerson, Robert M., Rachel I. Fretz, and Linda L. Shaw. 1995. *Writing ethnographic fieldnotes*. Chicago: University of Chicago Press.

Farnell, Brenda, ed. 1995. *Human action signs in cultural context: The visible and invisible in movement and dance*. Metuchen, NJ: Scarecrow Press.

Feintuch, Burt. 2003. *Eight words for the study of expressive culture*. Urbana: University of Illinois Press.

Feldenkrais, Moshe. [1972] 1990. *Awareness through movement: Easy-to-do health exercises to improve your posture, vision, imagination, and personal awareness*. San Francisco: HarperCollins.

Fisher, Seymour, and Sidney E. Cleveland. 1958. *Body image and personality*. Princeton, NJ: D. Van Nostrand.

Fletcher, Richard. 1992. *Moorish Spain*. Berkeley: University of California Press.

Fraleigh, Sondra H. and Penelope Hanstein, eds. 1999. *Researching dance: Evolving modes of inquiry*. Pittsburgh: University of Pittsburgh Press.

Fraser, Angus. 1998. *The Gypsies*. Oxford: Blackwell Publishers.

Frontain, Dick. 1966. *How to enjoy a bull fight*. Phoenix: Hooper Press.

García Lorca, Federico. 1935. *Llanto por Ignacio Sánchez Mejías*. Quoted in Arturo Barea 1958, 107–113 (English) and 170–174 (Spanish).

———. 1955. *Poet in New York*. New York: Grove Press. Quoted in Barea 1958.

Gardner, Howard. 1999. *Intelligence reframed: Multiple intelligences for the 21st century*. New York: Basic Books.

Gay y Blasco, Paloma. 1999. *Gypsies in Madrid: Sex, gender, and the performance of identity*. Oxford: Berg.

Geertz, Clifford. 2000. *Local knowledge: Further essays in interpretive anthropology*. New York: Basic Books.

Giurchescu, Anca. 1983. The process of improvisation in folk dance. *Dance Studies* 7:21–57.

———. 1991. Theory and methods in dance research: A European approach to the holistic study of dance. *Yearbook for Traditional Music* 23:1–10.

———. 2000. Interpreting a dancer's discourse on improvisation. In *ICTM Study Group on Ethnochoreology 20th Symposium Proceedings*, Istanbul, 259–274.

González Barrionuevo, Herminio. 1992. *Los seises de Sevilla*. Seville: Editorial Castellejo.

González Climent, Anselmo. 1953. *Andalucía en los toros, el cante y la danza*. Madrid.

———. 1961. *Bulerías: Un ensayo jerezano*. Jerez de la Frontera, Spain: Editorial Jerez Industrial.

———. 1964. *Flamencología: (toros, cante y*

baile). Madrid: E. Sanchez Leal. De Artes Graficas.

González Zaafra, David. 1991. *Flamenco y toros*. Linares, Spain: Ayuntamiento de Linares.

Goodridge, Janet. 1999. *Rhythm and timing of movement in performance: Drama, dance and ceremony*. London: Jessica Kingsley Publishers.

Gore, Georgiana. 1999. Textual fields: Representation in dance ethnography. In Buckland, ed., 1999, 208–220.

Grau, Andrée. 1995. Dance as part of the infrastructure of social life. In "Working with Blacking: The Belfast Years," a special issue, *The World of Music* 37 (20): 43–59.

Greenfield, Arthur, II. 1961. *Anatomy of a bullfight*. New York: Longmans, Green.

Grut, Marina. 2002. *The Bolero School: An illustrated history of the bolero, the seguidillas and the Escuela Bolera*. Hampshire, UK: Dance Books Ltd.

Guerrero Pedraza, José. 2002. *La dinastia rondeña de los Romero*. Seville: Centro Andaluz del Libro.

Guest, Ann Hutchinson. 1983. *Your move: A new approach to the study of movement and dance*. New York: Gordon & Breach.

———. 1998. Labanotation. In *International Encyclopedia of Dance*, Selma J. Cohen, ed., vol. 4, 95–105. New York: Oxford University Press.

Hackney, Peggy. 2002. *Making connections: Total body integration through Bartenieff Fundamentals*. New York: Routledge.

Hall, Edward T. 1959. *The silent language*. Garden City, NY: Doubleday.

———. 1969. *The hidden dimension*. Garden City, NY: Anchor Books.

———. 1975. A system for the notation of proxemic behavior. In Davis, ed., 1975, reprinted from *American Anthropologist*, 65 (1963): 1003–1026.

———. 1976. *Beyond culture*. New York: Anchor Books/Doubleday.

———. 1983. *The dance of life: The other dimension of time*. Garden City, NY: Anchor Press.

———. 1992. *An anthropology of everyday life*. New York: Doubleday.

Hanna, Judith L. 1979a. *To dance is human*. Austin: University of Texas Press.

———. 1979b. Toward semantic analysis of movement behavior: Concepts and problems. *Semiotica* 25 (1/2): 77–110.

———. 1983. *The performer-audience connection: Emotion to metaphor in dance and society*. Austin: University of Texas Press.

———. 2002. Reading a Universal Language? *DCA News* (Dance Critics Association) Spring: 6–15.

Hanna, Thomas L. 1986. What is somatics? In Johnson 1995, 339–352. (Originally published in *Somatics: Magazine-Journal of the Bodily Arts and Sciences*, 5, Spring-Summer 1986.)

Hayes, Michelle Heffner. 2009. *Flamenco: Conflicting Histories of the Dance*. Jefferson, North Carolina, and London: McFarland.

Headland, Thomas N., Kenneth L. Pike, and Marvin Harris, eds. 1990. *Emics and etics: The insider/outsider debate*. Frontiers of Anthropology. Newberry Park, CA: Sage Publications.

Hemingway, Ernest. [1926] 2003. *The sun also rises*. New York: Scribner.

———. [1939] 1994. *Death in the afternoon*. London: Arrow Books.

Herskovits, Melville J. 1964. *Cultural dynamics*. New York: Alfred A. Knopf.

Hillman, James. 1999. *The Force of Character and the Lasting Life*. Random House Audiobooks: Random House.

Hooper, John. 1986. *The Spaniards: A portrait of the new Spain*. London: Penguin Books.

Howson, Gerald. 1994. *The flamencos of Cadiz Bay*. Westport, CT: Bold Strummer.

Jablonko, Allison, and Elizabeth Kagan. 1988. An experiment in looking: Reexamining the process of observation. *Drama Review* 32 (4) (Winter): 148–163.

Jackson, Michael. 1989. *Paths toward a clearing: Radical empiricism and ethnographic inquiry*. Bloomington: Indiana University Press.

Johnson, Don H. 1992. *Body: Recovering our sensual wisdom*. Berkeley: North Atlantic Books.

———. ed. 1995. *Bone, breath & gesture: Practices of embodiment*. Berkeley: North

Atlantic Books and California Institute of Integral Studies.

Jones, Jo. 1969. Paintings and drawings. *The Gypsies of Granada*. Text by Augustus John, Laurie Lee, Sir Sacheverell Sitwell, Walter Starkie, and Marguerite Steen. London: Athelnay Books.

Kaeppler, Adrienne. 1972. Method and theory in analyzing dance structure with an analysis of Tongan dance. *Ethnomusicology* 16 (2): 173–217.

———. 1985. Structured movement systems in Tonga. In Spencer 1985, 92–118.

———. 2000. Dance ethnography and the anthropology of dance. *Dance Research Journal* 32 (1) (Summer): 116–124.

Kealiinohomoku, Joann W. 1970. An anthropologist looks at ballet as a form of ethnic dance. *Impulse* (1969–70): 24–33.

———. 1974. Review number one: Caveat on causes and correlations. *CORD News* (Committee on Research in Dance) 6 (July): 20–24.

———. 1976. Theories and methods for an anthropological study of dance. PhD diss., Indiana University.

———. 1979. Review of *Dance and Human History*, a film by Alan Lomax. *Ethnomusicology* 23:168–176.

———. 1990. Angst over ethnic dance. *CCDR Newsletter* (Cross-Cultural Dance Resources) 10 (Summer): 1–2, 5–6.

———. 2001a. Signatures embodied in dance: Their transformative power. In *Traditionalism and modernity in the music and dance of Oceania: Essays in honour of Barbara B. Smith*, ed. Helen Reeves Lawrence, Oceania Monograph 52. Sydney, AU: University of Sydney.

———. 2001b. The study of dance in culture: A retrospective for a new perspective. *Dance Research Journal* 33 (Summer): 90–91.

———. 2002. Back to basics: An anthropological retrospective on dance scholarship. *CCDR Newsletter* 19 (Summer): 1.

Kearney, Michael. 1984. *World view*. Novato, CA: Chandler & Sharp.

Kehoe, Vincent J. R. 1959. *Aficionado! The Pictorial Encyclopedia of the Fiesta de Toros of Spain*. New York: Bonanza Books.

———. 1961. *Wine, women & toros! The fiesta de toros in the culture of Spain*. New York: Hastings House.

Kirsch, Gesa E. 1999. *Ethical dilemmas in feminist research: The politics of location, interpretation, and publication*. Albany: State University of New York Press.

Knox, Cynthia. 1992. Embodied knowledge: The cultural patterning of movement and meaning. PhD diss., Union Institute and University.

Krupat, Arnold. 1992. *Ethnocriticism*. Berkeley: University of California Press.

Laban, Rudolph von. [1948] 1968. *Modern educational dance*. New York: Praeger.

———. [1950] 1971. *The mastery of movement*. Boston: Plays, Inc.

———. [1966] 1974. *The language of movement: A guidebook to Choreutics*. Boston: Plays, Inc.

Lalagia. 1985. *Spanish dancing: A practical handbook*. London: Dance Books.

La Meri [Russell Meriwether Hughes]. 1967. *Spanish dancing*. Pittsfield, MA: Eagle Print & Binding.

———. 1977. *Total education in ethnic dance*. New York: M. Dekker.

Landborn, Adair. 1989–1999. Spain travel journals (unpublished).

———. 1996. Shared movement elements: A style analysis of flamenco dance and bullfighting. Paper presented at the First Biannual Flamenco History Conference, Albuquerque, NM.

———. 2000. Cultural relativity: Views on passion in music and dance. *Visual Anthropology* 13 (3): 295–304.

———. 2002. Flamenco dance notation. Faculty working paper, Wesleyan University, Middletown, CT.

———. 2003. The flamenco *bulerías*: An improvisational site of negotiation between personal freedoms and familial constraints. Paper presented at the Annual Meeting and Conference on Romani Studies of the Gypsy Lore Society, University of Michigan, Ann Arbor. http://www.adairlandborn.com/flamenco-articles/2014/5/1/the-flamenco-buleras-an-improvisational-site-of-negotiation-between-personal-freedoms-and-familial-constraints.

_____. 2006. Kinesthetic culture: A comparative study of the movement practices of Spanish bullfighting and flamenco dance. PhD diss., Union Institute and University.

_____. 2010. Reflections on Intracultural Dance Research: Investigating the Kinesthetic Culture of Spanish Bullfighting and Flamenco Dance. *CCDR Newsletter* 33 (Summer 2010): 1, 4–7. Cross-Cultural Dance Resources, Inc., Flagstaff and Tempe, AZ. http://dance.asu.edu/research/ccdr/documents/issue33_2010fall.pdf.

Leblon, Bernard. 1995. *Gypsies and flamenco: The emergence of the art of flamenco in Andalusia*. Hatfield, UK: University of Hertfordshire Press.

Lomax, Alan. 1967. Special features of the sung communication. In *Essays on the Verbal and Visual Arts: Proceedings of the 1966 Annual Spring Meeting of the American Ethnological Society*, ed. June Helm, 109–27. Seattle: University of Washington Press.

_____. 1968. The choreometric coding book. In Lomax, ed. 1968, 262–273.

_____, ed. 1968. *Folk song style and culture*. Washington, D.C.: American Association for the Advancement of Science.

_____, Irmgard Bartenieff, and Forestine Paulay. 1968. Dance style and culture. In Lomax, ed. 1968, 222–247.

Lorca, Federico García. *See* García Lorca, Federico.

Malefyt, Timothy deWaal. 1998. Gendering the authentic in Spanish flamenco. In Washabaugh, ed. 1998, 51–62.

Maletic, Vera. 1987. *Body—space—expression: The development of Rudolph Laban's movement and dance concepts*. Berlin: Mouton de Gruyter.

_____. 1998. Laban Principles of Movement Analysis. In *International Encyclopedia of Dance*, 1998, Selma J. Cohen, ed., vol. 4, 95–105. New York: Oxford University Press.

Marcus, George E. 1998. *Ethnography through thick and thin*. Princeton, NJ: Princeton University Press.

Marrero, Vicente Suárez. 1959. *El enigma de España en la danza española*. Madrid: Ediciones Rialp.

Martínez Remis, Manuel. 1963. *Cancionero popular taurino: Antología*. Madrid: Editorial Taurus.

Matteo [Matteo Marcellus Vittucci] with Carola Goya. 1990. *The language of Spanish dance*. Norman, OK: University of Oklahoma Press.

Mauss, Marcel. [1902] 2001. *A general theory of magic*. London: Routledge.

McDowell, Bart. 1970. *Gypsies: Wanderers of the World*. Washington, D.C.: National Geographic Society.

McLane, Merrill F. 1987. *Proud outcasts: The Gypsies of Spain*. Cabin John, MD: Carderock Press.

McNamara, Joann. 1999. Dance in the hermeneutic circle. In *Researching dance: Evolving modes of inquiry*, 1999, eds. Sondra H. Fraleigh and Penelope Hanstein, 162–187. Pittsburgh: University of Pittsburgh Press.

Meeker, Joseph. W. 1997. *The comedy of survival: Literary ecology and a play ethic*. Tucson: University of Arizona Press.

Mitchell, Timothy. 1991. *Blood sport: A social history of Spanish bullfighting*. Philadelphia: University of Pennsylvania Press.

_____. 1994. *Flamenco deep song*. New Haven: Yale University Press.

_____. 1998. *Betrayal of the innocents: Desire, power, and the Catholic Church in Spain*. Philadelphia: University of Pennsylvania Press.

Moore, Carol-Lynne, and Kaoru Yamamoto. 1988. *Beyond words: Movement observation and analysis*. New York: Gordon & Breach.

Morca, Teodoro. 1990. *Becoming the dance: Flamenco spirit*. Dubuque, IA: Kendall/Hunt Publishing.

Myers, Thomas W. 2003. *Anatomy trains: Myofascial meridians for manual and movement therapists*. Edinburgh: Churchill Livingstone.

Nahachewsky, Andriy. 1995. Participatory and presentational dance as ethnochoreological categories. *Dance Research Journal* 27 (1) (Spring): 1–15.

Nash, Robert J. 2004. *Liberating scholarly writing: The power of personal narrative*. New York: Teacher's College Press.

Ness, Sally Ann. 1988. Understanding cultural performance. *The Drama Review* 32 (4) (Winter): 135–147.

North, Marion. 1971. *Introduction to movement study and teaching*. London: Macdonald & Evans. Quoted in Preston-Dunlop 1995, 286.

Novack, Cynthia J. 1990. *Sharing the dance: Contact improvisation and American culture*. Madison: University of Wisconsin Press.

Otero, José. 1987. *Tratado de bailes*. Seville: Asociación Manuel Pareja-Obregon.

Parra, Antonio. 1997. *Toros y flamenco*. Murcia, Spain: Concejalia de Cultura, Festejos y Turismo.

Pedraza Jiménez, Felipe B. 1998. *Iniciación a la fiesta de los toros*. Madrid: EDAF.

Phillips, Miriam. 1990. The "trained" and the "natural" Gypsy flamenco dancer. In *100 Years of Gypsy Studies*, ed. Matt T. Salo, 267–277. Cheverly, MD: Gypsy Lore Society.

Pike, Kenneth L. 1967. *Language in relation to a unified theory of the structure of human behavior*. The Hague: Mouton.

Pink, Sarah. 1997. *Women and bullfighting: Gender, sex, and the consumption of tradition*. Oxford: Berg.

Pocock, David. 1994. The idea of a personal anthropology. Special issue, *Journal for the Anthropological Study of Human Movement* 8 (1): 11–42.

Pohren, Donn E. [1962] 1984. *The art of flamenco*. Shaftesbury, UK: Musical New Services Limited.

——. 1964. *Lives and legends of flamenco: A biographical history*. Madrid: Society of Spanish Studies.

——. 1980. *A way of life*. Madrid: Society of Spanish Studies.

Polhemus, Lillian B. 1968. *Good-bye Gypsy: Living with the Gypsies of Spain, an account by Lillian B. Polhemus*. Glendale, CA: A. H. Clark.

Preston-Dunlop, Valerie. 1995. *Dance words*. Chur, Switzerland: Harwood Academic Publishers.

Puig Claramunt, Alfonso. 1977. *El arte del baile flamenco*. Barcelona: Ediciones Polígrafa.

Puri, Rajika, and Diana Hart-Johnson. 1995. Thinking with movement: Improvising versus composing? In Farnell 1995, 158–86.

Quintana, Bertha B. 1972. *!Qué gitano! Gypsies of southern Spain*. New York: Holt, Rinehart & Winston.

Ramón, José Luis. 1998. *Todas las suertes por sus maestros*. Madrid: Editorial Espasa Calpe.

Richardson, Laurel. 1994. Writing: A method of inquiry. In *Handbook of qualitative research*. eds. Denzin, Norman K. and Yvonna S. Lincoln, 516–529. Thousand Oaks, CA: Sage Publications.

Rosaldo, Michelle Z., and Louise Lamphere, eds. 1974. *Woman, culture and society*. Stanford, CA: Stanford University Press.

Rosenberg, Marshall B. 2003. *Nonviolent communication: A language of life*. Encinitas, CA: Puddle Dancer Press.

Ross, Dorien. 1995. *Returning to A*. San Francisco: City Light Books.

Royce, Anya P. 2002. *The anthropology of dance*. Hampshire, UK: Dance Books Ltd.

——. 2004. *Anthropology of the performing arts: Artistry, virtuosity, and interpretation in a cross-cultural perspective*. Walnut Creek, CA; Oxford: AltaMira Press.

Salguero, Susan. 2009. *The Gachí: My Gypsy Quest*. La Mesa, CA: Hickey's Books.

San Román, Teresa. 1976. *Vecinos Gitanos*. Madrid: Akal.

——. 1984. *Gitanos de Madrid y Barcelona: Ensayos sobre aculturación y etnicidad*. Bellaterra: Universidad Autónoma de Barcelona.

——. 1986. *Entre la marginación y el racismo: Reflexiones sobre la vida de los gitanos*. Madrid: Alianza Editorial.

Sánchez, Cristina. With Dulce Chacón. 1998. *Matadora*. Barcelona: Editorial Planeta.

Sánchez, Ricardo B. 2001. (Photographer.) *Passes, the Art of the Bullfight: Seduction, Deception, and Truth*. Essays by José Luis Ramón and Rosa Olivares. New York: Rizzoli.

Sánchez Ortega, María Helena. 1977. *Los gitanos españoles*. Madrid: Castellote.

Saura, Carlos. 1984. *Carmen: El sueño del amor absoluto*. Barcelona: Ediciones Folio.

Schechner, Richard. 1983. *Performative circumstances from the avant garde to Ramlila*. Calcutta: Seagull Books.

———. 2002. *Performance Studies*. London: Routledge.

Schreiner, Claus, ed. 1990. *Flamenco: Gypsy dance and music from Andalusia*. Portland: Amadeus Press.

Segall, Marshall H., Donald T. Campbell, Melville J. Herskovits, eds. 1966. *The influence of culture on visual perception*. Indianapolis: Bobbs-Merrill.

Sheets-Johnstone, Maxine. 1966. *The phenomenology of dance*. Madison and Milwaukee: University of Wisconsin Press.

———. 1990. *The roots of thinking*. Philadelphia, PA: Temple University Press.

———. 1999. *The primacy of movement*. Amsterdam/Philadelphia: John Benjamins Publishing.

Shweder, Richard A. 1996. *Quanta* and *qualia*: What is the "object" of ethnographic method? In *Ethnography and human development*, eds. Colby, Anne, Richard Jessor and Richard A. Shweder, 175–182. Chicago: University of Chicago Press.

Silverman, Hugh J., ed. 1991. *Gadamer and hermeneutics*. Vol. 4 of Continental Philosophy. New York: Routledge.

Sossin, K. Mark. 1987. Reliability of the Kestenberg movement profile. *Movement Studies: Observer Agreement* 2:23–28.

Spencer, Paul, ed. 1985. *Society and the dance: The social anthropology of process and performance*. Cambridge, UK: Cambridge University Press.

Spradley, James P. 1980. *Participant observation*. New York: Holt, Rinehart & Winston.

Steingress, Gerhard. 2002. El flamenco como patrimonio cultural o una construcción artificial más de la identidad andaluza. *Anduli: Revista Andaluza de Ciencias Sociales* 1:43–64.

Stolzenberg, Elke. 1992. (Photographer.) *Las Máscaras de lo Jondo*. Text by Ángel Álvarez Caballero. Madrid, Spain: Ediciones del Prado.

Strathern, Andrew J. 2004. *Body thoughts*. Ann Arbor: University of Michigan Press.

Taylor, Shelley E., Laura C. Klein, Brian P. Lewis, Tara L. Gruenwald, Regan A. R. Gurung, and John A. Updegraff. 2000. Biobehavioral responses to stress in females: Tend-and-befriend, not fight-or-flight. *Psychological Review* 107 (3): 411–29.

Tedlock, Dennis, and Bruce Mannheim, eds. (1995). *The dialogic emergence of culture*. Chicago: University of Illinois Press.

Thomas, Helen. 2003. *The body, dance and cultural theory*. New York: Palgrave Macmillan.

Thomas, Katherine. 2002. Dance research worldwide: Spain. *Dance Research Journal* 34 (Summer): 98–105.

Todd, Mabel Elsworth. [1937] 1972. *The thinking body: A study of the balancing forces of dynamic man*. Brooklyn, NY: Dance Horizons.

Totton, Robin. 2003. *Song of the outcasts: An introduction to flamenco*. Portland: Amadeus Press.

Truitt, John. 1997. Flamenco appreciation course presented at Festival Flamenco Internacional, University of New Mexico, Albuquerque.

Turner, Victor W., and Edward M. Bruner, eds. 1986. *The anthropology of experience*. Urbana: University of Illinois Press.

Tuser Vila, Gustavo. *Pases del toreo*. Medellín: Editorial Colina.

Van Manen, Max. 1990. *Researching lived experience: Human science for an action sensitive pedagogy*. Albany: State University of New York Press.

Van Zile, Judy. 1999. Capturing the dancing: Why and how? In Buckland, ed., 1999, 85–99.

Vavra, Robert. 1985. Photos and text. *The Sevilla of Carmen*. New York: William Morrow.

Vergillos Gómez, Juan. 1999. *Libertad o tradición: Una especulación en torno a*

la estética del flamenco. Cornella de Llobregat, Spain: Aquí+Más Multimedia.
Wacquant, Loïc. 2003. Ethnografeast: A progress report on the practice and promise of ethnography. *Ethnography* 4 (1): 5–14.
Wagner, Ann. 1997. *Adversaries of dance: From the Puritans to the present.* Urbana: University of Illinois Press.
Wang, Kirsten. 1996. *The story of Tío Carlos: The autobiography of a Spanish "Gitano."* New York: Peter Lang.
Washabaugh, William. 1996. *Flamenco: Passion, politics and popular culture.* Oxford: Berg.
———. 1998. Fashioning masculinity in flamenco dance. In Washabaugh, ed. 1998, 39–50.
———. 1998. Flamenco song: Clean and dirty. In Washabaugh, ed. 1998.
———, ed. 1998. *The passion of music and dance: Body, gender and sexuality.* Oxford: Berg.
Wheaton, Kathleen, ed. 1988. *Insight guide: Spain.* Hong Kong: APA Publications.
Wilkerson, William S. 1999. From bodily motions to bodily intentions: The perception of bodily activity. *Philosophical Psychology* 12 (1): 61–77.
Williams, Drid, ed. 1972. Review of *Choreometrics and Ethnographic Film-Making* (1971) by Alan Lomax. *Dance Research Journal* 6 (2).
———. 1996. *Signs of human action.* Visual Anthropology. Amsterdam: Taylor & Francis.
———. 1999. Fieldwork. In *Dance in the field: Theory, methods, and issues in dance ethnography,* ed. Teresa J. Buckland, 26–40. Houndmills, UK: Macmillan.
———. 2000. *Anthropology and human movement: Searching for origins.* Lanham, MD: Scarecrow Press.
———. 2004. *Anthropology and the dance: Ten lectures.* Urbana: University of Illinois Press.
Winnicott, Donald W. 1971. *Playing and reality.* London: Tavistock Publications.
Winter, Deborah Du Nann. 1987. Field studies of action profiling reliability. *Movement Studies: Observer Agreement* 2:21–22.
Wolf, Margery. 1992. *A thrice-told tale: Feminism, post-modernism, and ethnographic responsibility.* Stanford: Stanford University Press.
Woodall, J. 1992. *In search of the firedance: Spain through flamenco.* London: Sinclair-Stevenson.
Woodruff, Dianne L., ed. 1978. *Essays in dance research.* Dance Research Annual, vol. 9. New York: Congress on Research in Dance.
Yoors, Jan. 1974. *The Gypsies of Spain.* New York: Macmillan.
Zabala, Vicente. 1968. *La entraña del toreo.* Madrid: Editorial Prensa Española.
Zumbiehl, François, and Pepe Luís Vázquez. 2002. *La voz del toreo.* Madrid: Alianza Editorial.

Audiovisual References

Alga Editores. 2003. Rito y geografía del baile. Series of 12 videocassettes about flamenco and Spanish dance based on films performed and broadcasted by Radio Televisión Española (RTVE) between 1971 and 1973, supplemented with older flamenco film footage (1955–70) and more recent footage (1980). Each number in the series contains several titled films. Murcia, Spain: Alga Editores.
No. 1: *Baile del candil. Poesía y el flamenco. Tomás de Madrid.* 88 min.
No. 2: *Fiestas públicas. Sevilla Morena. Cejilla y Pañolón. El niño, único protagonista.* 72 min.
No. 3. *Café cantante (hasta 1900). Sentimento y linea. Paco Romero.* 82 min.
No. 4. *Primeros pasos en el teatro. Renuevos del árbol viejo. El baile hoy—1980.* 89 min.
No. 5. *El café cantante hasta 1930. Manuel Corrales, "El Mimbre." Matilde Coral.* 91 min.
No. 6. *Fiestas privadas. De Lebrija a los Madriles. Voz y baile. Patio de Banderas.* 81 min.
No. 7. *Folklore y flamenco. Del campo a la academia. Flora Albaicín.* 79 min.
No. 8. *Enseñanza y técnica. Estudio de*

Danza de Jerez. Fernando Belmonte (1 y 2). 90 min.
No. 9. *Consagración del teatro flamenco. Aires de Los Gabrieles. Carmen Mora.* 75 min.
No. 10. *Aportaciones actuales. "Ay, Musical Hondo." Terción y tacon.* 84 min.
No. 11. *Baile flamenco en la actualidad. Bronce añejo. Eduardo Serrano, "El Guito."* 80 min.
No. 12. *Culturas y razas. El Farruco. Dinastías gitanas—Los Farrucos.* 83 min.
Almodóvar, Pedro. 1986 (Spain). *Matador.* Motion picture, 107 min. Videocassette. New York: Cinevista.
Ajami, Jocelyn M. 1998. *Gypsy heart.* Videocassette, 48 min. U.S.: Kultur International Films.
Boetticher, Budd. 1950. *Bullfighter and the lady.* Motion picture, 87 min. U.S.: Republic Pictures.
Bryer, Chris. 1989. *The lady bullfighter.* Documentary film, 26 min. Princeton, NJ: Films for the Humanities & Sciences.
Canales, Antonio. 2002. *El torero.* DVD. n.p.
Cortés, Joaquín. 1997. *Pasión gitana.* Videocassette, 55 min. Madrid: Sagliocco Records. U.S.: Buena Vista Home Entertainment.
Figgis, Mike. 1997. *Flamenco women.* Videocassette, 52 min. U.S.: New River Media.
Films for the Humanities (Firm). 1988. *Matador.* 60 min. Princeton, NJ: Films for the Humanities, Inc.
Gatlif, Tony. 1993. *Latcho drom.* Videocassette, 103 min. France: Video France Film. New York: New Yorker Video.
_____. 2000. *Vengo.* DVD, 90 min. Spain, Home Vision Entertainment.
Guzman, Pilar Pérez de. 1986. *Show flamenco: Una noche de luz.* Videocassette, 40 min. Madrid: Alegrías Productions.
_____. 1991. *Danza flamenca de hoy.* Videocassette, 60 min. Madrid: Alegrías Productions.
Lomax, Alan. 1977. *Step style.* Documentary film on videocassette, 29 min. New York: The Project.

_____, and Choreometrics Project of Columbia University Dept. of Anthropology. 1976. *Dance and human history.* Documentary film, 40 min. Berkeley: University of California Extension Media Center.
_____, and Forrestine Paulay. 1977. *Palm play.* Documentary film on videocassette, 40 min. U.S.: Choreometrics.
_____, Forrestine Paulay, and Choreometrics Project of Columbia University Dept. of Anthropology. 1984. *The longest trail.* Documentary film, 58 min. Berkeley: University of California Extension Media Center.
Mamoulian, Rouben. 1941. *Blood and sand.* Motion picture, 125 min. U.S.: Twentieth Century–Fox.
Marre, Jeremy. 2002. Gypsy music into Africa. Romany Trail 1. Videocassette, 60 min. Newton, NJ: Shanachie Records.
Meyjes, Menno. 2011. *A matador's mistress.* Motion picture, 92 minutes. Santa Monica, CA: Xenon Pictures. Iberoamericana Films Production S.A.
Pachon, Ricardo. 1992. *The heritage of flamenco.* Documentary film, 60 min. Princeton, NJ: Films for the Humanities & Sciences.
Real Escuela Andaluza del Arte Ecuestre. 1989. *Un caballo jerezano.* Videocassette, 49 min. Seville: Savitel Productions.
Saura, Carlos. 1981 (Spain). *Bodas de sangre.* Motion picture, 68 min. Videocassette. U.S.: Siren Entertainment.
_____. 1984 (Spain). *Carmen.* Cinematheque Collection. Motion picture, 99 min. Videocassette. Los Angeles: Media Home Entertainment.
_____. 1986 (Spain). *El amor brujo.* Motion picture, 99 min. Videocassette. Universal City, CA: Universal Studios Home Video.
_____. 1992 (Spain). *Sevillanas.* Documentary film, 55 min. Los Angeles: Connoisseur/Meridian.
_____. 1997 (Spain). Flamenco. Documentary film, 100 min. U.S.: New Yorker Video.

Index

Page numbers in ***bold italics*** indicate pages with photographs.

a las cinco de la tarde (at five in the afternoon) 121
Abella, Carlos 45, 47
acculturation 15, 19, 29, 47, 67, 146, ***147***, 148, 149, 151, 155, 157–158, 163, 182, 244, 247, 251
adrenaline 64, 65, 80, 97, 121, 124, 133, 144, 196, 221, 231, 252, 255–256
aesthemics 134, 135, 138, 140–141, 205, 210, 253, 256, 276ch5n3
aesthetics ***2***, ***4***, 7, 10, 12, ***13***, 26, ***28***, 29, 33, 36–39, 41, 43–45, 47–48, 53, ***63***, 72, 75, 78, 82, 86, 104, 123, 125–127, 130, 132–***137***, 138–145, 148, 151, 153, 155, 157, 160, 164, ***166***, 171, 186, 188, 205, 208, 211, 212, 222, 229, 233, 238, 243, 246, 253, 255, 257; attributes, chart of 144; standards and expectations 12, ***13***, 47, ***63***, 75, 86, 123–127, 134, 138–141, 153, 205, 208, 229; *see also* romantic aesthetic
aficionados, bullfighting ***2***, 26, 29, 61, 97, 104, 117, 121, 126, 128, 133, 139, 175, 197, 250, 259
aficionados, flamenco and bullfighting 7, 61, 121, 125–126, 133, 139, 250, 259
age 10, 26, 73, 94, 148, 205, 248; children ***20***, ***101***, ***147***, 151, 153, 164, 182, 199, 247; influence on cultural change 152–153; older performers 205; teenagers 104
agency 10, 15, 64, 82, 154–155, ***203***, 244, 245, 249, 252–253
agricultural lifestyle 27, 54, 163, 250
Aguirre, Tere 1
Albaicín, Flora 40, 48
Albuquerque, New Mexico 1, 5, 208, 277n2
alegrías (flamenco music and dance form) ***11***, 86, 119, 122, 134, ***159***, 238
Álvarez Caballero, Ángel 40, 41, 47, 192, 206
Amaya, Carmen ***218***, 275n19
ambiente (atmosphere) ***79***, 123, 124, 134
Amor de Dios (dance studio in Madrid, Spain) ***13***, ***173***
Amparo, Nila ***118***
Andalusia, Spain 10, 15, ***17***, 43–44, 46, 52–54, 96; towns of 126
Andalusian lifestyle 15, ***17***, 73–74, 78, 80–***83***, 85, 93, 100, ***107***, 108, 117, ***118***, 120–122, 126–127, 133, 135–136, ***137***, 139, 141–142, 158, 161,

164, 190, 194, 198, 200, ***203***, 206–207, 209–211, 233, 236, ***239***, 241, 243, 248–251, 254, 257
Andalusian sensory patterns 81–***83***, 161, 200, ***203***, 243
androcentrism 198, 200
anecdote as evidence 38
anecdotes: conflict 248–249; sustained gaze 82–***83***; *toreando* 160–161
Ángel, Miguel ***193***
Anglo-American: behavior 135, 248–249; ethnocentrism 22; eye contact 82; perspectives ***28***–31, 60, 73, 81–82, 161, 248–249
Anglo-European ethnocentrism 22, 60
animal behavior 126, 176, 178–182, ***184***, 185, 234, 250–251, 275n3; *see also* critical distance; "fight or flight"
anthropocentrism 197
anti-bullfight activism (*anti-taurino*) ***3***
Antonio Gades Company 77, ***83***, ***156***; *see also* Gades, Antonio
Aposhyan, Susan 67
arcing (dance motif) 188, ***203***, 227, ***228***, 229, ***232***, ***235***, ***237***, 243
arm "runs long" (bullfight movement) ***88***, 176, 188, 189
arms moving in tandem (dance motif) 167–***168***
Arrebola, Alfredo 44, 78, ***79***
associative appreciation 123, 125; *see also* metonymy
audience 123, 132, 134, 165, 171–172, 175, 190, 200, ***214***, 216, 230, 234, 236, 238, 241–243, 246, 253, 257–258; foreign 135, 136, ***137***; indigenous ***107***, 135, ***137***, 138–140, 173, 194, 196–197, ***203***
authenticity ***13***, 26, 54, 61–62, 94, 105, ***115***–***116***, 128, 130, 138, 139, 144, 151, ***156***, 163, 205, 248
ayuda (wooden practice sword) 177–178, 277n11

back space (dance motif and in bullfighting) ***226***, ***228***
ballet ***28***, 40, 41, ***42***, ***89***, ***150***, 157, 191, 192, ***193***, ***195***, 205, 223, 233

291

Ballet Nacional de España 191
Ballet Teatro Español de Rafael Aguilar **42, 89, 150**
banderillero (torero who places barbs) **102**, 119, 185, 202, **203, 204, 218**
Barcelona, Spain 1, **4**, 47
Barea, Arturo 142
Barón, Javier **193**
Barras, Sara 152
"Barrier score" 30, 273n11, 276ch5n2, 280n5; *see also* personal boundaries
Bartenieff, Irmgard 52–53, 206, 254–255; with Dori Lewis 82, 84, 85, 202
Bartenieff Movement Fundamentals 157
bata de cola (long flamenco dress) **118, 129, 131**, 169–172, **174**, 210, 211
Bayeu y Subías, Ramón **102**
Behar, Ruth 49, 71
Belmonte, Juan 225, 231
Bennahum, Ninotchka D. 192
Biblioteca Nacional de España, Madrid, Spain 5, 36, 273ch1n1
biorhythms and interaction 120
Birdwhistell, Ray L. 50, 201, 206
Blacking, John 50
Blood Wedding (film) 1
Boas, Franz **17**, 75
body, attitude toward 29–30
body extenders 169, 172, 175, **193, 204**, 207, 209–211
Bonner, John Tyler 250
braceo (arm movements) 209, 233
Bretón de Cádiz, theater 192
Bruner, Edward M. 49, 50, 58, 70
Bryer, Chris 121, **137**, 140, 191, 208, 251
bulerías (flamenco music and dance form) **11**, 44, 53, **77**, 84, 86, 94–96, 97, 105, 119, 238
burladero (wooden barrier in arena) **66**, 104, 181, 185

el cabal or *los cabales* (experts, critics) 139, 153
Caballero Bonald, J. M. 41, 47
Cádiz, Spain 126, 134
Café de Chinitas, Madrid, Spain **79**
cafés cantantes (singing cafes) 40, **106–107**, 192, 194, 209, 275n2
California Academy of Tauromaquia 5, **63**, 87, 175
Campbell, Donald T. 74, 248
Campbell, Douglas G. **174**
Canales, Antonio 192–**193**, 208, 277n2
cantaor(a) (singer) 90, 99, 134, 173
cante (song) 38–41, 43–44, 54, **76**, 92–93, 96, 133, 225, **240**
cante jondo (deep song) 92, 133, 141, 259
capea (informal bullfight) **77, 101**, 103, 110, 120, 250
capote (large cape) 62, **113**, 119, **129**, 152, 163, **166**, 167, **168**, 169, **193, 195, 215, 235, 239**
carceleras (flamenco song style) 133
careo (dance motif) 194, 242

Carmen: dance productions **42, 77, 83, 89, 150, 156**; film **13**, 41, **42**
Carrasco, Manuela 130, **131**
Carrithers, Michael 49, 70, 73–75
Carse, James P. 201
Casa de Campo (city park in Madrid, Spain) 62
catharsis 60, 80, 84–85, 93, 96–98, 108, 120–121, 125, 134, 141–143, 145, 161, 219, 248, 251, 255–260; *see also* emotionality
Catholicism 110, 122, 198, 206–207
Choreometrics Project 14, 253–255, 262; criticisms of 253; critics of 255
Ciro (Diezhandino Nieto) **193, 195**
citación (bullfight movement) **113**, 170–171, 177, 189, **193**
citing (dance motif) **113**, 189, 241–242
Clara, Adela 169
class, social or economic 7, 10, 26–27, 40, 47, 127, 128, 139, 161, 182
Cleveland, Sidney E. 30–31, 49; *see also* "Barrier score"
Cohen, Bonnie Bainbridge 233, 245, 253
Cole, Joanna 75
Collins, Larry 27, 51–52, **77, 101–102**, 110
Colombia, S.A. 5, 62, 127, 163
commercialism 52, **69, 79**, 128
compás (musical structure) 86–87, 90–91, 119, 126, 158, **159**, 160, 196, 221, 236, **240**, 258; *see also* rhythm
competition **17**, 100, **107**, 134, 138, 144, 153, 161, 181, 183, **184**, 185, 197, 200
conflict 75, 100, **112**, 141, 164, 171, 179, 187, 189, 190, 201, 202; positive role of 31–32, 85, 200, 230, 238, 241, 248–249, 255–259
conformity 73, 91, 141, 144, 152, 155–**156**, 198, 244, 249, 257
Congress on Research in Dance (CORD) 5, 53
Connerton, Paul 49, 148–149; on variance and invariance 151–152
contoneo (proud walk) 164–165, 212, 243
Cooney, Coleman 5, **63**, 87, **88, 89**–90, **101**, 104, **112–113**, 170, 175–176, 178–179, 182, 185, 188
Córdoba, Spain 1, 126, 158, **159**
corrida, corrida de toros, or *fiesta de toros* (public bullfights) **2**, **4**, 27, **28**, 46, 48, **69**, 72, 74, 80, 97, **101, 102**, 104, **109, 113**, 120, 121, 124, **166**, 179, 181, 194, 201, 221, 223, 241, 243, 251, 256
La corrida (dance production) 192
Cortés, Joaquín **28**, 72, 75, 152
countertension: bullfight movement 62, 171, **174**, 207, 257; dance motif 171, **174**, 207, **214**, 233, 257; Laban term 165, **213, 214**, 229
courage 33, 51, 62, **63**–64, 97–98, 133, 138, 142, 144, **166**, 178, 182–183, **184**, 185–188, 194, 197, 222–225, 229, 257, 259
courtship 93–96, 198
critical distance **112–113**, 176; *see also* animal behavior; "fight or flight"

Crosby, Jill Flanders 53, 68
cross-cultural research 7, 14, 16, 21, 24, 26, **28**, 32, **42**, 52, 61, 67, 148, 158, 201, 254
Csordas, Thomas J. 50, 80, **203**, 252–255
cuadrilla (matador's team) 78, 180, 181, 185, 202
cuadro flamenco (semi-circle of flamenco performers) 78, **79**, **106–107**, **115**, 117, **150**, **213**
cultural complex 10, **11**, 12, 18, 26, 80, 93, 135, 192, 198, 252, 275*n*19; movement as integrative factor in 252
cultural continuity 7, 149, 155, 243
cultural hybridity 1, 148
cultural icon **4**, 10, 26, **42**, **56**, 125, 175, 188, 191, 221
cultural relativity 16, 31–32, 49, 60, 134, 248–249
culture: high-context 73, 78, 126, 135, **137**, 139, 145, 155, 161, 197, 249–250; low-context 135, 136, 197
culture group 9, 10, 146, 149, 152, 153, 155, **156**

dance and language 61–62, 163
dance enactments of bullfighting: cultural scripts 191–**193**; movement quotations **193–195**; theatrical productions 192–**193**; see also *paso caida*; *paso de muleta*; *vuelta torera*
dance events, "contained" and "extended" 120
dance motifs 227, **228**, 229–231, **232**, 233–234, **235**, 236, **237**, 238, **239**, **240**, 241–243
dance motifs (bullfight influence) *see* arcing; arms moving in tandem; back space; *careo*; citing; countertension; elbows; eye contact; fabric manipulation; facings; impactive phrasing; misdirection; near-to-but-not-touching; passing; peripheral spatial tension; *recoje*; *remate*; separation of upper/lower body; space hold; spiraling; *torcido*; trailing; wrist rotation
death **2**, 16, 32, 51, 96, 97, 103, 111, 119, 121, 124, 133, 142–143, 144, **166**, 189, 191, 196, 197, 199, 210, 223, 230, 231, 251, 259
desplante (extended *llamada*) 92, 173, 242, 280*n*13; see also *llamada*; signaling
deWaal, Frans 73, 87
Dils, Ann 53, 68
"Don Tancredo" (bullfighting stunt) 225
"don't move your feet" **224**, 225, 227, **232**–233, 279*n*4; exception to the rule 231
duende (spirit) 32, 99, 120, 123, 125, **131**, 132, 134, 140–145, 241, 256, 257; biological factors in 120–121; as a measure of performance 7, 140–141
Dumas, Alexandre 22
Duse, Elenora 212

Effort drives 217, **218**, 219
Effort phrasing (explosive, impactive, breath, swing) **220**
Effort qualities (Laban term) 202, 216, 257, 278*n*8; fighting qualities 216; indulging qualities 216

Effort states 217
elbows (dance motif) **63**, 202, **203**, **218**
"El Cojo" (Enrique Jiménez Mendoza) 30, 205–206
"El Cordobés" (Manuel Benítez) 52, **77**, 110
"El Estampío" (Juan Sánchez) 192
"El Farruco" (Antonio Montoya Flores) 205
"El Farruquito" (Juan Manuel Fernandez Montoya) 205
"El Fundi" (José Pedro Prados) **203**
embodied experiential research 55; see also somatic ethnography
embodiment 9, 21, 29, 37, 50, 55, 59, 70, 73, 105, 124, 151, 157, 169, **203**, 210, 252–257
emic perspectives 16, 24–**28**, 29, 30, 32, 35, 37–40, **42**, 47–49, 51, 52, 57, 60, 68, 134–135, 140–146, 148, 155, 158, 163, 188, 202, 241, 254, 255
emotion, theories of James-Lange and Cannon-Bard 59
emotionality 5, **23**, 29, 60, 72–75, 84–85, 104, **116**, 128, 130, 132–134, 142–143, 236, 247, 251, 254, 258; see also catharsis
emotions 5, 15, **23**, **28**, 32, 53, **116**, **118**, 121–122, 246; see also courage; pride
empathy for animals 87, 117, 187, 251; see also intraspecies and interspecies bonding
encierro (running with the bulls) **101**, 103, 104, 120, 121, 250
Enciñias-Sandoval, Eva 1
enculturation 15, **17**–19, **20**, **28**–32, 60, 73, 74, 81, 85–86, **101**, 134, 136, **137**, 138, 146, **147**, 148–149, **150**, 151–152, 154–155, 158, 199, 244, 247–249, 251; of rhythm and touch 85–86
endogamy 94
entrada (entrance) 92, 119, 275*n*14
entrainment 16, 87, 119, 144, 251; see also rhythmic entrainment; temple
equipo see *cuadrilla*
Escudero, Manolo 140, 191, 208
Escudero, Vicente 192
Esmeralda, Merche **173**, 275*n*19
espontaneo **69**, 110
estampa (personal style) 74, 128, 144, 152, 205, 243, 248; see also individuality
estocada (final sword thrust) 194, 238, 242
ethnicity 7, 10, 26, 127–130, 139, 205
ethnocentrism 16–19, **20**, 21, 49, 136, 158; see also Anglo-American ethnocentrism; Anglo-European ethnocentrism
ethnographic research 25, 65, 49; field research 5, 7, 94, 175–190; see also participant-observation research, levels of
ethnographic writing 6, **42**, 48–49, 51–52, 70–71
etic perspectives 16, 24–27, 29, 32, 37, 49, 50, 52, 57, 60, 148, 158, 188, 201–202, 255
eye contact 57, 64, 92, 173, 251; in circular formations 108, **109**, 110; cultural patterns of 81–**83**

eye contact (dance motif) 64, 82, **83**, 84, 171, 189, 194, **218**, 219, 233-234, **235**, 242-243, 260

Fabregas, Evelina 121, 196, 251
fabric manipulation 53, **166, 168,** 169, 171, 199, 210; see also *capote*; flamenco skirt; *muleta*
fabric manipulation (dance motif) 53, **166, 168,** 169, 171-173, 175, 210, **237**
facings (dance motif) 233-**235**, 243
faena, faena de muleta see *tercio de matar*
farruca (flamenco music and dance form) 53, 194
female, femininity (*hembra*) 27, **28**, 153, 157, 169, 170, 172, **174**, 191-**193**, 198, 200, 208-209; attitudes toward female sexuality 95, 96, 197-198; see also courtship; gender; gender roles in performance; gendered domains; *matadora*
feria del caballo (horse fair) **17, 20,** 122, 209
Festival Flamenco Internacional, Albuquerque, New Mexico 208
Festival of San Fermin, Pamplona, Spain **101**, 103
"fight or flight" **224**; see also animal behavior; critical distance
Fisher, Seymour 30-31, 49; see also "Barrier score"
flamenco dance notation 39, 48, 158-**159**; see also Labanotation; Language of Dance
flamenco footwork **13**, 91-92, 119, 124-125, 154, **159**, 206, 207, 209, **213**, 217, 219, **220**-222, 225, **240**, 242
Flamenco History Conference, First Biannual 5
flamenco puro 130
Flamenco Puro (dance production) **131**
flamenco skirt 53, **89**, 125, **166, 168,** 170-171, **173**, 199, 209-211, **214, 237**
flamenco social circle 64, **76, 77,** 96, 100, 103, 105, **106**, 108, **109**, 114, **115-116**, 117, **156**, 205, 259
flamencology, *flamencología* 35-36, 38-41, **42**, 43-45, 47, 48, 246
Fraser, Angus 94, 95
Fundación de Flamenco, Jerez de la Frontera, Spain 5, 36

Gades, Antonio 1, 41, **42**; see also Antonio Gades Company
Galvan, Israel 72, 152
Galvan, Pastora 152
ganadero (cattle rancher) 104, 117, 121, 178-180, 183
García Lorca, Federico 1, 43, 121, 141-143, **193**
Gardner, Howard 67, 70
Gay y Blasco, Paloma 22, 46, 211
Geertz, Clifford 31-32, 49
gender 6, 7, 26, 27-**28**, 46, 73, 94-95, 153, 186, 197-198, 205, 208-210; see also female; male
gender roles in performance 21, **28**, 100, 191, 200, 208-209, 231, 277n6, 278n15

gendered domains 100, **107**, 170, 172, 182-185, 210-211, 277n12
general space 165, 212, **213, 214**
gesture 16, 57, 68, 86, 91, 92, 117, 142, 143, **166**, 191, **193**, 196, **203**, 207-208, **213, 214**, 217, 229, 260
gitanesco (gypsy-like) 128
gitanismo (authentic gypsy performance style) 123, 127-128, 130
gitano (Spanish Gypsy) culture 7, 22, 26, 46-47, 60, 94, 127-128, 130, 133, 135, **137**, 139, 148, 205, 211; *gitano* wedding 94-96; *gitanos* as cultural arbiters 139
Giurchescu, Anca 50
González Climent, Anselmo 43-44, 47, 78, 80, **83**, 90, 139, 153, 196
Goodridge, Janet 75, 87
Goya, Carola 48, 62, 194, **232**, 233, 242
Goya, Francisco de (tapestries of) **101-102**
Greco, Carmela 167
Greco, José **204**; see also José Greco Company
Grut, Marina 209, **218**, 242, 243
Guest, Ann Hutchinson 231
Gusman Center for the Performing Arts, Miami, Florida **131**

Hackney, Peggy 221
Hall, Edward T. 19, 50, 73, 80, 81, **112**, 135, 197, 249
Hamada, Rika **173**
Hanna, Judith L. 50, 55, 61, 255
Hanna, Thomas 58, 245, 255
Hannan, Daniel 87, **88**
Hart-Johnson, Diana 61-62, 154
Hayes, Michelle Heffner 45
Hemingway, Ernest 51, 97, 111
Heredia, Yolanda 169, 170
Herskovits, Melville J. 10, **17**, 19, 31-32, 49, 51, 56, 74, 93, 146, 152-153, 161, 248, 252
"Hija del Ciego" (Salud Rodriguez) 192, 194
Hillman, James 59
homeostasis 18, 73, 93, 97, 154, 200, 206
Hooper, John 80
horns (of bull) **4, 13, 56, 101, 102,** 103, 111, 143, 163, **166**, 176-177, 181, **184**, 202, **203, 215**, 227, 231, 233, 236, 238, 246, 279n9
horses **2, 4,** 15, **17,** 22, 54, 80, 87, **102**, 119, **137, 159**, 160, 209, 233, 250, 251; see also *feria del caballo*
Howson, Gerald 43, 52
human universals 18, 61
humor 96-97, 133, 141, 144, 160, 179, 238, 256

Iberian Peninsula 148, 212
impactive phrasing (dance motif) **220**-222, 241, 242
improvisation 21, 39, 53, 61, **63**-64, **76**, 86, 92, 94, 95, 104, 130, 133, 134, 144, 152-155, 158-**159**, 160, 164, 186-187, 190, **224, 226,** 238-**239**, 241, 246

individuality 31, 32, 64, 73–74, 128, 130, 132, 151, *156*, 249, 257; see also *estampa*
innovation 49, 72, 136, 138, 140, 144, 149, 152–153, 155, *156*, 187, 223, 243, 254, 258
insider/outsider dichotomy 12, 26–27, 65, *109*, 135
international extent: of bullfighting *3*, 10, *11*, 127; of flamenco 10, *11*, *13*, *69*, 105, 126
intracultural research 7, 14, 24, 201, 254–255
intraspecies and interspecies bonding 87; see also empathy for animals

Jablonko, Allison 53, 68
jaleo (supportive sounds) 54, 64, *76*, *77*, 78, 90, 93, 96, *106–107*, 114, *115–116*, 117, 144, 151, 160
jazz 127, 157
Jerez de la Frontera, Spain 5, *17*, 36, 44, 73, 94, 104–105, 126, 161, 209
Jichen Theater in Chengdu, China *42*, *89*, *150*
José Greco Company *118*, *204*
juerga (flamenco party) *76*, 104, *109*, 120, 121, 161, 246
jurisdicción (territory) 110–111, *112–113*, 114, 117, 170, 171, 177, 179–180, 186, 189, 234, 236, 238, 241; see also *querencia*; territoriality

Kagan, Elizabeth 53, 68
Kealiinohomoku, Joann W. 14, 18, 21, 51, 59, 61, 75, 90–91, 93, 97, 99, 120, 130, *131*, 132, 136, 140–141, 149, 153–154, 163, 169, *204*, 205, 209, 247, 252–253, 255
Kearney, Michael 9–10, 49; see also *worldview*
"keep your eyes on the bull" *226*, 227, *232*, 233
Kehoe, Vincent J. R. 45–46
kinesphere *89*, 117, 119, 165, *166*, 167, 171, *174*, *193*, 207, 212, *213–215*, 216, 229–230, 244
kinesthetic culture 6, 7, 9, 14–16, 108, 146, 244–260
knowledge, esoteric and exoteric 146, 161, 236; see also syntactical appreciation
Knox, Cynthia 51, 67, 72–73, 81, 86, 87, 146, *147*, 148, 153, 165, 251

"La Argentina" (Antonia Mercé) 192
La corrida (dance production) 192
"La Cuenca" (Trinidad Huertas) 192, 194
"La Meri" (Russell Meriwether Hughes) 211–212, 223
La Mezquita, Córdoba, Spain 160, 276*ch*6*n*4
"La Yerbabuena" (Eva María Garrido García) 152
Laban, Rudolph von 25, 52, 82, 84, 85, *88*, 144, 165, 202, 206, 212–*213*, 217, *218*, 219, 229, 244
Laban movement analysis (Labananalysis) 7, 25, 50, 52, 68, 82, 84, 85, 158, 164, 165, 188, 201–202, *220*; overview of 261–262
Labanotation 25, 48, 231, 234, 261, 273*n*5; see also flamenco dance notation

language and gender 182, 264–265
Language of Dance 158, 231, 276*ch*6*n*3; see also flamenco dance notation
language use and style 7, 37–39, *42–43*
LaPierre, Dominique 27, 51–52, *77*, *101–102*, 110
Lerin, Juan Giralt *11*
letra (song verse) 38–39, 86, 133–134
linguistics 24, 33, 57, 61–62, 67, 70, 273*n*13
lived experience 6, 9, 39, 51, 54–*56*, 57, *63*, 68, 71, 78, 138, 157–161, 190
llamada (call or signal) 91–92, 173, 242; see also *desplante*; signaling
llamativo (showy) 144, 177, 242, 243
Lomax, Alan 14, 201, 206, 253–255
López-Chaves, Domingo *226*
Lopez, Pilar 153
Lorca see García Lorca, Federico
Low, Dalia *193*
Luisillo *218*

Madrid, Spain 5, *13*, 36, 46, 47, *56*, 62, 64, *66*, *69*, *79*, 82, *88*, *101*, *102*, 110, 158, 160–161, 163, 169, *173*, 175, 183, *184*, *193*, *195*, 196, *203*, 211, *224*, *226*, 248, 249
madrugada (*la madrugada*, the hours before dawn) 36, 121, 161
Magdalena, María *13*
male, masculinity (*macho, machismo*) 21, 27–*28*, 39, 41, *42*, 53, 62, 78, *83*, 92, 94, 95, 96, 100, *107*, 153, 161, 183, *184*, 185, 186, 191–192, 194, 197–198, 205, 209; see also courtship; gender; gender roles in performance; gendered domains
Malefyt, Timothy deWaal 45, 100, 105, *107*
maletillas (itinerant toreros) 110
maneo (hand movements) *173*, 209
Manolete (dancer, Manuel Santiago Maya) 217
Manolete (matador, Manuel Laureano Rodríguez Sánchez) 80
manton (shawl) *168*, *173*, *214*
marcaje (marking time) *116*, 225, 236, *240*
marriage 78; see also courtship
mastery 62, 133, 151–155, 164, *166*, 180, 257
matadora (female matador) *28*, 46, 51, *109*, 183, *184*, 185; *señoritas toreras* 183; see also Fabregas, Evelina; Sánchez dePablos, Cristina
matiz (dynamics) 82, *220*
Matteo 48, 62, 194, *232*, 233, 242
Maya, Belén 152
McNamara, Joann 57
media, public *3*, 27, 35, 38, 39, 104, 108, 127
Meeker, Joseph *102*, 103, 164, 258
metonymy 45, 196–198, 202, 212, 222, 230, 238, 243; see also associative appreciation
Mexico 5, *63*, 127, 154, 175, 177, 180, 182, 234
mimesis 117, *147*, 164, *166*, 172, 192, 197
mimetismo taurino (mimed bullfighting) 192, *193*, 194, *195*

misdirection (dance motif and in bullfighting) 84, 181, 188, 199
Mitchell, Timothy 43, 46, 92, 103, 110
Moors, influence of 22, 81, 96, 148, 274*n*9, 276*ch*5*n*1
morality 29, 60, 93, 132, 138, 192, 207, 211
Morca, Teodoro 1, 48, 119, 153
movement analysis 6, 25, 37, 39, 48, 50, 52–53, **56**, 68, 82, 84, 85, 158, 191–222
movement and culture 21, 71, 157, 244
movement in unison 108, **150**, **152**
movement vocabularies 6, 7, 9, 12, 53, 57, 67, 68, 71, **88**, 155, 157, 163, 167, 186, 188, 199, 202, 207, 219, 223, 234, 243, 247
muleta (small red cape) **63**, 80, **88**, **102**, **113**, 119, 126, 152, **166**, **168**–172, 175–178, 181, 182, **184**, 186, 188, 189, 199, 207, 210, 217; see also *paso de muleta*
multisystem use of body 124
music 6, 16, 22, 24, 39–40, 53, 64, 70, 85–87, 90–91, 94, 104, **106**, 117, 119, 122, 124–127, 130, 134, 138, 140, 142, 143, 148, 154, **159**–160, 173, 196, **214**, **220**–221, 236, 243, 246, 253, 257; for the bullfight 92; see also *cante*; *soniquete*; *toque*
music-dance dyad 25, **42**, 75, 90–92
music notation 25, 38–39

Nachos (dance studio in Madrid, Spain) **193**, **195**
near-to-but-not-touching (dance motif) **56**, **218**, **228**, 231
no dice nada (it says nothing) 134, 233, 236, 254, 255
North, Marion 221

oral tradition 38, 39

Paco Peña Festival Internacional de la Guitarra, Córdoba, Spain 1, 158
Palencia, Fernando de **79**
palillo (small stick) 175–177, 189
palmas (handclapping) **76**, 78, 90, 96, 104, 114, 117, 140, 160, 196
palmero (handclapping performer) 90, **115**–**116**, 140
Pamplona, Spain **101**, 103
Parra, Antonio 44, 78
participant-observation research, levels of 65, 66, 67; see also ethnographic field research
pases (cape movements) 154, 170–172, **174**, 243; *natural* 176, 189; *redondo* 176
pasión (suffering) 122; compared to English word "passion" 219
Pasión Gitana (dance production) **28**; *see also* Cortés, Joaquín
paso de caída (dance movement) 194
paso de muleta (dance movement) 194
paso doble (bullfight music) 92
passing (dance motif and in bullfighting) 170–172, **174**, 231, 241–243

patrones (patrons) 26, 139
patterns and pattern recognition 7, 12, 14–15, 29, 39, 48, 61, **63**, 68, 70, 73, 81–82, 85–87, 90–92, 117, 124–125, 136, 139, 141, 144, 146, 148, 151, 154–155, 157, **159**–162, 197, 247; developmental patterns 87, 151, 157; motifs as patterns 227; movement patterning 29–30, 163, 165, 167, **168**, 169, 189, 245; repatterning 148, 157, 161
Paulay, Forrestine 52, 206, 254
pedagogy 12, **13**, 47–48, 62–64, **66**, 149, 151, 153–155, 157–158, 175, 194, 223
Pedrito de Portugal 183
pena (pain, difficulty) 122
peña (social club) 38, **76**, 104, **109**
peña flamenca (flamenco social club) 104–105, **106**, **107**, 108, 120, 123
Peña Tío José de Paula, Jerez de la Frontera, Spain 105
perception 19, 31, 58–59, 73, 81, 90, 97, 245, 255; see also visual perception; visual perception of a bull
perceptual inference habits 30, 74, 247–248
performance contexts 7, 10, 32–33, 40, **69**, 75, **76**–**77**, 78, **79**, 94; formal and informal 78, **79**, 155, **156**, 205; in the round 213 (*see also* flamenco social circle); venues and institutions 99–108
performativity 16, 32–33, 45, 50, 64–65, 74, 93, 96, 127–128, 132–136, 153, 157, 161, **174**, 179, 187, 198–201, 211–212, 225, 251–252, 259
peripheral spatial tension (dance motif) **88**, **89**, 188, 229–231, 243
personal boundaries 84, **116**–117, 248; defined or undefined 30, 31, 248–249; see also "Barrier score"
phenotype 10, 61, **204**, 205, 208; nonmatching **156**; uniform **150**
Phillips, Miriam 48, 133
Pike, Kenneth L. 24, 25, 29, 49
Pink, Sarah 46, 104, 183, **184**, 191
plasticidad (plasticity) 223, 246
play 15, 21, 32, 51, 53, **56**, 64, 72, 91, 93, 97, 99, **101**–**102**, 103, 120, 132, 142, 145, **147**, 152, 161, 164, 172, **174**, 198–201, 230–231, 238, 243, 247, 256–259
Plaza de Toros de Las Ventas, Madrid, Spain **56**, 110, **203**, **224**, **226**
Plaza de Toros Monumental, Barcelona, Spain 1
Pohren, Donn E. 22, 43, 126
posture 12–**13**, 40, 57, 62, **63**, 68, 91, 117, **129**, **137**, 164–165, 169, 206–207, 209, 212, 227, 229, **232**, 250; of matador **63**, 165, **203**, **204**, **232**; vertical stress 164, 167, 206–207; *see also* separation of upper and lower body; *torcido*
praxis (practice) 37, **239**; incorporating or bodily practice 148–149, **156**; formal or informal 151–152, 155, **156**

pride *4*, 21, 22, 72, 97, 128, 130, *137*, 144, 164, 206, 212, 250
professionalism 27–*28*, 40, 47, 51, 78, *79*, *88*, *101*, 104–*106*, 127, 153–154, 164, 179, 180–181, 183, *184*, 185, 205, 250, 264
promenade *20*, 211, 212, 279n16
proscenium theater *77*, *106*, 108, 117, *150*, *213*; theatrical dance productions in 191, 205
proxemics 81–82, 230
public spectacles and public ritual life 22, *23*, 32, 65, *66*, *69*, 72, 75, *77*–78, 90, 96, 103, 110, 120, 122, 124, *137*, 145, 198, 244, 247, 251, 258
Puig Claramunt, Alfonso 40, 48, 192
Puri, Rajika 61–62, 154

qualitative versus quantitative research 254
querencia (sense of belonging) 110, 111, *112*–*113*, 114, *116*, 117, 236, 238, 259; see also *jurisdicción*; territoriality
quiebros (bullfight movement) *215*, 230–231, 238, *239*, *240*, 243

"Rafaelillo" (Rafael Rubio) *23*
Ramón, José Luis 46, 48, 154
Real Monasterio de San Lorenzo del Escorial, Madrid, Spain *101*-*102*
recoje (dance motif) 238, *239*, *240*; see also *quiebros*
redundancy as feature of culture 87, 120, 136, 138, 149, 153–155, *156*, 201, 253–255, 258
regionalism 126, 134
rejon (lance) *2*, *102*
rejoneo, toreo de rejones (bullfighting from horseback) *2*, *102*, *137*, 233
remate (bullfight movement) *129*, 170–172, *195*, 241, 243
remate (dance motif) 92, 172, *195*, 241, 243
research see cross-cultural research; embodied experiential research; ethnographic field research; intracultural research; participant-observation research; qualitative versus quantitative research; somatic ethnography
rhythm (*ritmo*) 16, 57–59, 75, 82, 85, 86, 91–92, 126, 140–141, 144, 158, *159*, 160, 207, 221, *240*, 257, 258; see also *compás*
rhythmic entrainment 85–87, *88*, *89*–90
risk taking *2*, 5, 7, 15, 32–33, *56*, *63*–64, *66*, 97–100, *101*-*102*, 103, 111, *113*, *116*, 117, 120, 128, 133, *137*, 140, 142, 144, 151–152, 170, 180–182, 185, 189–190, 194, 197, 202, 221, *226*, 229, 231, 238, 246, 248, 256–259
ritual *4*, 9, 10, 12, 15, 21–24, 29, *42*, 46, 57, 65, 72, *77*–78, 85, 86, *88*, 93, 96–97, 99–122, 132, 138, 142–145, 155, 172–*174*, 197–200, 245, 247, 251, 256–258
Rivera, Manolo 1
Romance del torero eterno ballet 41
romantic aesthetic 33, 37, 132–134, 141–142; see also aesthetics
Romería de El Rocío, El Rocío, Spain 76

Romero, Francisco *102*
Romero, Teresa Viera *218*
Ruíz, Joaquín *193*
rumba gitana (flamenco music and dance form) 86, 94, 238

Sánchez de Pablos, Cristina *28*, 46, 51, 183, *184*, 185
San Diego, California 5, *63*, 175
Saura, Carlos 1, *13*, 41, *42*, 205
Schreiner, Claus *42*, 122
Segall, Marshall H. 74, 248
Semana Santa (Easter Holy Week) 122
senses 59, 80–82
sensory experience 19, 55, 80, 81, *203*-*204*, 245–246
sensory-motor system 245
sensual appreciation 123–125
separation of upper and lower body (dance motif) 206–208, *232*, 233; see also posture
sevillanas (flamenco music and dance form) 17, *20*, 53, *76*, *83*, 94, 122, 209, 242
Seville, Spain *20*, *76*, 170
Sheets-Johnstone, Maxine 55
signaling 86, 91–92, *173*, 201, 242–243; see also *desplante*; *llamada*
siguiriyas (flamenco music and dance form) 86, 134, 259–260
social bonds 78, 94, 200; see also marriage; courtship
social class 26–27, 47, 127, 139, 161
social conformity 73, 141, 144, 152, 155, *156*, 198, 244, 249
social control 95, 96
social memory 49, 149
social status (ranking) 136, 153, 182, *184*–185, 187, 205
sociality 6, *20*, 32, 38, 49, 51, 57, 64–65, 72–75, *76*, *77*, 78–81, 85–86, 94, 95, 108, 110, 114, *115*-*116*, 123, 128, 144, 200, 248, 251, 258; female forms of *107*
sol o sombra (sun or shade, tickets at bullfight arena) *109*
soleares (flamenco music and dance form) 86, *118*, 134
somatic ethnography 55, *56*, 57–62, *63*, 64, 68, 71
somatic intelligence 59, 67–68, 70, 196
somatic perspectives (somatic studies) 6, 33, 51, 55–59, 149, 149, 157, 172, 198, 246, 253, 255
soniquete (resonance) 160
space hold (dance motif) 234–*235*
Spanish classical dance 40, 48, 191–192, 194, 205, 227, 274ch1n3
spatial dimensions 212–*213*, 244, 279n20
spatial parameters 7, *106*, 108–*109*; in bullfight arena *109*, 110–111, *112*, *113*, 114; in flamenco performance 114, *115*-*116*, 117, *118*
spatial tension *56*, *213*, *214*, 230; central spatial tension *213*, *215*; peripheral spatial ten-

Index

sion 165, *166*, 167, 176, 188, *214*, *215*, 216, 229–231, 242–243 (*see also* peripheral spatial tension [dance motif]); transverse spatial tension 214, *215*, 216, *239*
spiraling (bullfight movement) *2*, *4*, *23*, *129*, *137*, 167, 169, 172, *195*, 223, *235*
spiraling (dance motif) *131*, 169, 171–172, 210, 211, 231, *232*; see also *torcido*
Spradley, James P. 49, 65, *66*, 67, 158
Strathern, Andrew J. 50, 57, 169, 210, 257
Steingress, Gerhard 44–45
Stolzenberg, Elke *13*, 41, *173*, *193*, *195*
suit of lights (matador's) *63*, *66*, 124, 163, *203*, 209, *224*, *226*, 276ch7n3
super-ordinary 14, 60, 97, 99, *109*, 120, 130, *131*, 132, 141–144, 200, 211, 241, 243, 247–248, 251–255; transition between ordinary and super-ordinary 252–253
sword (*espada*) 10, *63*, 84, *88*, 119, 124, 169, 177, 194, 199, 207, 210, 217, 238, 242
symbolism *4*, 10, 90–91, 125, 173, *174*–175, 186, 189, 210, 243
synesthesia 75, 90
syntactical appreciation 123, 125–126, 136, 138, 139, 141, 155, 250, 253

tablao (flamenco nightclub) *79*, *106*, 108, *115*, 120, 121, 123
Talavante, Alejandro *224*
tauromachy, *tauromaquia* 12, 35–36, 38, 44–48, *88*, 97, 100, 140, 154, 158, 175, 180–182, 185–186, 188–189, 191, 207, 208, 223–227, 231, 234, 238, 246
Tecate, Mexico 5, *63*, 154, 177–182, 234
temple (in-sync timing) 90, 119, 188–189; *see also* entrainment; intraspecies and interspecies bonding
tercio de banderillas (second third of a bullfight) 119
tercio de matar (last third of a bullfight) 114, 119, *184*, 194
tercio de varas (first third of a bullfight) 114, 119
Teresa and Luisillo Ballets Espagnol *218*
territoriality 110, *116*, 117, 170, 171, 179; see also *jurisdicción*; *querencia*
tienta (testing bravery of yearlings) 62, *63*, 64, *77*, 96, 103–104, 175–188, 234, 250, 251
temporal parameters 7, *118*–120, 161
toque (guitar) 1, 27, 33, 39, 41, 43, 78, 86, 91–92, *115*–*116*, 119, 140, 158–*159*, 161, *173*, 259

torcido (dance motif) *129*, *131*, *195*, 233, *235*, 243; *see also* posture; spiraling (bullfight movement); spiraling (dance motif)
toreando (bullfighting) *101*-*102*, 103, 110, 120, *147*, 160, 164–*166*, 186–187, 196; formal and informal *193*, 250; *see also* anecdotes: toreando
Torero (dance productions) 192–*193*, *195*; *see also* Canales, Antonio; Ciro (Diezhandino Nieto)
toros bravos (fighting bulls) *4*
Torrero, Patricia 208–209
Torres, Mariano 158
Tortes, Manuel 141
Totton, Robin 43, 126, 130
tourism 1, *11*, 16, *69*, *79*, *159*
trailing (dance motif) *129*, *131*, 169, 170, 172, *195*, 211
transitional object *193*, 199, 210, 211, 230, 247
transitional phenomena 198–200, 247
Truitt, John 123, 132
Turner, Victor W. 50, 58
2010 Theater, Music and Dance Festival, Canary Islands, Spain *77*, *83*, *156*

Valle, Manuela 192, 194
Varela, Rachel *168*, *174*
Vargas, María 105
verónicas (*capote* techniques) 160
videography 39, 52–54, 65, 108, 127, 182
visual perception 73, 80–81, 124
visual perception of a bull *83*–84, 225
Vittucci, Matteo Marcellus *see* Matteo
vocalization *77*, 85, 92–93, *113*, 160, 177; see also *cante*; *jaleo*
vuelta torera (dance movement) 194

Wacquant, Loïc 49, 65
Wang, Kirsten 94, 95
Washabaugh, William 45, 54
Williams, Drid 24–25, 50, 59, 65, 255
Winnicott, D. W. 198–199, 247
Woodall, James 43, 126, 143, 148
worldview *2*, 16, *28*, 32, 47, 55, 73, 99, 128, 146, 148, 160, *195*, 200, 256; *see also* Kearney, Michael
wrist rotation (dance motif) 62, *166*, 167, *168*, 175, 176, 207, 208

zarzuela (Spanish light opera) 191, 194, 205

www.ingramcontent.com/pod-product-compliance
Ingram Content Group UK Ltd.
Pitfield, Milton Keynes, MK11 3LW, UK
UKHW041925140426
5217IPUK00014B/323